God's Gentlemen

George Augustus Selwyn. (From the Beattie Collection. Permission Auckland Institute and Museum)

Other UQP Epress books in the Pacific Studies Series

God's Gentlemen
A History of the Melanesian Mission, 1849–1942
David Hilliard

Workers in Bondage
The Origins and Bases of Unfree Labour
In Queensland 1824–1916
Kay Saunders

Papua New Guinea
Initiation and Independence
Don Woodford

Race and Politics in Fiji
(Second Edition)
Robert Norton

Tax Havens and Sovereignty
In the Pacific Islands
Anthony Van Fossen

God's Gentlemen

A History of the Melanesian Mission, 1849–1942

DAVID HILLIARD

PACIFIC STUDIES SERIES

An imprint of UQP

First published 1978 by University of Queensland Press
PO Box 6042, St Lucia, Queensland 4067 Australia
This edition was created from a facsimile of the original
Published 2011 by UQ ePress, an imprint of University of Queensland Press

www.uqepress.com.au
www.uqp.com.au

© 1978 David Hilliard

This book is copyright. Except for private study, research, criticism or reviews, as permitted under the Copyright Act, no part of this book may be reproduced, stored in a retrieval system, or transmitted in any form or by any means without prior written permission. Enquiries should be made to the publisher.

Ebook produced by Infogrid Pacific Pte Limited
Cover design: Kate Barry

UQ ePress Pacific Studies Series Editorial Committee:
Professor Clive Moore (Chair)
Professor Brij Lal
Andrew Schuller

Cataloguing-in-Publication Data available from the National Library of Australia God's gentlemen: a history of the Melanesian mission 1849-1942 / David Hilliard UQ ePress pacific studies series

ISBN (pbk) 9781921902000
ISBN (pdf) 9781921902024
ISBN (epub) 9781921902017

Contents

List of Illustrations and Maps	vii
Abbreviations	ix
Preface	xi

1. "Visionary and Impracticable Principles" 1
2. Foundations 30
3. The Martyr 54
4. "God is Never in a Hurry" 79
5. Old Methods, Slightly Adapted 121
6. The Tide Turns 163
7. Towards a Melanesian Christianity 190
8. Dreams and Disenchantment 214
9. "The Redemption of the Whole Man" 258

Epilogue	293
Biographical Notes	297
Bibliography	303
Index	329

Illustrations

frontispiece	George Augustus Selwyn
16	J.C. Patteson, as captain of the Eton First XI
25	New Zealand General Synod of 1865
32	St Andrew's College, Kohimarama, Auckland
38	Joseph Atkin
39	Charles Bice with a group of New Hebridean mission scholars, St. Barnabas' College, Norfolk Island
42	Dining-hall, St. Barnabas' College
42	Morning drill, St Barnaba's College
55	John Coleridge Patteson
70	Patteson memorial cross, Nukapu
74	Interior of St. Barnabas' Chapel, Norfolk Island
80	John Richardson Selwyn
84	Taki, chief of Wango, San Cristobal
94	Alfred Lombu
99	Walter Woser, with his wife and children
113	John Palmer
128	Cecil Wilson
148	Mission-house at Loh, Torres Islands
148	On Board *Southern Cross V*
152	Girls' sewing-room, St Barnabas' College
152	Women's mission-station at Honggo, Nggela
168	Christian "school people" and village church at Fagani, San Cristobal
172	Clement Marau
175	Dr Henry Welchman
175	Bishop Wilson dedicating a church at Pirihandi Santa Isabel
197	Interior of St Paul's Church at Heuru, San Cristobal

200	Robert Pantutun
207	Melanesian schoolgirls, St. Barnabas' College
209	Cecil John Wood
216	John Manwaring Steward
220	Hugo Hembala
228	Ini Kopuria
229	Bishop Steward with the original seven members of the Melanesian Brotherhood
250	Frederick Merivale Molyneux
260	Walter Hubert Baddeley
271	Melanesian Mission headquarters station at Siota, Nggela
274	Charles Elliot Fox
282	Richard Prince Fallowes

Maps

xii   Solomon Islands

following page 9

New Hebrides
South-west Pacific

Abbreviations

A.B.M.	Australian Board of Missions
A.N.U.	Australian National University, Canberra
B.S.I.P.	British Solomon Islands Protectorate, Resident Commissioner; General Correspondence
C.M.S.	Church Missionary Society
C.O.	Colonial Office
F.O.	Foreign Office
I.V.	Melanesian Mission, *The Island Voyage*
L.M.S.	London Missionary Society
M.L.	Mitchell Library, Sydney
M.M.R.	Melanesian Mission, *Annual Report*
M.M.R.&I.V.	Melanesian Mission, *Annual Report* and *The Island Voyage* (combined issue)
N.H.	New Hebrides, British Resident Commissioner; General Correspondence
N.L.A.	National Library of Australia, Canberra
P.R.O.	Public Record Office, London
Q.K.M.	Queensland Kanaka Mission
S.C.L.	*Southern Cross Log*, Australian and New Zealand edition
S.C.L.E.	*Southern Cross Log*, English edition
S.P.C.K.	Society for Promoting Christian Knowledge
S.S.E.M.	South Sea Evangelical Mission
U.M.C.A.	Universities' Mission to Central Africa
U.S.P.G.	(United) Society for the Propagation of the Gospel
W.P.A.	Western Pacific Archives, Suva
W.P.H.C.	Western Pacific High Commission; Inward Correspondence

Preface

On 26 January 1975, almost twelve months before the British Solomon Islands Protectorate became an internally self-governing state, the Church of Melanesia was inaugurated as an autonomous province in the Anglican Communion. The purpose of this study is to examine the process by which the religion of the Church of England was extended to the islands of the southwest Pacific through the agency of the New Zealand-based Melanesian Mission. It begins with the first Anglican missionary voyage in 1849 and concludes with the Japanese invasion of the region in 1942, which remains a fundamental dividing-line in twentieth-century Melanesian history. To produce a full account beyond this date would necessarily involve the use of church and official records that are not yet open to researchers. In the meantime, the interested reader should consult Professor W.P. Morrell's summary of post-war events in the diocese of Melanesia in his history of the Anglican Church in New Zealand.[1]

Mission, with its ship *Southern Cross*, was among the best-known of all Christian missions in the South Pacific. It therefore invites attention, not only as a significant religious institution in the modern history of the Pacific Islands but also as a case-study in the British missionary movement of the nineteenth and early twentieth centuries. In this book, I have focused on the attitudes, objectives and achievements of the Anglican missionaries; the distinctive doctrines and ethos of the religion they taught; the problems they encountered in Melanesia and the methods they

---

1. W.P. Morrell, *The Anglican Church in New Zealand*, ch. 9. See also A.R. Tippett, *Solomon Islands Christianity*, which is primarily a study of the Anglican and Methodist churches in the Solomon Islands, based upon field research done in 1964.

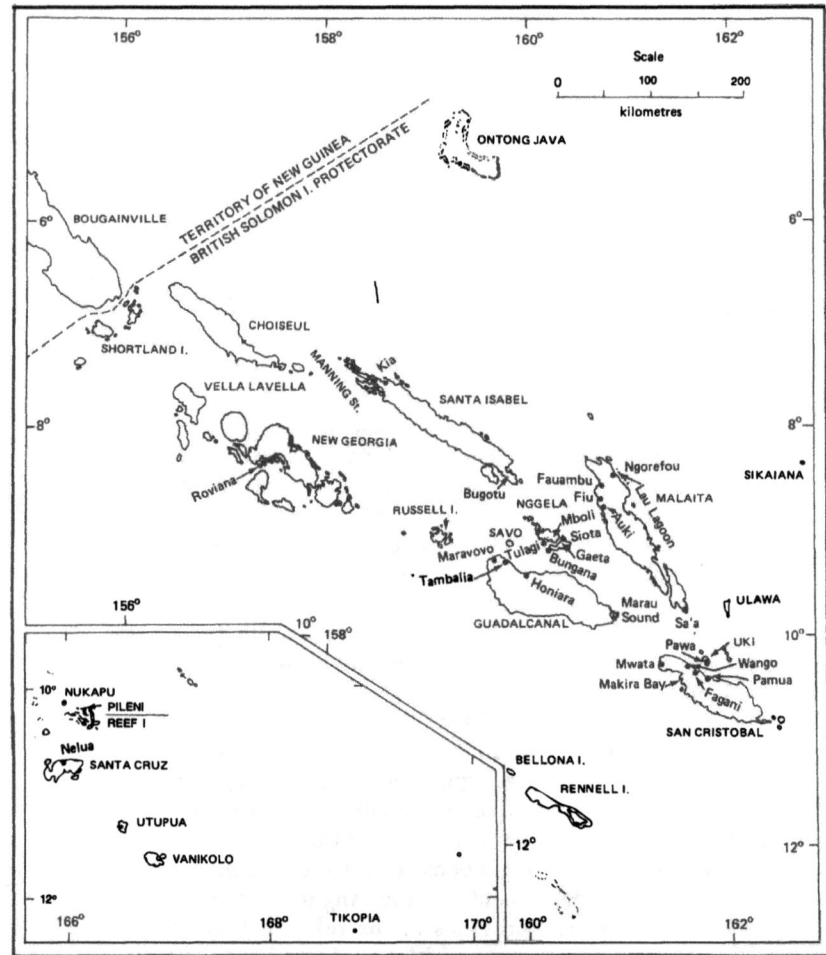

Solomon Islands

evolved—and modified—to meet them; their interaction with colonial powers, secular Europeans and representatives of other Christian denominations; the extent to which the Anglican mission collectively reflected broader currents in Christian missionary theology and strategy. Consideration of these themes has involved an examination of the varying Melanesian responses to Christianity, the consequences of conversion and the emergence of indigenous leadership in the Church. However, the book is primarily about missionaries; it is only indirectly concerned with the complex phenomenon of Melanesian Christianity.

The Melanesian Mission formally defined its field of work as "the Islands of Melanesia", though its actual operations were confined almost entirely to the northern New Hebrides, the Santa Cruz group and the Solomon Islands. The term "Melanesia" is itself only a little older than the Mission. It was first used in the 1830s, to describe that region of the south-west Pacific, extending from New Guinea to Fiji and New Caledonia, that is inhabited by people with dark skin and frizzy hair. The total population of those islands within the Anglican sphere of influence was estimated at the beginning of the twentieth century to be "anything between" 100,000 and 150,000.[2] It has not been my purpose to summarize the diverse peoples and cultures of Melanesia, for there are already many adequate works on the area to which the reader may refer.[3]

There is an enormous popular literature dealing with the Melanesian Mission: books of reminiscences, biographies, pamphlets, annual reports, and, from 1895, the Mission's monthly journal, the *Southern Cross Log*. There are also two substantial narrative histories: Mrs E.S. Armstrong's *History of the Melanesian Mission*, published in 1900, and *Lord of the Southern Isles* by the Reverend Dr C.E. Fox, published in 1958.

---

2. W.G. Ivens, "Melanesia and its People", in Appendix to *Dictionary and Grammar of the Language of Sa'a and Ulawa* ... , p. 179.
3. Among the best summaries is Ann Chowning, *An Introduction to the Peoples and Cultures of Melanesia*, An Addison-Wesley Module in Anthropology, no. 38 (Reading, Mass.: Addison-Wesley, 1973). For details of published works relating to Melanesia, see C.R.H. Taylor, *A Pacific Bibliography* (Oxford: Clarendon Press, 2nd edn, 1965); and the annual "Bibliography of Current Publications" in the *Journal of Pacific History*.

The special value of this material for the historian lies in its preservation of original correspondence and lengthy reports received from the field, and in the light it throws on missionary personalities and attitudes. On the other hand, much of it suffers from the characteristic defect of missionary literature, in that it has been written primarily to encourage and edify its readers. "The Logs and reports tell you nothing of the inner life of the Mission," admitted a newly arrived missionary in 1910. "The Bishop hates a dismal report and tells you so, and so everyone writes as cheerfully as possible."[4] To minimize this disadvantage, I have therefore drawn extensively on unpublished and non-Mission sources that have not been used by previous writers on the Melanesian Mission. These include the few surviving administrative records of the pre-war Mission (most of which, alas, were accidentally destroyed after the war), the private correspondence and diaries of former missionaries, official records of the British administrations in the New Hebrides and Solomon Islands, the writings of anthropologists and travellers, the archives of other missionary societies and the papers of successive archbishops of Canterbury.

During the writing of this book, I have been helped by many people and institutions. I am particularly grateful to the librarians and archivists of the Mitchell Library, Sydney; the Auckland Institute and Museum; the Western Pacific Archives, Suva; and the United Society for the Propagation of the Gospel, London. The administrative staffs of the Australian Board of Missions and the Church of Melanesia have also been of great assistance. For permission to consult private papers and other manuscripts, I am indebted to the Reverend W.F. Browning, Mrs Mary Clift, Mrs Qona Clifton, the Reverend E.A. Codd, the Reverend R.P. Fallowes, the Reverend D. Lloyd Francis, the Reverend H. Selwyn Fry, O.B.E., the Reverend W.J. Pinson, Mrs Rosemary Rowland, the Reverend Michael Tavoa and the Melanesian Mission English Committee.

Many individuals have generously answered my questions on the Melanesian Mission. I am especially grateful, in this regard, to the late Reverend Dr C.E. Fox, C.B.E., the Right Reverend Derek

---

4. J.W. Blencowe to his father, 19 June 1910, Blencowe Papers, in possession of Mrs M. Blencowe.

Rawcliffe and the late Mr H.W. Bullen. For suggestions and criticism, I should like to thank Dr Peter Corris, Dr Niel Gunson, Dr Hugh Laracy, Mr J.M. Main, Professor Francis West and Dr David Wetherell.

I gratefully acknowledge the support provided for this research by the Australian Research Grants Committee, the Department of Pacific and Southeast Asian History at the Australian National University and the Flinders University of South Australia.

Finally, my thanks to Jean Stokes, who patiently typed my drafts, and to Ian Maidment, who helped in a number of ways.

DAVID HILLIARD
Adelaide
1977

1
"Visionary and Impracticable Principles"

Victorian Anglicanism entered Melanesia not as the result of an upsurge in missionary interest within the Church of England, but through the imagination and restless energy of one man: George Augustus Selwyn, first Bishop of New Zealand.[1]

In 1840, Christian missionary activity in the South Pacific, from Tahiti westward to Fiji, was dominated by English Protestants of the (largely Congregational) London Missionary Society and the Wesleyan Missionary Society. At the same time, French Roman Catholic missionaries of the Society of Mary (Marists) were seeking island bases from which to challenge the Protestant monopoly. The Church of England, by contrast, was confined to a single diocese—the diocese of Australia, which embraced both the British colonies of Australia and New Zealand and the flourishing Maori mission of the Church Missionary Society.

In May 1841, the newly created see of New Zealand was offered to Selwyn, then curate of Windsor. Selwyn was a product of Eton and St John's College, Cambridge; thirty-two years old and happily married to the daughter of a judge. The formal cause of the entry of the Church of England into the Pacific Islands was an error in the Letters Patent of 14 October 1841 by which Selwyn was appointed, which defined the northern boundary of his diocese as 34° 30′ *north* instead of south. The effect of this was to extend the diocese far beyond New Zealand to include many of the islands of Melanesia. As a legal claim, it convinced no one but Selwyn himself. However, there was also a valedictory letter from Archbishop Howley of Canterbury, writing on behalf of the Colonial Bishoprics Council, who exhorted the new bishop to regard New Zealand as "a fountain diffusing the streams of salvation over the islands and coasts of the Pacific"—an image that echoed John Williams' widely-read description of the Tahitian mission of the L.M.S. as a "fountain from whence the streams of salvation are to flow to the numerous islands and clusters scattered over that extensive ocean".[2] It was on the secure authority of this archiepiscopal command rather than the questionable warrant of a Colonial Office clerk that Selwyn later preferred to justify his spiritual claim to the Melanesian islands. His belief that this "dark expanse" was an integral part of his diocese never wavered. He left England in December 1841 knowing nothing of the Pacific Islands, but on the outward voyage to New Zealand he studied navigation and Polynesian grammars, and soon he was envisaging a central missionary college drawing pupils from all parts of the South Pacific.

The founder of the Melanesian Mission was an old-fashioned High Churchman in his views on the sacraments, the succession of bishops from the Apostles and the excellent *via media* of Anglican tradition. Though influenced by the Tractarian theologians of the Oxford Movement, who were his contemporaries, in their appeal to the God-given authority of the Church and their opposition to state interference in religious affairs, he proudly proclaimed that he belonged to no church party. His missionary philosophy was as much ecclesiastical as evangelical. It followed logically from his unquestioned conviction that, despite accidental imperfections, the Church of England uniquely combined the pure doctrines of the early Church with the principles of apostolic order. Missionary work was essential for the vigour of every church, he proclaimed, but especially of colonial churches, which having themselves received the gospel from others, had a special obligation to their own neighbourhood. Most influential at the time, however, was his glowing vision, powerfully expounded to huge congregations in England in 1854, of the mission field as a potential source of new power to revitalize the dissension-ridden and erastian church at home. The mission field offered an outlet for the energies of sensitive spirits who sought in vain for ecclesiastical perfection, a refuge from sterile theological controversy and a sure sign, against Dissenting or Papist detractors, of the inherent vitality of the English Church:

> if our Missionaries in foreign lands do their duty in reclaiming the waste, then we may defy any one to say that ours is not a true branch

of the Church; when all theological discussion is come to an end, there will be proof that our doctrine was the truth.³

The Melanesian islands were thus seen by Selwyn as a religious *tabula rasa*—a place where the Church of England could freely demonstrate the validity of its spiritual claims and rebuild itself on a more perfect model, closer to the church of antiquity.

These were the same goals that he was pursuing in New Zealand: "to mould the institutions of the Church from the beginning according to true principles", to be deduced from the records of the first three centuries of the Church.⁴ If his ideal ecclesiastical system were fully implemented, unhampered by the state connection and with free power of expansion, he dreamed, "the Church of England would speedily become a praise upon the whole earth".⁵ Accordingly, he laid careful plans for an independent colonial church. In 1844 and 1847, he called synods of clergy, which were the first such independent assemblies by nineteenth-century Anglicans outside the United States of America, despite the opposition of those who feared that the Royal Supremacy was thereby infringed. Ecclesiastical self-government was finally achieved in 1857 by the constitution of the United Church of England and Ireland in New Zealand, later (from 1874) entitled the Church of the Province of New Zealand.

The delay in embarking on the Melanesian Mission was not due to lack of determination, but to other demands on Selwyn's energies. He travelled ceaselessly throughout New Zealand, by sea and on foot. There were unedifying disputes with the entrenched Evangelical missionaries of the Church Missionary Society over their qualifications for ordination and the internal organization of the Maori mission. There was a Maori rebellion in the far north, unrest in the south, and the supreme difficulty of finding assistant clergy who shared his High Church sympathies and were prepared to submit to his authoritarian rule. "I have really led a very perturbed life for the last four years", he wrote in 1846, "and am only just now beginning to feel as if there were some solid ground under my feet."⁶ His opportunity finally came in December 1847, when he was able to visit the Pacific Islands for the first time, as acting-chaplain to the cruising warship H.M.S. *Dido*.

Selwyn's ten weeks' voyage on the *Dido* was to be of seminal importance in the evolution of a strategy for his proposed mission. Principally, it enabled him to observe the methods of two of the most successful missions in the South Pacific—the Wesleyan mission in Tonga and the L.M.S. mission in Samoa. His visit to Samoa was particularly significant. As a High Churchman, he regarded non-episcopal bodies as lying outside the divinely constituted church and therefore declined to share in their public services. Nevertheless, he was a warm admirer of the achievements and writings of John Williams, Samoa's pioneer missionary, who had been killed on his first mission voyage into Melanesia, at Erromango in 1839. Although he privately deplored the evidences of missionary paternalism, personal contacts were cordial enough. He was deeply impressed by the expansive energy of Polynesian Christianity and by the sending of evangelists to the Loyalty Islands and southern New Hebrides: "we shall be indeed disgraced, if the older Mission of New Zealand cannot do as much for Melanesia, as its younger brethren in Samoa and Rarotonga".[7] This view was reinforced by his meeting with John Geddie and Isaac Archibald, missionaries from the Presbyterian Church of Nova Scotia, who were waiting in Samoa for a passage to their projected new mission field in the New Hebrides. "This was a striking lesson for our New Zealand Church; for I believe this was the first instance of any Colonial Body sending out its own Mission to the heathen, without assistance from the mother country."[8]

From Samoa and Tonga, the *Dido* sailed westward into Melanesia, to the New Hebrides and New Caledonia. In this part of the Pacific, European contact was just out of its initial phase. Since the 1820s, whalers, traders for bêche-de-mer and shell, and trading vessels from Port Jackson bound for China had called regularly at a few favoured bays and anchorages, as far north as the Solomon Islands, New Ireland and the Admiralty group. However, it was not until 1841, when large quantities of sandalwood were found at the Isle of Pines, and later on adjacent islands, that the region became drawn into a regular European trading network. The discoveries led to a "sandalwood rush" and during the next ten years at least 150 sandalwood voyages were made to New Caledonia, the Loyalty Islands and the southern New Hebrides.[9]

The search for sandalwood was a highly competitive and often hazardous enterprise, though it scarcely deserves its subsequent missionary-fostered reputation for unmitigated violence and fraud. The Melanesian islanders were already familiar with the concept of exchange and throughout the trade they showed themselves fully capable of using it for their own advantage. By the time of Selwyn's first visit in 1848, the boom was over; the coastal inhabitants of south-western Melanesia were becoming accustomed to sustained European contact, "sandalwood English" was widely understood and there was a growing demand for labour-saving metal tools and other favourite European goods.

Selwyn's knowledge of Melanesia was very limited, for in New Zealand, accurate information had been almost impossible to obtain. He had studied James Cook's published journal of his exploratory voyage through the New Hebrides in 1774 and James Burney's *Chronological History of the Discoveries in the South Sea or Pacific Ocean*, published in 1803-17. From reports derived from traders and whalers, he had heard that the Melanesians were to be feared for treachery and cannibalism, and that there was scarcely an island in the region where a stranger could land in safety. Then at the Isle of Pines he met the veteran sandalwooder James Paddon, who in 1844 had established the first permanent trading-station in the south-west Pacific, at Aneityum. Despite the forbidding reputation of the New Hebrideans for hostility to foreigners, Paddon seemed safe enough. This state of affairs was due, so he told Selwyn, to his humane treatment of the neighbouring peoples and generous payment in food and trade goods for services rendered. "Don't waste time in learning the languages," was his advice, "but teach the natives English." "I confess", Selwyn noted at the time, "that I was not ashamed to ponder well upon this wisdom of the children of this world, and to draw from it many hints for the guidance of our future operations."[10]

Selwyn was further encouraged by his friend Sir George Grey, Governor of New Zealand, whose fertile imagination envisaged the infant colony as a natural centre for the extension of British power throughout the South Pacific. During 1848, Grey was attempting—unsuccessfully as it turned out—to persuade the Colonial Office of the immense commercial, strategic and political benefits that would follow from the immediate annexation of

Tonga and Fiji. As a shrewd politician, he was anxious to assist any mission that might assist his own design. He subsidized mission schools in New Zealand, on condition that Pacific Islanders as well as Maoris would be eligible for admission, and he wrote letters of greeting for Selwyn to carry to the "Chiefs" of the Isle of Pines and New Caledonia, urging them to return with the bishop to New Zealand, to receive presents and become acquainted with English ways.[11]

Selwyn himself saw the political issues rather differently. Like Grey, he had no doubt that English Christianity and English civilization marched forward together, with the rule of law as an essential concomitant of true religion, but this did not imply the direct extension of British rule. Rather, he saw Britain's role in the South Pacific as one of stewardship. A great and wealthy power, whose subjects predominated among Europeans in the islands, had a primary responsibility before God to prevent injustice and violence between the races, especially on the Melanesian frontier. Such police work should be carried out by a patrolling warship, under an "enlightened" naval officer, which would radiate "moral influence and good example" in place of the customary techniques of retaliatory bombardment. Thus would British naval justice serve as a *preparatio evangelica* for the pagan islands of the south-west Pacific.[12]

It was against this background that Selwyn drew up plans for an Anglican mission to the Melanesian islands. Unfortunately for him, the Church of England was no means the first on the scene. The martyrdom of John Williams had stimulated the L.M.S. to continue the work he had begun, and during the 1840s, Samoan and Rarotongan teachers were left with their families at various places in the southern New Hebrides, New Caledonia and the Loyalty Islands. At the Isle of Pines and Futuna, some of the foreigners were killed, and many others died of fever and dysentery. Melanesia was also being entered by French Marist Fathers, who in 1848, after disastrous attempts to found missions in New Caledonia and the Solomon Islands, were trying to establish bases on the Isle of Pines, Aneityum and Murua, midway between the Solomons and New Guinea. When the Solomons missionaries withdrew from Makira Bay, San Cristobal, in September 1847, they had lost their leader, Bishop Epalle, and six other men by disease and violence in the previous twenty-one months. Also at Aneityum were Presbyterians from Nova Scotia, who arrived there in July 1848.[13]

Selwyn was not deterred. His own plan rested on the assumption that Nature, by dividing the Pacific into separate islands and archipelagoes, had "marked out for each missionary body its field of duty".[14] Wasteful competition and sectarian controversy could thus in principle be avoided. He himself had no doubt that God had summoned the Church of England in New Zealand, through Howley's commission, to lead the evangelization of the whole of Melanesia—"all the *News*", he announced to his old friend W. E. Gladstone, in an extraordinary flight of episcopal fantasy: New Caledonia, New Hebrides, New Britain, New Ireland, New Hanover, New Guinea, where, "if it please God, I hope in ten years to shake hands with the Bishop of Borneo".[15] Missions of other churches, British Nonconformist or Roman Catholic, would have their own portions of this work (for they could scarcely be excluded), but he expected that their role in Melanesia would be a subordinate one. He drew comfort from the fact that the French priests, despite their numbers, had made no headway. "Now then is the time to shew by fruits which is the better tree."[16]

Such reasoning, with its overtones of Establishment arrogance, was hardly likely to commend itself to the L.M.S. As his first mission field, Selwyn selected New Caledonia, together with the Loyalty Islands and the Isle of Pines, which were the closest of the Melanesian islands to New Zealand. "Bishoplike," snorted one of the L.M.S. missionaries, "his Lordship says that he looks upon the inhabitants of that group as *his* people."[17] Collision was initially averted by an agreement in June 1848. In return for Selwyn's assurance that he would leave the New Hebrides (exactly which islands, it was not stated) to the L.M.S. or its allies, the Samoan mission committee unanimously consented to the transfer of its Polynesian teachers already on Mare and Lifu in the Loyalties to an Anglican mission directed by Selwyn. This they assumed—and later insisted—would be conducted by sound Evangelicals of the C.M.S., whereas Selwyn was already planning his mission on lines quite different from those favoured in New Zealand. This unfulfilled condition, and episcopal attempts to evade it, was to be the source of a bitter religious squabble.

Melanesia, as Selwyn saw it in 1849, was still a virgin mission field, but one that offered no likelihood of speedy results and dramatic mass conversions. At those places where Polynesian Christian teachers had already been stationed, the native peoples were proving to be indifferent to the new religion. Its agents were at best barely tolerated; at worst, they had been driven out or massacred. Furthermore, the number of islands between New Caledonia and New Guinea was very large and their inhabitants spoke an "amazing multiplicity" of different languages, so that, unlike Polynesia, mastery of one did not open the way to a knowledge of the rest.

> In Islands, not larger than the Isle of Wight [Selwyn wrote from Aneityum], we find dialects so distinct, that the inhabitants of the various districts hold no communication one with another. Here have I been for a fortnight, working away, as I supposed, at the language of New Caledonia, by aid of a little translation of portions of Scripture, made by a native teacher sent by the London Mission from Rarotonga; and just when I have begun to see my way, and to be able to communicate a little with an Isle of Pines boy, whom I found here, I learn that this is only a dialect used in the southern extremity of the Island, and not understood in the part which I wish to attack first.[18]

There were other formidable obstacles to missionary activity. Beyond the southern New Hebrides, the "pestilential" tropical climate, and especially the presence of endemic malaria, appeared to prevent permanent residence by any foreigner, whether Polynesian or European. If attempted, the likely result would be "a great and unprofitable waste of human life". In any case, there was the practical impossibility (and the huge expense) of obtaining from England a succession of suitably qualified clergymen to station on more than one hundred major islands, in competition with even greater demands from other new missions in India, China and Africa. The solution, as Selwyn conceived it, lay in a new method, thoroughly grounded in the principles of the early Church. Unlike other missions, who were relying on resident European missionaries or on evangelists from Polynesia, he would work through a Melanesian "Native Ministry"—Melanesian teachers who would Christianize their own communities from within.[19]

The Northern Mission, as it was initially known, was to be

commenced under Selwyn's close personal supervision. By virtue of his episcopal office, he saw himself as a commanding general of an advancing Christian army. Because the Melanesian enterprise seemed to depend upon himself alone, and because his headquarters were fixed in New Zealand, he made it a department of the centralized collegiate institution that he had inaugurated in 1843 by the foundation of St John's College, located in Auckland since 1844. This was a large rambling establishment, comprising bishop's residence, boarding-school for European and Maori youths, printing office, hospital and theological college. In 1846, the college community numbered 146. For all scholars, a formal education was interspersed with training in agriculture or a useful trade, through which, it was hoped, the institution would eventually become self-supporting. Each day was regulated by a quasi-monastic timetable, for in the bishop's view, a college without daily services was "like a body without breath or circulation of blood"[20]—which was one of the reasons why C.M.S. men regarded St John's with suspicion as a nest of Tractarian error.

It was Selwyn's hope that from this "central reservoir"—an antipodean Iona or Lindisfarne—would radiate true religion, sound learning and useful industry throughout New Zealand and beyond. From his Auckland headquarters, he proposed to cruise for up to six months each year among the Melanesian islands, opening up friendly relations with as many peoples as possible, persuading them to entrust to him "a few promising youths" who would be taken for the summer to St John's and there taught the English language, arithmetic, writing, "all social and civilized habits" and the saving truths of the Christian faith. At the onset of winter, when Auckland became cold and wet, the Melanesian "scholars" would be returned to their own villages, where it was expected that they would begin to pass on knowledge of the new religion and awaken a desire for further teaching. If they proved to be intelligent and adaptable to the mission system, they would be brought back again in the following years, to resume schooling; if not, others would be obtained in their place. For each youth, the process would be repeated until he was baptized and sufficiently instructed to return permanently to his home as an evangelist, to convert his own people. The selection, collection and return of the Melanesian scholars would be directed by the

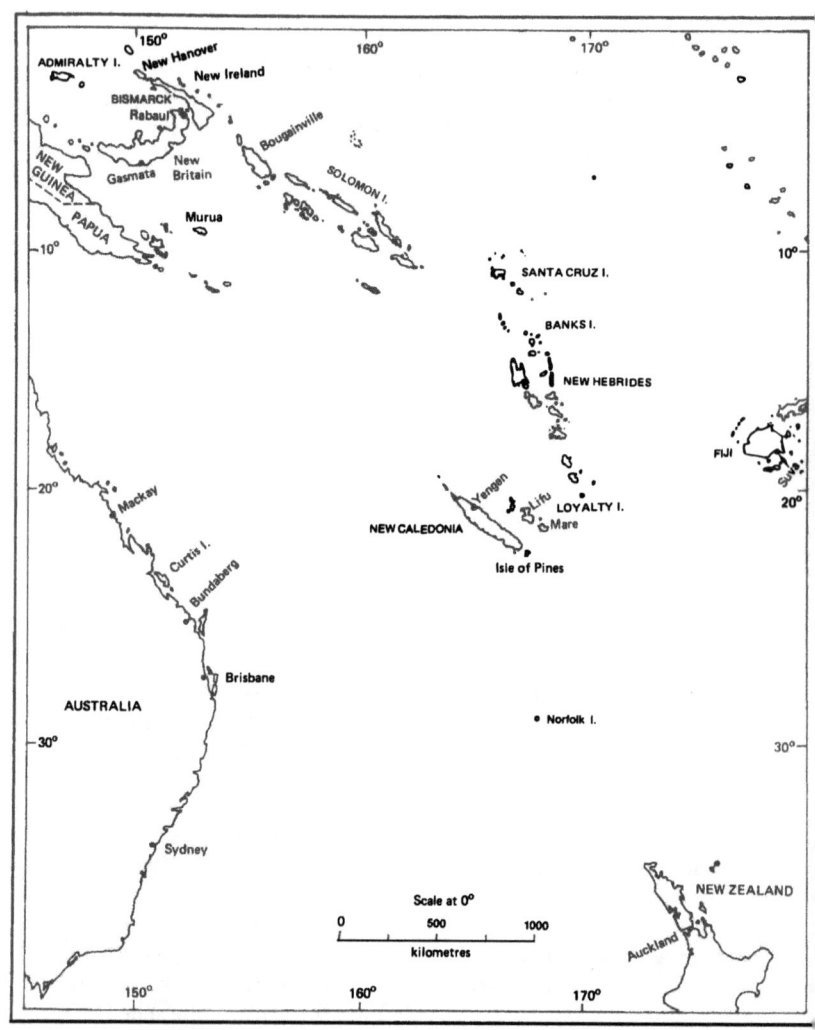

South-west Pacific

bishop himself on his "floating Mission House", while a small band of carefully chosen English assistants would undertake the educational work at the central school. These were compared to "white corks" unholding a "black net".

This was merely "the ground plan of a great design".[21] Reflecting the optimism of his time, Selwyn envisaged continued growth and progress under his successors. He was confident, moreover, that Melanesians had the "intellectual power" and "moral earnestness" to become effective teachers for their own islands, with the support of Europeans needed only for a time. Ultimately, he believed, there would arise a Melanesian church, independent of foreign oversight, led by its own English-educated élite of deacons, priests and bishops, and free to evolve its own forms of worship and discipline—though what this ideal might involve in practice was not clear.

In August 1849, Selwyn set sail on his first real missionary voyage, on the 21-tonne schooner *Undine*. Escorted for protection during part of his journey by H.M.S. *Havannah*, under Captain J.E. Erskine, he visited the southern New Hebrides, New Caledonia and the Loyalty Islands. Triumphantly, he then returned to his anxious wife in Auckland, with five recruits for his missionary college—Siapo, Uliete and Kateingo from Mare, Thol from Lifu and Dallap from Yengen on New Caledonia. The two months' voyage of more than 5000 kilometres aroused attention, in that the *Undine* was small, unarmed, without accurate charts and (although the vessel carried a captain) was often navigated by Selwyn himself. An admiring assistant wondered how many Right Reverend Lord Bishops could take a little vessel so far across the Pacific, like "George Augustus New Zealand". But the voyage was no trail-blazer, for everywhere Selwyn went he found that the sandalwooders had preceded him. He could only lament the entrenched position, superior numbers and resources of these "emissaries of the world" as a standing reproach to tardy Christians. The obliging Royal Navy granted its assistance again in 1850, when under the watchful eye of H.M.S. *Fly*, Selwyn returned his first scholars to their homes, while Erskine, in the *Havannah*, delivered to Selwyn three young men he had brought from the New Hebrides and a Solomon Islander named Didimang from San Cristobal. In 1851, with no warship at hand, Selwyn sailed in the new *Border Maid* to Malakula, in the company of Bishop William Tyrrell of Newcastle, collecting and returning scholars. In the following year, the Mission's frontier moved forward again to embrace the Banks Islands, Santa Cruz and San Cristobal, 3500 kilometres north-west of Auckland.[22]

At Mare, the Anglican party found that Polynesian evangelists, under the protection of the great chief Yiewene Kicini Bula, had established three stations, and already there were "probably more Christians than anywhere else in these seas".[23] In fulfilment of what was believed to be the spirit, if not the letter, of the 1848 L.M.S. resolution, a trusted clergyman assistant named William Nihill and a Maori helper, Henry Taratoa, were left at Netche, in the Christian chiefdom of Si Gwahma, for three months in 1852. Nihill co-operated amicably with the Samoan and Rarotongan catechists. He taught school, collected specimens of flora and fauna, walked around the island exhorting pagan villages to accept Christianity and produced an accomplished series of translations of religious texts.

> Every night we translate for about an hour and a half ... The natives supply us with food in abundance, yams etc. at all times, fowls very frequently, pork occasionally. They treat us just as they do their own chiefs, attending to our wishes, saluting us etc., and their teachableness is shown by the congregation on Sunday usually amounting to a thousand, and by Henry and I securing each a regular attendance of about 25 youths & boys, who spend two hours most patiently and attentively in being instructed by us ...[24]

During this voyage, the first island baptisms were also held. Four scholars were baptized at Netche before a congregation of a thousand in the coral-block chapel; John Thol received baptism in the chapel at Mu on Lifu and Didimang took the Christian names William Nihill at a ceremony on shipboard at his home village of Mwata on San Cristobal. During 1853, Selwyn made two further missionary voyages, but covering familiar ground. Nihill, in an advanced stage of tuberculosis, was returned with his wife to the warmth of Mare, only a few months before the long-delayed arrival of the L.M.S. resident missionaries S.M. Creagh and J. Jones. He died there in April 1855.

The Mission's first contacts with the Melanesians reflected Selwyn's intensely personal style. In the northern New Hebrides and beyond, where Western contact had been localized and intermittent, he carefully evolved a high-minded technique of approach. A primary principle of Christianity, he argued, was not to suspect strangers of evil motives, but to trust in the common goodness in human nature: goodwill begat goodwill. As a means of gaining the confidence of the islanders, despite the lack of a common language, he used "stray words", gesticulations, presents of beads, fish-hooks, hatchets and Jew's harps. He displayed mission scholars from other islands, and collected vernacular words and phrases. At the same time, on the universal missionary assumption that all unexpected attacks by Melanesians were acts of revenge for previous European aggression, especially for injuries inflicted by traders—"they can draw no distinction between one white man and another, however different they may be in calling or even in country"—he proceeded with caution, always watching for hostile reactions.[25] He made it a rule to swim ashore from the ship's boat unarmed though never alone (with a vocabulary notebook safely inside his bishop's shovel-hat), to keep the mission ship in a place of safety, always to obtain the consent of parents or kin before taking boys, and never to go anywhere or do anything out of mere curiosity. His blanket interpretation of Melanesian motives for violence may be questioned, but as a practical policy, it was justified by its results. Only once, while filling water casks at Port Sandwich at Malakula in 1851, was the mission party in real danger of attack.

At St John's College, too, where the bishop himself often took classes, his commanding personality made a profound impression upon the Melanesian pupils.

> They all think and talk much of him [wrote Mrs Martin, wife of the Chief Justice], and with pleasure of his going to the Islands, and how their friends will welcome him; and they laugh about "Picopo *oui-oui*", as they call the French Bishop, coming in "large ship, guns here, guns there—go *bomb, bomb*. He no land. Our Bishop come little ship, no guns! he land, everybody say, Come here." They think the Bishop can do everything, ... that he wrote all the books they see; ...[26]

In their home villages, when they returned, the name of "Bishop" or "Bishop of New Zealand" was reported to be a "passport and security" for wandering Europeans.[27]

In Auckland, the Melanesian Mission (as it was called from

about 1852) aroused mild interest, but little real support beyond an élite circle of friends and devotees of Selwyn centred on St John's. Chief Justice Martin and his wife took a deep interest and often visited the college. In 1853, Sir George Grey received the Melanesian scholars at a Queen's Birthday levée at Government House and gave presents of axes and hammers. Vicesimus Lush, an Auckland parish clergyman, entertained eleven Melanesian scholars at a vicarage dinner of curried meat and rice, potatoes, broad beans and plum pudding, and marvelled at their respectful behaviour:

> ... I don't believe eleven labouring men taken from any village in England and invited to dine with the local clergymen would have conducted themselves with half the propriety these black fellows did —and yet not six months ago they had not seen a knife and fork and knew nothing of sitting at table to eat their food.[28]

Yet even among friends there was endless criticism of the bishop's restlessness, his apparent eagerness to take refuge in the islands from the unsolved administrative and racial problems of the New Zealand church, and of the risk to his life and health in dangerous places. In the three years from 1849, ordinary New Zealand subscriptions for support of the Melanesian work did not exceed £350.[29]

Nor did Selwyn achieve lasting success at home in his attempt to introduce a new mode of missionary organization. Against the practice existing within the Church of England, by which missionary work was undertaken without co-ordinated planning by semi-independent voluntary societies, he favoured a design already adopted by American Anglicans, based upon the High Church idea that missions should be an enterprise of the whole church in its corporate capacity, led by the bishops. In New Zealand, his theological objection to the society system had been fortified by unhappy relations with the C.M.S. Accordingly, at a meeting of the five Anglican bishops of Australia and New Zealand, held in Sydney in October 1850, he played a leading part in setting up an Australasian Board of Missions, which was intended to be the sole official missionary agency of the colonial churches, thereby bypassing the C.M.S. The new board, with Selwyn and Tyrrell designated as its missionary bishops, was charged with the conversion and civilization of the Australian

Aborigines and the "Heathen races in all the Islands of the Western Pacific", through the careful training in English of a "select number ... at a distance from their own tribe".[30] His plan at last had the episcopal endorsement that he considered essential. Soon afterwards, diocesan boards of missions were set up in Sydney and Auckland. But when, in a bid to unite all church parties around his new organization, Selwyn invited G.A. Kissling, an Auckland C.M.S. missionary of irenic temper, to accept office, the Parent Committee of the C.M.S. in London, distrustful of Selwyn's intentions and sensing competition, descended in full-throated opposition. No loyal missionary could serve two masters. The bishop's mission principles, as embodied in the Australasian Board's resolutions, were denounced as at variance with all the experience and practice of the C.M.S. and bound to bring discredit upon "real" missionary work.

> To this Society it has ever appeared that uncivilized pupils trained at a distance from home in a civilized land will return to their native home very unsuitable Missionaries & that the truths of religion can be taught only in the vernacular langage of the country. We see not how our Agents can properly identify themselves with so opposite a system to that of the C.M.S.[31]

Kissling, chastened, withdrew. Selwyn's allies were outraged at the C.M.S. decision. After a brief flurry of activity, the diocesan boards disintegrated, while the Australasian Board continued only in name.

It was a decisive point in the early evolution of the Melanesian Mission. The Mission could not be truly described as Tractarian, but it was now abundantly clear that few Evangelicals of the conventional mould would be taking an active part in it. It was thus cut off from that party of the Church of England in which missionary fires burned brightest. From what quarter, therefore, was its principal support in money and manpower to come? When Selwyn, in the company of Grey, left New Zealand at the end of 1853 on a visit to England, one of his objects was to place his Melanesian work on a sound financial basis and to select "a few coadjutors" who would relieve him of the need for constant supervision.[32]

In this quest, he was partially successful. When he returned to New Zealand in 1855, he had acquired capital funds from well-connected friends, a new mission ship and a sympathetic missionary chaplain. The chaplain was John Coleridge Patteson, Old Etonian son of a well-known judge, who had been combining an Oxford Fellowship with a village curacy near his family's seat in Devon. Selwyn's formidable exterior and imperious will made him a difficult partner in any enterprise. Patteson was one of the few men who could work harmoniously with him, initially as a devoted disciple and later in a position more resembling equality. Patteson had "the greatest admiration and affection" for Selwyn, recalled R.H. Codrington, who knew him well, "and I believe the two men were as attached as men can be".[33] Although the bishop sailed to the islands each year from 1856 to 1859 on the principal voyages of the new mission schooner *Southern Cross* (the first of that name, wrecked off northern New Zealand in 1860), he soon committed to Patteson the responsibility for the internal management of the Mission and the annual return of scholars to their homes. For the meantime, the original method of work remained unaltered.

Reinforced by Selwyn's accumulated island experience and Patteson's remarkable linguistic abilities, the exploratory voyages of the *Southern Cross* in the late 1850s were remarkable for the number of new places where friendly contacts were established. In 1856, there was an exploratory cruise through the eastern Solomons and the first large party of Solomon Islanders was taken to Auckland—seven of them from Marau Sound at the eastern end of Guadalcanal and from coastal villages in north-western San Cristobal. On the second voyage of 1857, a record number of islands was visited—sixty-six in all, with eighty-one landings or an average of one each day for much of the journey. By this time, Selwyn and Patteson between them could speak the languages of eight islands and communicate in some way with "many more". In an attempt to find common ground, they expounded Christian teaching on the choice between eternal life or death to curious listeners with reference to familiar things. Man was not like pigs or dogs or fishes, Patteson told them, for these could not speak or think. Because man was different, he would not die like them, but rise up again. If he learnt to obey "the great spirit", he would go to him, but the man who did not obey would go into pain and sorrow.[34]

At the Polynesian outliers of Rennell and Bellona, and a few

J.C. Patteson as captain of the Eton First XI (From Jesse Page, *Bishop Patteson, the Martyr of Melanesia*)

other places, the missionaries appear to have been the first white visitors. At Port Patteson on Vanua Lava in the Banks Islands (named by Selwyn after Sir John Patteson, the father of his assistant), the people believed that the white men they were seeing for the first time were returning ancestral spirits, a common interpretation at the time throughout Melanesia. A fifteen-year-old boy named Sarawia, drawn by curiosity, paddled out to the strange ship and was called and beckoned to climb on board, where the two missionaries asked questions and wrote down the names of the local people, the islands and various pronouns in the island's language. "The ship appeared to me like a village," Sarawia wrote towards the end of his life, "and I thought that it had not been made by man but perhaps by spirits."[35] He was alarmed by the leather shoes he saw: "I said to myself that these men were made partly of clam-shell, and my bones quaked." But in this case, fear was soon dispelled by signs of confidence and kindly words. Later he returned to the ship with five companions, to sleep on board, attend prayers for the first time and to receive coveted presents of fruit, fish, biscuits, fish-hooks and calico.

However, at islands already frequented by commercial vessels for food and sexual hospitality, the *Southern Cross* was no novelty. The missionary visitors therefore found themselves at a disadvantage, for the whalers gave tobacco and spirits and "don't speak to them [the islanders] about any need of altering their habits".[36] The Polynesian chiefs of Tikopia, already well provided, were scornful of mere hatchets and fish-hooks, and when the bishop told the assembled people in Maori that he had not come for pigs or yams, but to teach about the "great God" who dwelt above and his son Jesus Christ, his listeners were bored. Even less promising was the situation at Ulawa, where Patteson was so shocked when asked in broken English whether he and his crew wanted women for the night that he forced his prospective host overboard. It was becoming clear that the best opportunities for Christianity lay among inhabitants of isolated localities and small islands, "uncorrupted" by whalers and other agents of Western commerce.

Between 1849 and 1860, 152 Melanesians were brought to the Auckland mission school for at least one season, and 39 of these came twice or more. The Loyalties had supplied the most, mainly in the earliest years—22 from Mare, 14 from Lifu. There had been 22 from Guadalcanal (none of whom had come more than once), 18 from San Cristobal, 11 from Mota in the Banks group and 10 from Eñae in the New Hebrides. The rest had been drawn from twenty different places. In the islands, however, there was little enough to report in the way of tangible achievements beyond the establishment of friendly contacts. Neither Selwyn nor Patteson was distressed, for both were confident that in such a difficult field, secure foundations inevitably required "a long and persevering effort".[37] Episcopal self-assurance and breadth of vision even won over some influential observers, who publicly lauded Selwyn's uniquely comprehensive strategy, so unlike other plans for mission work, as the one most feasible for Melanesia and the most likely to prove successful. Hard-headed members of other societies were not impressed. Henry Venn, secretary of the C.M.S., who was a leading thinker about Protestant missionary principles, privately criticized the methods of the new mission as "visionary and impracticable". A Presbyterian missionary in the New Hebrides, John Inglis, concluded that Selwyn's new modes were in general not successful, whereas his successful modes were not new. And in fact, there was ample evidence for those not blinded by episcopal eloquence that Selwyn's ambitious scheme in its original form contained serious practical defects that largely nullified its well-publicized advantages.[38]

It suffered firstly from the unreal expectation, shared by virtually all nineteenth-century British missionaries, that Western-style classroom instruction, commonly through the medium of the English language, could be utilized effectively to impart the doctrines of an alien religion to children drawn from a non-literate culture, and that this method of teaching could offset the entire network of indigenous education through parental and societal influence. The Mission's earliest pupils were usually no more than boys—anyone who would come, whatever their motive, whose word carried no weight in their homes. The average age rose. By the late 1850s, only four out of forty-two were thought to be under sixteen years old, a dozen were young men aged between nineteen and thirty, but "so manageable that they *can* be moulded as easily as boys".[39] In the English-speaking and restrained environment of St John's College, with its ordered timetable of prayers and chapel services, school, recreation and "useful industry", it was clear that they had little choice. Patteson himself had no illusions. He recognized that his charges had no inducement to exhibit themselves in any but a favourable light, and that they listened to him from curiosity and not from conviction. He nevertheless anxiously watched for encouraging signs, proudly reporting the acquisition of steady methodical habits, an aptitude for learning and the growth of a "real sense of duty" not very different from that of the best type of English public schoolboy. Sapandulu from Erromango delighted Mrs Martin by summing up his catechism: "Me say, One God; God very good; all good; God made you, made me, made everything. You good, God love you." Petere and Laure from Emae announced that they would "talk, talk, talk, night, night, night, day, day, day", to tell their people all that they had seen and heard.[40]

Yet any expectation that young Melanesians, after only a few months of continuous instruction, could as individuals successfully challenge the existing system of beliefs and behaviour, was doomed to disappointment. Only one of the first generation of scholars was of high rank. This was John Cho, half-brother of the great chief Bula, of Mu at Lifu, where much of the population had already accepted the externals of Christianity through Samoan and Rarotongan evangelists of the L.M.S. Others, returning to their homes with a temporary prestige based on their knowledge of English, European dress and boxes of presents accumulated in New Zealand, had little or no lasting influence, while it is likely that their new conceit made them positively unpopular. Visiting San Cristobal in 1857, Patteson thought he saw signs that "some vague imperfect ideas" had been conveyed to the islanders, "who had heard from our old pupils what they could remember of the teaching they had received at the College"; but the process clearly went no further.[41]

For returned scholars, the most common reaction was one of compartmentalization. Christianity as they had heard of it in New Zealand was an exotic, and on returning to "real life" they shed it as easily, and for much the same reason, as they parted with their unsuitable new clothes. A few tried to teach, only to find that no one would listen to them. When transposed to the

English situation by a missionary who had witnessed ten years of failure in the New Hebrides, the inadequacy of the method was obvious.

> I wonder how a young man from one of our public schools would set to work to teach the old ideas in his neighbourhood the tenets of a new, strange, and thoroughly uncongenial religion. It is not to be supposed that a nation is to be converted from the error of their ways all at once by the desultory and timid teaching of a few boys.[42]

Moreover, the essential principle of "constant interchange" proved unexpectedly difficult to maintain. A few scholars were found too dull to learn much. A few more died in New Zealand or on the voyage, which had the effect of predisposing their people against supplying more. More frequently, mission scholars found that one or two trips abroad were enough to satisfy their curiosity, and they disappeared into the bush when the bishop's ship reappeared. Others married after returning, thereby assuming full responsibilities within their own society, or for some unknown reason were prevented by their families from going away again.

One by one, the first generation of Melanesians taken to school in Auckland disappeared from view—"swept away once more", Patteson sadly noted, "by the torrent of heathenism in their own homes";[43] though in their own view, it was more likely to have been seen as the restoration of a desirable *status quo*. Some, like Benjamin Gariri, Hiriha and Sono of San Cristobal, survived to the end of the century, resolutely pagan, to surprise later missionaries with reminiscences of their time in New Zealand with Selwyn and Patteson.[44]

The eventful career of William Didimang, a spectacular failure in the eyes of the Mission, well illustrates the predicament of a young Melanesian mentally torn between two opposing systems. In September 1850, he had come on board H.M.S. *Havannah*, then cruising along the coast of San Cristobal, and as he insisted on staying, was taken to Sydney and there handed over to Selwyn. In August 1852, he was brought home to Mwata and baptized in the presence of his friends and relatives.

> A book of prayers and some Scripture lessons had been translated by his assistance, and a supply of school lessons and stationery were

left with him, in the hopes that he might conduct family prayer and school with his own relations ..."[45]

In July 1856, when the *Southern Cross* called, there was distress on board when it was learned that Didimang, the Mission's most distant scholar, had done no teaching and refused to come away again. A few months later, "smitten apparently with remorse", he shipped on board a Sydney-based trading vessel with a friend, hoping to find his way back to New Zealand. Instead, the ship sailed to China, where his companion died. Didimang then found his way back to Sydney and worked a passage across to Auckland, where, at the end of 1857, he was received as a returning prodigal back into the fold. Returning to Mwata in 1858, he again did no teaching, but joined the crew of another vessel. There are passing references in mission sources to his living in the area in 1866 and 1875, but what became of him after that is not known.[46]

Another weakness in the Mission's approach was inherent in the Melanesian culture-contact situation. In common with other European visitors, the most obvious attribute of the missionaries in the eyes of the islanders was their possession of seemingly unlimited stores of wealth. To gain a hearing, Selwyn and Patteson had been compelled from the first to follow traders' precedent and fulfil expectations by giving presents (though Selwyn refused to give tobacco) to the leading men of each place as an expression of goodwill. Not to do so would be to alienate goodwill and make it impossible to obtain scholars. There was also a need to trade, in order to obtain yams and other food for the *Southern Cross*. An immediate result, however, was to create in the minds of the islanders an indelible impression that the Mission was the pathway to material prosperity. George Sarawia, who went away from Vanua Lava in 1858, recalled his own motives for going with the strangers:

> I had made up my mind at the beginning to go with the bishops for this reason: I wanted to go myself to the real source of things, and get for myself an axe and a knife, and fish hooks and calico, and plenty of other such things. I thought they were just there to be picked up, and I wanted to get plenty for myself ... Also I wanted to see where the white people's country was, and what it was like.[47]

Far from the Mission's original purpose, the acquisition of trade goods soon became an end in itself, in no way connected with the new religion. Visits from the *Southern Cross* were welcomed because of the opportunity thus afforded to trade and travel to other lands, while fervent exhortations to accept the Christian religion, with its promised spiritual benefits, were quietly ignored. Later, as traders multiplied, offering superior articles and more exciting and profitable ways of seeing the outside world, so the Mission found itself steadily pushed into a position of permanent inferiority.

Although Selwyn did not intitially realize it, no single method could have accomplished the rapid evangelization of Melanesia. A primary reason was the general absence of political cohesion, for north of the Loyalty Islands there were no powerful hereditary chiefs who could compel thousands of their subjects to adopt the Christian religion—as had been the case in the Polynesian societies of Tahiti and Tonga. Political units in the New Hebrides and Solomon Islands were small in scale and settlement was dispersed. On the larger islands contacted by the *Southern Cross*, the bulk of the population lived in the interior, in isolated hamlets of two or three households. Villages in coastal societies usually contained between one and two hundred inhabitants. It was this "comparative scantiness of the population", observed the missionary-anthropologist W.G. Ivens sixty years later, that was "the real difficulty in the evangelization of Melanesia".[48] From present-day knowledge of the region—its complex languages, divergent subcultures and egalitarian social groupings—Selwyn's confident expectation that he could engineer the conversion of up to 200,000 people by means of a central school, a cruising schooner and an army of youthful English-trained evangelists—and at a time before the invading European political and economic order had begun to interact on a decisive scale with the indigenous cultures—must be seen as a quixotic exercise, foredoomed to failure.

Nevertheless, Selwyn's grandiose vision of an Anglican Melanesia, counterbalancing the Congregational and Wesleyan empires of the central and eastern Pacific, did significantly shape the course of the Christianization process. It pre-empted for the Church of England a large portion of the south-west Pacific as a sphere of religious influence, which, despite boundary disputes, other British missions for the next fifty years refrained from challenging. This practice of non-interference was not because of a written or formal "compact", as was popularly believed in later years; it was a gentleman's agreement based on a tacit understanding. The dream of an Anglican Melanesia thus lingered on, a religious mirage to encourage and justify successive generations of English missionaries in their struggling efforts to achieve it.

In 1861, the Melanesian Mission, hitherto under the auspices of Selwyn's now subdivided diocese of New Zealand, became the responsibility of a new missionary diocese of Melanesia, with Patteson as its first bishop. Its foundation was surrounded with legal and theological controversy concerning the place of bishops of the Church of England in relation to overseas missions. The state church had been consecrating bishops to govern existing churches in British colonies since 1787; ten such overseas bishoprics had been created by 1841, and after the establishment in that year of the Colonial Bishoprics Fund, another thirty— including New Zealand—were endowed and founded within the next generation. As the idea of colonial sees came to be universally accepted in England, another debate was looming over the sending of bishops as pioneer missionaries into unevangelized territories beyond the British flag.[19]

There were two opposing points of view. Evangelicals and old-fashioned erastians foresaw difficulties with the Royal Supremacy, for from whom were such bishops to receive their commission and to whom would they be responsible? To send a bishop into lands beyond the British dominions might be seen as a first step toward formal annexation. Furthermore, the office of bishop was essentially that of chief pastor of a settled flock, which had no meaning on the mission field until converts had been gathered and congregations organized. Against the arguments of law and expediency was set another view, based on a high concept of the episcopal office, which was first expounded by the American Bishop Doane in the 1830s and taken up semi-independently by the Tractarians: that missions should in principle be led from the first by a bishop, as a successor of the Apostles, to whom Christ had given the missionary commission and who thus personified the Church "in its integrity": "A Church without a Bishop, a Clergy and people without a Bishop, were things absolutely unheard, unthought of, in the early and purest ages of Christianity."⁵⁰

The leading English exponent of the theological and practical necessity of missionary bishops was Samuel Wilberforce, Bishop of Oxford. In 1853, he introduced an unsuccessful missionary bishops Bill into Parliament, but seven years later his ideas received endorsement within the church from Convocation. Prominent among his supporters was Selwyn, whose own journeyings through New Zealand and Melanesia had done much in England to change stereotyped attitudes by building up the image of bishops as modern apostles.⁵¹

Much of the debate of the 1850s concerning missionary bishops was conducted with an eye to southern Africa, where Bishop Gray of Cape Town was planning to dispatch a bishop at the head of a new mission to the tribes of the Zambezi. Its outcome was equally relevant to Selwyn's early plan to have a bishop for the islands of the western Pacific. On his visit to England during 1854, he had privately collected £10,000 to endow a Melanesian see. To satisfy the lawyers, it was at first proposed to base the diocese at Norfolk Island, just as the British island of Labuan had in 1855 become the see for the Borneo Mission. This plan, however, was thwarted by Sir William Denison, Governor of New South Wales, who regarded Selwyn's scheme for an island bishopric as "crude and undigested" and smelt the threat of "ecclesiastical tyranny" over the 200 newly arrived Pitcairner descendants of the *Bounty* mutineers.⁵²

At this point, it seemed that the Melanesian see would be within New Zealand, possibly at the Bay of Islands. Then, with reference initially to Central Africa, and in 1860 to Melanesia, the Colonial Office finally conceded that a bishop of the Church of England might in fact be legally consecrated for work beyond the Queen's Dominions, with no authority or jurisdiction within them, though the imperial government could accept no responsibility for such a venture. The five bishops of the now autonomous Anglican Church in New Zealand were therefore free to exercise their "inherent power" of consecration.⁵³ The Archbishop of Canterbury was informally consulted and made no objection. Patteson's privileged education, impeccable family connections and substantial practical knowledge marked him out as well suited for the position. Although troubled by doubts of his fitness,

At the new Zealand General Synod of 1865; *Left to right:* Bishops G.A. Selwyn, H.J.C. Harper (Christchurch), C.J. Abraham (Wellington), J.C. Patteson (Melanesia). *Seated:* W. Williams (Waiapu) (From the John Kinder Album: Permission Auckland Institute and Museum)

his assent had been anticipated. There was no other candidate, and in any case, he was Selwyn's choice. On 24 February 1861, he was consecrated in Auckland by Selwyn, as Primate of New Zealand, and the Bishops of Nelson and Wellington—"three Eton bishops ... consecrating a fourth Eton man"—as a missionary bishop for the "Western Islands of the South Pacific Ocean".[54] The new bishopric was to become an associated missionary diocese of the Church of the Province of New Zealand, with representation in General Synod equal to that of the mainland dioceses. Its territorial boundaries were undefined.[55]

For supporters of Wilberforce and Selwyn, the year 1861 was a remarkable one for the Church of England, as the year in which it first extended its episcopate beyond the limits of the British

Empire.[56] C.F. Mackenzie was consecrated for Central Africa in January, Patteson for Melanesia in February and T.N. Staley for Hawaii in December. Precedent had been set. There were high hopes that this new mode of organization, by planting the Church in its integrity, would create a new era in Anglican missions: that an apostolic mission would indeed achieve apostolic results.

NOTES AND REFERENCES

1. The principal biographies of Selwyn are: H.W. Tucker, *Memoir of the Life and Episcopate of George Augustus Selwyn, D.D.*, 2 vols.; G.H. Curteis, *Bishop Selwyn of New Zealand, and of Lichfield*; John H. Evans, *Churchman Militant*. There are numerous popular works. For the most recent study of his New Zealand episcopate, see W.P. Morrell, *The Anglican Church in New Zealand*, chs. 2-5.
2. Tucker, *Selwyn*, vol. 1, p. 85; John Williams, *A Narrative of Missionary Enterprises in the South Sea Islands: With Remarks upon the Natural History of the Islands, Origin, Languages, Traditions and Usages of the Inhabitants* (London, 1840), p. 2. On the boundaries of Selwyn's diocese, see Angus Ross, *New Zealand Aspirations in the Pacific in the Nineteenth Century*, pp. 12-15.
3. *Colonial Church Chronicle* 8 (1854-55): 217. Selwyn's Cambridge sermons on missionary work, *The Work of Christ in the World*, were especially influential.
4. Henry Jacobs, *Colonial Church Histories: New Zealand*, pp. 109-10.
5. Tucker, *Selwyn*, vol. 1, p. 250.
6. A.B. Webster, *Joshua Watson: The Story of a Layman* (London: S.P.C.K., 1954), p. 170.
7. G.A. Selwyn, *Letters on the Melanesian Mission in 1853*, p. 33.
8. ibid., p. 26.
9. For the New Hebrides sandalwood trade, and early European contact in south-western Melanesia generally, see Dorothy Shineberg, *They Came for Sandalwood*; and *The Trading Voyages of Andrew Cheyne, 1841-1844*, ed. Dorothy Shineberg (Canberra: A.N.U. Press, 1971). On the Solomon Islands: Peter Corris, *Passage, Port and Plantation*, ch. 1; Colin Jack-Hinton, *The Search for the Islands of Solomon, 1567-1838* (Oxford: Clarendon Press, 1969). An important contemporary account of the region is Andrew Cheyne, *A Description of Islands in the Western Pacific Ocean, North and South of the Equator: With Sailing Directions, together with their Productions: Manners and Customs of the Natives and Vocabularies of their Various Languages* (London, 1852).
10. *Colonial Church Chronicle* 7 (1853-54): 384; Selwyn, *Letters*, p. 42.
11. Ross, *New Zealand Aspirations*, ch. 4.
12. Tucker, *Selwyn*, vol. 1, pp. 310-14; G.A. Selwyn to W.E. Gladstone, 31

October 1848, 17 November 1850, Selwyn-Gladstone Correspondence, Alexander Turnbull Library.
13. For accounts of these missions, see William Gill, *Gems from the Coral Islands: Western Polynesia, comprising the New Hebrides Group, the Loyalty Group, New Caledonia Group* (London, 1855); A.W. Murray, *Missions in Western Polynesia: Being Historical Sketches of these Missions, from their Commencement in 1839 to the Present Time* (London, 1863); Hugh M. Laracy, *Marists and Melanesians*, ch. 2.
14. Tucker, *Selwyn*, vol. 1, p. 255.
15. Selwyn to Gladstone, 2 December 1850, 20 July 1853, Selwyn-Gladstone Correspondence.
16. G.A. Selwyn to W.B. Clarke, n.d. [1853], G.A. Selwyn Letterbook, Selwyn Family Papers, in possession of Rev. H. Selwyn Fry. See also Lewis M. Hogg, *A Letter to His Grace the Duke of Newcastle ... on behalf of the Melanesian Mission*, p. 8.
17. G. Drummond to A. Tidman, 26 February 1848, L.M.S. South Seas Letters, box 21, 4A, Council for World Mission Archives, School of Oriental and African Studies, University of London.
18. Tucker, *Selwyn*, vol. 1, p. 293.
19. Selwyn's early plans are expounded in his letters to Edward Coleridge, a master at Eton College, 12 August and 21 December 1849, published as *Two Letters from Bishop Selwyn*; reprinted in Tucker, *Selwyn*, vol. 1, pp. 286-94, 317-19. See also Selwyn's letters to his father, 15 September and 6 December 1849, ibid., pp. 300-304, 305-11.
20. Tucker, *Selwyn*, vol. 1, p. 251.
21. ibid., p. 289.
22. For accounts of the first four mission voyages, see Tucker, *Selwyn*, vol. 1, pp. 311-17; John Elphinstone Erskine, *Journal of a Cruise among the Islands of the Western Pacific, including the Feejees and others inhabited by the Polynesian Negro Races, in Her Majesty's Ship Havannah* (London, 1853), pp. 310-402; William Nihill, "Journal of a Voyage to the New Hebrides, New Caledonia and the Loyalty Islands ..." (1850); and id., "Journal of a Voyage from Auckland, N.Z. to the New Hebrides and Loyalty Islands" (1851), Auckland Public Library; *Gospel Missionary* 2 (1852): 145-57; *New Zealand Church Almanac*, 1852 and 1853 (pages unnumbered); R.G. Boodle, *The Life and Labours of the Right Rev. William Tyrrell, D.D.*, ch. 8.
23. *New Zealand Church Almanac*, 1852. For the social context, see K.R. Howe, "Culture Contacts on the Loyalty Islands, 1841-1895" (Ph.D. thesis), ch. 2.
24. William Nihill to his father, 1 August 1852, Nihill Letters, Hocken Library; also in *Colonial Church Chronicle* 6 (1852-53): 423-28.
25. Bishop Tyrrell in Tucker, *Selwyn*, vol. 1, p. 367; *Sydney Morning Herald*, 21 July 1853.
26. [Mrs Martin] to S.P.G., 6 July 1851, in "Letters from the Bishop of New Zealand and Others, 1842-1867", p. 822, Selwyn Papers, Auckland Institute and Museum Library; also in *Gospel Missionary* 2 (1852): 97-112.

27. *Gospel Missionary* 5 (1855): 58-59.
28. Alison Drummond, ed., *The Auckland Journals of Vicesimus Lush, 1850-63* (Christchurch: Pegasus Press, 1971), p. 183.
29. A.E. Prebble, "George Augustus Selwyn, the Apostle of Melanesia" (M.A. thesis), p. 44.
30. Church of England in Australia, *Minutes of Proceedings at a Meeting of the Metropolitan and Suffragan Bishops of the Province of Australasia ... 1850*, pp. 23-24.
31. H. Venn to G.A. Kissling, 19 February 1852, C.M.S. Outward Letterbooks, New Zealand, C N/L5, C.M.S. Archives.
32. *Letter from Bishop Selwyn* [St Barnabas' Day, 1853], p. 8.
33. R.H. Codrington to his aunt, 1 October 1872, Codrington Papers, Rhodes House Library.
34. *The Island Mission*, p. 159; J.C. Patteson to his sisters, 22 July 1866, Patteson Papers, U.S.P.G. Archives.
35. George Sarawia, *They Came to My Island*, p. 2.
36. J.C. Patteson, journal-letter, September [1857], Patteson Papers.
37. Tucker, *Selwyn*, vol. 2, p. 29.
38. R.H. Codrington, *Lecture delivered at Nelson, N.Z., September 25, 1863*, p. 3; Erskine, *Journal of a Cruise*, pp. 22, 317-18; Mrs [S.M.] Smythe, *Ten Months in the Fiji Islands* (Oxford, 1864), pp. 5-6, 174-76; J.J. Halcombe in *Mission Life* 2 (1867): 158-59. Cf. John Inglis, *In the New Hebrides: Reminiscences of Missionary Life and Work, especially on the Island of Aneityum, from 1850 till 1877* (London, 1887), pp. 309-18; H. Venn to Admiral Vernon Harcourt, 2 April 1852, C.M.S. Outward Letterbooks, Home, G/AC 1/9, C.M.S. Archives.
39. J.C. Patteson to his father, 28 April 1859 (continuation 13 June), Patteson Papers.
40. "Letters from the Bishop of New Zealand and Others", pp. 317, 822.
41. Melanesian Mission, Account of Second Voyage, 1857, in *M.M.R.*, 1857 (pages unnumbered).
42. *M.M.R.*, 1876, p. 15.
43. *M.M.R.*, 18 March 1861, p. 9.
44. See, e.g., *I.V.*, 1897, p. 34; *S.C.L.*, September 1906, p. 46.
45. *New Zealand Church Almanac*, 1853 (pages unnumbered).
46. On Didimang, see Philip D. Vigors, "Private Journal of a Four Months Cruise ... in H.M.S. 'Havannah' ", pp. 187-88, Auckland Institute and Museum Library; *S.C.L.*, June 1898, pp. 1-4.
47. Sarawia, *They Came to My Island*, p. 8.
48. W.G. Ivens, "Melanesia and its People", in Appendix to *Dictionary and Grammar of the Language of Sa'a and Ulawa ...*, p. 191.
49. Eugene Stock, *The History of the Church Missionary Society: Its Environment, its Men and its Work* (London, 1899), vol. 1, pp. 408-10; vol. 2, pp. 19-21; Hans Cnattingius, *Bishops and Societies: A Study of Anglican Colonial and Missionary Expansion, 1698-1850* (London: S.P.C.K., 1952), pp. 195-206; Owen Chadwick, *Mackenzie's Grave* (London: Hodder & Stoughton, 1959), pp. 20-23; Gavin D. White, "The Idea of the Missionary Bishop in Mid-nineteenth Century Anglicanism"

(S.T.M. thesis, General Theological Seminary, New York, 1968).
50. *Colonial Church Chronicle* 14 (1860): 125.
51. ibid., 7 (1853-54): 98-99; 13 (1859): 263-66; 14 (1860): 73-75, 245-51; 15 (1861): 154-57, 287-96, 328-37.
52. *Norfolk Island: Correspondence between His Excellency Sir W. Denison ... and the Bishop of New Zealand*; Sir William Denison to H. Labouchere, 12 June and 21 July 1856, Denison Correspondence, M.L.; Selwyn Papers, Auckland, folder 3.
53. Duke of Newcastle to Governor Gore Browne, 26 June 1860, in Melanesian Mission, *Records and Documents relating to the Consecration of a Missionary Bishop for the Western Islands of the South Pacific Ocean*, pp. 3-4. See also Selwyn Papers, Auckland, folder 2.
54. Tucker, *Selwyn*, vol. 2, p. 212.
55. Church of the Province of New Zealand, *Proceedings of General Synod*, 1862, pp. 16-17, 68-70.
56. H.W. Tucker, *Under His Banner: Papers on the Missionary Work of Modern Times* (London: S.P.C.K., 8th edn, 1904), p. 253.

2
Foundations

The headquarters of the new Pacific diocese was not in Melanesia but in Auckland. In 1859, the Melanesian school had been moved from St John's College, on its exposed hilltop, to Kohimarama, a sheltered bay on the southern shore of Auckland harbour, where expensive stone buildings were erected to form three sides of a collegiate quadrangle. Most of the cost was met by Patteson's cousin, Charlotte Yonge, from the proceeds of her then famous novel *The Daisy Chain*, first published in 1856, into which she had incorporated a missionary theme as well as fragments of various accounts of life in the Loyalty Islands. It was in romantic allusion to a fictional church in *The Daisy Chain* that the college was dedicated to St Andrew.

At Kohimarama, the new bishop pondered much over his teaching objectives and methods. According to his own High Church school of Anglican theology, Christianity embodied the authoritative transmission of divine revelation in the form of "positive" dogmatic truth. The instruction of young Melanesians therefore required enormous care. In 1863, he wrote to John Keble:

> *Now* is the time when they are in the receptive state, and *now* especially any error on our part may give a wrong direction to the early faith of thousands! What an awful thought! We are their only teachers, the only representatives of Christianity among them. How inexpressibly solemn and fearful![1]

Patteson disliked much of what he had seen of the L.M.S. The Polynesian teachers in the Loyalty Islands had been trained, he alleged, by a defective system, which laid too much stress on emotional catch-phrases and simple texts, with the result that there was a widespread profession of the new teaching, but "no knowledge of what that new teaching really is".[2] The need was for depth of knowledge and not a mere religious exuberance. Effective teachers should be masters of their subject, equipped to remain alone in a hostile environment, perhaps for years at a time, reproducing without distortion the principal tenets of Christian orthodoxy. This concern for dogmatic purity and the rational comprehension of solemn truths inevitably led to a heavily didactic atmosphere within the school. Patteson devoted himself to the provision of simple grammars and phrase-books of native languages, catechetical literature and translations of scripture. The Melanesians were taught a simple catechism and were questioned rigorously on their understanding of translated books of the New Testament: "What means did the Lord employ to make known His will to Saul?" "He sent a disciple to tell him." ... "Mention another instance of God's working in the same way recorded in the Acts." "The case of Cornelius, who was told by the angel to send for Peter." ... "But what is the greatest instance of all, the greatest proof to us that God chooses to declare His will to man through man?" "God sent His own Son to become Man."[3]

The white staff at Kohimarama was, of intention, kept small. Not many were needed for the teaching work; even fewer were judged to be suitable. Patteson's ideal missionary was a man of similar stamp to himself: a young English gentleman, public school (preferably Eton) and university-educated, "free from preconceived notions", who would go anywhere, could learn a native language and who held "no taint of the common and fatal heresy concerning the natural inferiority of the black races", which he saw in every mission but his own.[4] Men from a lower-middle-class background, who predominated among recruits for the Wesleyan, L.M.S. and C.M.S. missions—jumped-up tradesmen who did not pronounce their *h's*—would not do, he sniffed, for they too easily became petty tyrants when put in a position of power over others. However, the "best men" by his own definition did not know about Melanesia and would not come anyway. For the Mission to survive and expand, he was therefore compelled to make do with colonial or English recruits from respectable non-university backgrounds, who could be trained to adopt his mission's assumptions and mode of living. In the early 1860s at St Andrew's, there were two lay teachers —Benjamin Dudley, son of a Christchurch clergyman, and

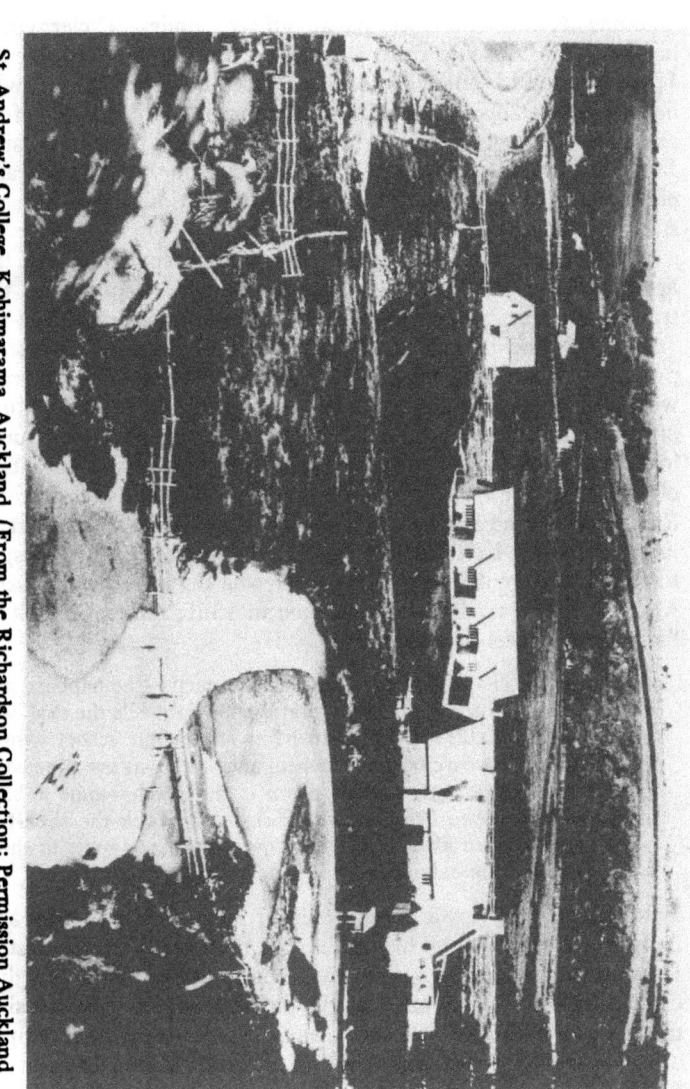

St. Andrew's College, Kohimarama, Auckland (From the Richardson Collection: Permission Auckland Institute and Museum)

Thomas Kerr, a former naval officer, under a clergyman headmaster, Lonsdale Pritt, who was a Cambridge graduate. In 1863, Kerr and Dudley left, to be replaced by John Palmer, who had worked at his uncle's C.M.S. station in the Waikato before studying theology at St John's. (He remained in the Melanesian Mission until his death in 1902.) Others came, to be tried and often found wanting, but the social composition of the mission staff remained much the same.

Under Pritt's headship, the school ceased to be an appendage of Patteson's private household. Expanding the tradition begun at St John's, there was much emphasis on "training" the young Melanesians in habits of industry, punctuality and responsibility by means of systematic manual work, for three hours daily. The boys were divided into groups of ten or a dozen, each under its own leader, who took turns in cooking, assisting in the printing office and in the operation of an 80 hectare farm supplying dairy and agricultural produce for the Auckland market. Outwardly, St Andrew's College ran like clockwork. Kohimarama became a favourite excursion spot for Auckland gentry to admire what was being achieved. Lady Martin, who stayed there for a time in 1861, remembered it as "a happy, peaceful place".

> At 7 a.m. the chapel bell rang, and all the party—the baptised and catechumens—assembled. "Now that the daylight fills the sky" was sung daily to Tallis's Ordinal, in Mota, the whole school joining heartily. By twelve o'clock, after school and work was over, the boys, fifty in all, would come rushing down to the beach—some to bask in the sun, some to fish from the rocks, or to cook the shell-fish which they groped after in the mud over tiny fires, some to shoot up and down the calm blue water in a native canoe.[5]

Patteson himself was a patient teacher, generous with gifts and money, greatly loved by his pupils, but Pritt was a harsh master, waspish to his colleagues, always complaining about lax discipline. When it came out that the oldest scholars were refusing to return to New Zealand because they feared his violent temper and beatings, he was asked to resign. He left the Mission in 1867.

There were other changes in the internal organization of the central school. During 1865, to avoid interruption to teaching and thus minimize the losses through "relapses" into paganism after only brief periods of Christian instruction, it was developed into a permanent institution. Only the first scholars from a new island or those who displayed little ability were now kept for one season, as formerly; the others remained initially for eighteen months and later for much longer periods—up to six or eight years, with only one visit to their homes—before finally being sent out as mission teachers. Whereas the number of pupils had previously been limited by the capacity of the *Southern Cross*, the size of the school was now governed solely by the Mission's never adequate income. The roll rose from 35 in 1863 to 69 in 1865, 134 in 1869, 181 in 1874. Included in the total were a dozen or more girls, who were brought from the islands to be trained by Mrs Pritt and her successors in the household arts of sewing, cooking, washing and ironing, to fit them to become "Christian wives for our Christian lads".[6]

A concurrent development was the discarding of English as the medium of instruction. Selwyn had made English the *lingua franca* of the Mission, in the absence of an alternative, hoping that it would some day occupy in the linguistically fragmented islands a position analogous to Latin in medieval Europe. Patteson doubted the wisdom of this policy, for not only was English unlike any Melanesian language in construction, but it also presented unusual difficulties in spelling and pronunciation. His own ability to acquire new languages was remarkable. For private religious instruction, he therefore committed to writing the six or seven principal languages then represented in the school, translated the Apostles' Creed, short catechism and selected prayers, and taught Christian doctrine to his pupils in their own tongues. This clumsy dual system lasted until the early 1860s, when the leadership of older youths from the Banks Islands and Pritt's inability to master more than one Melanesian language led to the spread of the language of Mota throughout the school. Despite the differences of vocabulary, it was found to be easily acquired by scholars from other islands. By 1867, English had fallen into disuse, to be supplanted by Mota as the Mission's common language: "not that we made it so," Patteson declared, "or wished it rather than any other to be so ... but so it is".[7] Only the English word "God" remained in use, on account of the "enormous difficulty ... of finding an adequate native expression in any one language".[8]

Soon after the adoption of Mota came the removal of the central school from New Zealand to Norfolk Island, 1200 kilometres nearer Melanesia. Auckland's advantages, which were a "tolerably settled state of society" and the attractiveness of its novel sights—cows and sheep, large buildings, shipping and soldiers—were increasingly outweighed by its drawbacks. Its distance from the islands made frequent trips impossible, thereby limiting the size of the school, and Solomon Islanders in particular found the annual six weeks' 3500-kilometre voyage from their homes, the latter part through cold and stormy seas, an unrelieved misery. From 1864, there was talk of transferring the Mission's headquarters to Curtis Island, off the coast of Queensland, only ten days' sailing from the Solomons, where the colonial government was prepared to grant land on condition that the school enlarged its scope to include the local Aborigines. Then came the offer of land at Norfolk Island from a new and sympathetic Governor of New South Wales, Sir John Young. Aware that Selwyn disapproved of removing the mission headquarters from New Zealand, Patteson agonized over the process of decision. At length, mainly because of the opportunity to "improve" the morals and intellects of the Pitcairners, Norfolk Island was chosen in preference to Queensland. The mission establishment was to remain there for another half century.

The new station (*vanua*) was named after St Barnabas. Wooden buildings were erected on a less-ambitious scale than at Kohimarama, and a farm was commenced before the first party of sixty-two began schooling at the end of 1867. The physical advantages of the new site were immediately obvious. It was warmer than New Zealand, though cool enough to require the wearing of flannel shirts and trousers, and the lush subtropical climate made it possible to save money by growing sweet potatoes, yams, bananas and other Melanesian foods. The Pitcairners living in the former convict settlement at Kingston, five kilometres distant, were outwardly friendly but inwardly angered by the intrusion; for they resented the high-handed manner in which the New South Wales colonial government had granted and sold to the Mission some 400 hectares of land that they insisted was theirs in perpetuity by Royal donation. The grievance was never forgotten.

In the late 1860s, this Mota-speaking school, located on a small cliff-bound island hundreds of kilometres from both Australia and New Zealand, far beyond the borders of Melanesia, seemed to symbolize the Mission's social and religious isolation, even twenty years after Selwyn's first voyages. Apart from a few dying infants, the only Melanesians so far baptized had been scholars at the central school in Auckland, and their number was not large. Up to the middle of 1868, Patteson's baptized converts totalled only twenty-six, of whom one had died and two (Benjamin Gariri and William Didimang on San Cristobal) were mourned as having fallen back into "habits of indifference, if not utter neglect of their teaching".[9] Of these, twelve were sufficiently advanced in Christian faith and conduct to have offered themselves for confirmation and admission to Holy Communion. Until 1871, the picture did not substantially alter.

The Norfolk Island station was more than a religious training institution. It was also the seat of the bishop, the locus of familial affections and personal feuds, and the living embodiment of the Mission's distinctive customs and traditions—*lingai* was the Mota word—and as such it had enormous influence on the early shaping of Melanesian Anglicanism. As the pivot of the Mission, it thus retained its priority as the one department in which every member of the white staff was compelled to participate and from which voyages on the *Southern Cross* and annual residence in the islands were seen essentially as incidental breaks.

The dominant figure at St Barnabas' was Pritt's successor as headmaster. This was Robert Henry Codrington, a clerical Fellow of Wadham College, Oxford, who had first come to New Zealand in 1860 to work in the Nelson diocese and had later been considered by Selwyn as a possible bishop for Dunedin. Having undertaken an initial voyage through Melanesia on the *Southern Cross* in 1863, he went to Norfolk Island out of a sense of obligation to Patteson, full of gloomy forebodings about his intellectual and social exile. There, his combination of remarkable erudition with personal geniality gave him a crucial role among the English staff as the one person who could talk on equal terms with both the bishop and the younger clergy. "He is so bright," enthused Patteson, "so sociable, so pleasant, such an element of usefulness, & such a bond of union for us all ..."[10] Codrington was to stay at Norfolk Island for twenty years, proud of his intellectual pre-eminence, a caustic commentator on the foibles of his colleagues, himself eventually to become a legendary character about whom affectionate stories were told.

Outside the religious world, Codrington achieved lasting fame. At the head of the uniquely polyglot school, he utilized his position to make a systematic investigation through trusted informants of the cultures of the Banks Islands and other places within the orbit of the *Southern Cross*, with the intention "to set forth as much as possible what natives say about themselves, not what Europeans say about them".[11] As a scholar, he was cautious, contemptuous of hasty conclusions, aware of the difficulties inherent in cross-cultural enquiry, concerned above all to portray Melanesian society not as grotesque barbarism but as a particular expression of certain common human experiences and traditions. His principal published works were recognized immediately in England and Europe as authoritative pioneer works of Pacific anthropology and linguistics: *The Melanesian Languages* (1885), *The Melanesians* (1891) and *A Dictionary of the Language of Mota* (1896). His classic account of *mana* ("supernatural power") in *The Melanesians* has been a stimulus to all subsequent investigators and theorists in the field of comparative religion.

> This is what works to effect everything which is beyond the ordinary power of men, outside the common processes of nature; it is present in the atmosphere of life, attaches itself to persons and to things, and is manifested by results which can only be ascribed to its operation ... But this power, though itself impersonal, is always connected with some person who directs it; all spirits have it, ghosts generally, some men ...
>
> All Melanesian religion consists ... in getting this Mana for one's self, or getting it used for one's benefit—all religion, that is, as far as religious practices go, prayers and sacrifices.[12]

Under Codrington, the internal organization of the central school at Norfolk Island continued broadly on the lines already laid down by Pritt. An important influence was the Arnoldian public school; hence the emphasis on corporate spirit, delegated authority to older pupils, the alternation of work and recreation, and the house system, by which each English missionary clergyman had special responsibility for twenty or thirty boys from one

Joseph Atkin (Permission Church Missionary Society, London)

particular island group. He would teach them during the summer, thereby learning one of the principal languages, and in the cooler season, would take a small party back to their home as the nucleus of a new village school. Codrington and Palmer were together in charge of the Banks Islanders, who by this time comprised almost half the total roll; Joseph Atkin, son of an Auckland settler, whose all-round abilities were impressive, taught boys from the eastern Solomons; Charles Brooke, an effervescent Irishman, had those from the central Solomons; Charles Bice, who had trained for the mission field at St Augustine's College, Canterbury, was responsible for the New Hebrideans. Senior scholars took classes as assistant teachers.

The aim of the Norfolk Island school was avowedly religious —"the selection and the training of native teachers and clergy".[13] As at St John's and Kohimarama, there was a characteristic High Church stress on regular and dignified liturgical worship, for

Charles Bice with a group of New Hebridean mission scholars, St. Barnabas' College, Norfolk Island (Permission Church Missionary Soceity, London)

it was to remain a principle of the Mission that the doctrines of the Bible should be interpreted only according to the traditional Christian creeds and forms of prayer. There were holidays on major saints' days, and convivial celebrations of the principal church feasts of Christmas and Easter. For the daily chapel services, Patteson arranged a connected series of selected psalms, Bible readings and narrative hymns in Mota, composed by himself, to commemorate each week the main sacred events and doctrines. On Sunday, the theme was the Resurrection ("Jesus rose again today", began the special hymn), followed in order by the Gift of the Spirit, the Nativity, Epiphany, Betrayal (a hymn on Judas was considered to be so terrifying that it was later omitted), Ascension, Crucifixion and Burial.[14]

The days were regulated by bells. A school day began at six o'clock; there was Mattins at seven, breakfast in the hall at seven-thirty and school work for an hour and a half from eight. From then until lunchtime, there was manual work for all in the gardens. Dinner was at one o'clock, with both whites and Melanesians eating "pretty much the same" meal of sweet potatoes, yams and vegetables, occasionally with meat. At two o'clock there were more school classes, followed at three by singing for an hour on the sol-fa system—"one of the most spirited schools of the day". The rest of the afternoon was free for recreation until tea (a "very plain meal") at six. Evensong was at six-thirty, evening school from seven to eight and private study until the final bell at ten.[15]

"A Melanesian's book is mostly his constant companion," observed Bice, "be it the Primer, or Prayer Book and Gospels."[16] No other books had yet been translated into the Mota language. Secular subjects, therefore, did not exist, apart from the essential tools of reading, writing and simple arithmetic. Codrington took a regular class for older boys on the "things of this world", teaching them "with more confidence than wisdom about tides & eclipses & what not".[17] The paucity of translations limited also the scope of religious instruction, but Patteson saw this as no disadvantage. There should be no hurry about printing the entire Bible, he argued, for the Gospels of St Luke and St John and the Acts of the Apostles contained "quite as much as any ordinary person can *really* and *thoroughly* know" of the life and work of Christ.[18] With his senior class, he devoted much time to expounding the meaning and interpretation of each doctrine and gospel event, even reading to them from his favourite work of sixteenth-century Anglican theology, Richard Hooker's *Of the Laws of Ecclesiastical Polity*. As lectures, Codrington observed, they were "quite as advanced as students get in the best theological colleges in England", though whether they were understood in the sense intended was a matter for conjecture.[19]

Norfolk Island was isolated from the outside world, linked only by the *Southern Cross* and ships every six months or so from Sydney or Auckland. For members of the mission staff, the combination of a closed environment, infrequent communications and a continuous routine easily became oppressively monotonous, from which it was possible to escape only through the occasional picnic, concert, tennis match or supper party among themselves and with the leaders of the Pitcairner community. For their Melanesian pupils, life at Norfolk Island offered satisfactions obtainable nowhere else. The peaceful routine, with its new friendships, new games (cricket and football), annual festivals, access to books, clothes and small sums of money paid for extra tasks, and the participation in a European way of life were together powerful inducements to eventual identification with the

Mission's goals and aims. Bice thought they soon preferred the school to their own homes. Codrington detected in the older Banks Islands scholars an "air of perfect ease and self-contentment", but this was not yet so among the others, especially the Solomon Islanders, who were obviously "thinking of their island life with regret more or less active and conscious".[20] Clement Marau, who first came to Norfolk Island from Mere Lava in the Banks group in 1869, at the age of twelve, remembered his astonishment that "there was nothing but peace in the place".

> I never heard of fighting, or quarrelling, or bad conduct. I saw that the girls kept properly by themselves, and that Palmer and his wife looked well after them; that the boys kept properly by themselves, and were well looked after at meals, sitting down and rising up all together; and that the white teachers all taught us properly, taking good care of us to prevent our going out in the rain, looking well after us to see that we washed ourselves properly, and dressed ourselves properly in our clothes, and forbidding us from quarrelling, or following after any bad heathen practices, or speaking bad words. And I heard continually the sound of the bell ringing to call people together, and I saw everything done regularly and in good order; and then I thought quietly within myself that this was a different way of living, and a thoroughly good one.[21]

The Mission's self-image placed particular importance on the principle of inherent equality of the races, shown in practice by the distribution of kitchen, farming and other duties among the whole mission community, without classification into higher tasks befitting a white man and menial tasks for the black—though there are no recorded examples of the latter occupying a supervisory position over the former. There were no servants. Everyone did an allotted share in accordance with his special skills; no one was exempt from some kind of manual labour, apart from the bishop himself, who spent his days and nights deep in the study of native languages and making translations.

Patteson was inclined to be self-satisfied as to the uniqueness of his equality principle. Indeed, he so often unfavourably compared the practice of other missions with his own, on the basis of unpleasing incidents that he had witnessed on C.M.S. or L.M.S. stations in the 1850s, that at least one of his readers became embarrassed and urged him to stop.[22] In fact, the ethos of the Norfolk Island school was less egalitarian (as it was

Dining-hall, St. Barnabas' College, Norfok Island (From the Beattie Collection: Permission Auckland Institute and Museum)

Morning drill, St. Barnabas' College, Norfolk Island (From the Beattie Collection. Permission Auckland Institute and Museum)

sometimes described) than it was that of a benevolent clerical paternalism. The model was the family, with the bishop ("Besope") as the unquestioned head and governing mind, the clergy as older brothers and the Melanesians as children in civilization at various stages of development, to be helped, encouraged, taught, weeded out and carefully disciplined by the "unwritten law of love". Church visitors were invariably delighted by what they saw, returning to their homes in the colonies to write glowing reports of the spirit of "brotherly and christian co-operation", the devotional atmosphere of the chapel services, and the easy access of pupils to the private rooms of their teachers

> ... sitting quietly by their side in their rooms, handling with much care their lesson-books, doing no injury to the furniture, and keeping their fingers from the private property of the missionaries which lies about them on every side. In the countenances of several of these hopeful scholars I thought I could discern signs of more than a glimmering of "sweetness and light".[23]

Old things were passing away. Here surely, it seemed, was the nursery of a new and Christian Melanesia.

By transferring its headquarters from Auckland to Norfolk Island, the Melanesian Mission became totally invisible to its potential supporters in New Zealand, as well as in Australia. Far from Selwyn's intention to establish Melanesia as the primary missionary object of the antipodean Anglican Church in its corporate capacity, it had become instead—and was to remain—a semi-private organization, headed by a bishop in the field, but receiving the bulk of its support, like any voluntary missionary society, from like-minded groups of personal friends, and the specially devout.

It is not hard to find reasons for the failure of this aspect of Selwyn's master-plan. Fundamentally, it was due to the strength in both Australia and New Zealand of the diocesan principle, with its deep-rooted sense of local independence and distrust of centralized church organizations of any kind. In every colonial diocese, moreover, parochial needs predominated, for as immigrants poured in from Britain there was a constant cry for money and men to supply the material demands of new churches in growing towns and scattered rural settlements. There were also doctrinal reasons for the lack of support. Evangelicals of conservative theology who became strong in Sydney and Melbourne under Bishops Barker and Perry, did not really approve of a mission consciously founded upon "church principles" that lacked the imprimatur of the C.M.S. and that counted among its English friends the Tractarian leader John Keble. In Australia, too, many pious people wondered why they should give money to foreign missions only to repeat elsewhere the spectacular failure of missions sent to their own Aborigines. The result of all this was that during the 1860s, less than half, sometimes only a third, of the Mission's £3000 annual income derived from individuals and parishes in the various dioceses of Australia and New Zealand. This pattern of support was to remain basically unchanged for the remainder of the century. Survival was therefore dependent upon other sources: revenue from the see's endowment fund, transferred to the control of the New Zealand General Synod in 1862 as the Melanesian Mission Trust (invested in English securities and farm land at Kohimarama), and donations from England. These comprised the handsome but dwindling royalties from Charlotte Yonge's *The Daisy Chain*, an annual grant of £300 from the Society for the Propagation of the Gospel (discontinued after 1879) and a similar sum from the exclusive Eton Association, which had originated in 1850 among a group of university and ecclesiastical friends of Selwyn, who pledged themselves to support the church in New Zealand and its extension to the Melanesian islands. The association met at Eton College each year on St Barnabas' Day (11 June) for a service, sermon, luncheon and meeting—a date that eventually became the acknowledged annual festival day of the whole Mission. Additional funds were later raised by another committee, the English Committee, set up in 1872 expressly to represent the interests of the Melanesian Mission in England. The deficit, which averaged £300 a year, and in 1866 was as high as £1100, was met by secret transfusions from Patteson's substantial private income—without which, he admitted, "we can't get on".[24]

The quasi-proprietary character thus assumed by the Mission was reinforced by Patteson's extreme reticence in publicizing his work abroad by popular reports or addresses. He disliked the idea of vulgarizing his daily activities and the religious experiences of his converts. Moreover, with an eye to the tragic failure of Bishop Mackenzie's much-heralded mission to Central Africa, he feared the prospect of pressure from enthusiastic supporters craving speedy results. Australasian support was admitted to be the ideal, but in the meantime, to work on quietly was best. It was only extreme financial necessity that compelled him to undertake tours of eastern Australia in 1864 and 1865, to arouse interest and obtain regular subscriptions. These involved tiring rounds of public welcomes, Sunday sermons and missionary meetings. He left behind a string of diocesan and parochial missionary organizations to raise money for Melanesia, promises of anniversary sermons and collections, and Sunday Schools pledging £10 a year to support assigned scholars at Norfolk Island. Enthusiasm, inevitably, was found to be easy to arouse in a crowded meeting after the singing of "From Greenland's Icy Mountains" and a stirring though studiously unsentimental address on the bright prospects in Melanesia, but it proved difficult to maintain. Donations fell off, as illustrated by the Norwood Melanesian Missionary Association, founded during Patteson's first visit to Adelaide in 1864. It collected £24 in its first year, £34 in its second, but only £10 in 1866 and £8 in 1867. There were no longer enough collectors and the attendance at the annual meeting was reported to be small.[25]

Likewise in New Zealand, continued financial support was dependent upon regular tours through each diocese by missionaries with dramatic stories to tell. The first of these, by Bice, was not until 1875. In Auckland, after the Mission's removal to Norfolk Island, there was much personal interest in Patteson and his work among a handful of high-ranking clergy and church-minded laity (the subscription list for 1870 included £10 from the governor, Sir George Bowen, and £5 from Sir William Martin). Among ordinary church-goers in the country as a whole, however, despite synod resolutions, semi-compulsory annual collections and episcopal exhortations to a "truly Christian spirit", there was understandably little interest in an exotic enterprise of which they knew virtually nothing and from which they could see no tangible advantage. The annual sum raised in New Zealand for the Melanesian Mission, averaging £600 in the twenty years after 1861, did not surpass Australian contributions until the early 1890s.[26]

In the islands, during the 1860s, the Mission was struggling to find a permanent foothold. It was still an article of orthodoxy that the "unhealthy" climate of northern Melanesia precluded continuous European residence, but this did not mean that a few missionaries could not live there for up to six months each year, in carefully selected places, during the cooler season of south-easterly trade winds between April and November. Certainly, in the south, there was no difficulty on this account. There was an early opportunity for a permanent mission-station at Yengen, a favourite port of call for European traders to New Caledonia, where the powerful chief Bwarat (or Bwaxat) made persistent requests for a "Missionary English" after his first meeting with Selwyn in 1849. However, Selwyn could find no "faithful and discreet" clergyman for the post, and in 1858, when Bwarat was deported to Tahiti by the French colonial authorities as a troublesome subject, Yengen was closed to all foreigners.[27]

In the adjacent Loyalty Islands, the obstacles were neither physical nor political, but religious. Nihill had already lived, and died, at Mare, while Patteson was anxious to retain Selwyn's connection with Lifu, where the L.M.S. had sent Polynesian teachers but no white missionary. It was a confrontation between High Anglicanism and Dissent, and feelings ran high. The Samoa missionaries of the L.M.S., hearing stories of the lamentably unprotestant ("Puseyite") character of the Australasian Board of Missions because it lacked C.M.S. participation, had already reversed their 1848 decision to cede the Loyalties to Selwyn. Creagh of the L.M.S. complained of the growth of dissension among his Mare flock when Selwyn's supporters, with an eye to profitable visits to New Zealand, proclaimed that "the bishop's ship is the best":

> We fear not for the *ultimate* triumph. It may do injury to our cause for a time, & subject us to annoyance, but I feel comfort in the thought that God is more honoured by the hearty service of one sincere & humble Christian man than by a thousand brought over by worldly considerations.[28]

Patteson wrote bitterly of the pettiness of the L.M.S. agents and their unreasonable suspicion of Selwyn's noble intentions. The arrival of a French Marist mission made action even more urgent. Accordingly, in 1858, he conducted a "winter school" on Lifu for twelve of his northern scholars between the two annual voyages of the *Southern Cross*, in the confident expectation that the people themselves, realizing the superior advantages of the bishop's system, would change their allegiance and demand an Anglican station. But the four months' experiment was not a success. Food for the party was in short supply, and Lifu was found to offer none of the novel attractions of school in Auckland. In the following year, as two L.M.S. missionaries were on their way to Lifu, he reluctantly withdrew the Anglican claim to the Loyalties for the sake of peace and because of his rival's undoubted "priority of occupation".[29]

In the New Hebrides, the Presbyterians had already established European stations on the southernmost islands of Aneityum, Tanna and Erromango. Their relations with the Anglicans were friendly. To avoid sectarian conflict, Patteson therefore confined his attention to those islands lying north of Efate. Thus reduced in size, from 1860 the Anglican mission field in Melanesia consisted of four distinct groups: the large islands of the northern New Hebrides, the Banks and Torres Islands (the northernmost extension of the New Hebrides island chain), the Santa Cruz group, with its adjacent Polynesian outliers, and the Solomon Islands. For another generation, no more was heard about expansion to New Britain and New Guinea.

In northern Melanesia, Selwyn's original plan was found to require modification. Although the emphasis was still on trained Melanesian converts as "the permanent element" in the Mission's work, the spectacular failure of the entire first generation of mission scholars to carry out formal teaching when they returned to their homes pointed to a need for a supportive European presence during their vulnerable early years. In 1861, therefore, Patteson outlined his intention to station at a central spot in each archipelago one or more English clergymen, who would live there for three or more months each year—perhaps for much longer—"visiting in their boat the adjacent islands, training up teachers, and keeping school in the different villages, winning the good-will and confidence of the people, and by their example recommending the Gospel of Peace to the heathen".[30] By 1871, Anglican missionary clergymen were itinerating annually from Omba in the New Hebrides, from Mota in the Banks

Islands and from San Cristobal and Nggela in the Solomons.

At the same time, as a step towards a "real hold" on the people, the initial phase of exploration gave way to one of concentration on those accessible and populous places that supplied the largest parties of scholars.[31] The early 1860s had seen the Mission's sphere of contact finally embrace the central Solomons: the Bugotu district of Santa Isabel, which Patteson first visited in 1861 as a passenger on the cruizing warship H.M.S. *Cordelia*, and the Nggela group, where the first scholar was obtained in 1862. Brooke began work there in August 1867. The last major exploratory voyage of the *Southern Cross* was in 1866, when it reached as far as the Marovo Lagoon on New Georgia in the western Solomons. Initial contacts were also made with the peoples of Savo Island and Sa'a, an important place at the southeast extremity of Malaita. During the same voyage, Patteson also spent ten days at Wango, a large village on the northern coast of San Cristobal. "Satisfied with Waño as a good position for a station," he noted in his diary. "Water, no mosquitoes or sand flies, sandy soil, soon dry after heavy rain."[32] Atkin stayed there for the first time in 1869, for nineteen days, accompanied by Stephen Taroaniara, a newly confirmed convert from the nearby village of Tawatana.

It was not in the Solomons, however, that the Melanesian Mission achieved its earliest success. The first island conversions occurred in the Banks Islands, which were neither the largest nor the most populous nor the closest to New Zealand of the principal island groups within its sphere of work. On his voyage through the Banks in 1857, Selwyn had been struck by the sight of canoes in peaceful passage from one island to another and by the absence of sandalwooders and whalers. "They have little or no knowledge of European commodities," he wrote approvingly; "no desire for tobacco; none of that vulgar swagger which is acquired by intercourse with ships ..."[33] Here, surely, was primitive Melanesia in its natural state, inhabited by "native gentlemen of the best class", and the prospect for Christianity seemed more promising than elsewhere. This was a sound argument for the concentration of mission resources, especially after the renunciation of Anglican claims to the Loyalty Islands. Port Patteson on Vanua Lava, which seemed to be a meeting-place for the whole Banks group, was first thought of as a suitable site for a regional headquarters. Then in September 1859, Patteson spent a night on Mota (or Sugarloaf Island), fifteen kilometres to the east, and convinced Selwyn of its overwhelming natural advantages for their purpose: "the dry soil, the spring of water, the wondrous fertility, the large and remarkably intelligent, well-looking population, the great banyan tree, twenty-seven paces round".[34] The issue was settled, and eleven scholars were taken to New Zealand to help prepare the way.

Mota was almost circular in shape, with a twin-peaked hill 300 metres high at the centre, surrounded by a narrow plain of uneven width fifteen kilometres around. There was a landing-place on the north side, but no harbour. The population, estimated at about 1400, was scattered throughout nine defined districts. Patteson held his first "winter school" there for five months in 1860, accompanied by Benjamin Dudley, Mano Wadrokal (a former scholar from Mare), two Lifu men and six Solomon Islanders from the Kohimarama school.

This first extended visit did not bring the quick results hoped for. It was not an asupicious time, for the arrival of the missionaries happened to coincide with a two months' ceremony of initiation, behind a sacred enclosure, for boys taking low rank in the *sukwe* or graded society. One of the Mission's pupils, Utagilaba, was immediately taken away—"very unhappy"—to participate. Others disappeared to tend their gardens or were found to have discarded their clothes and to be joining in pagan dances. Despite this, the Mota people were willing enough to have the foreigners living among them. Patteson's speedy command of their language was already a cause for admiration, as Robert Pantutun, one of the first Christian converts, recalled many years afterwards:

> When he came to visit us he would sit quietly in the boat and write down words. He would hold out a fish-hook, and if anyone said "Give me the hook, I will buy it," he would write down *gau*, fish-hook; *wol*, buy; *le ma*, give; *tagai*, no, etc. After that we saw then that he went about the *vanua*, and gave medicine to the sick; and the people said he was a good man, and wanted to help us.[35]

Accordingly, they agreed to give up about a hectare of land for a wooden frame house brought down from Auckland. They bartered yams for hatchets (one hatchet in exchange for 36 kilograms weight of yams), bottles and bars of iron. Some diligently attended the daily school classes, in order to qualify for fish-hooks, clothes and other coveted presents. In the evenings, visitors crowded into the missionaries' tiny room, to ask about the Word of God, their eyes fixed upon the stores of trade goods; after which, Patteson complained, they would "go off laughing with the idea that they have deceived me into supposing that they are anxious to be taught".[36]

The missionaries were accepted with excitement as objects of curiosity and a source of trade goods, but their role was restricted. Their attempts to demonstrate by argument the logical inconsistency of traditional beliefs produced only silence. Direct confrontation, stressing the "distinct opposition" between Satan-inspired superstition and God's truth—Patteson even refusing to accept a gift of breadfruit from a leader of the initiation rites proceeding nearby—brought polite evasion: "By and Bye we will listen to the Word of God, when we have finished these ceremonies."[37] Verbal assent was freely given. "Yours only is the good teaching", the Mota people told their teachers, with apparent equanimity.

> In talking with them [wrote Dudley] they always allow that their old superstitions are wrong, & that the new religion is the good one, but there they end. They go on just as ever with the [*sukwe*] & heathen feasts. There is nothing for it but patient waiting until it pleases God's Holy Spirit to shine into their hearts, & then their whole religious system will fall together.[38]

Almost every year thereafter, a mission party—always including either Patteson or Palmer—returned to teach school for up to three months at a time, increasingly cautious in approach but uncompromising in opposition to the traditional religion. The influence of Wadrokal was openly disruptive. He demanded that the islanders give up their *sukwe*, polygamy and separation of the sexes for eating, and when he carried an uninitiated child on to a sacred dancing-ground, the feeling ran so high that Patteson himself was in danger of being killed in punishment —a threat that he evaded only by calmness and gentle words.[39] Unease was compounded by disastrous epidemics of influenza and dysentery in 1863, which were throught to carry off about one-tenth of the population.

Each year, nevertheless, the Mota people were said to become more friendly. Despite the difficulty of finding suitable words to express Christian concepts, Patteson and Palmer found that their teaching on the Resurrection and Judgement provoked much interest: "This is a subject that will nearly always make them attend. They often ask 'When I die where shall I go to?' thinking more of the locality than of how they will then exist."[40] By 1867, it was reported that there was "much more desire to understand our teaching, much less reserve in speaking to us of themselves, and their habits and superstitions".[41] The most obvious sign of change was the decrease of fighting. Bows and arrows almost disappeared, except for hunting, due to a vague belief that the missionaries were supported by a British warship and to their persistent exhortations to end fighting. Visiting Mota in 1870, Codrington found no understanding among the islanders of what "the new teaching" involved, except that they should believe in peace and quietness and that Sunday was to be kept without work; but "they see that our scholars are immensely improved and want all the young people to be like them".[42]

In June 1871, Patteson became tired of waiting. He told his hearers that the time had come to decide between the two religions and set about baptizing the infant children of pagans, upon receiving an assurance from their parents that they would be allowed to attend a new Christian school taught by George Sarawia. "Why withhold the Baptismal gift and blessing from the little ones?", he wrote to his sisters. This triggered a mass movement to Christianity, in which parents followed their children into the Church, because, they said, they wanted to belong to the "same system".[43] During the next three months, some 230 infants and 58 adults were baptized and given English Christian names. The adult converts had learned by heart the general confession from the Book of Common Prayer, the Lord's Prayer, the Creed, a short version of the Ten Commandments and the Te Deum. For Patteson, it was a triumph, but it was little enough to show for more than twenty years of Anglican missionary work in the islands. To outward appearances, the conversion of northern Melanesia was almost as distant as it had been in 1849.

NOTES AND REFERENCES

1. Charlotte Mary Yonge, *Life of John Coleridge Patteson*, vol. 2, p. 41.
2. J.C. Patteson to his sister Frances, 25 October 1858, Patteson Papers, U.S.P.G. Archives.
3. *M.M.R.*, 1 January 1865-9 May 1866, p. 2.
4. J.C. Patteson to Warden, St Augustine's College, 7 February 1866, S.P.G. Letters Received, vol. 29, U.S.P.G. Archives; J.C. Patteson to Samuel Wilberforce, 2 January 1867, Wilberforce Papers, Bodleian Library; Yonge, *Patteson*, vol. 2, pp. 25-30, 53-57, 66-68.
5. Lady [Mary] Martin, *Our Maoris*, pp. 198-99. Chapter 13 of this book is an account of the Melanesian Mission.
6. J.C. Patteson to his sister Frances, 6 February 1864, Patteson Papers.
7. Yonge, *Patteson*, vol. 2, p. 256.
8. R.H. Codrington, *The Melanesians*, p. 121n.
9. J.C. Patteson, undated report, 1868, S.P.G. Letters Received, vol. 40/3.
10. Patteson to his sister Frances, 14 October 1867, Patteson Papers.
11. Codrington, *Melanesians*, p. vi.
12. ibid., pp. 118-19. For assessments of Codrington, see the memorial articles in *S.C.L.E.*, October 1922, pp. 114-22; obituary by S.H. Ray, *Man* 22 (1922): 169-71; Robert B. Lane in *Journal of the Polynesian Society* 84 (1975): 95-96; Charles E. Fox, *Lord of the Southern Isles*, pp. 219-22. The Oceanic concept of *mana* is analysed in: H. Ian Hogbin, "Mana", *Oceania* 6 (1935-36): 241-74; Raymond Firth, "The Analysis of 'Mana': An Empirical Approach", *Journal of the Polynesian Society* 49 (1940): 483-510. Codrington's views on the relationship between Christianity and Melanesian paganism are discussed below, p. 191.
13. *M.M.R.*, 1874, p. 10.
14. Yonge, *Patteson*, vol. 2, p. 329; *S.C.L.E.*, June 1927, p. 90.
15. *Mission Life*, n.s. 1 (1870): 504.
16. *Gospel Missionary*, n.s. 1 (1871): 108.
17. R.H. Codrington to his aunt, 16 December 1867, Codrington Papers, Rhodes House Library.
18. Yonge, *Patteson*, vol. 2, p. 593.
19. Codrington to his aunt, August 1867, Codrington Papers.
20. R.H. Codrington to W.T. Bullock, 4 April 1867, S.P.G. Letters Received, vol. 29.
21. Clement Marau, *Story of a Melanesian Deacon*, pp. 23-24.
22. Codrington to Bullock, 4 April 1867.
23. Bishop W.G. Cowie in *Church Gazette* 2 (1873): 3-5; also published separately as *Notes of a Visit to Norfolk Island ... in November 1872*. Other visitors' accounts are: Charles Hunter Brown, *The Melanesian Mission*, pp. 4-6; Melanesian Mission, *Consecration of Memorial Chapel*; Walter Coote, *The Western Pacific*, pp. 12-16; "A Visit to Norfolk Island", by a naval officer, *Mission Field* 24 (1884): 382-85; H.H. Montgomery, *The Light of Melanesia*, pp. 11-21; Vice-Admiral Boyle Somerville, *The Chart-Makers* (Edinburgh and London: W. Blackwood, 1928), pp. 90-91; P. Stacy Waddy, *A Visit to Norfolk*

Island. The school as it was in 1902 was recalled by Charles E. Fox, *Kakamora*, ch. 1.
24. Patteson to his sisters, 26 March 1868 (continuation 26 May), Patteson Papers. From January 1865 to May 1866, the total income of the Mission was £3790, of which £1139 came from Australian contributions, £620 from New Zealand, £650 from England and £300 from the Melanesian Mission Trust. In 1869, income was £4198, of which Australia supplied £992, New Zealand £631, England £1212 and the Trust £380.
25. *South Australian Register*, 23 February 1864, 25 January 1865, 21 February 1868.
26. See, e.g., Wendy Patricia Clark, " 'A Truly Christian Spirit?': Christchurch and the Melanesian Mission, 1868-1875" (M.A. long essay).
27. G.A. Selwyn to his sons, 17 October 1857, in "Letters from the Bishop of New Zealand and Others, 1842-1867, pp. 384-87, Selwyn Papers, Auckland Institute and Museum Library; David Hilliard, "Bishop G.A. Selwyn and the Melanesian Mission", *New Zealand Journal of History* 4 (1970): 132. On Bwarat, see Dorothy Shineberg, *They Came for Sandalwood*, pp. 74-79. The French had annexed New Caledonia in September 1853.
28. S.M. Creagh to A. Tidman, August 1857, L.M.S., South Seas Letters, box 27/2A, Council for World Mission Archives, School of Oriental and African Studies, University of London.
29. Patteson to his father, 12 May 1858 and 28 April 1859, Patteson Papers.
30. Melanesian Mission, *Isles of the Pacific: Account of the Melanesian Mission and of the Wreck of the Mission Vessel*, p. 23.
31. Patteson to Bullock, 16 August 1866, S.P.G. Letters Received, vol. 29.
32. J.C. Patteson, Diary, 28 July 1866, G.A. Selwyn Papers, Selwyn College Library.
33. G.A. Selwyn to his sons, 17 October 1857, in "Letters from the Bishop of New Zealand and Others", p. 346.
34. Yonge, *Patteson*, vol. 1, p. 423.
35. *S.C.L.*, October 1898, p. 3.
36. Patteson, journal-letter, 4 June 1860, entry 16 August, Patteson Papers.
37. ibid., entry 16 June.
38. B.T. Dudley, "Journal of a winter spent on Amota, Banks [Islands] ...", entries 17 and 22 June 1860, Hocken Library.
39. George Sarawia, *They Came to My Island*, pp. 17-18.
40. J. Palmer, Journal, 27 July 1866, Church of Melanesia Archives.
41. *M.M.R.*, 1867, p. 3.
42. Codrington, letter fragment, October 1870, Codrington Papers.
43. Patteson to his sisters, 16 June 1871, Patteson Papers; *Mission Life*, n.s. 3 (1872): 78-79. On Sarawia's school and the aftermath of the initial conversion, see below, pp. 58-61.

3
The Martyr

By the time the Melanesian Mission moved its headquarters to Norfolk Island in 1867, its distinctive methods and style were assuming a fixed pattern. An over-optimistic visitor from New Zealand reported in 1868 that it had "almost passed from the stage of tentative doubtful experiment, to that of ascertained success, of proved practability".[1]

The structure of the Mission was centralized and autocratic. For the next half-century, everything revolved around two focal points—the Norfolk Island school and the person of the bishop. Theoretically, the Mission *was* the bishop. In internal matters, he alone dictated policy, bound by no diocesan synod or council and responsible only to the New Zealand General Synod for the use of income derived from the Melanesian Mission Trust. The English clergy were technically his chaplains, receiving no parochial licence (as would have been issued in New Zealand), because for the greater part of each year they were resident at Norfolk Island.[2]

Patteson himself was the source of intellectual activity as well as practical policy. Brooding among his books at St Barnabas' or in the mission-house on Mota, he wistfully pondered the problems of presenting Western Christianity to a non-literate pagan society. He was a cautious and not a notably original thinker, but he was unusual among Pacific missionaries of the time in his attempt to supply his policies with a theological justification derived from first principles. His view of Melanesian pagan beliefs and religious rites was not sympathetic. They were irrational superstitions, he believed, full of error, whose only significance for Christianity lay in the underlying religious instincts of awe and "faith in powers and beings invisible".[3] His correspondence with Friedrich Max Müller at Oxford, famous

The Martyr 55

John Coleridge Patteson, *c*. 1865 (From the Beattie Collection: Permission Auckland Institute and Museum)

philologist and pioneer of the modern comparative study of religions, concerned the structure of Melanesian languages and not the diffusion of divine revelation through Melanesian religious systems.

At the centre of his mature missionary philosophy lay the principle of accommodation: that Christianity, as an inherently universal religion, should seek to adapt and assimilate itself to the modes of thought and social needs of each race or society. This implied a distinction between the fundamental and unchangeable doctrines of Christianity, which could never be compromised, and its secondary or human accretions, which, as products of particular societies, were open always to intellectual speculation and should not be universally reproduced without modification.

> I have for years thought that we seek in our Missions a great deal too much to make *English* Christians of our converts. We consciously and unanimously assume English Christianity (as something distinct I mean from the doctrines of the Church of England), to be necessary; much as so many people assume the relation of Church and State in England to be the typical and normal condition of the Church ... Evidently the heathen man is not treated fairly if we encumber our message with unnecessary requirements.[4]

When Melanesians adopted Christianity, therefore, it was not necessary that they should be encouraged to "denationalize" themselves in the process, assuming all outward habits of a nineteenth-century Englishman. As little as possible should be changed: "only what is clearly incompatible with the simplest form of Christian teaching and practice".[5]

This was not in fact a novel view, for the limits of Christian accommodation were already being debated with reference to polygamy in Africa, caste in India and the changing intellectual climate within Europe itself. However, it did not command wide assent in the higher levels of the Victorian Church of England, where there was a good deal of robust confidence in the supreme virtues of English Christianity and a distrust of local variation. This attitude was exemplified by Bishop Tait of London, whose view of overseas Anglican churches was that "the more they remain like ourselves the better".[6] Only at the end of the century, when the Church of England had confronted ancient civilizations and tribal societies in many parts of the world, often with scant success, did the principle of accommodation receive sanction from the highest quarter. This was at the Lambeth Conference of Anglican bishops in 1897, which urged that the Church should be adapted to local circumstances, and the people brought to feel in all ways that no burdens in the way of foreign customs are laid upon them, and nothing is required of them but what is of the essence of the Faith, and belongs to the due order of the Catholic Church.[7]

The problem was always to distinguish between what was essential and what was peripheral. In application of his accommodation principle, Patteson was not adventurous. He did not challenge the confident assumption of his time that the conversion of a primitive people must necessarily involve their introduction to a new social and economic order—although the civilization he envisaged in Melanesia would be of a modified and humbler form.

Among other British missionaries of the nineteenth century, the doctrine of Christianity-with-Civilization was almost axiomatic. In 1814, Samuel Marsden had sent skilled tradesmen as missionaries to the New Zealand Maoris to prepare a new social context, without which, he believed, the gospel could not take root. From the South Seas, John Williams asserted that true religion awakened new wants: "Until the people are brought under the influence of religion, they have no desire for the arts and usages of civilized life; but that invariably creates it."[8] David Livingstone had described his journeys of exploration in Africa as the opening of a "path for commerce and Christianity" and the Universities' Mission to Central Africa, led by Bishop Mackenzie, was founded explicitly to implement Livingstonian ideals.[9] The linkage between Christianity and civilization was variously justified. Whereas Evangelicals were inclined to be utilitarian—"The whole civilized world, and our own countrymen especially, share the advantages"—High Churchmen characteristically appealed to the teaching of the apostolic Church. Selwyn, for example, saw civilization implied in the gospel account of the demoniac sitting at the feet of Christ "clothed, and in his right mind" and symbolized by the sacrament of Holy Communion, in which man-made bread and wine required the prior existence of agriculture and commerce.[10]

For Patteson, too, the acceptance of Christianity ideally involved material as well as spiritual "improvement", within the context of a visible and industrious community that exemplified in "actual daily actions the teaching of the Bible".[11] In the

Melanesian Christian society of the future, the traditional daily occupations of garden work, cooking and so on would continue much as before. In domestic life, however, arrangements of "decency and propriety" would be needed: coral-lime cottages, with interior partitions and windows; light, loose clothing; crockery pots, tables and chairs; and lamps to enable reading and writing by night—though towards the end of his life, he was privately questioning the traditional Protestant association between Christianity and literacy, and discouraged adult catechumens on Mota from unnecessary book learning.[12]

Where Patteson was nearest the frontier of mid-Victorian missionary thought was not in his views on what social changes were necessary, but on how they should come about. The initiative was to lie with the Melanesian converts. New customs should not be imposed (or old ones banned) from without by ecclesiastical edict. Ideally, they should follow naturally from the islanders' deeper comprehension of Christian truth or through absorption of the example of civilized ways set before them at Norfolk Island. For missionaries to exercise secular power or to use their religious authority to demand immediate conformity in the matter of Sunday observance, the prohibition of smoking or the wearing of European clothes—as he had seen in the Loyalty Islands and southern New Hebrides—would produce only unreasoning obedience, inevitably to be followed by resentment and hypocrisy. To Christianize was to civilize, but not to anglicize; toleration of Melanesian "nationality" was ever to be preferred to legalism and suppression.

It was not until 1867 that his interest in the problem took a practical turn, when a group of Mota scholars led by George Sarawia suggested the formation of a separate Christian village on their island: "where we all can live together; where we can let the people see what our mode of life is, what our customs etc. are which we have learned from you".[13] Patteson was delighted, seeing the proposed community as another step towards success in the evangelization of Melanesia through a Melanesian agency. Called Kohimarama (after the site of the school in New Zealand), located on land bought by the Mission between the villages of Maligo and Veverau, it sprang into existence in 1869, comprising Sarawia, his wife and two other Christian couples, all of them with Norfolk Island training. As leader, Sarawia was liberally supplied with simple domestic furniture, kitchen utensils and clothing—for "all help to carry on the general work of religion & civilization".[14] The Christians lived together around a new wooden mission-house, cultivated their own gardens and began a "boarding-school" for some thirty boys and young men, to prepare them for Norfolk Island.

In 1871, a parallel venture commenced among the hundred inhabitants of Ra, an islet attached to Mota Lava, fifteen kilometres north of Mota. This was led by the brothers Henry Tagalad and Edwin Sakelrau and their brother-in-law William Kwasvarong (from Rowa), with their wives. Unlike Mota, however, the Ra Christians did not live apart from the wider community.

> They live in one house, the best in the village ... After bathing in the morning they have prayers and a hymn, which, as they are all singers, sounds very well. They spend the days variously, sometimes working, sometimes making visits in the two districts of the main island ... In the evening, after prayers, which people stand outside the house to hear, Henry and William go and sit in the two or three principal places and talk to the people, many ... coming to [Ra] on purpose.[15]

Within five years, the Ra people had all been baptized. They were said to be "more active-minded, more energetic than the Mota men, and they furnish in proportion very many more competent teachers than the larger island".[16] It was from Ra, and through its teachers, that Christianity spread into Mota Lava and later to Vanua Lava, where Sakelrau began a school at Pek in 1873.

During its first few years of existence, the tiny Christian village at Kohimarama was the Mission's brightest spot in the islands. Palmer, paying a surprise visit in 1870, found everything "most satisfactory", the house "nice and clean", with school and church services held daily at regular hours, on the pattern of Norfolk Island.[17] After the baptism of nearly three hundred infants, children and adults in 1871, Sarawia's original group was augmented by married couples and others who wished to live near the school. By 1872, Kohimarama was a flourishing Christian settlement of a dozen houses, clustered around the coral-lime church. Some 150 people attended daily school for an hour morning and evening, to be taught by Sarawia and other

Norfolk Island scholars, in addition to three new schools in other districts, while the sole Sunday School drew over 330, or a quarter of the island's population. Codrington was vastly impressed with the enthusiasm of the evening school he witnessed. There were three classes meeting on the verandah, seven inside the house, "covering every inch of space", "reading where there was light enough, and spelling where there was not", and three more outside in the open air: "One of little boys I found spelling under a cocoa nut tree, the teacher making out with difficulty his word in the moonlight, and then getting the boys to spell it."[18] The forty-eight members of the senior class of baptized adults were said to come from distant places in all weathers, "in wet weather and dark nights, sheltering themselves with palm leaf umbrellas, and seeing their way with cocoa nut torches". They were anxious for further knowledge and fascinated by biblical stories. In the first week of his stay, Palmer was asked to explain a reference to the Pharisees, the story of Zacharias and Elizabeth, the woman of Samaria, and to teach the Te Deum.[19]

During the following year, the enthusiasm suddenly evaporated. Not excluding an explanation in terms of declining novelty and failed expectations, it is certain that many people regarded the new teaching as linked in some way with a series of calamities that struck Mota within a few months: a severe hurricane in January 1873, which destroyed food gardens and created a food shortage, followed by heavy rains and epidemics of dysentery and influenza, in which about one-seventh of the population died, including George's wife Sarah and some seventy of those recently baptized. Schools and church services were little attended and the baptismal class ceased to meet. The mission report for 1874 conceded that Mota "does not answer any sanguine anticipations". The huge attendances at the Kohimarama school had fallen away permanently: "There is a want of zeal and energy, and the evangelization of the whole island languishes."[20] The picture did not change. Commodore J.G. Goodenough, who visited Mota in 1875 on H.M.S. *Pearl*, found at Kohimarama not a shining embodiment of Christian truth and social virtues, as Patteson had envisaged, but a dilapidated European house in a clearing in the bush, its verandah rotting and roof shaky, and a tiny church. He described the natives as "pleasing-looking people, but very dirty compared with those of Samoa, or Fiji even".[21] Patteson's ideal Christian village had been a theological construction, and when put to the test, the romanticism of the original concept was easily exposed.

Another aspect of the problem of accommodation concerned the qualifications of the Melanesian clergy. The question of educational standards for the "native ministry" produced wide differences of opinion and practice among mid-nineteenth-century English missionaries, and in missionary periodicals, old policies and new experiments were eagerly dissected. Some missions deliberately related effective leadership in the indigenous church to the local context, stressing the prime importance of a candidate's spiritual power and the respect of his fellows rather than a high level of Western book-learning. The majority was cautious, easily deterred by the risk of "failures" or unforeseen consequences. It was common practice not to ordain non-European converts until they were two or three generations removed from the taint of paganism, and in opposition to the creation of a vernacular ministry of inferior status, to insist on a uniform intellectual standard for all, based upon a full course of theological reading. Selwyn, at least in New Zealand, inclined to the second view; the first Maori deacon was not ordained until 1853, a Maori priest not until 1865. Patteson saw the issue as one of adjustment to local needs, with the qualifications of "native clergy" related to the work they would be doing in their own society. It was a precedent that his successors did not dispute.

> They have not to teach theology to educated Christians, but to make known the elements of Gospel truth to ignorant heathen people. If they can state clearly and forcibly the very primary leading fundamental truths of the Gospel, and live as simple-minded humble Christians, that is enough indeed.[22]

The first Melanesian clergyman was George Sarawia, ordained deacon in December 1868, eleven years after he had gone from Vanua Lava to Patteson's winter school on Lifu to learn about the alphabet and the Christian God. He was given the name George after Bishop Selwyn, who had baptized him in 1863, and was among the first group of Melanesians to be confirmed in 1865. He then assisted Palmer with a school at Mota for a few months each year. After the Mota Christian village scheme was mooted, Patteson announced his intention to ordain him. Sarawia initially resisted the idea: "... I was not clever enough for that work; it was a very serious thing, and I was not worthy of it." But Patteson insisted:

> "... You will do this because we are not there, and it is your duty to do this work. It is not good just to bury someone without prayer, and it is not good for someone to die as a heathen without Baptism." When the Bishop said that, I no longer opposed him ... Someone might hear him speaking gently, but without fail, it must be as he said.[23]

Sarawia's early success on Mota, with the corresponding growth of the Christian community, seemed to be a sufficient qualification for his advancement to the priesthood, to which he was admitted in Auckland in 1873. Meanwhile, three more Banks Islanders had been made deacons: Robert Pantutun, Henry Tagalad and Sarawia's brother, Edward Wogale. In accordance with Patteson's principle that the Melanesian clergy should be not only effective teachers but harbingers of a higher mode of social life, a regular scale of pay was laid down, generous for Pacific Islanders by the standards of the time. Whereas Melanesian plantation labourers received £6 per annum in Queensland, £3 in Fiji, a priest was to be paid £25 annually, a deacon £20, while village teachers would receive between £10.15.0 and £3.10.0, depending upon their experience and degree of responsibility.

At the same time, the overall pace of the Mission began to slacken as Patteson's control visibly weakened. The strains of solitary leadership, the long and uncomfortable voyages on the *Southern Cross* year by year and his habit of living on shore almost entirely on native food had left their mark. The first serious signs of physical decline appeared in 1867, in his forty-first year, when he admitted to his sisters that he did not expect to last "overlong" at his strenuous work.[24] Among his Melanesian pupils, he was spoken of habitually as "the old man". A critical illness early in 1870 compelled him to visit Auckland for professional medical treatment, and friends there were shocked by his haggard appearance and obvious deterioration since their last meeting two years previously.

A profound sense of isolation may have contributed to his physical decline. He had never married. An emotional blow fell in August 1864, when two devoted Norfolk Island assistants, Edwin Nobbs and Fisher Young, were fatally wounded in an unexpected and unexplained arrow attack on the ship's boat at Graciosa Bay, Santa Cruz. This disaster left a permanent scar on his memory. Selwyn's return to England in 1868, to take up the see of Lichfield, depressed him still further. In the same year, a typhoid epidemic at Norfolk Island caused the deaths of four schoolboys and prevented the annual mission voyages. He hungered for the small group of intimate friends who remained in Auckland, and in relation to his colleagues became taciturn and peevish, withdrawing permanently into the company of his books and his senior Melanesian pupils, with whom alone he felt entirely at ease. In 1871, he rejected an appeal by the five New Zealand bishops, urging extended leave in England for the sake of his health. Melanesia now held him like a magnet; he expected to die there.

At the same time, the Mission was encountering for the first time an external hindrance to its influence in the Banks Islands, in the form of recruiting vessels seeking labourers for the cotton and sugar plantations of Fiji and Queensland. These began moving northwards from their favourite recruiting-grounds of Tanna and Malakula in the late 1860s, and in pioneering new places, they inevitably ran into the difficulty of explaining their intentions to people with whom they could not easily communicate. There was no common language, the islanders had no understanding of wage labour or terms of engagement, and some unscrupulous recruiters were fully prepared to use deception and force to override the reluctant and ensure a full ship. On their voyage through the Banks Islands in 1869, the missionaries on the *Southern Cross* were besieged with reports of unsuspecting men being lured away by false pretences, though Patteson admitted that he knew of "no actual violence" that would enable him to bring a direct charge of kidnapping. He heard that his own name had been used to assist recruiting, the people having been told that "the Bishop is ill—has broken his leg getting into his boat—is at Sydney—and has sent us to bring you to him".[25] Stories of deceit and abduction multiplied over the next two years, producing a visible growth of distrust and suspicion towards all foreign vessels and reports of retaliatory attacks. In five months of 1871, fifteen crew members of Fiji labour ships were reported to have been killed at different places in the New Hebrides.[26]

The principal objection of the Melanesian Mission to the early labour trade lay in the "disgraceful" methods by which recruits were often obtained. Recruiting as actually carried on in many places, Patteson privately claimed, was "practically kidnapping men into slavery"—though he realized that this would be difficult to prove under the existing laws.[27] Another objection was the disruption of its near-monopoly of contact with the people of the Banks Islands, for the islanders were going from the prospect of Christian instruction to an environment generally unsympathetic to religion just at a time when the Mission's first village schools were being established. Codrington, always the most vehement of Anglican critics of the labour trade, admitted as much:

> It is very trying certainly to have to encounter all the hindrances of a slave trade just when we thought we had got things into train for carrying out our own scheme ... A teacher who could have got at hundreds in their own home, and in their natural state, can now hardly get at tens & in unnatural and disturbed condition, and with the prejudice against missionary teaching which intercourse with the lower class of Europeans always gives.[28]

He wrote darkly, but with exaggeration, of islands in the Banks group, desolate and "almost depopulated".

More cautious than Codrington, and unlike fervent propagandists for total abolition such as John Inglis and John G. Paton of the New Hebrides Presbyterian mission, Patteson could never bring himself to condemn the trade root and branch. In view of the long-established practice of his own organization, he could scarcely object in principle to planters—apparently dependent for their economic survival on an assured and cheap labour supply—taking young men away from their homes for three years. For pagans, if they were "properly treated" and could see for themselves a functioning Christian society, it could be "a great advantage".[29] Furthermore, he knew well enough from experience that some young Melanesians were eager to leave their homes for temporary work abroad, drawn by motives of curiosity and "the spirit of adventure". In such cases, it would be inaccurate to apply the umbrella-name kidnapping or "blackbirding". As befitted the son of a Westminster judge, he put his faith in British law. He favoured a system of imperial regulation that would permit voluntary recruitment while effectively protecting the Melanesians from violence, fraud and murder: the "employment of a limited number of licensed vessels under the management of certified masters, and under the watchful control of a man-of-war, with stringent regulations summarily enforced against offenders".[30] Until this was enacted, however, he would encourage those islanders under his influence not to recruit. This belief in the possibility of effective regulation rather than outright suppression was to remain the fundamental principle in the approach of the Melanesian Mission to the labour trade for as long as the latter was carried on.

In London, the Colonial Office was already considering the question of imperial legislation. A Polynesian Labourers Act passed by the Queensland Parliament in 1868 contained (until 1870) no provision for control of recruiting in the islands. British subjects who engaged in the trade were controlled only by an Act of 1817, with later amendments, and the slave trade Acts. Further than this, the imperial authorities were reluctant to proceed. A Bill first drafted by the Colonial Office as early as 1862, aimed at remedying the obvious deficiencies in the existing legislation by creating new offences under law, was opposed by the Treasury, determined to enforce rigid economy in all public expenditure, and the proposal was deferred indefinitely.[31]

Patteson sailed from Norfolk Island on 27 April 1871, half-expecting to be attacked. He was in a weak and depressed condition, and thoughts of death were often on his mind. He first spent three months at Mota, where thirteen years of missionary contact climaxed in the first mass baptisms. The *Southern Cross* picked him up on 19 August and proceeded to the Solomons to collect Atkin and Brooke, who had been living on San Cristobal and Nggela respectively for the previous ten weeks. Labour vessels from Fiji had moved into the region only in 1870, but already there were familiar stories of blackbirding, with consequent appeals to the missionaries for help. When twenty young men were carried off by a recruiter from Ulawa in 1870, the people had no doubt that the bishop would succeed in bringing them back. In the following year at Nggela, where within a few months recruiters had taken over fifty men and reportedly killed eighteen, Brooke was confronted by two hostile chiefs:

> Why does not Bishop take us on board and take us to these places that we may kill these killers? ... You two Bishop have deceived us: you came and told us not to kill, &c., and then these vessels come and kill us![32]

When all possible allowance is made for Brooke's highly developed sense of the dramatic, it is clear that by the August of 1871, retaliation was in the air. A few days before his departure from Wango, Atkin had spoken with the master of a Fiji-based recruiting-ship, *Emma Bell*, which was sailing eastward in the direction of Santa Cruz. The *Southern Cross* followed. On 20 September, it anchored off the reef-enclosed island of Nukapu, in the Reef Islands, north of the large and populous mainland of Santa Cruz. The Melanesian schoolboys on board were having lessons on the Acts of the Apostles, and that morning Patteson had told them the story of the death of St Stephen.

It was not the Mission's first contact with the Polynesian inhabitants of this small, flat, bush-covered island. The *Southern Cross* had called at Nukapu in 1856 and 1857, when Selwyn and Patteson had found it possible to make themselves understood in the Maori language. Patteson's next visits were probably in 1866 and 1867, and again in 1870, as the first step in an old plan to use the Reef Islands as a spring-board for the evangelization of Santa Cruz, to which they were closely linked by trade and interchange of visits.

At noon, the ship's boat was lowered and Patteson was rowed ashore. With him were Atkin, Stephen Tarpaniara and two Mota youths, John Ngongono and James Minipa.[33] As they approached the reef, they were met by canoes from the shore, two kilometres distant. Because the tide was low, they were unable to cross the reef, so the bishop boarded a canoe belonging to a chief named Moto, whom he knew from his visit of the previous year, leaving the others to follow when the tide rose. He landed, entered a palm-leaf hut in the village and lay down on a mat reserved for the use of guests, while his host went out to procure food. When Moto returned, he found the bishop lying dead, having been struck from the rear on the right side of the skull with a heavy wooden mallet. According to most accounts, the assailant, named Teandule, hid in the bush and later fled to Santa Cruz. Women of the village proceeded to prepare the body for burial and carried it to a canoe on the beach. On top of the body, according to Nukapu burial custom, they placed a frond of sago palm tied in five knots. Meanwhile, the ship's boat had been lying beyond the reef, surrounded at about ten metres distance by four canoes. About three-quarters of an hour after Patteson had gone ashore, the men in the canoes began shooting arrows at those in the boat. Atkin was struck in the left shoulder, Taroaniara was pierced in his shoulders and chest by six arrows; only Minipa escaped injury. The boat retreated to the *Southern Cross*, but soon returned with a new crew, led by Atkin, to rescue the bishop. By this time, the rising tide enabled them to pole across the reef and approach the island. Inside the lagoon, they saw a laden canoe being brought out from the shore and cast adrift. It was found to contain the bishop's body, wrapped in native matting. A week later, both Atkin and Taroaniara died, in acute agony, of tetanus. So completely had the Mission been identified with Patteson that the young Melanesians on board the ship took it for granted—as did the newly baptized people of Mota—that their new religion had died with him, and that they would have to return to their old homes and former ways. It was only with difficulty that they were persuaded that "school" would continue.[34]

In normal circumstances, the violent death of a well-known missionary, even a bishop, would have evoked more than token reaction only among the devout supporters of missions. However, because of its supposed connection with the Melanesian labour trade, the deaths of Patteson and his companions immediately acquired more than a religious significance. Few contemporaries, it seems, doubted that the killing of the bishop was in some way the result of the labour trade. He had been well received on his visit to Nukapu in 1870. Therefore, it was inferred, the hostility of the Nukapu people must have been provoked in the intervening period by the violent behaviour of a visiting labour recruiter, and in accordance with the "universal law of savage life", Patteson had been murdered as a blind act of retaliation.[35] "Bishop Patteson's murderers killed him as they would kill a great chief against whom they had no personal animosity," pronounced the Wesleyan missionary-anthropologist Lorimer Fison; but for tribal reasons, it had been necessary to put him to death.[36] Writing a few hours after the news reached Norfolk Island, Codrington expressed the unanimous interpretation of the mission staff:

> There is very little doubt but that the slave trade which is desolating these islands was the cause of this attack ... Bishop Patteson was known throughout the islands as a friend, and now even he is killed to revenge the outrages of his countrymen. The guilt surely does not lie upon the savages who executed, but on the traders who provoked the deed.[37]

The precise truth is still far from clear. An attempt in Fiji to trace some Nukapu men, alleged to have been kidnapped from the island, produced only rumours of their whereabouts, and they were never located. It was also revealed, much later, that the *Emma Bell* had recruited five men from somewhere in the region of Santa Cruz before reaching Havannah Harbour at Efate on 25 September, but the name of the island was not known. In Fiji, the recruits had mysteriously escaped.[38] There was no firsthand investigation into the affair by members of the mission staff until 1876, when John Still, a young English missionary, made contact with two castaways from Nupani in the Reef Islands, at Ulawa. These men said that a labour vessel had come to Nukapu shortly before the bishop, killing four men, wounding four and carrying away four; hence the reprisals. Still admitted, however, that the castaways had talked "very fast" in a mixture of Santa Cruz and Ulawa, so that it was difficult to understand them. An account collected from Pileni in the Reefs through a Nifiloli informant in 1877 seemed generally to confirm the accepted story: five men had been kidnapped. It was also said that in Fiji, the men had stolen a whaleboat, in which they had navigated themselves homeward by way of Tanna and Ambrym, bringing dysentery, which swept through the neighbouring islands and was attributed to the anger of the bishop's god. In 1878, the *Southern Cross* called at Nukapu for the first time since

1871. Canoes came out from the shore, the people seemed friendly, though "they did not like talking about the Bishop", and no landing was made.[39] Further investigations made by Lister Kaye, missionary on Santa Cruz in the early 'eighties, and by John Selwyn, Patteson's successor as bishop, who in 1884 was the first European visitor to land at Nukapu since 1871, yielded no fresh information. Although Selwyn met an old man who was said to be a survivor of those kidnapped, it is doubtful whether confident questions from Europeans, transmitted to the chastened Nukapu people through several interpreters, would by this time have brought answers at variance with the popularly accepted explanation, which already had established a life of its own quite independent of empirical evidence.[40]

The principal weakness in the revenge theory is that it was born not out of investigation into the actions of the Nukapu people themselves, but out of a desire to condemn the activities of labour recruiters. Not all attacks on Europeans by islanders were reprisals, yet other possible reasons for the murder were ignored. Did Patteson unintentionally violate a local custom? Such an explanation was in fact put forward in 1894 by a lay missionary, A.E.C. Forrest, who had been based at Santa Cruz since 1887, had stayed on Nukapu for a month and was the first European to acquire a fluent knowledge of a Santa Cruz language. He claimed that Patteson had been killed not by the people of Nukapu, but by a native of Santa Cruz, out of jealousy and anger, "because the Bishop gave a present to the Nukapu chief and either a smaller one or none at all to the Santa Cruz man who conceived himself the more important personage".[41] Although Forrest's version was immediately discounted by his fellow-missionaries, it was welcomed by Sir John Thurston, then High Commissioner for the Western Pacific, who as captain of a Fiji recruiting-ship, had met Patteson at Mota in 1871, only two months before his death. "I have for many years heard something of this nature", he wrote in his diary, "and for years have felt assured that the old story of Kidnapping for Fiji was a mere surmise."[42] His own investigation, moreover, revealed that John Selwyn's much-quoted story of the escaped labourers returning to their home in a stolen boat referred not to men kidnapped from Nukapu—thus demolishing a vital piece of supporting evidence—but to some Tikopia recruits, who had

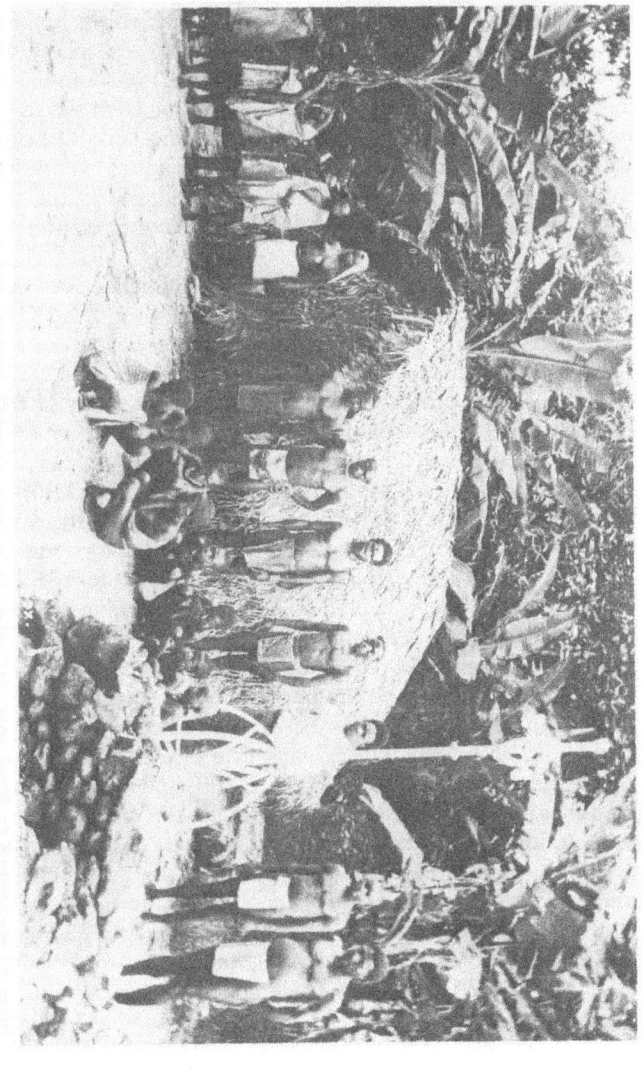

Patteson memorial cross at Nukapu, 1906 (From the Beattie Collection: Permission Auckland Institute and Museum)

eventually ended up in Santa Cruz, where they were killed. In the absence of positive evidence of blackbirding at Nukapu, Forrest's explanation is the more plausible, especially in light of a similar incident recorded at Ulawa in 1880, in which John Selwyn unwittingly provoked hostile reaction from a leading man by publicly giving a present to a person of low rank.[43] Its principal weakness is its failure to account for the attack on the waiting ship's boat. Nevertheless, twenty-three years after the event, it was too late to dislodge the established interpretation.

When the news of the tragedy at Nukapu reached New Zealand and eastern Australia at the beginning of November 1871, there was an immediate and emotional uproar. Newspapers reported the incident from eye-witness sources, and special editorials on conventionally pompous lines eulogized the memory of the dead bishop. His two companions, about whom little was known, disappeared into the background.

There was no hesitation in explaining the killing as a customary act of revenge for a previous kidnapping incident. This explanation in turn provoked a unanimous cry for long-delayed British intervention, to suppress or at least to regulate the recruitment of Pacific Islands labour. New Zealand indignation culminated in the colonial Parliament, where both Houses adopted addresses for presentation to the Queen, deploring the "cruel deed" and urging the imperial government to act without delay.[44] In church circles, the news inspired elaborate expressions of grief: church bells tolled, black drapes were brought out and special sermons preached before tearful congregations in many churches laid heavy stress on the example set by the dead bishop's self-sacrificing life and devotion to duty. Anglican diocesan synods, religious societies and representative assemblies of the major Protestant churches passed resolutions of sympathy, coupled with demands for an immediate end to the "new slave trade", while in Auckland, Sydney, Melbourne and Hobart, there were large public meetings to demonstrate sorrow and protest. A Bishop Patteson Memorial Fund was founded in Sydney, to raise an endowment for the Mission (£1015) and to erect a monument, a life-sized effigy that was eventually placed in the city church of Christ Church St Laurence.[45]

In England, the news caused much less stir in the secular press at large. Patteson's sixteen-year absence meant that beyond a small circle of relatives and personal friends, many of them highly placed in public life (his cousin, Sir John Duke Coleridge, was Attorney-General in Gladstone's first Cabinet), he was no more than a name or a distant memory. As in the colonies, however, his death was taken up by those who sought to combat blackbirding.

The incident at Nukapu certainly hastened, though it did not cause, the passage of imperial legislation to regulate recruiting by British subjects. Even before the rallying of outraged public opinion in the colonies was heard of, the news of Patteson's death proved sufficiently dramatic to turn the scales decisively in favour of immediate action. The killing of a bishop, the archetype of an innocent victim, seemed to be evidence enough that the Melanesian labour trade had become a scandal. A series of articles in the religious press, petitions and a special meeting in London mobilized church and humanitarian public opinion.[46] Treasury objections faded into insignificance. In February 1872, the long-discussed draft Bill was introduced into the new session of Parliament. Moving the second reading of the Bill in the Lords, the Earl of Kimberley, Secretary of State for the Colonies (himself an Eton contemporary of Patteson), described the bishop's murder as "the crowning atrocity", decisive proof of the evils produced by unregulated recruiting. In June 1872, the Bill became law as the Pacific Islanders Protection Act.[47]

As a prominent Christian missionary struck down in the course of his work, Patteson—and by association, the Melanesian Mission—achieved an assured place in the gallery of Christian martyrs, destined to be the subject of numerous short *lives* and pious articles, and to rank alongside William Carey, John Williams, David Livingstone and James Chalmers as a hero-missionary of the nineteenth century. Not surprisingly, it was among those who shared his High Anglican faith that his death made its deepest impression. For followers of the Oxford Movement, the violent death of a missionary bishop was a glorious demonstration of the apostolic foundations of the Church of England: "an honour reflected for the first time in this age on the office of a Bishop in our Church".[48] In Patteson, the English Church now had a hero which hitherto it had lacked, but of which the early Church (and the Church of Rome) had no shortage: an episcopal missionary-martyr. Charlotte Yonge, herself a devoted disciple of John Keble, when requested by the Patteson family to write the "life and letters", found the prospect "very awful, for it is embalming the Saint for the Church"— though the two-volume biography that she produced was more honest than mere hagiography.[49] The death of Patteson was among the influences prompting the Society for the Propagation of the Gospel to request the Archbishop of Canterbury to appoint an annual Day of Intercession for missions, first observed in Anglican churches throughout the English-speaking world on 20 December 1872. The society also sponsored a Patteson Memorial Fund, approved by the archbishops and powerfully backed by G.A. Selwyn as Bishop of Lichfield. It raised £7000, which was allocated to the purchase of a new mission ship, a memorial chapel at Norfolk Island and a permanent endowment. For devout readers, there was a spate of ephemeral commemorative pamphlets and fulsome devotional verse on the theme of the Christ-like martyr hero:

> In that canoe of vengeance
> He lay, so grandly calm;
> His face—one benediction,
> And on his breast the palm;
> As if the prayer "Forgive them!"
> Scarce sown on earth's dim bounds,
> Had blossomed in praise as his raptured gaze
> Fixed on the Five Dear Wounds.[50]

Friends and admirers of Patteson subscribed to erect permanent monuments: stained-glass windows; an elaborate wall tablet in the chapel of Merton College, Oxford, where he had been a Fellow; and a carved stone pulpit for Exeter Cathedral, where he had been ordained, that depicted the martyrdom in carved stone.

Supporters of the Mission were still in mourning when news arrived in England of the bombardment of Nukapu by a British warship. They were scandalized by this apparent reprisal for Patteson's murder, and even more so when the actual events came to light. On 29 November 1871, H.M.S. *Rosario*, commanded by Lieutenant A.H. Markham, arrived off Nukapu to investigate the tragedy. At Norfolk Island, he had already been petitioned by the surviving missionaries not to avenge the bishop. Three

Interior of St. Barnabas' Chapel, Norfolk Island (From the Beattie Collection: Permission Auckland Institute and Museum)

attempts at a peaceful landing were repelled by a hail of arrows. For "protection" and as a demonstration of power, lest the "savages" should boast that they had beaten off a man-of-war, Markham therefore shelled the island and sent in a well-armed landing-party, which burned the village and destroyed canoes. The loss of life among the Nukapu people was not known, though Markham himself thought it to have been severe. For the islanders, it was a traumatic experience. Thirty-five years later, however, when the Mission had at last established a school on the island, it was the death of Patteson that the older inhabitants had become accustomed to regard as the great tragedy in their history, whereas they laughed as they recalled their bombardment.[51]

At Norfolk Island, Patteson's memorial was the lofty stone chapel of St Barnabas. Completed in 1880, it was exquisitely furnished with a floor of Devonshire marble, a pipe organ (given by Charlotte Yonge and played by a succession of Melanesian organists), stained-glass windows by Burne-Jones, a carved reredos, and collegiate seating inlaid with shell. It was a striking expression of that mid-Victorian High Anglicanism, whose essential ethos Patteson had secretly aspired to recreate in Melanesia.

> Sometimes I have a vision ... of a small but exceedingly beautiful Gothic chapel, rich inside with marbles and stained glass and carved stalls and encaustic tiles and brass screen work ... It may come some day, and most probably long after I am dead and gone ... And yet a really noble church is a wonderful instrument of education, if we think only of the lower way of regarding it.[52]

NOTES AND REFERENCES

1. Charles Hunter Brown, *The Melanesian Mission*, p. 8; also *I.V.*, 1877, p. 53.
2. W.G. Ivens, "Some Historical Notes concerning the Melanesian Mission", in Appendix to *Dictionary and Grammar of the Language of Sa'a and Ulawa ...*, pp. 199-200.
3. J.C. Patteson, " 'Christian Principles' ...", *Australasian Church Quarterly Review* 1 (1910-11): 231.
4. Charlotte Mary Yonge, *Life of John Coleridge Patteson*, vol. 2, p. 166.
5. ibid., p. 167.
6. Randall Thomas Davidson and William Benham, *Life of Archibald*

Campbell Tait, Archbishop of Canterbury (London, 1891), vol. 1, p. 331.
7. Church of England, *Conference of Bishops of the Anglican Communion holden at Lambeth Palace, in July, 1897* (London, 1897), p. 37.
8. John Williams, *A Narrative of Missionary Enterprises in the South Sea Islands* (London, 1840), p. 152.
9. A.E.M. Anderson-Morshead, *The History of the Universities' Mission to Central Africa, 1859-1909* (London: U.M.C.A., 6th edn, rev., 1955), ch. 1; Owen Chadwick, *Mackenzie's Grave* (London: Hodder & Stoughton, 1959), pp. 13-18.
10. Williams, *Missionary Enterprises*, p. 152; H.W. Tucker, *Memoir of the Life and Episcopate of George Augustus Selwyn, D.D.*, vol. 1, p. 288.
11. J.C. Patteson to his sister Frances, 25 August 1858, Patteson Papers, U.S.P.G. Archives.
12. Yonge, *Patteson*, vol. 2, pp. 359, 532-33. Cf. "Christianity and Civilisation in Relation to Each Other", in Church of England, *Authorised Report of the Second Missionary Conference ..., 1877*.
13. Patteson, journal-letter, May-June 1867, entry 4 June, Patteson Papers.
14. J.C. Patteson to W.T. Bullock, 21 December 1868, S.P.G. Letters Received, vol. 40/3, U.S.P.G. Archives.
15. *Mission Field* 16 (1871): 175.
16. *The Net*, March 1874, p. 40.
17. St Augustine's College, Canterbury, *Occasional Papers*, no. 135 (1871), p. 3.
18. *The Net*, February 1873, p. 20.
19. J. Palmer to S.P.G., 30 June 1872, S.P.G. Missionary Reports, vol. 27, U.S.P.G. Archives.
20. *M.M.R.*, 1874, p. 14.
21. J.G. Goodenough, *Journal of Commodore Goodenough, R.N., C.B., C.M.G., during his Last Command as Senior Officer on the Australian Station, 1873-1875*, ed. with a memoir by his widow (London, 1876), p. 298.
22. Yonge, *Patteson*, vol. 2, p. 494.
23. George Sarawia, *They Came to My Island*, pp. 27-28.
24. Patteson to his sisters, 23 November 1867, Patteson Papers. See also C.H. Brooke's reminiscences of Patteson's last years in *Mission Life*, n.s. 4 (1873): 116-23.
25. *Colonial Church Chronicle* 24 (1870): 123. See also George Palmer, *Kidnapping in the South Seas: Being a Narrative of a Three Months' Cruise of H.M. Ship Rosario* (Edinburgh, 1871), pp. 186-88.
26. *Brisbane Courier*, 27 November 1871.
27. J.C. Patteson to his brother James, 14 January 1871, Church of Melanesia Archives.
28. R.H. Codrington to his aunt, 15 October 1871, Codrington Papers, Rhodes House Library.
29. J.C. Patteson to Captain C.W. Hope, 26 May 1868, G.A. Selwyn Papers, Selwyn College Library. Cf. the case for "complete suppression" of the labour trade by the Presbyterian John Inglis, *In the New Hebrides* (London, 1887), pp. 198-221.

30. Letter to Canon Vidal, 25 April 1871, *Sydney Morning Herald*, 11 November 1871. See also his influential "Memorandum to the General Synod of New Zealand", 11 January 1871, Great Britain, *Parliamentary Papers*, vol. 43, 1872 [C.496], pp. 107-9.
31. O.W. Parnaby, *Britain and the Labor Trade in the Southwest Pacific*, pp. 3-24.
32. Great Britain, *Parliamentary Papers*, vol. 50, 1873 (244), p. 10. The initial phase of labour recruitment in the Solomons is described by Peter Corris, *Passage, Port and Plantation*, pp. 24-29.
33. For biographies of Atkin and Taroaniara, see *Mission Life*, n.s. 3 (1872): 131-45, 221-22; *S.C.L.*, July 1898, pp. 1-5.
34. *New Zealand Herald*, 1 November 1871; *Sydney Morning Herald*, 7 November 1871; *Mission Life*, n.s. 3 (1872): 10-12; Yonge, *Patteson*, vol. 2, pp. 566-76; *S.C.L.*, September 1896, p. 7; July 1905, pp. 5-7; H.N. Drummond, *John Coleridge Patteson: An Account of his Death at Nukapu* ..., pp. 10-18; Charles E. Fox, *Lord of the Southern Isles*, pp. 24-26; William Davenport, "Notes on Santa Cruz Voyaging", *Journal of the Polynesian Society* 73 (1964): 141-42.
35. *Guardian* (London), 6 December 1871, p. 1443.
36. *Sydney Morning Herald*, 18 November 1871.
37. *Mercury* (Hobart), 18 November 1871.
38. William Floyd to R.H. Codrington, 16 August 1873, S.P.G. Letters Received, vol. 40/3; J. Harding to E.L. Layard, 7 October 1875, enclosure in Layard to F.O., 26 October 1875, F.O. 58/147, P.R.O.
39. *M.M.R.*, 1876, pp. 9-10; 1877, pp. 31-32; 1878, p. 12; *I.V.*, 1876, pp. 30-31.
40. *I.V.*, 1884, pp. 12, 43-44.
41. J. Thurston, Diary, 4 November 1894, Thurston Papers, N.L.A.
42. ibid.
43. Walter Coote, *The Western Pacific*, pp. 123-24.
44. Great Britain, *Parliamentary Papers*, vol. 43, 1872 [C.496], pp. 97-107.
45. *New Zealand Herald*, 1, 10, 20, 30 November 1871, 7 December 1871; *Daily Southern Cross*, 1 November 1871; *Wellington Independent*, 6 November 1871; *Lyttleton Times*, 6 November 1871; *New Zealand Church News*, December 1871, January 1872, February 1872; *Australian Churchman*, 18 November, 16 December 1871; B.T. Dudley, *The Martyrs of Santa Cruz*. For accounts of meetings, see *New Zealand Herald*, 17 November 1871; *Argus* (Melbourne), 16, 25 November 1871; *Sydney Morning Herald*, 29 November 1871; *Mercury* (Hobart), 11 December 1871. Resolutions etc. are in Great Britain, *Parliamentary Papers*, vol. 43, 1872 [C.496]; vol. 50, 1873 (244). The New Zealand reaction is described in P.J. Stewart, "New Zealand and the Pacific Labour Traffic, 1870-1874", *Pacific Historical Review* 30 (1961): 47-59; Angus Ross, *New Zealand Aspirations in the Pacific in the Nineteenth Century*, pp. 80-84.
46. See Aborigines Protection Society, *The Polynesian Labour Traffic, and the Murder of Bishop Patteson*; *The Times*, 1 December 1871, 9, 19 February 1872; *Colonial Church Chronicle* 26 (1872): 81-87; *Guardian*

(London), 3 January 1872, p. 9; *Mission Life*, n.s. 3 (1872): 1-13; S.P.G. Standing Committee Minutes, 30 November, 14 December 1871, 11, 18 January, 21 March, 11 April 1872, U.S.P.G. Archives; G.A. Selwyn to W.E. Gladstone, 27 November 1871, Gladstone to Selwyn, 28 November 1871, Gladstone Papers, Add. MS 44299, f. 175, 44540, ff. 181-82, British Museum Library; Tait Papers, vol. 186, 1872 Foreign, Lambeth Palace Library. The S.P.G. petition is in R.P. Flindall, *The Church of England, 1815-1948: A Documentary History* (London: S.P.C.K., 1972), pp. 221-22.

47. Great Britain, Hansard's *Parliamentary Debates*, 3rd series, 211 (1872): 184-89; Parnaby, *Labor Trade*, pp. 25-27.
48. *Mission Field* 17 (1872): 62. See also Bishop Wilberforce's Convocation speech on Patteson's death, 10 February 1872, in *Speeches on Missions by the Right Reverend Samuel Wilberforce, D.D.* (London, 1874), pp. 325-26. The only other Anglican missionary bishop of the nineteenth century to meet a violent death was an Evangelical, James Hannington, first Bishop of Eastern Equatorial Africa, who was killed in Uganda in 1885.
49. Letter from Charlotte Yonge, 28 December 1871; quoted in C.A.E. Moberly, *Dulce Domum. George Moberly (D.C.L., Headmaster of Winchester College, 1835-1866, Bishop of Salisbury, 1869-1885): His Family and Friends* (London: John Murray, 1911), p. 245. On Yonge's biography of Patteson, see Georgina Battiscombe, *Charlotte Mary Yonge: The Story of an Uneventful Life* (London: Constable, 1943), ch. 11.
50. *In Memoriam: J.C.P., St Matthew's Day, 1871. Poem by the Rev. Jackson Mason ...* (London, 1872). For other commemorative poems, see *Sydney Morning Herald*, 18 November 1871; *Guardian* (London), 6 December 1871, p. 1456; Thomas Williamson, *In Memoriam: Bishop Patteson. A Prize Poem recited in Rugby School, June 29th, 1872* (Rugby, 1872); H.A.S. [pseud.], *A Martyr-Bishop of our own Day*, London, [1881].
51. Great Britain, *Parliamentary Papers*, vol. 39, 1872 [C.542], p. 11; Albert Hastings Markham, *The Cruise of the "Rosario" amongst the New Hebrides and Santa Cruz Islands, exposing the Recent Atrocities connected with the Kidnapping of Natives in the South Seas* (London, 2nd edn, 1873), pp. 145-56; Markham to Selwyn, 13 May 1872 and subsequent correspondence, G.A. Selwyn Papers, Selwyn College Library; *Mission Life*, n.s. 4 (1873): 124-25; *S.C.L.*, August 1907, pp. 35-36.
52. Yonge, *Patteson*, vol. 2, p. 79.

4
"God is Never in a Hurry"

The violent death of Patteson brought fame to the Melanesian Mission at the price of a crisis in internal organization. For not only had the bishop been the acknowledged administrative and intellectual head of the Mission but he and Atkin alone had "a complete and general knowledge" of the people and places visited by the *Southern Cross*.[1] The immediate problems were quickly overcome. A former master of the *Southern Cross* returned to assist in navigation through the islands, donations from sympathizers to various memorial funds produced a rise in income and two young graduate clergymen from Wolverhampton were moved to volunteer as missionaries: John Selwyn, second son of Bishop G.A. Selwyn, and John Still, his curate.

The question of a successor to Patteson was paramount. By canon of the New Zealand General Synod, the appointment of a missionary bishop for Melanesia lay ultimately with the synod, though members of the mission staff (later defined as meaning only those in priest's orders) had the right to recommend a candidate. Codrington, who had become acting-head, declined nomination. He was a poor sailor, disliked island food and advocated the appointment of "a first-rate man straight from England".[2] So strong was the sense of tradition and family association, that John Selwyn was himself elected to the vacant see in January 1874, only two months after his arrival at Norfolk Island. He was only twenty-nine. This haste was unacceptable to the General Synod of 1874, which refused to confirm the nomination and deferred his appointment until its next meeting in 1877.[3] His father, the founder of the Mission, died in the following year.

John Selwyn was a representative of late-Victorian muscular Christianity. He was unquestionably broad in his doctrinal

John Richardson Selwyn (From the Beattie Collection. Permission Auckland Institute and Museum)

views, accustomed to take command, generous-hearted and impetuous to the point of folly. "Just what does him most harm is what he likes," lamented Codrington.[4] At the same time, he was noticeably lacking in his father's intellectual ability and powers of organization, and he was either remote or hearty in his relations with the Melanesians, whom he believed he had come to serve, whereas Patteson had been warm and intense. Despite a powerful sense of vocation, the inevitable comparison with his famous predecessors constantly oppressed him. "I sometimes long with all my heart that they had not made me Bishop," he confided to his mother. "The routine outside work I find no difficulty in—but the inner spirit of it which my Father and Bishop Patteson had so strongly is ... lacking utterly."[5] It was this deep sense of inadequacy that discouraged him from initiating change in any detail of the existing method of work.

The pace of the mission organization under John Selwyn was not vigorous. Until the late 1890s, the Anglican presence in Melanesia remained unchanged in outline. It was centred upon the Norfolk Island-trained "native agency" (the "black net"), whose teaching work was supplemented by annual visitations, ranging in duration from a few weeks to six months, by English missionaries (the "white corks") who were assigned to superintend particular island "districts".

For the six or so clergymen who came up from Norfolk Island on the *Southern Cross* each April or May, missionary life in the Melanesian islands was pleasantly varied. It embraced a regular round of public prayers each morning and evening, instruction of candidates for baptism and confirmation, preparation of Sunday sermons, language study and translation work, doctoring of sores and other ailments, and excursions by foot or canoe to inspect the progress of neighbouring schools and advise their teachers. "The natives are quite capable of thinking for themselves, and of carrying on an intelligent conversation," wrote Arthur Brittain from Pentecost in 1884, "and to one whose aim is to gain an accurate philological knowledge of their language, and some insight into their customs and beliefs ... there is but little unoccupied time, and no need to feel loneliness a burden."[6] Missionaries with scholarly interests took the opportunity to study the New Testament in Greek and to read the latest works of English theology. For relaxation, they went swimming, dynamited fish, shot pigeons, and in the evenings, following the custom of the Norfolk Island school, they taught their hosts to sing English glees, rounds and popular songs—"The Keel Row", "The Anvil Chorus" and pieces from Gilbert and Sullivan—set to vernacular words. Daily meals, as for Bice at Maewo in 1886, might comprise a breakfast of rice and sugar, coconut milk and coffee; biscuit or roasted yam at midday; fried bacon and potted meat in the evening, with taro, potatoes and tea. On special occasions, there would be a boiled fowl. Whether a missionary lived in the village school-house or had a separate dwelling erected, open house was the rule; no one lived apart.[7]

The least pleasant aspect of the work, by common consent, was the long, slow passage on the crowded *Southern Cross*, especially across the rough seas between Norfolk Island and the tropics, and against the south-east trade winds between the eastern Solomons and Santa Cruz. "Beating up to Torres. Foul weather," was David Ruddock's sole diary entry for ten successive days on a return voyage in August 1880. W.G. Ivens recalled the dismal voyages of the 1890s on the fourth *Southern Cross*. "Coming from the hot tropics, we felt the cold; our blood was thin and malaria insistent; supplies were apt to run short and we were perchance but poor exponents of Christian or even of Spartan fortitude."[8]

In the Solomon Islands, the Mission's precarious foothold at San Cristobal had been most affected by the tragic events of 1871, through the loss of the three men who alone were familiar with the Arosi people of the western end of the island and their language.[9] On his last visit, Atkin had been optimistic. He had attracted a following among the young men of Wango and began a small farm, with calves and poultry, as the nucleus of a proposed model mission-station, to be led by Taroaniara, on the lines of Sarawia's at Mota. Contrary to pious hopes, the blood of the martyrs was not destined to be the seed of the San Cristobal church. The islanders were hospitable to the successive missionaries (R.S. Jackson, John Still and R.B. Comins) who went there each year, but their welcome depended upon a constant supply of trade goods, and their reaction to Christian teaching was one of unchanging indifference. After his first visit in 1872, Jackson asked the Wango people if they wished him to come again:

> "Yes", cried they, "and bring very much tobacco, and axes, and beads, and red braid." "Ah!" said I, "You do not want *me* really; you only want tobacco." At which they laughed.[10]

Despite the severe loss of life in a dysentery epidemic several years before (Patteson counted 110 houses at Wango in 1866, yet the population in 1872 numbered only forty-four), intergroup warfare, head-hunting and seasonal ceremonials were carried on with vigour during the 1870s, which seems to indicate no loss of satisfaction in the traditional social order.

In any case, the coastal inhabitants of San Cristobal were already familiar with Europeans. By 1860, at least a dozen beachcombers had lived for a time at various places around the island. Makira Bay was a favourite port of call for whalers and traders, and from 1845 to 1847, it had been the headquarters of the ill-fated Marist mission. The anchorage at Wango itself was a well-known watering-place. Nearly every young man in the district was employed on a trading vessel at one time or another, which made it unusually difficult to attract recruits for Norfolk Island. For his practical services, the "chief" of Wango, Taki, had been taken on a voyage to Sydney and had accumulated an impressive store of European goods—trading articles, saucepans, clothes, sailor's chests and guns. His house, as Jackson saw it in 1872, had a small glass window at one end and the interior walls were lined with pages of the *Illustrated London News*.

Accordingly, the Wango scholars who returned from Norfolk Island were scarcely in a position to withstand the pressures from their own society. A remnant met intermittently in the evenings for prayers and held irregular school classes for anyone who would come, but most quietly dropped out of attendance at Christian worship. The line between the Christian community and traditional paganism was blurred. In 1885, Comins found that his first class of baptismal candidates had been offering sacrifices to ancestral spirits to ensure a good yam crop. The faltering Christian presence at Wango nevertheless brought about some changes to the pattern of village life. Sunday was generally observed as a day of rest; fighting became less common and weapons were freely brought out for sale to European visitors; cannibalism and infanticide were practised secretively rather than openly. In 1886, the first adult converts were baptized.

Taki himself hovered between the new religion and the old. Having befriended every missionary who stayed at Wango— John Selwyn thought he behaved like "a thorough English gentleman"[11]—he was fond of displaying to British naval captains his special connection with the English mission as a badge of respectability. He permitted his only son to receive schooling at Norfolk Island and in 1875, was taken there himself on a special visit. But when the youth returned home as a baptized Christian, Taki compelled him to renounce school and to take part in warring expeditions against neighbouring villages. (He

Taki the chief of Wango, San Cristobal, *c.* 1891 (From the Beattie Collection: Permission Auckland Institute and Museum)

subsequently died of wounds from a shark attack.) Although Taki first attended school for a few months in 1888—probably as a gesture of submission to the new way of life that was enveloping his village—it was not until 1895 that he consented to receive baptism, taking the Christian names of John Still, in honour of the popular pioneer missionary. His motives for conversion were known to be mixed. C.E. Fox, missionary on San Cristobal from 1915 to 1924, who knew Taki in his last years (he died in 1917), compared him to a "nominal Anglican" who "came to church & helped the school; but I think he always loved the old ways, the old sacrifices, ceremonies, fighting".[12]

Meanwhile, small schools commenced in the adjacent villages of Heuru and Fagani followed a similar pattern, growing and then languishing by turn. Despite forty years of mission contact, the annual reports from San Cristobal presented a melancholy picture. It was not possible, conceded Bishop Montgomery after his visit in 1892, to "boast yet of the effect produced upon this island by the Mission".[13]

Christianity made even less headway on Malaita, which was the most heavily populated—and for labour recruiters the most dangerous—island in the Solomons. Opposition to the alien religion was intense. The Mission's sole foothold was a struggling school at Sa'a in the south, which came to an end in 1880 when its teacher, Joseph Wate, was suspended from office on taking a second wife after his first partner had left him for another. To the missionaries, it was a bitter disappointment, especially as Wate—one of Atkin's protégés—had been held up as the outstanding convert from the Solomons. In 1886, two years after its resumption by Andrew Doraadi, the school was subject to a ban by the chief Dorawewe, reinforced by a priestly curse in the name of a powerful spirit. When the Christian party refused to pay the fine of pigs and shell money to enable the sacrifices necessary to remove the taboos, the school was forced to disperse to a place beyond Sa'a and was not permitted to return until after Dorawewe's death in 1890. There were no baptisms until 1896.[14] Another coastal place contacted by the *Southern Cross* was Alite Island on the west coast, which was the centre of the Langalanga Lagoon shell-money industry. There the door was closed by the death of a mission scholar after his return home, which was attributed by his relatives to the mysterious book-learning he had acquired at Norfolk Island. "He go along ship belong missionary," Comins was told afterwards; "too much book, him kill him."[15]

The people of Ulawa were closely linked with Sa'a by language and kinship. A school was begun there in 1880 by Walter Waaro, who was joined in the following year by Clement Marau, from Mere Lava. Marau found the Ulawa language "strangely difficult", observed Comins, "and the customs of the people in many ways very different from what he was accustomed to"; but to "win Solomon Islanders he was willing to become one himself".[16] Full of proselytizing zeal, Marau actively courted opposition by destroying charms and emblems associated with spirit worship, desecrating sanctuaries and sacred stones, and chopping down a sacred grove, as he himself recalled:

> When the heathen people heard of all this they were exceedingly afraid that something would happen, that some calamity would before long come upon the island, because the things that they had been used to venerate so much had been treated with disrespect.[17]

The pagan majority, understandably hostile, took food from the gardens of Christian converts, killed their pigs, and when the yam crop failed, sought to starve them out altogether. Marau's party refused to withdraw, and a stalemate situation resulted in which the Christians slowly gained followers and extended their influence.

On the small island of Savo, the Mission found that its teachings held no attractions to a people whose way of life was already based on warfare and trade. Ships called regularly; every chief was said to be a trader's agent, and since 1870, the island had been the seat of the first permanent trading-station in the Solomons. In the early days of the labour trade, many Savo men recruited for Fiji and Queensland returned with powerful Snider rifles, with which they terrorized the coastal peoples of the western end of Guadalcanal. Proud of their formidable reputation as warriors, they were unimpressed by the unsupported claims of the Christian religion, nor would they allow boys to go away to Norfolk Island. Two attempts in the early 1880s to found a school among them were given up because of opposition. In their failure, disgruntled missionaries described Savo grimly as "the Sodom of the district", whose inhabitants were "prepared to do any enormity for the sake of gain"; no teacher "seems inclined to live among such people".[18]

On Santa Isabel, by contrast, warfare and the custom of head-hunting ultimately facilitated the islanders' acceptance of Christianity. The island had been the scene of head-hunting raids since the 1850s. Expeditions came over from the New Georgia group, seeking slaves and human heads, and other raids were initiated within Isabel itself. By the 1870s, the central coastline was almost totally desolated by constant raids and warfare, while most of the remaining population was concentrated in the Bugotu district at the southern corner, in strongly fortified hilltop villages. For protection against head-hunting attacks, the Bugotu people had built tree-houses on bamboo platforms up to thirty metres above the ground, where they could take refuge and stone their attackers. However, when the raiding parties came to be armed with rifles, such defences became ineffective and tension ran high. Alfred Penny, missionary in the central Solomons from 1876 to 1886, observed: "These constant raids have so demoralized the people that they live in constant dread, and have no sort of unity among themselves or trust in each other."[19] The first school for Santa Isabel people had been started by the redoubtable Loyalty Island teacher Mano Wadrokal, among a colony of refugees and former Norfolk Island scholars on Savo. These returned in 1874 to their original home, to live under the direct protection of Bera, a powerful head-hunting leader, whose own assistance to labour recruiters and traders for bêche-de-mer, copra and shell at Thousand Ships Bay had enabled him to amass a formidable armoury of more than a hundred rifles and revolvers, and ammunition.

Wadrokal's arrogant manner and violent temper did not attract many to the religion he taught. His reports were said to consist chiefly of "repetitions at short intervals of two words, 'Vus' and 'Gol', meaning respectively 'Beat' and 'Scold' ".[20] He was ordained deacon in 1875, but had to be removed from his post three years later when he ran foul of Bera, two companions from Mare having killed two of the great man's followers. He left three schools in Bugotu, the largest (numbering 100 pupils) at the bush village of Tega, which moved later to the coast at Pirihandi.

Bera himself, until his death in 1884, tolerated the Mission's presence, but held aloof from its demands. Although he was the "one man whose influence and power could have welded the area together", his unabated head-hunting raids were directly responsible for much of the insecurity.[21] Penny regarded him as a principal obstacle to the progress of Christianity. "The news of Bera's death has come from Ysabel," he wrote in his diary; "it seems too good to be true."[22]

Soga, who was the stronger personality of Bera's two sons, did not want a Christian school in his own village of Sepi. To establish himself with the authority of his father, he proceeded to lead a series of head-hunting expeditions to the north of Santa Isabel. The symbolic turning-point for Christianity in Bugotu came in 1886, when Soga was cured of a serious bout of influenza by Bishop Selwyn's home-made concoction of brandy and quinine, after exhortations to follow the example of Cakobau of Fiji: to become a strong chief, revered as a saviour of his people and not as a destroyer. "Go and tell them", had been Cakobau's public message to Selwyn's Melanesians when he met the bishop in Fiji in 1880, "that I have fought battles and killed many men, but that this teaching is the true one."[23] Soga apparently found the prospect of prestige through peace rather than war an attractive one. In the years following, he sailed on no more marauding expeditions, refused to hand over heads when demanded by raiders from the west and in 1888, tried unsuccessfully to arrange a truce in a bloody war between Savo and Vaturanga. He also reluctantly allowed Hugo Gorovaka, a Guadalcanal-born teacher, to begin a school at Sepi. In 1889, having attended classes regularly, he embraced Christianity to the extent of publicly renouncing pagan worship and sending away all but one of his wives, and was baptized by the name of Monilaws (the second name of the then missionary, R.M. Turnbull), together with seventy people of his village. Bice, who administered the baptism, was jubilant:

> A more important and encouraging event has perhaps never occurred in Melanesia, and it is hoped, and much to be prayed for, that by God's grace and continued blessing Monilaws Soga may hereafter become a second Ethelbert to his people at Ysabel.[24]

He did. In obedience to Soga's expressed wish, hundreds of his Bugotu followers immediately accepted Christianity. The alliance was crucial, as Selwyn recognized: "It is very true and very helpful to us when Church and State run together."[25] By the early 1890s, with Soga's paramount authority in partnership with the missionary–doctor Henry Welchman, the conversion of Bugotu's two thousand inhabitants appeared to be only a matter of time. Behind the religious success, however, lay the terrorism of head-hunting, which had concentrated the population in Bugotu and had enabled the rise to dominance of Bera and Soga, both as fighting leaders and as defenders against external enemies.

It was the Nggela group (Florida) that became the most important centre in the Mission's chain of operations in the Solomons, When Brooke first stayed there in the late 1860s, trading vessels were already frequenting the harbours of its indented coastline. The Nggela people were eager traders and receptive to outside influences, so that "the force of original habit [had] been to some extent diminished and new views entertained". "They are a lively, energetic people," Codrington observed, "and when they begin to move they will move quickly."[26] There were the unusual advantages of a common language, large settlements and the prospect of protection by several conspicuous *vunagi* (chiefs), who had achieved by their personal abilities and fighting prowess a position of local dominance. But at the same time, there was internal unrest. Until 1873, the peoples of Mboli and Honggo were at war; there were several instances of blackbirding, and in 1872, the crew of the *Lavinia*, trading for bêche-de-mer, was massacred near Mboli —an enterprise led by Patteson's first Nggela scholar.

Brooke lived for a few months each year at Mboli, where there was a safe harbour for the *Southern Cross*. Takua, his protector, used the novelty of a resident European to great advantage. He collected a fee from anyone who entered the missionary's house and demanded payment of iron, tobacco and beads from those boys who went through Mboli to Norfolk Island, and again when they returned. Later, in a bid to monopolize the trade goods that Brooke distributed so lavishly, Takua tried unsuccessfully to prevent him from travelling to places beyond Mboli. Brooke's enthusiasm impressed his missionary colleagues. He wrote wordy articles for English religious papers on his various visits, recounting the saga of where he went and what he did. Each Sunday, he preached fluently in the Nggela language to audiences of hundreds. Always, he revelled in the singular position he occupied in Nggela society: "There was I, the only white man on the Island, without so much as a pop-gun to defend myself with, dwelling amidst that crowd of eager bloodthirsty savages, but without the slightest fear or misgiving ... The romance of the life appealed to me strongly."[27] Part of the romance for Brooke lay in the emotional relationships that he established with his male pupils. In 1874, when overt homosexuality was discovered, he was abruptly dismissed from the Mission. Afterwards, he incorporated his personal experiences of Melanesia into a fictional autobiography of a Nggela boy—melodramatic in plot, but accurate in its details of island life. It recounted the story of "Percy Pomo" of "Pombuana" (Nggela), who was taken on the mission ship "Aurora" to "Happy Island" and was subsequently kidnapped as labour for New Caledonia, from where he was rescued by his beloved missionary teacher, Percy Wakefield.

Brooke left behind him at Mboli an elaborate schoolhouse, 18 metres long by 13 metres wide, but no permanent school. Each year, a party of some thirty young and old scholars, including Takua, had assembled for teaching, for as long as the party from Norfolk Island was on the spot. But when the ship went south, recalled Penny, who took over in 1876, the school collapsed, "because there were no teachers old enough and reliable enough to carry it on by themselves, and no native converts to Christianity to rally round them and back up their efforts".[28] The permanent nucleus that Christianity needed before it could expand arose not at Mboli, where Takua was becoming disillusioned with the missionaries' confident claim that "the people would be much better for the new religion", but in the Gaeta district.[29] There a school had been founded by Charles Sapimbuana (whose sister was one of Takua's six wives), on his return home from Norfolk Island. The baptism in 1878 of the first adult converts, members of Sapimbuana's immediate family, led to the formation of a separate Christian village at Langgo.

A crisis followed in October 1880, during the absence of Penny and Sapimbuana at Norfolk Island, when Kalekona, the "chief" of Gaeta, apparently angered by a series of personal grievances, called for a human head to "restore him to his accustomed equanimity".[30] This instigated an attack by his son, Vuria, with four companions, on Lieutenant Bower and four sailors from the man-of-war schooner *Sandfly*, who were surveying the Nggela coastline. Bower and three of his men were killed. At the end of the year, a landing-party from H.M.S. *Emerald* wrought punishment by massive destruction of canoes, houses and coconut trees throughout Gaeta, so that "the whole district was in ashes".[31] They spared only Langgo, which was distinguished by its schoolhouse, with its bell, slates and books, and by a grave marked with a white cross. Then in May 1881, H.M.S. *Cormorant* was sent to investigate officially. Selwyn, who arrived on the *Southern Cross* at the same time, offered to mediate between the naval officers and the Gaeta elders, in a bid to prevent the promised bombardment. He arranged a compromise by which Kalekona—a friend of the Mission—would be spared and Vuria temporarily held as hostage until the other murderers were given up. Three were brought in, "tried" and executed; the fourth evaded capture by escaping into the bush. Selwyn had cause to be uneasy about the inherent injustice of his solution, for the two who were most guilty had escaped without punishment; indeed Vuria later openly boasted of his exploits. Selwyn nevertheless defended his intervention by its practical consequences: it had saved the whole people from wholesale bombardment and had given them and all the islands around "a very salutary lesson". Publicly, he always considered the action to have been one of the highlights of his episcopate, but privately, he regretted it.[32]

The *Sandfly* affair, and the fear of naval reprisals that it engendered, had a profound effect upon the internal politics of Nggela. The morale of the Nggela people had suffered a massive blow, so that years later the news that a warship had anchored nearby could cause an instant panic. Warfare finally came to an end; there was a new freedom of movement between rival localities; and the prestige of the pagan *vunagi* was diminished. Moreover, the Melanesian Mission had been demonstrated to be a political agent, linked on terms of friendship with the all-powerful British man-of-war. Not surprisingly, its position was thereby strengthened, as was shown by the remarkable popularity it attained during 1883.

In that year, the movement towards Christianity that had begun at Langgo culminated in the destruction by Kalekona and his followers of the emblems and shrines of their *tindalo* (ancestral spirits). As the news of Kalekona's dramatic defiance of the *tindalo* spread, native observers confidently predicted that the apostates would be punished by death. When nothing unusual happened, the *mana* of Christianity was conceded to be superior, but localized at Gaeta. Such a drastic break with the past, however, could not safely be confined to one place and Kalekona's band went on to destroy *tindalo* emblems belonging to a neighbouring leader. This was interpreted as a decisive demonstration of the superior power of "the new report" over the old. The consequences were described by Penny:

> Ground once held to be sacred was fearlessly trodden upon: certain places along the beach, where only the initiated dared walk or land from canoes without payment of a fine, became public property: sacrifices were dropped, because the priests were either under the influence of Christian teaching and refused to perform their functions, or because the people no longer troubled about that which was found to be of no avail ...[33]

There had been nothing on such a scale since the Mission began. Between 1882 and 1885, schools grew in number from seven to sixteen, in every major district. Some 2600 people—more than half the population of Nggela—were then receiving some kind of Christian instruction, of whom 750 attended school classes daily. Two hundred or more adults were being baptized annually. The number was large because Penny—gratified by the mass movement—demanded no high standard of Christian knowledge. His successor, J.H. Plant, found the baptismal candidates to be "extraordinarily ignorant", and for the sake of religious purity, he wished that Christianity had not become so popular.[34]

The Christian assault on paganism was directed with skill and severity by Sapimbuana.[35] He was ordained deacon in 1882. Almost everything the missionaries admired in the Gaeta church "had their origin, or their adaptation and improvement from him". He was "such a gentleman," Penny enthused, "and one can make a friend of him".[36] After Kalekona's death in 1884, when it was due mainly to Sapimbuana's efforts that Gaeta unity was maintained, his prestige increased still further, so that he became a *vunagi* in all but name. He died in 1885, only thirty years old, at Norfolk Island, where he had been preparing for priests's orders. When the news reached Gaeta, Codrington was told, "there was a silence in the whole place, no-one cooked food. The loss is felt throughout the island ... but of course chiefly at Gaeta, where in fact for some time they had not thought of anyone else as a leader."[37]

There were no successors of equal ability, trusted by both Europeans and Melanesians, to lead the Nggela church. Years afterwards, the people still looked back to Sapimbuana as a model teacher and exemplar of Christianity: "Why were there not more like him?" Instead, there was said to be a "dangerous" inclination among newly appointed village teachers to become "lords over God's heritage".[38] Each year, the missionary arriving from the south was met with accusations against teachers of sexual misconduct, neglect of services and school, and arrogant misuse of their religious authority. Some were found to be driving their people out of school for trifling offences and then demanding fines before admitting them back. Pagans were insulted, and in one celebrated case, a village and its gardens were destroyed at the behest of teachers because its inhabitants refused to have a school imposed upon them.[39] In 1884, Alfred Lombu deserted his post at Halavo only six weeks after his ordination as deacon, apparently because of a minor quarrel with the local people, and in 1891, he was suspended for three years after charges of adultery.

As the people of Nggela accepted Christian ideas, there were changes—though "fewer changes than one would expect"—in the indigenous social and political order. Land once regarded as sacred was brought under cultivation. Without fear of enemy attacks, people moved their dwellings from hilltops and ridges to the shore, "where they could get their salt water for cooking, and fish, and move about and see their friends".[40] At each village where Christianity was taught, there was a new schoolhouse in a prominent position—often on the site of the *kiala*, where war canoes had been kept. As on Mota, there were new communal activities: a daily class in reading, writing and translated extracts from the New Testament for children, morning and evening prayers for baptized people, and oral instruction in the Creed, Lord's Prayer and Catechism for adult candidates who were too old to learn to read. Sunday was a day without garden work or fishing, given up to church services, Sunday School and the

Alfred Lombu, 1906 (From the Beattie Collection: Permission Auckland Institute and Museum)

proud display of European dress. Apart from a few adaptations to local custom—everywhere in Melanesia, men sat on one side of the church, woman on the other—public worship was thoroughly English in content, conducted as at Norfolk Island in strict accordance with the Book of Common Prayer of 1662. C.M. Woodford, a travelling naturalist who attended a service at Halavo in 1888, found Alfred Lombu reading from the Nggela Prayer Book "in the most grave and proper manner" and he was "surprised at the manner in which all joined in responses and chanting the psalms".[41]

Contemporaries agreed that the rapid adoption of Christianity on Nggela had weakened the traditional moral sanctions and leadership system. According to Codrington, this was because the power of the *vunagi* was based on belief in their special relationship with the *tindalo* and their possession of "that *mana* whereby they [were] able to bring the power of the *tindalo* to bear".[42] Consequently, when a *vunagi* renounced his *tindalo*, he effectively renounced his customary power to levy fines in punishment for offences and his authority was undermined. Both the missionaries' fear of impending anarchy and their quasi-constitutional solution echoed the situation in the older missions of Polynesia, ever since the mass conversion of the Tahitians in the years after 1815. There, Wesleyan and L.M.S. missionaries had sought to create stability through the introduction of codes of law and representative institutions. To Plant, likewise, the vacuum demanded a new political institution to unify the whole of Christian Nggela and in which the new authority of the Christian teachers would be duly recognized. In 1887, he inaugurated an annual "parliament" (*vaukolu*), attended by "Christian chiefs" led by David Tambukoro of Honggo, senior teachers and representatives of the male population of each school village. It was intended as a supreme authority, empowered to fix new penalties for adultery and other crimes formerly punishable by death, as well as a forum for the discussion of matters of common concern. At the 1888 *vaukolu*, laws were passed concerning the fines to be imposed for breaches of the Seventh Commandment and the trespassing of pigs, and there was a discussion of a common grievance of older people against the labour trade—the recruiting of very young boys without their family's consent.[43] To the disappointment of its founder, the *vaukolu* soon became an occasion for feasting, attended by a thousand people, rather than a solemn deliberation of affairs of state. Nevertheless, it was sufficiently embedded in the life of Nggela to survive Plant's death in 1891, with the nominal addition of a "supreme council" of *vunagi* and teachers to guide proceedings and judge disputes. Thereafter, the only issues to be referred to a missionary for decision were those such as murder or disputed fishing-grounds, on which public feeling ran high.

Meanwhile, in the Banks Islands, the number of baptized Christians had exceeded a thousand by 1881, or about one-fifth of the total population. Half of these were concentrated on Mota (1879 population: 869), where paganism was dominant only in one district. In all other respects, however, the spiritual state of the "leading Christian island" failed to live up to expectations.[44] Enthusiasm for Christianity had clearly reached its zenith in 1870–72, and afterwards had rapidly ebbed away. Sarawia himself enjoyed considerable local prestige, but as a church leader he was not energetic; his health was poor and he seldom travelled beyond Kohimarama, which was supplanted by Navkwoe as the leading Christian village. The population slowly declined. School numbers decreased as teachers became rusty in their learning, attendance at church services was irregular and Christian functions were invariably eclipsed in importance by *sukwe* (graded society) and *tamate* (secret society) ceremonies, still uneasily tolerated by the Mission.[45] No one could diagnose the precise cause of the discontent. When Palmer and other visiting missionaries sought to revive the "lifeless" church, their exhortations brought no response. Nevertheless, it was Norfolk Island-trained converts of the first generation of Christian Mota who established Mota-speaking schools at many different places in the region: John Ngongono at Mere Lava (1873), Robert Pantutun (1873), Edmund Kwaratu (1874) and Maros (1878) at Santa Maria, Thomas Ulgau at Pentecost (1877), Gororagwia at Maewo (1878) and Edward Wogale at Loh in the Torres Islands (1879).

Much closer to the Mission's ideal was Henry Tagalad's village at Ra, which with its out-stations on Mota Lava, seemed like a Melanesian counterpart of the devout English country parish of Tractarian romance.

> The bell was ringing for Evening prayers as we went ashore, and we slipped into the little Church as Henry was reading the Confession. It was very pleasant and cheering to find all things going on so quietly and orderly, as they did not in the least expect us, and the bright little Church was like a bit of home.[46]

Tagalad himself was held in high esteem by his missionary mentors. He was described as "a perfect native clergyman": "He lives a priest and patriarch amongst his people. In him one sees what a Melanesian may become. In his school one sees what a Melanesian teacher can do, and the kind of education that can be given in the islands."[47] Equally to be admired was the missionary zeal of his Mota Lava converts, who for years supplied more teachers than any other Christianized island for new schools elsewhere in the Banks and in the Solomon Islands. By 1908, there were thirty-four of "Tagalad's boys" working in the Mission away from their home.

During the 1880s, the first church buildings used solely for worship were erected outside Mota. The first church was at Pek, Vanua Lava, where Codrington marvelled at the sight of a congregation armed with prayer-books, "all of them singing hymns and chanting canticles, in respectable dresses, as if they had been used to it all their lives".[48] Villages throughout the Banks Islands proceeded to compete in the erection of elaborate churches, larger than ordinary buildings, usually of timber, bamboo and leaf construction, which were furnished in traditional Anglican style with lamps, altar, prayer desks in the chancel and benches for the congregation on either side of a central aisle. Teachers who had learnt to play the organ at Norfolk Island pressed their congregations to make huge amounts of copra for sale to traders, to raise money to buy harmoniums, though the instruments inevitably succumbed to the ravages of heat, damp, cockroaches and rats.

For ambitious converts who built in coral-lime, the model was St. Barnabas' Chapel at Norfolk Island, with its lofty timber roof and semi-circular apse. The first such structure was on the tiny island of Rowa, where the twenty-six inhabitants laboured under the direction of their teacher, William Kwasvarong, to build a much-admired church with interior seats, altar, sanctuary rails, and exterior walls all of coral, smoothly plastered over with lime. Twenty years later, they built an even grander church with a roof twelve metres high and large enough to hold two hundred people.

The construction of village churches was probably the most visible symbol of the social changes that accompanied the spread of Christianity in the Banks Islands. As in Nggela, there was also a new vogue for European clothing, begun by teachers who had acquired the habit at Norfolk Island and fostered by traders and returning labourers from Queensland. Sunday was preceded (as at St Barnabas') by a Saturday *wurvag* or clean-up of the village, and at Mere Lava there originated a custom of having a communal meal each Sunday for the congregation, after the morning service. Intergroup fighting became confined to Santa Maria, apparently stimulated by firearms introduced by returning labourers; polygamy and infanticide were less common, but traditional dancing was forbidden to Christians only within the context of pagan festivals. Christmas was celebrated everywhere by up to a week of feasts and dances, the participants sleeping during the day and dancing all night. Throughout the Banks group, Mota became the sole language for church services and translations, and among those who had learnt to read and write, there was a new opportunity through the common language to transmit private information. On one voyage of the *Southern Cross*, as early as 1875, some two hundred letters were given in by Banks Islanders for delivery to scholars at Norfolk Island.[49]

Such changes, however, were not spectacular. Naval officers on visiting warships were invariably disappointed, for they saw nothing new or imposing to impress them. There were no model Christian villages, no commanding mission-stations like those of the Presbyterians in the south. "Their homes and cultivations have but little if at all improved from former times," reported Palmer in 1881, after almost twenty years' contact with the Banks Islanders, "although many of our Teachers set them a good example, in having well built houses with separate rooms."[50] At Santa Maria, for example, Maros had made a table of reeds with seats of bamboo; there was a clock on the centre-post of his house and photographs of his friends hung around the walls. Clearly, the Banks Islands as a whole did not yet display that wholesome Melanesian variant of European civilization for which Patteson had hoped.

The beginnings of Christianity in the northern New Hebrides paralleled its early stages in the Banks, but without the equivalents of Mota or Mota Lava. As elsewhere, coastal peoples had been contacted and a few boys taken away by G.A. Selwyn in the early 1850s. Under Patteson, the process recommenced on a more systematic basis, the first of a new succession of scholars being obtained from Eṁae in 1857, Espiritu Santo in 1857, Pentecost in 1862, Omba in 1865, Ambrym in 1867 and Maewo in 1870. Early contact with Espiritu Santo was never followed

Walter Woser, a Mota Lava deacon, with his wife and children, Norfolk Island, c. 1895 (Permission Mrs. Mary Clift)

up, and an attempt to establish a foothold for a permanent station on Ambrym brought no success, due mainly to a constant state of warfare. What was described as an "open and promising field" in 1874 was two years later dismissed as "a hopeless sort of place".[51] The long-standing Anglican interest in Eṁae, which went back to the first Bishop Selwyn, was finally withdrawn in 1880, when the island was ceded to the Presbyterian mission, whose work had already extended farther northward to embrace Epi. By an adjustment of boundaries, suggested by John Selwyn and accepted by the Presbyterian synod in 1881, the Melanesian Mission was in future to confine its work to the three northeastern islands of Omba, Maewo and Pentecost, in order to allow the Presbyterians an uninterrupted field from Aneityum to Ambrym and a primary claim to Malakula and Espiritu Santo.[52]

When Bice stayed at Walurighi, on the northern coast of Omba, for ten days in 1871, he was probably the first white man to have lived on the island. By the end of the decade, however, Omba's large population and coconut groves had made it a favourite place for labour recruiters and copra traders. By 1886, there were at least four trading-stations. Bice itinerated vigorously by boat and on foot, sharing with the local people in their fishing and feasting, so that the name "Bicie" was soon known everywhere; but he accomplished little of consequence during his short annual visits. "I can't see any entrance to their hearts," he wrote after his second visit. "They hold such curious notions, are so diffident, and live in such out-of-the-way places, and so inaccessible, that I fear it will be a long, weary, and toilsome process to bring them to a sense of their needs."[53] His lack of optimism was justified. Charles Taribwatu, a leading teacher who was looked to as the future mainstay of the Omba church, was killed in 1888 in a gun accident. When Bice left the Mission at the end of 1891, there were only four struggling Christian schools in north-eastern Omba. At the same time, there were four school villages on Pentecost, all but one of them in the far north (Raga), where there was frequent contact with adjacent east Omba. A beginning had been made in the north in 1877, at a bush village called Bwatvenua, by a locally-born teacher, Louis Tariliu, and Thomas Ulgau from Mota.

Only at Maewo, where there was no resident trader and recruiters seldom called, did the Mission achieve any marked success in this period. Since the 1860s, the island had been on the regular route of the *Southern Cross*, after the discovery of a coastal waterfall where the ship's tanks could easily be refilled. In 1878, a school was commenced seven kilometres inland at Tanoriki (or Tanrig), in the midst of some seven hundred bush people, far removed from the troublesome influences of secular civilization. Bice, who had encountered little to encourage him at Omba or Pentecost, wrote with enthusiasm of this peaceful and Christian Shangri-la—the women decently clad, old men puzzling over sheets of letters; and its attractive church, surrounded by brightly coloured shrubs imported from Norfolk Island, as the focus of village life.

> A more orderly or better conducted community it would be hard to find ... The simple childlike confidence and trust of these people is very touching, and religion seems to be the chief interest of their lives. Frequent services and instructions produce no weariness, and

there is a ready acquiescence in the requirements of the law of Christ.[54]

This idyllic phase did not last long. By the end of the 1880s, Tanoriki was reported to be dull and lifeless. The population of the district had been "much thinned" by labour recruitment and a high death-rate caused by new diseases, which seemed to be prevalent wherever schools were located.[55]

As European traders extended their activities into areas where the Anglicans were already at work, there was much talk among the missionaries about the proper relationship between Western commerce and the Christian religion. Before 1870, there had been no permanent trading-stations in the Solomons, but during the next decade, they sprang up throughout the group on every major island except Choiseul and Malaita. The largest concentration was at the western end of San Cristobal and on the north-eastern coast of Guadalcanal. Most of these stations were agencies collecting copra, tortoise-shell and other island produce for Sydney and Auckland firms. The best-known of the early traders was Captain Alexander Ferguson (killed at Bougainville in 1880), who maintained a dozen stations, linked by a fleet of four ships, headed by the schooner-steamer *Ripple*.[56]

There was no doubt in mission circles in the 1880s of the partnership between Christianity and civilization in Melanesia. Economic independence through "legitimate trade" and the cultivation of crops; civilization shorn of its abuses, without spirits, gun-powder and firearms: these were worthy goals. Selwyn believed that the Mission had a duty to "raise the people by giving them something to work for as well as by shewing them something to live for in the world to come".[57] But how? To provide an adequate economic basis for a civilized life, he toyed with the idea of a mission trading company, only to conclude that a distinctly religious body ought not to undertake such a work. Penny gave cordial support to trading when "fairly" carried on and rejoiced in the resulting adoption of European clothing on Sundays by his converts on Nggela and Santa Isabel.

> The men are then clad in shirts and trousers, some even with the addition of a straw hat. The women modestly dressed in petticoats and jackets, neatly made by themselves from fancy prints of

unaesthetic shades. That this is a step in the right direction all will admit.[58]

Anglican attitudes towards individual traders were governed simply by their supposed moral example: did they deal fairly with the local inhabitants and adhere to the Christian sexual code or did they not? The few substantial and "respectable" traders like Alexander Ferguson or Captain Oscar Svensen, whose employees attended church services or contributed to mission funds, were thus seen as allies. However, little was expected of the smaller agents, many of whom were hard-drinking ex-seamen, consorting with Melanesian women who were not their legal wives. The social gulf was rarely crossed. When Selwyn exhorted all traders he met on shore to avoid setting an evil example to the impressionable peoples around them, an attitude of condescension was implicit. He described one he met on Guadalcanal as "the best man of his class I have seen yet".[59] Penny opposed his *bête-noire* at Bugotu with the confident assumption of social as well as moral superiority:

> That scamp "Lorrie" was on board. I tackled him about his grog and woman [and] of course he had nothing to say—he was as servile as a thrashed dog. I am thankful to say that he is not going to stay on shore here.[60]

The majority of traders, he subsequently proclaimed, were "generally idle fellows, who have tried and failed at almost everything requiring industry or energy" and they constituted "a source of both bodily and spiritual danger".[61]

The real objection was to "spiritual danger". For it was no coincidence that at those places where regular traders flourished —Savo, Uki, San Cristobal, Guadalcanal and Omba—the cry was "no want missionary".[62] Annoyed by their failure to obtain footholds, the missionaries were quick to blame the traders themselves for their anti-religious and demoralizing influence. "The whalers and traders have done their work effectually," lamented a mission-inspired visitor to Mwata on San Cristobal in 1880, "and the missionaries feel it impossible to make any stand against their influence."[63] But the real reason lay with the islanders who lived near the stations, who were able to maintain their traditional customs and religious practices alongside an assured supply of Western manufactured goods and an opportunity for profitable short-term employment as boats' crews or station labourers. The prospect of a school therefore held no positive attraction for them.

In cultural impact, the thirty or so traders in the Solomon Islands and the northern New Hebrides in the 'seventies and 'eighties were exceeded only by labour recruiters. Kidnapping and violence declined, partly because of imperial legislation and the appointment of government agents on Queensland and Fiji vessels, but mainly because the islanders themselves had become aware of what was involved. From the late 1870s, the centre of the trade moved northwards and the percentage of Solomon Islanders recruited increased dramatically. Between 1878 and 1882, they comprised one-half of the 8300 labourers introduced into Fiji and one-seventh of the 11,400 recruits for Queensland, which was the generally preferred destination because the wages of £6 per annum were double those of Fiji. Between 1894 and 1904, the Solomons supplied four-fifths of those taken to Fiji and about half of Queensland's intake. By the mid-1880s, coastal dwellers had virtually ceased from direct participation in the trade, preferring the more profitable role of middleman. They were supplanted as recruits by the more numerous bushmen from the larger islands, mostly from Malaita and Guadalcanal. In 1884, the Fiji and Queensland governments banned the supply of arms and ammunition as recruiting presents—a reform that the Melanesian Mission had advocated since 1872. Mortality rates on the plantations declined.[64]

As conditions in the trade visibly improved, so the prevailing attitude of the Mission softened. Codrington's early blanket denunciations of the "slave trade" were not followed up by his colleagues, and by 1880, any such generalized complaints of irregularities and "outrages" were met by the Colonial Office with stiff requests for more precise information.[65] Furthermore, unlike the more militant Presbyterians, the urbane ethos of the Anglican mission did not encourage political belligerency. John Selwyn, following the precedent set by Patteson, refused to condemn the trade as an unmitigated evil. He objected to the recruiting of woman and of under-age boys, the supplying of firearms, the returning of time-expired labourers to the wrong "passage" and the depletion of the male population of some smaller islands. But overall, he conceded, the regulated trade had the potential for more good than harm. It was no bad thing for a young man to leave his "narrow island home", to learn to work steadily and to use his labour to obtain what he wanted. Many such recruits, he believed, returned to their homes with "a better idea of work" than they had formerly, as well as having "some notion of *law* founded on a policeman".[66] His was the voice of the muscular Christian:

> Do what we will we cannot keep those islands wrapped up in cotton-wool. There is evil in the world, and in some form or another they will come in contact with it. Our duty is to try and strengthen them morally and physically, that they may be able to resist it.[67]

By transferring the business of recruiting from private to government hands, limiting the numbers taken away each year, and increased efforts to educate and Christianize the Melanesians on the plantations, so he argued, the remaining abuses could be eliminated entirely and the trade transmuted into a total benefit to the islands as well as to Queensland.

But behind the tolerence lay always an English gentleman's disdain for the world of Pidgin English and profit-minded commerce. "Fancy a clergyman's son in such a berth!" Selwyn exclaimed after his astonished discovery that a friendly government agent was a fellow Old Etonian and son of a country rector.[68] Penny, Comins, Palmer, Bice and the other island missionaries expressed similar views. They accepted the trade without enthusiasm as a fact of life: a legitimate if grubby commercial enterprise and a convenient outlet for restless spirits anxious to see the world. They did not seek its abolition, but thought it would die a natural death when the Melanesians had exhausted its advantages. Personally, they were often on friendly terms with individual recruiters who carried mail, supplied stores and provided passage to neighbouring islands.

Always a high proportion of Melanesian labourers came from Malaita and other large islands where Christian influence was slight or non-existent. But in places where the Mission had gained converts and was anxious to keep them under its influence, there was a potential for confrontation. In the early 1870s, when feelings were running high, each teacher in the Banks Islands was instructed by Codrington "to do his best to prevent any natives from engaging in foreign labour" and to explain "the ruin of their country and race which follows".[69] Their efforts certainly diminished the flow of recruits from these islands. At Nggela, where mission teachers were much less successful in deterring their male converts, an exceptionally high level of recruitment during the 1890s provoked a wave of vigorous opposition. In 1895, it was claimed that five hundred Nggela men (from a total population estimated at four thousand) were absent in Queensland. This migration had led to a depletion of the upper classes of village schools, in some places to the virtual disappearance of able-bodied young men. Accordingly, in 1896, six Christian "chiefs" signed a letter drawn up by two deacons petitioning the British government to close Nggela for recruiting: "Because we beget children, and when they are grown big the ships that trade in men carry them all off to Queensland and other places, and not many of them come back here, and many of them die, and many, too, stay there for ever."[70] However, the Colonial Office saw "no special reason" for making an exception in the case of Nggela, and the request was refused.

One objection to the labour trade remained constant: that Melanesian labourers were allowed to remain as pagans while living in Christian countries. At the time of his death, Patteson had been planning to visit the new cotton plantations of Fiji—which was believed to lie within his jurisdiction—to see what might be done. In 1872, Codrington made a tour of Queensland and was angered to find that *"absolutely nothing is done by the Church"*.[71] He concluded that the dispersion of the Melanesians throughout the colony, and the variety of languages represented on each plantation, made it impracticable to send Mota-speaking teachers even to selected centres. For Anglican teachers to impart Christian truth through the crude medium of Pidgin English was out of the question. Moreover, the "natural first duty" of the Melanesian Mission was to Melanesians in their island homes, and the scope of its work could not easily be changed.[72] Mission work on the plantations should therefore be the primary responsibility of the churches of Queensland. He urged the synod of the diocese of Brisbane to appoint white catechists to conduct English schools for the labourers. Bishop Edward Tuffnell, however, showed no interest in the proposal, and his successor, Mathew Hale, was frustrated by the colonists' deep prejudice against missionary work among the non-Europeans in their midst, whether Aborigines, Chinese or Pacific Islanders. When, during the 1880s, individuals began special evening and Sunday classes for pagan Melanesians, those few schools associated with the Church of England were soon eclipsed in success and evangelistic fervour by the undenominational Queensland Kanaka Mission, founded by Florence Young at Bundaberg in 1886.[73]

Fiji was thought to offer an environment more favourable to Christianity. In addition to the influence of the Christian Fijians themselves and the dominant Wesleyan mission, the Church of England clergyman at Levuka, William Floyd, held regular Sunday services for labourers working in his district. Edward Wogale, sent from Mota, assisted him for three years from 1875, and in 1880, Selwyn himself paid a three weeks' visit to conduct confirmations and an ordination. He rejected a proposal to send more Anglican teachers to the Fiji plantations, for they could not be supplied in worthwhile numbers, he claimed, and their work would be thrown away on a polyglot and transitory population. Moreover, he insisted, to extend his oversight to Fiji's imported labourers (and white population) would require regular annual visits from Norfolk Island, a practical impossibility.[74]

There were problems of staffing, finance and communication. Nevertheless, it was an unimaginative decision, which failed to take account of the changes that had occurred in Melanesia since the 1840s. Between 1863 and 1914, altogether about 100,000 Melanesians were engaged as indentured labourers for Queensland, Fiji, Samoa and New Caledonia. Of these, at least one-half came from islands in the Solomons, Santa Cruz, Banks and New Hebrides that were formally within the sphere of the Melanesian Mission. During the 1890s, it was demonstrated that many of those islanders, whose hearts had been stirred by their contact with "enthusiastic" Christianity in Queensland and Fiji, returned to their homes to become zealous evangelists. If the Melanesian Mission had adapted its machinery to embrace the thousands of receptive Melanesians on colonial plantations, it is probable that it could have extended its influence through returning labourers, both to augment existing Christian communities and to establish new schools in villages beyond the reach of the *Southern Cross*.

In the meantime, the spiritual state of the Pidgin English-speaking and swearing, returned labourer was to be a constant cause for pious lament. It was generally agreed that their sophistication made them more difficult to deal with than islanders "totally ignorant but innocently heathen".[75] The ex-Queenslander "does not believe in offerings to the church in the shape of pigs, fowls, yams, or bread-fruit", observed the recruiter W.T. Wawn, with approval. "He knows how clergymen are regarded by the white workmen with whom he has come in contact."[76] A school at Fagani, San Cristobal, was deserted after an ex-labourer told the people that there was no need to go to church and pray, for it was not done in Queensland; while the Mota deacon Robert Pantutun complained that returned labourers "talk only of those things that are not good which they have done in evil living, and in doing this, they do harm to some of the children of our schools".[77] Before the 1890s, the number of labourers returning as Christian converts was rather smaller than the number of mission teachers, neglected and dissatisfied with their pay or anxious to escape from a position of tension, who themselves recruited for the colonies.

The Melanesian Mission was the largest body of Europeans, and the only Christian mission, operating in the huge area between New Britain and the central New Hebrides. British authority was represented on behalf of the Fiji-based High Commissioner for the Western Pacific by men-of-war of the Australian Station. These warships cruised through the Melanesian islands between May and October each year to enforce British law among those planters, traders, seamen and labour recruiters subject to it, and to punish islanders for offences committed against British subjects.[78]

In relation to British power, the Melanesian Mission pursued the phantom of a political *via media* between fervent imperialism and total neutralism. "Missionaries don't go as British subjects but as Ministers of [Christ] to the heathen, & must not mix up the two characters," Patteson had declared, and later missionaries echoed his viewpoint.[79] During the 1880s, when Presbyterians were leading an aggressive campaign in the Australasian colonies to preserve the New Hebrides from French rule, the Anglican mission declared itself opposed to territorial annexation by either France or Britain, on the ground that the islanders themselves had a right to be consulted how and by whom they should be ruled—although a "Protectorate which the natives could feel was exercised for their benefit, as well as for that of the white man" was not felt to be open to the same objection.[80] The ideal role of Britain in the South Seas was seen as that of policeman rather than of territorial ruler. John Selwyn's own solution to the problems of law and order in the western Pacific—a permanent "peripatetic officer" with a trained force and full powers—was almost the same as that put forward by his father forty years earlier.[81]

It followed from this semi-neutralist position that missionaries who went to the Melanesian islands for reasons of their own had no right to expect special armed protection in their work. If "missionaries can only be maintained upon an island by the guns of a man-of-war, they had much better leave it", wrote Patteson in 1866, on hearing of the naval bombardment of villages on Tanna and Erromango at the request of aggrieved Presbyterian missionaries.[82] The shelling of Nukapu by H.M.S. *Rosario* after his murder in 1871 was publicly deplored for the same reason.

But independence of the force of British arms was one thing; mutual assistance, advice and friendly association were another. From the 1870s, a regular pattern of informal co-operation evolved, based on practical necessity and common British loyalties. In their investigations into murders of Europeans and breaches of the recruiting regulations, naval commanders habitually turned to a local missionary as the most trustworthy European in the area for reliable information and for the supply of guides and interpreters. Anglican missionaries everywhere in the islands volunteered their assistance with enthusiasm. Like Selwyn in the *Sandfly* affair, their primary aim was to obtain a peaceful settlement, to avoid the necessity for punishment of whole communities by an act of war. They agreed in principle that missionaries should not be seen to be personally associated with bombardments or other punitive actions, though in Melanesian eyes, this distinction was understandably not obvious. For Anglican churchmen, moreover, the visit of a British warship was a welcome link with their homeland. It brought letters and newspapers, and an opportunity to dine on board with the officers —"our old friends"— in civilized surroundings. "How refreshing it is to meet a party of genial English gentlemen under our isolated circumstances, no one who has not been in the same case can know."[83] The friendship of the man-of-war was usually extended to include Melanesians attached to the Mission, who were treated to displays of gunnery and searchlights, hearty choral singing, tours of the ship, and in later years, games of cricket.

Missionary mediation sometimes prevented injustice or led to redress, as in two cases of wrongful bombardment at Omba and Pentecost. Its consequences could also be embarrassing. In an inquiry in 1889 into the murder of a trader at San Cristobal, Plant misinterpreted a Pidgin English "confession"—an error that led to the wrongful imprisonment of the alleged murderer.[84] In 1892, in a naval investigation into the murder of Fred Howard, a trader at Uki, Comins obtained some Christian converts from Sa'a to guide the warship's punitive expedition to the assassins' village in the Maramasike Passage. The Maramasike people later descended on the Sa'a Christian village, armed with rifles and threatening to kill for revenge. Missionaries took up the cause of the Sa'a Christians and sought weapons for their protection. Joseph Wate and his followers were living in constant danger, Selwyn told the First Lord of the Admiralty, solely because they had "aided the forces of the Crown" and "trusted in the honour of England".[85] Naval captains diagnosed the conflict, more correctly, as only part of a more complex struggle on Malaita between Christians and pagans, and therefore refused to intervene. The incident confirmed Sir John Thurston, the High Commissioner, in his resolve to avoid in future accepting assistance from "any missionaries whatever", with their unjustified claims to "particular and special protection".[86]

The official dissociation was too late, for already the idea had taken root in many Melanesian coastal communities that Anglican missionaries and British warships worked in concert. As early as 1860, Dudley learned to his surprise that the people of Mota firmly believed that "if they do not behave well while we are here, a man of war will come & blow up their island".[87] Subsequent participation by missionaries in naval investigations throughout the region reinforced the equation. By the 1890s, neutrality, as Patteson had envisaged it, was a dead letter. Missionaries of that imperialist decade felt no qualms about using the fear of a warship to back up their position. This was demonstrated on Pentecost in 1898 by W.H. Edgell, district missionary from 1897 to 1903, who was eager to accept a naval offer to punish a pagan chief who had attacked a Christian teacher: for it showed "that I could call in a man-o'-war if I wished to, which before he had been inclined to scout as a wild fancy".[88]

The predominance of British missionary and trading activities in the southern Solomons was recognized by the Anglo–German agreement of 1886, which divided New Guinea and its adjacent islands into two spheres of influence. A protectorate was formally proclaimed in June 1893, prompted partly by humanitarian concern for full control over the centre of labour recruiting, principally by fear of possible French intervention. It was extended to include the Santa Cruz group in 1898, Santa Isabel and Choiseul (ceded by Germany) in 1899.[89] Publicly, the Melanesian Mission accepted the establishment of British rule calmly, as the correct and inevitable culmination of previous imperial policy in the region. In the case of Santa Cruz, there was relief that possible French or German intervention had thereby been forestalled. On Santa Isabel, Welchman had found that the shadowy German administration centred in distant New Guinea had been a practical hindrance to his freedom of action. The two missionaries resident in the Solomons in 1893, C.W. Browning and R.B. Comins, who were being appealed to as judges and mediators, welcomed the prospect of an early release from the exercise of secular functions. There was an expectation of assistance from a friendly British administration, which would advance the "spiritual interests" as well as the "social and moral character" of the islanders.[90]

Converts of the Melanesian Mission in the Solomons were already familiar with the idea of benign British protection. Church of England missionaries were men of their time, proud of their country's supreme position in the world, and themselves had engaged in a little flag-waving. On the occasion of Queen Victoria's Golden Jubilee in June 1887, Plant called together the Christians of Nggela for a day of feasting, sports and a firework display, after which he talked to them of "our dear Queen, and the meaning of a protectorate and other matters on which they wanted information".[91] Two years later, he wrote to Lees Knowles, an old Cambridge University friend who was a Member of Parliament:

> Why can't these islands be annexed? Guadalcanal and Florida wd. soon be very profitable possessions ... The Florida people want annexation—they are afraid of the Germans & more so of the French. I have purposely avoided giving advice on the subject & the request comes from themselves.[92]

It is symbolic of the relationship existing between the English mission and British naval authority that Comins, who was already well known to visiting commanders, should be taken on board H.M.S. *Curaçoa* to advise on the best places to hoist the flag and personally to explain to island observers the significance of the ceremony. They were instructed to raise the flag whenever a ship visited, and if there were any cause for complaint against a trader, they were to show the papers of declaration and report the matter to the next British warship. On Comins' recommendation, the proclamation was made in both Christian and pagan districts of Nggela, lest it be assumed that the protectorate was connected only with the Mission and its schools.[93]

In other respects, the early 1890s was an unhappy period for the Melanesian Mission. Selwyn's refusal to take reasonable care of himself during his sojourns in the islands led eventually to a complete breakdown in health. Permanently crippled by malarial sciatica, he returned to England in 1891 with his wife and family, and resigned the see. For the next three years, the Mission was administered by John Palmer as senior missionary, assisted by Codrington, who returned to take charge of the 160-pupil Norfolk Island school for a year during the interregnum. He found the Mission's slender resources squeezed to the limit by "distressing poverty".[94] In 1890, when expenditure exceeded income for the first time in more than twenty years, it was rescued only by £1000 in special donations from Selwyn and Archdeacon Samuel Williams of New Zealand. In the following year, income fell again by a further £1100 to £5250, of which one-third went to run the *Southern Cross*. One reason for the decline was the acute economic depression that had affected New Zealand since the 1880s and came to a crisis in eastern Australia in 1892–93, which cut parish contributions as well as income from mission investments. Furthermore, the interest in Melanesia inspired by Patteson's martyrdom was dying from lack of home organization and colourful propaganda. English contributions were drifting to new fields. The Australian Board of Missions (successor to the defunct Australasian Board, formed in 1850) had been founded in 1872 as the official missionary agency of the newly constituted Church of England in Australia and Tasmania, but it remained dormant and ineffectual. "Where is the Board of Missions?" rhetorically asked Bishop Cecil Wilson, of Melanesia, at the Adelaide Church Congress in 1902. "Does it ever meet? Is it anything more than an idea, not a reality at all?"[95] In addition, there was new competition for the allegiance of existing supporters, from the (predominantly Anglo-Catholic) New Guinea Mission, founded in 1891, and the (Evangelical) Church Missionary Associations of New South Wales, Victoria and New Zealand, formed in connection with the English C.M.S. in 1892.[96]

In 1892, Bishop H.H. Montgomery of Tasmania made a three months' tour of the diocese in the *Southern Cross*, to administer confirmations. His book, *The Light of Melanesia*, in which he recorded his impressions for the church-going public, was the first independent account of the Melanesian Mission since Yonge's biography of Patteson and the consequent *lives*. It was no pious treatise. Montgomery was a perceptive observer, later (1901–18) to become secretary of the Society for the Propagation of the Gospel, a trusted adviser of the Archbishop of Canterbury, Randall Davidson, and highly regarded in the Church of England as a far-sighted missionary strategist. He wondered if the limited success of the Melanesian Mission was due in part to outmoded methods of organization, inefficient deployment of its staff and a fear of new approaches. Full of confidence, he briskly listed the problems that needed debate: the establishment of permanent European stations in the islands, with a consequent division of the white staff into full-time teachers at Norfolk Island and island missionaries; central schools in the major island groups; the employment of women missionaries; extension of schools to the Melanesian labourers in Fiji and Queensland; the future of Mota as the sole *lingua franca*; and possible revision of the Mission's traditionally tolerant attitude towards indigenous customs.[97]

"*God is Never in a Hurry*" 113

John Palmer, c. 1895 (Permission Mrs. Mary Clift)

Secular-minded travellers were mixed in their judgements. The explorer-scientist H.B. Guppy, in 1887, had praised the "quiet heroism" of Anglican missionaries in the Solomons, which was the kind of tribute church people wanted to hear.[98] In 1900, an appeal for funds to build the fifth *Southern Cross* was backed by a pamphlet containing glowing testimony from former commanders and admirals of the Australian Squadron to the success of the Melanesian Mission in "Humanising, Civilising and Christianising" the savage and treacherous peoples of the south-west Pacific. C.M. Woodford, by contrast, privately recorded the opinion of the local traders—which he also shared — that the Mission was "utterly futile": "I do not believe there is in the whole group one genuine convert, who if the Mission were to retire for a year would remain faithful to it."[99] Its method of work was a "very bad one", simply because single missionaries who spent only three to five months in the group annually were unable to associate closely enough with the islanders to gain any real knowledge of what was happening around them or during their absence. Thurston, who toured the new protectorate in 1894, had no doubt that the Anglican mission was a failure. He was repelled by the "very dirty" appearance of its Nggela converts, who smoked trade pipes and wore ragged articles of European clothing. Its teachers and churches he found unprepossessing. "It seems as hard to find a white missionary as it is to find a crocodile," he grumbled in his diary; and "little or no permanent effect had been produced anywhere".[100] His official report was no less critical:

> ... although some twenty five years have elapsed since the Mission first established its station in this group, it would be a delicate, as well as a really difficult task, to offer any positive opinions upon the results attained. I found the native mind, everywhere possessed with a very strong feeling against the Mission, and in many places the natives, upon my expressing surprise and regret, very frankly gave their reasons ... I merely observe that judging from appearances the Mission has done very little.[101]

Thurston was already prejudiced against the Melanesian Mission. He was enraged by John Selwyn's recent public criticism of the "cumbersome" machinery of the Western Pacific High Commission, and his social assumptions were affronted by the rough equality between the races, which he witnessed on the *Southern Cross*, where "it seemed to me that the natives ... treated their Pastors with scant courtesy".[102] Yet the kernel of his indictment contained truth. The leisurely system by which each missionary divided the year between Norfolk Island and his island district had long since outlived its usefulness. The mood of the Mission was routine-bound and complacent. Slow progress was excused and justified, on the grounds that large-scale conversions were invariably shallow and that any "secure and lasting result" would require infinite time. Haste in missionary work was to be avoided, for "God is never in a hurry".[103]

From what they had seen of the results of the Mission, moreover, pagans outside Nggela and Bugotu saw no reason to doubt the continuing validity of their own religious system. The arrogance of certain Nggela mission teachers, the recurrence of dissension and sickness within Christian communities, and unfavourable reports of some individual missionaries were not attractive to the pagans who were Thurston's informants. They were prepared to admit a limited validity for the Christian religion, without feeling bound to accept it for themselves; Christianity might even be good for Nggela and Santa Isabel, they said, but it would not do in New Georgia or Malaita or Guadalcanal.

At the beginning of 1894, twenty-three years after Patteson's death, the Melanesian Mission was once again leaderless. It then claimed 8929 baptized converts out of an estimated population of 150,000 on islands where it was working. Of these there were 1111 communicants; another 3200 were under some kind of Christian influence. There were 122 schools and 381 teachers —double the number ten years before. Just over one-half the total number of teachers and schools were in the Solomons. The largest Christian community was on Nggela where 3000 were baptized. Next largest in order was Santa Isabel with 1200, Mota Lava 1013, Mota 770, Santa Maria 644 and Maewo 500. On no other islands did Christian converts number more than 350. The Melanesian clergy comprised two priests (Sarawia and Tagalad) and seven deacons. The white missionary staff numbered eight, with a few others employed solely at Norfolk Island.[104]

In absolute terms the numbers were not an impressive return for almost forty years' continuous operation over a wide area. Optimistic churchmen nevertheless compared Melanesia with other missions and discovered victory in failure. The Presbyterians in the New Hebrides, who had always worked on conventional mission-station lines, claimed about the same number of adherents, but precise comparison of progress is difficult because the dwindling population in southern Melanesia was in some places cancelling out the annual gains through baptism.[105] Among Anglican missions elsewhere in the world in the 1890s, the Melanesian Mission was overshadowed by the great C.M.S. missions of India and West Africa, but it was similar in size to the U.M.C.A., whose foundation it had paralleled, and it was considerably larger than the struggling Borneo Mission. There were almost as many baptized Anglicans in Melanesia as there were in China (10,200) and three times as many as in Japan (2910).[106] For devout members of the Church of England, the "island mission", sanctified by a martyr bishop, had never lost its romantic aura. Hardly anywhere, it was claimed, had the gospel been more faithfully and effectually preached; no other mission in modern times had "attracted more enthusiasm or enlisted more noble workers" than the Melanesian Mission.[107]

NOTES AND REFERENCES

1. *M.M.R*, 1872, p. 4.
2. *S.C.L.E.*, October 1922, p. 115.
3. Church of the Province of New Zealand, *Proceedings of General Synod, 1868*, pp. 77-79; 1874, pp. 38-39; F.D. How, *Bishop John Selwyn: A Memoir*, pp. 62-64, 92-95, 109-16.
4. R.H. Codrington to his aunt, 10 November 1876, Codrington Papers, Rhodes House Library.
5. Selwyn to his mother, 21 July 1880 (continuation 19 August), 1 November 1883, J.R. Selwyn Letters, Selwyn Family Papers, in possession of Rev. H. Selwyn Fry; How, *John Selwyn*, pp. 83-85.
6. St Augustine's College, Canterbury, *Occasional Papers*, no. 237 (1885), p. 16.
7. See, generally, the detailed reports by missionaries in the Melanesian Mission annual, *Island Voyage*; and C. Bice and A. Brittain, *Journal of Residence in the New Hebrides, S.W. Pacific Ocean ... 1886*. For private accounts, see: Alfred Penny, Diary, 1876-86, M.L.; David Ruddock, Diary, 1880-84, Bishop Patteson Theological Centre Library; W.H. Edgell, Diary, 1897-1901, in possession of Mrs R. Rowland. Ruddock's list of provisions for his four months' stay in the Solomon Islands in 1881 included twelve dozen tins and boxes of meat, sardines, pickled salmon, marmalade, cocoa, coffee and biscuits, a dozen bottles of port, a case of brandy and a 18 kilogram box of tobacco.
8. Ruddock, Diary, 16-26 August 1880; W.G. Ivens, " 'Yachting' in Melanesia", in Appendix to *Dictionary and Grammar of the Language of Sa'a and Ulawa ...*, p. 216.
9. For a more detailed account of the Melanesian Mission in the Solomon Islands, with full references, see D.L. Hilliard, "Protestant Missions in the Solomon Islands, 1849-1942" (Ph.D. thesis), chs. 3-5.
10. *Mission Life*, n.s. 4 (1873): 281.
11. J.R. Selwyn to R.S. Jackson, 23 July 1877, R.S. Jackson Letters, Auckland Institute and Museum Library.
12. C.E. Fox to P.A. Selth, 30 June 1970, quoted by P.A. Selth, "European Contact with Wango Bay, San Cristobal, and the Life of John Still Taki" (B.A. Hons research essay, A.N.U., 1970), p. 24. See also H.B. Guppy, *The Solomon Islands and their Natives*, pp. 15-16; and R.B. Comins in *S.C.L.E.*, January 1918, pp. 6-8.
13. H.H. Montgomery, *The Light of Melanesia*, p. 164.
14. *M.M.R.*, 1886, p. 13; W.G. Ivens, *Melanesians of the South-east Solomon*

Islands, pp. 260-62. On Wate, see *S.C.L.*, November 1905, pp. 8-10; August 1913, pp. 203-5.
15. *M.M.R. & I.V.*, 1893, p. 36.
16. *S.C.L.*, May 1904, pp. 23-24. For a biography of Waaro, see *S.C.L.*, November 1898, pp. 6-9; December 1898, pp. 3-5.
17. Clement Marau, *Story of a Melanesian Deacon*, p. 74.
18. *I.V.*, 1883, p. 61; John Gaggin, *Among the Man-Eaters* (London, 1900), pp. 193-94; *Church Gazette* 15 (1886): 104.
19. *I.V.*, 1886, p. 15.
20. *Mission Life*, n.s. 4 (1873): 602.
21. K.B. Jackson, "Head-hunting in the Christianization of Bugotu, 1861-1900", *Journal of Pacific History* 10 (1975): 66-71.
22. Penny, Diary, 16 May 1884.
23. *I.V.*, 1886, p. 10.
24. *M.M.R.*, 1889, p. 5.
25. J.R. Selwyn to his mother, 2 September 1890, Selwyn Family Papers.
26. *M.M.R.*, 1873, p. 22; R.H. Codrington to W.T. Bullock, 5 August 1875, S.P.G. Letters Received, vol. 42, U.S.P.G. Archives.
27. *S.C.L.E.*, January 1924, p. 10. One of Brooke's articles, "The Last Cruise of the Second 'Southern Cross' ", was serialized in *Mission Life*, n.s. 4 (1873); 5 (1874).
28. Alfred Penny, *Ten Years in Melanesia*, p. 43.
29. *I.V.*, 1877, p. 36. Takua remained a pagan until his death in the late 1890s.
30. Penny, *Ten Years*, p. 157.
31. Captain W.H. Maxwell to Commodore J.C. Wilson, 3 January 1881, enclosure in Admiralty to C.O., 31 March 1881, C.O. 225/8, P.R.O.
32. Report of Proceedings, 20 July 1881, enclosure in Sir Arthur Gordon to C.O., 2 December 1881, C.O. 225/7, P.R.O.; How, *John Selwyn*, pp. 190-93; *M.M.R.*, 1881, p. 7; C.M. Woodford, Diary, 14 June 1887, Woodford Papers, bundle 19, 1/7, Department of Pacific and Southeast Asian History, A.N.U.
33. Penny, *Ten Years*, p. 192.
34. *Church Gazette* 15 (1886): 104; *I.V.*, 1890, p. 54.
35. There is an account of Sapimbuana's life in *S.C.L.*, August 1898, pp. 1-6; September 1898, pp. 1-4.
36. Penny, Diary, 22 July 1879.
37. Codrington to his aunt, 29 July 1886, Codrington Papers.
38. *Church Gazette* 15 (1886): 104; Melanesian Mission, *Occasional Paper*, February 1893, p. 4.
39. R.B. Comins to C.M. Woodford, 29 June 1897, enclosure in Sir George O'Brien to C.O., 7 September 1897, C.O. 225/52, P.R.O.
40. *M.M.R. & I.V.*, 1891, p. 84; Cecil Wilson, *The Wake of the Southern Cross*, pp. 169-70.
41. Woodford, Diary, 23 September 1888, Woodford Papers, bundle 29, 1/8.
42. R.H. Codrington, *The Melanesians*, p. 52.
43. The Nggela *vaukolu* laws are enclosed in Comins to Woodford, 29 June 1897, C.O. 225/52, P.R.O.

44. *M.M.R.*, 1885, pp. 5-6.
45. On missionary attitudes to *tamate* and *sukwe*, see below pp. 198ff.
46. *I.V.*, 1876, p. 22.
47. *M.M.R. & I.V.*, 1895, p. 28. See also *M.M.R.*, 1908, pp. 28-29; Charles E. Fox, *Lord of the Southern Isles*, p. 137.
48. *I.V.*, 1881, p. 66.
49. *Mission Life*, n.s. 6 (1875): 232. By 1906, the *Southern Cross* was taking up to 900 letters to Norfolk Island on each voyage.
50. Report of J. Palmer for 1881, S.P.G. Missionary Reports, vol. 36, U.S.P.G. Archives.
51. *M.M.R.*, 1874, p. 12; *I.V.*, 1876, p. 4.
52. New Hebrides Presbyterian Mission, Synod Minutes, Session beginning 26 May 1881, microfilm, Pacific Manuscript Bureau, A.N.U.
53. *Mission Field* 18 (1873): 194.
54. *Mission Life* 15 (1884): 249.
55. *M.M.R.*, 1890, p. 9.
56. Peter Corris, *Passage, Port and Plantation*, pp. 99-106.
57. Selwyn to Jackson, 30 June 1875, Jackson Letters.
58. Penny, *Ten Years*, p. 143.
59. *I.V.*, 1877, p. 11.
60. Penny, Diary, 3 October 1879.
61. Penny, *Ten Years*, pp. 142-43.
62. J. Thurston, Diary, 27 September 1894, Thurston Papers, N.L.A.
63. Walter Coote, *The Western Pacific*, p. 127.
64. Corris, *Passage*, ch. 2, appendix 1; Charles A. Price, "Origins of Pacific Island Labourers in Queensland, 1863-1904 : A Research Note", *Journal of Pacific History* 11 (1976): 106-21.
65. E.g., *M.M.R.*, 1879, p. 13; C.O. to Sir Arthur Gordon, 5 September 1880, C.O. 225/6; J.R. Selwyn to Gordon, 7 February 1881, C.O. 225/7, P.R.O.
66. Selwyn to Jackson, 30 June 1875, Jackson Letters.
67. Letter in London *Guardian*, 4 May 1892; quoted in Great Britain, *Parliamentary Papers*, vol. 56, 1892 [C.6686], pp. 6-9.
68. Selwyn to his mother, 26 October 1884, Selwyn Family Papers.
69. Codrington to Bullock, 13 October 1873, S.P.G. Letters Received, vol. 40/3.
70. Petition of "Christian chiefs of Gela" [Nggela], 8 August 1896, enclosure in Cecil Wilson to C.M. Woodford, 8 December 1896, C.O. 225/52, P.R.O.; also in *S.C.L.*, August 1897, p. 10. On the "runaways" from Nggela, see Corris, *Passage*, pp. 54-55.
71. Codrington to Bullock, 10 April 1872, S.P.G. Letters Received, vol. 40/3.
72. *M.M.R.*, 1872, pp. 13-14; Codrington to his aunt, 15 May 1873, Codrington Papers.
73. On the Q.K.M., see Florence S.H. Young, *Pearls from the Pacific*, pp. 37-48, 106-10, 127-83; David Hilliard, "The South Sea Evangelical Mission in the Solomon Islands: The Foundation Years", *Journal of Pacific History* 4 (1969): 41-44; Corris, *Passage*, pp. 92-96. The difficulties facing Anglican mission work in Queensland are described by A. deQ. Robin, *Mathew Blagden Hale: The Life of an Australian Pioneer Bishop*

(Melbourne: Hawthorn Press, 1976), pp. 173-77.
74. *M.M.R.*, 1880, pp. 6-7; *Mission Field* 26 (1881): 34-37.
75. C. Bice to Warden, St Augustine's College, 8 November 1873, Student Files, St. Augustine's College, Canterbury.
76. William T. Wawn, *The South Sea Islanders and the Queensland Labour Trade: A Record of Voyages and Experiences in the Western Pacific, from 1875 to 1891* (London, 1893), p. 18.
77. *M.M.R.*, 1882, p. 8; *S.C.L.*, October 1895, p. 12.
78. See W.P. Morrell, *Britain in the Pacific Islands*, pp. 332-37; Deryck Scarr, *Fragments of Empire*, chs. 6-7.
79. J.C. Patteson, Diary, 16 October 1866, G.A. Selwyn Papers, Selwyn College Library.
80. *M.M.R.*, 1883, pp. 14-16; 1886, p. 6. The Melanesian Mission English Committee, however, was opposed to French annexation: English Committee Minutes, 18 June 1886, Melanesian Mission English Committee Office. On the New Hebrides "crisis" of 1886, see Angus Ross, *New Zealand Aspirations in the Pacific in the Nineteenth Century*, pp. 218-29; J.A. Salmond, "New Zealand and the New Hebrides", in *The Feel of Truth: Essays in New Zealand and Pacific History*, ed. Peter Munz (Wellington: A.H. & A.W. Reed, 1969), pp. 113-35.
81. J.R. Selwyn, "The Islands of the Western Pacific", *Journal of the Royal Colonial Institute* 25 (1894): 587-607.
82. *Guardian* (London), 20 June 1866, p. 634.
83. L.P. Robin (Torres Islands), in *I.V.*, 1890, pp. 38-39. See also Penny, *Ten Years*, pp. 150-73.
84. W.P.A., file nos. W.P.H.C. 191/1889; 82/1890; 125/1890; 230/1890; 273/1890; 354/1890.
85. J.R. Selwyn to Earl Spencer, 10 January 1894, enclosure in Admiralty to C.O., 16 January 1894, C.O. 225/46, P.R.O.
86. Sir John Thurston to Lord Ripon, 22 December 1894, C.O. 225/45, P.R.O.
87. B.T. Dudley "Journal of a winter spent on Amota, Banks [Islands] ...", entry 30 September 1860, Hocken Library.
88. Edgell, Diary, 27 September 1898.
89. Morrell, *Britain in the Pacific Islands*, pp. 343-47; Scarr, *Fragments of Empire*, pp. 252-56.
90. *M.M.R. & I.V.*, 1893, pp. 4, 36, 40; *S.C.L.*, February 1900, p. 18; February 1901, p. 141.
91. *I.V.*, 1887, p. 56.
92. J.H. Plant to L. Knowles, 28 October 1889, Fergusson Papers, F.O. 800/26, P.R.O.
93. Special Report of Proceedings, enclosure in Captain H.W.S. Gibson to Rear-Admiral N. Bowden-Smith, 10 August 1893, enclosure in Admiralty to C.O., 6 October 1893, C.O. 225/43, P.R.O.; "Hoisting the Flag in the Solomon Islands", *Mission Field* 38 (1893): 447-52.
94. R.H. Codrington to H.W. Tucker, 27 August 1893, S.P.G. Letters Received.
95. Cecil Wilson, "Missions to the Heathen in and near Australia", in *The*

Official Report of the Proceedings of the Adelaide Church Congress ... 1902, p. 195.
96. On the New Guinea Mission, see David Wetherell, *Reluctant Mission*. The Evangelical Anglican societies are described by Keith Cole, *A History of the Church Missionary Society of Australia* (Melbourne: Church Missionary Publications, 1971); and Kenneth Gregory, *Stretching Out Continually: A History of the New Zealand Church Missionary Society, 1892-1972* (Christchurch: N.Z.C.M.S., 1972).
97. Montgomery, *Light of Melanesia*, pp. 251-54.
98. Guppy, *Solomon Islands*, p. 271.
99. Woodford, Diary, 25 September 1886, Woodford Papers, bundle 30, 1/4. Woodford's private observations on the work of the Melanesian Mission do not appear in his published account of the Solomons, *A Naturalist among the Head-Hunters*.
100. Thurston, Diary, 3 and 26 September 1894, Thurston Papers.
101. Sir John Thurston to Lord Ripon, 22 December 1894, C.O. 225/45, P.R.O.
102. Thurston, Diary, 3 September 1894, Thurston Papers.
103. E.g., C. Bice in *Gospel Missionary*, n.s. 7 (1877): 155.
104. *M.M.R. & I.V.*, 1894, p. 25.
105. New Hebrides Presbyterian Mission, *"Dayspring" and New Hebrides Mission: Report for Year 1895* (Sydney, 1896), pp. 12-22.
106. See the statistics in Church of England, *Reports of the Boards of Missions of the Provinces of Canterbury and York on the Mission Field* (London, 1894).
107. Eton Association of the Melanesian Mission, *Annual Report*, 1884, p.5; Alfred Barry, *The Ecclesiastical Expansion of England in the Growth of the Anglican Communion: The Hulsean Lectures for 1894-95* (London, 1895), pp. 384-85; H.W. Tucker, *The English Church in Other Lands, or the Spiritual Expansion of England* (London, 1886), p. 96.

5
Old Methods, Slightly Adapted

In the Church of England in the late nineteenth century, the circle of those who contributed to foreign missions was wider than at any time previously. Outside the Evangelical party, however, missionary enthusiasm had been slow to develop. In 1871, the sum contributed to missionary causes by members of the national church (£325,000) was only slightly larger than the income of the various Nonconformist societies (£291,000);[1] missionary candidates were in short supply and there was a sense of discouragement and loss of zeal. The turn of the tide coincided with the aftermath of the death of Patteson. It was widely attributed to the first Day of Intercession for missions on 20 December 1872 (later observed around St Andrew's Day, 30 November), which achieved unexpected success. In a sermon at Westminster Abbey, Dean Stanley, the leading Broad Churchman of the day, argued that the weakening of the old doctrine of everlasting Hell for unbaptized heathen—the "doctrine which for a thousand years it was thought impious to doubt, it was now thought impious to believe"—did not destroy the missionary impulse, but rather gave it new force as an activity of hope.[2] New missionary enterprises were inspired in 1873 by the withdrawal of the public proclamation against Christianity in Japan and by the death in Africa of David Livingstone. A change in attitude towards missions and missionaries was much remarked on. There were many new donations and many more volunteers for service. Public opinion, as expressed in political and literary periodicals, seemed to become more favourable. In 1884, the total income of the various Church of England missionary societies was £492,000. In 1907, it was £750,000— one-tenth of the entire sum raised from congregations for church purposes.[3]

As interest in missions grew and the number of Anglican dioceses outside the British Isles multiplied (there were ninety-seven by 1900), so missions achieved a place in the central organization of the Church of England. During the 1880s, provincial boards were set up by the Convocations of Canterbury and York for study and advice on missionary matters, and in 1908, these were combined into a Central Board of Missions. In 1894, the United Boards organized the first missionary conference of the Church of England and published the first comprehensive survey of Anglican missionary work throughout the world.[4]

Foreign missions also became a primary subject on the agenda of the decennial conferences of the bishops of the Anglican Communion at Lambeth. At the first two such conferences, in 1867 and 1878, there had been virtually no discussion of missionary subjects, whereas in 1897, they occupied fourteen out of sixty-three resolutions. There was new, if vague, recognition of the possibility of liturgical variation within the Anglican Church, as an expression of cultural diversity and national character. At the Lambeth Conference of 1908, the committee on foreign missions (which included the Bishop of Melanesia) supported the principle that Western forms of marriage and public worship should be adapted to the requirements of different races and customs, even if this meant departure from the Book of Common Prayer. In Melanesia, however, as in most other dioceses, nothing was done along these lines.[5]

The later Victorians rejoiced in the signs of the advance of Christianity, both at home and on the mission field. At the time of Constantine's conversion, it was calculated, Christians composed only 1/150th of the human race, but by the 1880s, they numbered almost one-third, and that percentage was increasing annually. The non-Christian world was everywhere reported to be more accessible, more "responsive" than ever before. From the United States, came the slogan "the evangelization of the world in this generation".[6]

Victorian Christians were confident of ultimate success, but not complacent. In the last quarter of the century, and especially during the 1890s, the scope of British Protestant missionary work widened to include new departments and methods to achieve old goals.[7] There was a multiplication of industrial and medical missions; the C.M.S., for example, ran three medical institutions in 1877, forty-nine in 1908. The number of single women, in all British societies, increased sevenfold between 1884 and 1900. There were many more opportunities for laymen with technical skills. To promote the missionary cause at home, there were special intercession services, cycles of prayer, drawing-room meetings, lantern-slide lectures, children's pageants, sales of work, exhibitions of "curios" sent from the field, collecting-boxes and summer schools. Amongst the committed, the insatiable appetite for facts and results stimulated a vast output of popular literature: children's books for Sunday School prizes, histories, reminiscences, and especially biographies. On the Melanesian Mission alone, more than forty books and pamphlets were published in England between 1894 and 1930, in addition to its regular reports and periodicals.

There was a new interest in the "science of missions", their history and strategy. On becoming secretary of the S.P.G., Bishop Montgomery founded in 1903 a new periodical, *The East and the West*, for the scholarly study of missionary problems and methods, which considered such issues as the attitude of the white man towards darker races, the Chinese character and missionary methods, the need for industrial missions and whether missions to Moslems were justifiable. Much discussion was devoted to "racial problems", self-government in the "native church" and the Christian significance of the British Empire, then at the zenith of its power. Influential writers and preachers argued that the record of history showed that the national vocation of Great Britain was not material but spiritual: that its duty was to bring its millions of subject peoples to acknowledge the authority of Christ as their chief allegiance. As the national church, the Church of England therefore had a special responsibility to take up the work of imperial evangelization as a significant step towards the salvation of the whole world. "Shall we say that the sway of Rome was useful in God's good providence for the spread of His gospel," asked Bishop John Selwyn in a course of pastoral lectures at Cambridge in 1896, "and yet despair of using our far more widely spread influence for the self-same purpose?"[8]

Ecclesiastical strategists and administrators worried over the lack of co-ordination in the missionary organization of the

Church of England. Missions were supported by more than eighty independent societies, with layers of separate organizations for genteel ladies, laymen, clergymen and children. Following the examples of the C.M.S. and the S.P.G., each major society had its own network of national committees, organizing secretaries and parochial branches, which in turn overlapped with associations formed to raise English funds for particular missionary dioceses. Interest in any such diocese, it was tartly observed by the Bishop of Auckland in 1908, doubtless with an eye to Melanesia, invariably climaxed whenever a new bishop was consecrated:

> The Home Church, or the Colonial, General or Diocesan, Synod, is quite keen and excited, and in earnest for the time being. The people say quite honestly: "We really must back-up so and so; he is such a good fellow, a perfect saint, just the man for a missionary bishop. What can we do? Why, we will give his work the collection at his consecration; it is sure to be good, and it will be an encouragement to him. Then, of course, he must start an association for his diocese; we will help him all we can because it really is grand work, and he is such a dear fellow, and knows such a lot of people and is so much loved—why, the thing will go splendidly."[9]

But such enthusiasm was inherently fickle. To maintain and enlarge his home support amidst the babble of competing publicity was a major preoccupation of every English missionary bishop.

Complaints about Anglican parochialism and parsimony were legion. Parish clergymen pressed missions on the poor or on the children in their Sunday Schools, it was alleged, but they neglected the rich, whose donations to the missionary cause— the "conventional annual guinea"—"fall strangely below the standard of their contributions towards domestic needs".[10]

It was the same with the supply of missionary recruits. There was a vague belief in high places that universities were—or should be—the "natural centres of the Church of England's missionary work".[11] Anxious bishops, returning to England on leave, pressed the urgent need for "first-rate men", products of public schools and ancient universities; for surely England should send abroad only its best and noblest? Because linguistic studies and translations demanded trained minds, declaimed Bishop Wilson of Melanesia at a meeting at Oxford University in 1908, "we must have men of education; we must have University men; we must have public school men".[12] However, undergraduate interest was ephemeral, and many English diocesan bishops were thought to discourage their ablest clergy from going abroad. Whereas three-quarters of those ordained in the Church of England during the 1870s and 1880s held a university degree (and some bishops refused to accept non-graduate ordinands), this proportion was never reflected among those who volunteered for colonial or missionary service. Missionary theological colleges, like St Augustine's College at Canterbury, were founded specifically for non-graduates; and it was non-graduates—who would have been regarded as second-rate men in English parishes —who predominated among clerical recruits for Anglican dioceses overseas. Missionary societies increasingly looked to this source for their rank-and-file recruits.[13]

The Melanesian Mission broadly reflected this trend. Of those who joined its staff from England between the 1850s and 1900, either as clergymen or as laymen who were afterwards ordained, there were 13 graduates, 11 non-graduates; between 1901 and 1920, 12 were graduates and 16 were non-graduates, and there was a growing, if reluctant, recognition that in future it would need to rely upon recruits from "a different class" than that hitherto favoured.[14] Nevertheless, the proportion of university men in the Melanesian Mission was always regarded as exceptionally high; indeed, Bishop Winnington-Ingram of London once compared it to a "crack regiment". In the U.M.C.A., one-quarter of the male missionaries had university degrees, which was probably nearer the average for Church of England missions.[15]

It was suggested with increasing vehemence that one reason for the short supply of well-educated missionary recruits was the failure of the Church of England to show by its actions that it recognized the missionary vocation as an honourable one. Salaries were inferior to those paid at home, clergy pension funds did not recognize service outside England and the societies made no adequate provision for those who returned home in broken health. For a man to have been a missionary, lamented a secretary of the S.P.G., was "a disqualification and a bar to his advancement in life".[16] English bishops were notoriously reluctant to present former missionaries to comfortable livings or positions of ecclesiastical dignity. Therefore, ambitious men saw that to accept a post in the colonies or the mission field was probably to miss preferment at home.

Some observers felt that the widespread reluctance to volunteer for missionary service was due to lack-lustre bishops themselves: that "the appeals of missionary bishops who never moved a muscle to become missionaries until a bishopric came their way leave men cold".[17] For it was a cardinal weakness in the appointment of bishops to Anglican missionary dioceses that experienced men on the spot who lacked the accepted social and academic background were so often bypassed in favour of men imported directly from England who were so qualified. Until the mid-twentieth century, the Anglican missionary episcopate, like the English episcopate itself, was virtually limited to graduates of Oxford or Cambridge. Few protested against the practice. Dr R. N. Cust of the C.M.S., who advocated an indigenous episcopate, attacked the assumption that "every Englishman, selected by chance out of an English curacy", was somehow fit to become a missionary bishop, but his words went unheeded.[18] In missionary dioceses unattached to an ecclesiastical province, the appointment ultimately rested with the Archbishop of Canterbury, whose advisers inevitably singled out men whose work, character and background they themselves knew and trusted. Yet even when missionaries had a voice in the nomination of their bishop, the result was scarcely different, because the expectation was always to receive a university-educated gentleman, usually direct from England. To be led by anyone else, it was feared, might lower their mission in public esteem.

For Melanesia, the issue arose again after John Selwyn's resignation in 1891. The English missionary clergy, few in number and depressed by mounting debt, delegated their right of nomination to the vacant see to their former bishop, together with Codrington and Archbishop Benson of Canterbury. An appointment was delayed until the debt was reduced. The special qualifications required of a bishop for Melanesia were that he should be young—a little under thirty-five if possible (Patteson had been consecrated at thirty-three, Selwyn at thirty-two), active, manly, "attractive to lads" and likely to win the support of Australasian colonists. Canon Edgar Jacob, Vicar of Portsea (Portsmouth), the largest parish in England, recommended an excellent former curate, Cecil Wilson, who had a suburban church in Bournemouth. The choice seemed ideal. Wilson was thirty-three, already interested in a missionary vocation, "very manly" (a former Kent county cricketer) and a "thorough churchman" of known moderate views.[19] After his nomination was approved by the six New Zealand dioceses, he was consecrated in Auckland in June 1894, with Sarawia, Tagalad and a party of scholars from Norfolk Island taking part in the service. Some thought it was a drawback that the old Melanesian connection with Eton had not been maintained, admitted the Mission's annual report, "but that interest which has been so valuable in the past will not, we hope, be allowed to die out because our new Bishop was trained at another school".[20] Wilson had attended Tonbridge School and immediately founded a Tonbridge Association of old school friends, parallel to the ageing Eton Association, to raise funds for the Melanesian Mission.

In contrast with the strong and assertive personalities among his staff, the new bishop was a gentle, unassuming man, constantly homesick, often to be accused of vacillation and excessive caution. Unlike his predecessor, he came to Melanesia with an open mind, unfettered by personal loyalties and feelings of inadequacy to uncritical maintenance of the existing order. He entered upon the headship of a faction-ridden, backward-looking mission still dominated by the memory of its near-legendary founders, thinly spread over 2800 kilometres, with a small and diminishing circle of faithful supporters. There was urgent need for a transfusion of men and money.

Accordingly, Wilson's first action was to recruit additional missionaries (the number rose from eight in 1894 to fourteen in 1899) and to extend the basis of support for Melanesia, both in England and in the dioceses of Australia and New Zealand. The English Committee, removed from the pocket of the Selwyn family, was enlarged and strengthened, and in 1899, an office with a paid staff was opened in London. An organizing secretary was appointed for Australia in 1903. In 1895, the *Southern Cross* made a three months' tour around the New Zealand coast for sermons and meetings in each port, and the exhibition of twenty-two Melanesian schoolboys as the living fruits of the Mission. At each meeting of the triennial New Zealand General Synod,

Cecil Wilson (From the Beattie Collection: Permission Auckland Institute and Museum)

church support for Melanesia was ritually reaffirmed as a "primary duty", but without spectacular effect.[21] In 1906, there were only three New Zealanders out of twenty-seven on the white staff, and a subsequent proposal to send Maori lay evangelists to the Polynesian outliers of the Solomons came to nothing. For publicity, there was a new monthly journal, the *Southern Cross Log*, first published in Auckland and later in a separate English edition. A network of fund-raising associations sprang up, by extension into the parishes of an existing (hitherto exclusive) St Barnabas' Association, whose members were committed to pray and work for Melanesia and pay an annual subscription of sixpence. There was a new "Island Scheme", by which groups of supporters, each led by a "chief", paid £10 per annum for the work on a designated island or station. Income revived and doubled in the next ten years to £15,000, half of which was derived from England, one-quarter from New Zealand and only one-tenth from Australia. Virtually all the increase had occurred in English subscriptions, and the prospect of the Melanesian Mission ever being supported wholly by parishes in Australia and New Zealand seemed further away than ever before.

As a means of propagating Christianity, the labour trade could no longer be ignored. By the 1890s, there were some eight thousand Pacific Islanders working on Queensland plantations, more than half of them having come from islands where the Melanesian Mission had schools. Accordingly, one of Wilson's first administrative acts was to send Arthur Brittain, missionary in the northern New Hebrides, to Queensland to inquire into religious and physical conditions on the plantations and to suggest what should be done. Anglican efforts had hitherto been scanty, unco-ordinated and perpetually short of money. A mission near Mackay, conducted by Mrs Mary (May) Goodwin Robinson since 1882, was the oldest continuous Christian school for Pacific Islanders in the colony, but hers was a devoted private venture for which money and gifts were sought in England rather than in Queensland. "Her instruction is all given with the view of making the Melanesians full Church members," reported Brittain (although he disapproved of her use of Pidgin English), "and Baptisms are frequent ... She works quite single-handed, and without any intermission as a rule even for an evening, from year to year, and without any fund from which to supply the ordinary school materials."²² Official church involvement was virtually non-existent. Most parish clergy did nothing, the few classes run by voluntary workers were "as a rule ... not vigorous efforts", and the only clergymen working full-time among the Melanesians in Queensland were J.E. Clayton at Bundaberg and F.D. Pritt at Herbert River in the far north.

Brittain's report was almost a turning-point for the Melanesian Mission in its approach to the Melanesians in Queensland. It contained a belated recognition that returning labourers would have "a considerable effect either in hindering or in furthering our efforts in their own islands"; hundreds of labourers had been converted in Queensland, whereas so far the Mission had gained only five teachers from this source.²³ He recommended a Queensland branch of the Melanesian Mission co-ordinated with the work in the islands, which would evangelize pagan Melanesians as well as retain contact with the growing number of Christians among those recruited.

In 1895, Wilson himself visited Queensland, on the invitation of the colony's three bishops, to examine the prospects for such a mission. Like Patteson and Selwyn, he did not oppose the trade in principle: "Queensland may be a good Public School for Melanesians, and the traffic may do good to their characters ... Encourage schools, civilize and evangelize the people, and we shall not object to it."²⁴ Persuaded during his visit that the colony was in fact a "bad school", essentially because it made no effort to "raise" the islanders "morally and intellectually" while they were there, he advocated the establishing of three "colleges" in Queensland on the Norfolk Island model, where time-expired labourers could be educated and prepared for work as Christian evangelists, both for the plantations and for their island homes.²⁵ This ambitious scheme, however, he later rejected as impracticable, for he had no suitable staff to spare and the difficulties of communication between Norfolk Island and Queensland would make co-ordination impossible. Furthermore, the primary duty to convert the labourers still lay with the church in Queensland. "We have only to say that we will do it," he complained to Montgomery, "& they will wash their hands of them altogether. We must force them to care for them by refusing to do so, & by helping them with grants out of a special fund."²⁶ In 1896, he sent P.T. Williams, for a period of two years, to organize the mission at Bundaberg, which became the "Melanesian Mission in Queensland", a self-supporting branch of the island work, under the Bishop of Brisbane. Small subsidies were also paid to the existing plantation schools. Mrs Robinson's school at Mackay, renamed the Selwyn Mission, attended by a hundred or more labourers, remained a principal centre of Anglican work. The number of Melanesians who attended Anglican services and classes in the whole colony rose to about 400 by 1898, but this number was far surpassed by the very successful Queensland Kanaka Mission, which then had eleven schools throughout the sugar belt, with a weekly attendance of more than 2000, 7000 in 1905.

In Fiji, there were small Anglican schools for labourers at Levuka and in Suva, where a separate church had to be built after complaints from the white congregation that "the Melanesians were ousting them from their own church".[27] In 1894, Comins was allowed by Thurston to take six Malaitan Christian "boys" for training as teachers at Norfolk Island.

The principal innovation of the early years of Wilson's episcopate was the establishment of the first permanently manned European centre in the islands. As early as 1879, Comins had advocated residential stations for Nggela and Mota.[28] However, because Selwyn had insisted on the annual return of the island missionaries to Norfolk Island, it was only in 1893 that he was free to go ahead and purchase land for £10 at Siota, at Mboli harbour, Nggela. By this time, St Barnabas' College, even at its maximum feasible size of 200 pupils, was able to produce only twenty teachers annually, enough to maintain the existing village schools, but not to increase them, and there was urgent need for a supplementary central school. St Luke's School at Siota, under Comins and Welchman, was to be a junior Norfolk Island of the Solomons. In a bid to attract recruits, Siota scholars were given a uniform of red shirts and blue trousers and were taught elementary English as well as Mota. But the venture was dogged with misfortune from the start. Welchman's young wife died there in January 1897, only six months after their marriage. In 1898, eleven boys—one-quarter of the school—died in an epidemic of dysentery. When more sickness followed in 1899, coupled with reports of heavy garden work and lack of food,

Christian villagers on Malaita and elsewhere refused to permit their sons to go there. Incorrectly convinced that the Siota site was inherently unhealthy, the bishop closed the school and leased the land for planting coconuts.

Meanwhile, the Nggela group surrounding Siota was posing pastoral problems that no one knew how to solve. On his first visit to the Solomons in 1894, Wilson saw Nggela in a romantic light as a "fountain of life", displaying the "arts of civilization" and maintaining its pristine fervour in the faith by sending missionaries to the adjacent unevangelized islands, just as the Celtic and Saxon churches had sent forth Aidan, Columba and Boniface.[29] Closer knowledge revealed a less idyllic state of affairs. Stories were in constant circulation about the misbehaviour of the new Christian élite of village teachers. C.W. Browning, missionary during the 1890s, attributed the growing indifference to church and school to the pace of the conversion movement in the previous decade: "Christianity was much more extensively adopted in outward profession than in principle" and most people had "all the while retained their old ideas and motives".[30] Worship of pagan *tindalo* was found to be widespread in Christian villages; charms and sorcery were "largely used"; while among European traders, the Nggela people, because of their keen business instincts, had already acquired a reputation as "the biggest liars and thieves in the group". "What is wrong with Florida?" bewailed another missionary. "The average white man has not a good word to say for its people, as a rule; and the enemies of the Mission point triumphantly to it as a proof of our inefficiency."[31]

Nor was Nggela destined to remain an undisturbed Anglican enclave. Because of its central location and peaceful condition, it was admirably suited to become the seat of government for the new British Solomon Islands Protectorate. In 1896, C. M. Woodford, who had been appointed as first Resident Commissioner, set up his headquarters on the small island of Tulagi, near an existing trading-station at Gavutu, and set about creating the nucleus of a modest district administration.

Woodford took up his work influenced by Sir John Thurston's doctrine that the "Administration should protect and aid all Missions to the utmost of its possibilities, but lay itself under obligation to none".[32] Infant administration and insecure mission eyed each other across the water with suspicion. Woodford interpreted the stories that came to his ears about aggressive teachers wielding political powers as evidence of a deliberate plan by the Melanesian Mission "to gradually make chiefs of their teachers"—a charge that was untrue because it presupposed more political ambition and intimate knowledge of Nggela than any missionary then possessed.[33] In 1898, he inaugurated an administration for Nggela in which teachers and clergy were to be excluded from the exercise of secular authority. At a gathering of *vunagi* and their followers at Tulagi, the Nggela group was divided into five districts, each governed by a principal "chief" directly responsible to the Resident Commissioner. The *vaukolu* was deprived of its governmental functions, eventually to become a church conference for discussion of marriage customs and ecclesiastical matters, by the introduction of a new code of laws. Modelled on the laws of the Ellice Islands, it decreed penalties of imprisonment and fines for murder, theft, lying reports, adultery and other breaches of the sexual code. Unlike the Ellice code, however, and partly reflecting the more tolerant ethos of Anglican Christianity, there were no laws for drunkenness, Sunday observance or attendance at school.[34]

There was an opinion among the Anglican missionaries that Woodford was unreasonably critical—even prejudiced—towards their mission and all its works. "He does not seem to love the Mission much & disagrees with our system," wrote Edgell after a dinner at the Tulagi residency. "Woodford is a critic, but no friend of M.M.," was Wilson's private view. "He puts me always on defence with his veiled attacks."[35] They themselves had welcomed the establishment of British rule in the expectation of positive assistance for their work and were "grievously disappointed" by the lack of tangible benefits. The government was not even neutral, Welchman alleged, but actually biassed against those of its subjects who followed the religion of England: "we felt that the Christians were at a discount & the heathens at a premium. The Christians were not believed & the heathen were."[36]

There were many occasions for friction, especially on Nggela, but in the long term, these were outweighed by a basic harmony of interest. In common with the majority of British colonial administrators of his generation, regardless of their personal views on the truth or falsity of the Christian creed, Woodford had a pragmatic appreciation of the social function of a religion that sanctioned a "civilized" code of moral behaviour. His administration was too small and too poor to do much by itself. Because the Colonial Office insisted on financial self-sufficiency, he was compelled to seek out big companies that would undertake large-scale plantation development in the Solomons, in order to raise essential revenue through indirect taxation. Likewise, he looked to Christianity to lay a foundation in Solomons villages of peace, literacy and an understanding of Western institutions, preparatory to the inauguration of a regular district administration. This recognition of the imperial utility of Christian missions was essentially the same policy as that followed by British, German and Australian colonial administrators in New Guinea. Sir William MacGregor (Administrator of British New Guinea, 1888-98), had governed on the assumption that the Christian religion and good order were synonymous, and that chiefs, policemen and missionaries were interchangeable in the work of pacification. Sir Hubert Murray (Lieutenant-Governor of Papua, 1908-40) frequently endorsed the work of Christian missions as "absolutely essential to the development of backward races".[37]

During his term of office, Woodford welcomed four new missions to the protectorate: French priests of the Society of Mary in 1898, Australian Methodists in 1902, a branch of the Queensland Kanaka Mission (later renamed the South Sea Evangelical Mission) in 1904 and Seventh-day Adventists, also from Australia, in 1914.[38] In the early years, in order to maximize the diffusion of civilizing influences and to avoid the social disruption of sectarian warfare, he directed the first three missions to begin work on separate islands. He prevented invasion of localities where another mission was already in effective occupation by the simple means of disallowing purchases of land intended for European stations. In this unofficial "sphere of influence" policy—echoing the religious partition of British New Guinea in 1890—there were no favourites, and all missions were treated alike. The propagation of the doctrines of the established Church of England received as such no special assistance. Woodford's policy effectively prevented the Marists from establishing a station on Santa Isabel. However, he was prepared to invite Methodists to north Malaita if the Melanesian Mission did not quickly send a European missionary (A.I. Hopkins was accordingly stationed there in 1902), and he refused to sanction Wilson's purchase of land in the Shortland Islands adjacent to a newly founded Roman Catholic station. He and his successors recommended mission schools of any variety to the Solomon Islanders as in accordance with the will of the government: "Christianity stands for all that is good," announced an official circular to the subjects of the protectorate, "no matter by whom it is taught."[39]

An aura of official protection surrounded the Anglican entry into Guadalcanal. In 1900, a party of teachers led by P.T. Williams invaded the north-west of the island to support Hugo Gorovaka's Christian school at Maravovo, which was in danger of being dispersed by Sulukavo, a powerful warrior-leader who was hostile to missions of any kind. This was the first occasion on which the Melanesian Mission had forced entrance to a place against the wishes of the local inhabitants. The tactic succeeded essentially because Williams was explicitly backed by the authority of the government, for Woodford had lent rifles to deter attackers and promised armed police to protect Maravovo if necessary. Sulukavo eventually withdrew his open resistance, convinced that the missionaries possessed a secret protecting power against which his own sorcery and charms were useless. The attitude of the local people changed, and the way was opened for Anglican expansion, under Nggela teachers, from Maravovo to villages along the west coast of Guadalcanal.

The Melanesian Mission was increasingly drawn into a qualified alliance with the Solomons administration. By the end of Woodford's term of office in 1915, it was secure in an unofficial position of pre-eminence over the other denominations. This was partly a result of local circumstances. The Anglican mission had preceded the government in time, and though outpaced by the S.S.E.M. on Malaita and by the Marists on Guadalcanal, it remained the largest and best-known Christian body in the protectorate. The *Southern Cross*, with the bishop on board, was a familiar visitor at Tulagi, where it called on arriving from the south two or three times each year for quarantine and customs inspection. There were also less tangible reasons for the affinity. Anglican missionaries, whether from England or the colonies, were as a rule sympathetic to the imperial ideal, innately respectful of lawful authority and its representatives. The close identification of the Melanesian Mission with the Crown had been assumed by Melanesians since the days of cruising men-of-war; among Pidgin English-speakers it was known as the "English mission", whereas the Marists were "French" and the S.S.E.M.—for reasons which are obscure—"Scotch". Moreover, there was a community of mind. Both Wilson and Woodford were Old Boys of Tonbridge. Successive bishops and many of the English clergy associated easily wih senior government officials who shared the same upper-middle-class values and conventions. Because both parties were assured of their position in the social hierarchy, their rare meetings were occasions for borrowing books, swapping Test-cricket scores, drinking together and reminiscing about mutual friends at home.

Deep in the consciousness of the Melanesian Mission was the conviction that it was "God's instrument" for the evangelization of northern Melanesia. At stake in this claim was nothing less than the honour of the Church of England—"the richest, the most influential Church in the whole of the world":

> A Church which believes herself to be purer in doctrine than others, in that she not only "adheres to the doctrine of the Cross, but also stands apart from Papal and Puritan innovations", would surely come under the greater condemnation if, having the best, she allowed the world to have what she considers to be the less good.[40]

The advent of other missions was therefore a humiliating blow to the self-image of the Anglicans, for it visibly demonstrated what had long been apparent to first-hand observers: that the Anglican mission had made a substantial impression on very few islands within its recognized sphere. Every Protestant society in the South Pacific had virtually occupied its own special territory, Wilson lamented, whereas the Melanesian Mission, despite a monopoly of fifty years, had not yet commenced work on fifteen out of forty-two islands in a field already "small enough". "Our traditions are noble—none more so in any part of the world," wrote Montgomery in 1903; but compared with the 160,000 Pacific Islands adherents of the L.M.S., Methodist and Presbyterian missions, Anglicans were "numerically an almost negligible quantity". Nor was there a practical possibility of "bringing all our people to a knowledge of Christ within this generation, or even the next".[41]

To retain an exclusive occupation indefinitely was impossible, for there were signs that other missionary bodies were becoming interested in what they regarded as a neglected field. At the Hobart Church Congress in 1894, Bice sounded a warning: "I can quite see that before long we shall have the jingle and clash of sects within the Church of England portion of Melanesia, the brighest and purest jewel in the crown of the Australasian Missionary Church."[42] Twenty years earlier, in 1874, the Wesleyan missionary George Brown had asked John Selwyn how far he expected the Melanesian Mission to have advanced in the next hundred years. "Give me the Solomons as the limit of my sphere," replied Selwyn, which he took to include all islands as far north as Bougainville. "Very well," said Brown, "then we will enter New Britain"—where he proceeded to found a Methodist mission in 1875.[43] At the General Conference of the Australasian Wesleyan Methodist Church in 1888, the Solomon Islands were again mentioned as a potential mission field, but the sending of a mission at MacGregor's invitation to eastern Papua in 1891 absorbed the expansionist energies of the home church until the late 1890s, when a series of petitions were sent to Sydney by a group of Christianized labourers in Fiji, urging a Methodist mission to accompany them on their return to Guadalcanal. These Wesleyan converts dismissed the Melanesian Mission as torpid and unevangelical:

> Concerning the Church which is at N'gela and Bugotu, we did not disrespect that Church, but we know that it has been a long time there, it has been thirty years there, but does not grow up and spread rapidly to Christianise all the people that they may know the true Light as we know the truth of the Gospel.[44]

Their repeated representations, combined with Brown's personal report on the "dreadful" spiritual condition of the Solomons and the unwelcome news that Bishop Alfred Willis, formerly of Honolulu, was planning to go to Tonga to begin an episcopal mission at the invitation of a congregation of ex-Wesleyans, were together sufficient to overcome the deep Methodist reluctance to break the unwritten comity agreement. In May 1901, the

Wesleyan General Conference resolved to found a mission in the Solomon Islands, "on such parts as may seem most desirable and practicable, and at the earliest possible time".[45] Conciliatory and anxious to avoid direct collision, Brown preferred to begin among the head-hunting inhabitants of the Roviana Lagoon in the New Georgia group, for according to the map in E.S. Armstrong's then newly published *History of the Melanesian Mission*, New Georgia was beyond the Anglicans' "present field of work".

Wilson, confronted with a choice between Guadalcanal, Malaita or New Georgia, refused officially to "give up" territory, but conceded reluctantly that a Methodist mission to New Georgia would not be a "distinctively unfriendly act", in direct violation of the existing compact. He had no immediate plans to begin work there, he told Brown at a meeting in Sydney in January 1902, "and I should certainly not take it up at all if you had a strong and effective mission work there".[46] Because of the small population of New Georgia, he confidently expected that the Methodist foundation would remain a small one. He was therefore furious when it expanded, following a route traditionally used by Roviana traders and head-hunters, to the adjacent island of Choiseul, where the *Southern Cross* had already taken a few boys from Sasamungga on the west coast in the years after 1900. It was an "abominable" breach of trust, he fumed to Montgomery.[47] In retaliation, he launched an offensive against islands claimed by the Methodists, encouraging Welchman to follow up some earlier exploratory voyages into the west by placing Bugotu teachers in pagan villages on Vella Lavella and Choiseul. However, the demand for teachers elsewhere in the Solomons compelled their withdrawal in 1907 —"not yielding our claim," wrote Welchman in gloomy self-justification, " & ignoring the Wesleyan claims until such time as it shall please God to open the way for us".[48] Thereafter, the Manning Strait between Santa Isabel and Choiseul became the accepted boundary between the two missions.

The Methodists had entered the Solomons mission field by the path of consultation and prior consent. Not so the Marist Fathers, who would recognize no externally-imposed limitation on their obligation to plant the Catholic religion wherever people would receive it. Returning in 1898 to the islands their predecessors had abandoned in 1847, they worked initially through a school at their headquarters on the islet of Rua Sura, off the north-east coast of Guadalcanal, from where they eventually established a ring of mission-stations around the island. They extended to San Cristobal in 1909 and to Malaita in 1912. When a Marist station was founded at Visale in 1904, only a few kilometres from Maravovo, the western end of Guadalcanal became a scene of intense religious rivalry as each mission raced the other to secure the allegiance of confused and uncommitted villagers.[49]

For such a struggle, the Melanesian Mission was ill-prepared. Fifty years of undisputed monopoly had made it complacent. From 1900 onwards, it had only one or two missionaries on Guadalcanal to supervise new schools thinly spread along more than 130 kilometres of coastline. The French priests, by contrast, were aggressive and numerous (nine in 1904, twelve in 1910), eager to draw heretics as well as pagans into the true church. They saw the English "Protestant" mission in the stark light of their own narrow Tridentine theology, as a rival to be blocked at every turn and dislodged from its strongholds wherever possible. There were Anglican complaints of unscrupulous tactics: that rather than go to places where there was no Christian influence at all, Roman Catholic teachers were deliberately settling adjacent to Anglican schools, to draw away malcontents, who were then subjected to rebaptism. "They have spoken against our faith and our workers," wrote one aggrieved missionary, "have harassed our people, and in one case at least have tried to pervert a teacher, telling him that we purposely neglected him and had taught him what we knew to be lies."[50]

The circumstances did not favour generosity of spirit, though the Anglicans, who held to a less exclusive concept of the Church, found it possible to recognize Roman Catholicism as a valid if erroneous expression of Christianity, whereas the reverse was not the case. When French Marists founded a small mission on Pentecost in 1898, Edgell was inclined even to welcome their presence, "because I feel that it is better to bring Christianity to the natives in any form (except Arian & other early heretical forms) rather than that they should not have it", and he was successful in arranging a short-lived no-trespass agreement.[51]

In the village propaganda war, followers of each church justified their own position by stressing differences and attacking the other's weakest points. The Church of England had been founded by an adulterous king and was no part of the Church of God, ran the popular Catholic argument; therefore its followers could not hope for salvation. In later years, Anglicans sought to counter this through an outline history of the Church of England, written in Mota for the use of teachers, which concluded with a table tracing the episcopal succession from Jesus Christ, through Pope Gregory the Great, Augustine of Canterbury and G.A. Selwyn, to the successive bishops of Melanesia. Anglican missionaries warned of the errors of Roman doctrines and devotions. Welchman gave Nggela teachers special lessons on the subject: "Nine came", he recorded in his diary after such a class, "& were much interested in the Rosary, Celibacy of the clergy, Confession, Mortification, the Inquisition & the House of Loreto."[52] Anglican converts boasted of their own mission's prestige. It had a mighty steam ship (the 500-tonne *Southern Cross V*) and was the church of the King, whereas the Marists, because they were French, would soon be expelled by the British government. On Guadalcanal, it was an unashamed struggle for local paramountcy, but with their superior numbers, the Marists were from the outset in a position of advantage, and eventually they claimed more than half the population.

It was a consequence of the Anglican *via media* that the Melanesian Mission, which was attacked by the Marists as Protestant and heretical, was also looked at with suspicion by Evangelical Protestants for being too Catholic. The Queensland Kanaka Mission had extended its activities to the Solomons in 1904 only after advice from leaders of the Church Missionary Association, who suspected that a reputedly High Church mission was stressing the sacraments at the expense of conversion of the heart. The Anglican attitude towards the undenominational South Sea Evangelical Mission, whose unordained missionaries worked largely through the medium of Pidgin English and were not supported by one of the historic Protestant denominations, was always rather condescending. For its part —like the Marists, who were its doctrinal antithesis—the S.S.E.M. initially refused in the name of Truth to enter into comity agreements, and its missionaries doubted whether many converts of the Melanesian Mission were really numbered among the saved.

The southern boundary of the Mission was no more inviolable. In the New Hebrides, the continued failure of the Anglicans to complete the evangelization of Omba, Maewo and Pentecost (for most of the 1890s, there was only one missionary for the three islands) led to a rumble of dissatisfaction among the Presbyterians, who felt frustrated in their advance by the formal agreement of 1881. In 1899, there was a proposal to begin a new mission in the German Solomons. Then in 1901, Peter Milne, Presbyterian missionary on Nguna since 1870, took militant action on his own account and settled among pagans at Nduindui in west Omba, protesting that the Melanesian Mission had done "nothing" on the island. (It had six schools in east Omba.) His action provoked a cautious resolution from the Presbyterian synod of 1902, requesting Wilson to avoid "all unhappy friction" by ceding at least the island of Omba. The offer was refused, Milne was withdrawn and the 1881 agreement reaffirmed.[53] But the Anglican monopoly in the north was already broken, first by Roman Catholics on Pentecost and Omba and later by Australian missionaries of the Churches of Christ, who founded missions among returned Queensland labourers at Pentecost, Omba (Nduindui) and Maewo in the years after 1903.

Relations between Anglican missionaries and those of other denominations varied according to persons and circumstances. Sometimes they were more friendly than might have been expected. Welchman gave a set of Nggela prayer-books and gospels to the newly arrived Marists, to assist their language studies. Edgell regarded the French priests at Pentecost as his "good friends" and exchanged books and food. Even on strife-ridden Guadalcanal, J.M. Steward publicly acknowledged the "brotherly spirit" of the priests at Visale, and Hopkins praised the generous hospitality and zeal of the S.S.E.M. on Malaita.[54]

But mutual hospitality and assistance in cases of physical need marked the limits of Christian co-operation throughout Melanesia until well into the mid-twentieth century. Isolated examples of European fraternization did nothing to modify the mutual suspicion and crude point-scoring that habitually marred relations between neighbouring adherents of different missions. After twenty-five years in the Solomons, Hopkins observed that Melanesians found it "hard to understand, but easy to imitate, our differences",[55] though the ultimate responsibility in fact lay with the polemical orientation of much missionary instruction. In addition to those disputes which arose directly out of half-understood doctrinal divergences, social cleavages tended also to assume a religious dimension. Traditional hostilities between adjacent villages commonly found expression in membership of rival missions, and quarrels within a Christian village sometimes resulted in one faction seeking a teacher of its own from elsewhere. In a society in which a particular Christian affiliation was so often determineed by geography, the fact of the diversity of missions at least gave the Melanesians a small degree of choice and bargaining power. The Anglicans, who had upheld the principle of non-interference when they were in sole possession, eventually found it expedient to adopt a more militant posture. The "explosion", as one observer called it, finally came in 1924, when a conference of European clergy agreed that in future they would be morally justified in starting a school in any village where one was requested, regardless of whether another body had a school there already or claimed the territory as its own. Comity was dead.

The fact of religious competition had meanwhile achieved what nothing else could have done. It compelled the Melanesian Mission to abandon for ever the time-honoured practice by which the missionaries divided each year between Norfolk Island and their island districts. During the 1890s, Welchman led the way, taking up continuous residence at Bugotu because of the year-round pressure of pastoral work. A few others experimented for a season or two, but most members of the staff still returned to Norfolk Island each year in the *Southern Cross*, at the onset of the wet season, to take up their share of classroom teaching. As the trading, planting and official population of the Solomons protectorate grew from a dozen in 1893, to fifty in 1896 and 110 in 1905, the continuance of a policy designed for Melanesia of the 1840s became increasingly anachronistic. Innate conservatism was defended against mounting internal criticism on the radical ground that the periodic absence of Europeans gave the Melanesian church an opportunity to develop the habits of self-reliance and independence. It was a policy for a non-competitive world. Circumstances were changed dramatically by the arrival of Roman Catholic missionaries on Guadalcanal and

Pentecost in 1898. Although the Melanesian teachers, Wilson conceded, were effective when working in isolation among their own people, they could not hold their ground against constant pressure from the "clever French priests", for it was "natural" to expect that some islanders would follow the teaching of those Europeans who were always on the spot. The conclusion was inescapable:

> We must have men settled on all these islands which we have not yet touched. We must have men settled also in the islands where, for fifty years, we have sown the seed, or else others will gather in our harvest.[56]

To critical observers like Woodford, the move to permanent residence from 1900 onwards was long overdue. At the head of the S.P.G., Montgomery was blunt:

> I have no doubt whatever that were the Selwyns and Patteson alive to-day they would show their statesmanship by adapting themselves to the changed conditions. It is no real loyalty to those great men to keep blindly to their methods in times which have changed so completely as ours have since they planned the Mission.[57]

However, the reform was undertaken reluctantly. Wilson emphasized the dangers of going ahead too fast. He explained the break with hallowed past practice as in reality a continuance of "old methods, slightly adapted to our new circumstances".[58]

The immediate consequences of the change were threefold. Because district missionaries no longer returned to Norfolk Island each year, the principal school acquired a permanent, therefore more effective, teaching staff. In the islands, the Mission assumed for the first time the visible characteristics of a permanent European institution, as dwellings of bamboo and sago palm hitherto used by itinerating missionaries were supplanted by small prefabricated wooden houses. Twelve such residences had been erected by 1907 at the various district headquarters, each of them on one or two hectares of mission-owned land. At the same time, the inauguration of a bi-monthly commercial steamer service from Sydney to the New Hebrides and Solomons, the more general availability of tinned provisions and the universal adoption of mosquito nets (the link between the anopheles mosquito and malaria was not finally proved until the turn of the century), were easing the worst physical problems associated with prolonged European residence in northern Melanesia. Permanent "central schools" for boys, each with forty or fifty pupils, were established in the islands as feeders for Norfolk Island, on the lines originally planned for Siota. These were set up at Vureas, Vanua Lava, in 1905 to serve the Banks Islands and New Hebrides; at Bungana, an islet in the Nggela group in 1910; and at Pamua on San Cristobal in 1911. The future of the latter two was seen romantically as "the Harrow and the Eton of the Solomons".[59]

These changes in organization required more missionaries. Accordingly, for the first time in the history of the Mission, a Bishop of Melanesia descended into the ecclesiastical marketplace to appeal publicly for recruits from the Australasian colonies and from England. In 1899, Wilson called for twenty additional men—the "best men"—to enable at least two missionaries for each large island and two for every group of small islands, as well as subscriptions for a new and faster mission ship. (Its predecessors had been paid for entirely by rich private donors.) He received £23,450 for *Southern Cross V* (£14,150 from England) and fifteen recruits.

By 1911, at the end of Wilson's episcopate, there were twenty-nine male missionaries on the staff. All but seven were ordained; all but five were from England; only five were married. Their social origins were less homogeneous. Twelve men were university graduates: ten of them from Oxford or Cambridge, one from London University, and one (C.E. Fox) from the University of New Zealand. P.T. Williams was a grandson of the pioneer New Zealand C.M.S. missionary Henry Williams and a Cambridge Rugby Blue. R.P. Wilson had been a solicitor before university and ordination. Eton, it was complained, was not doing "her duty" towards Melanesia, for after the departure of C.W. Browning, missionary at Nggela from 1892 to 1899, the nearest the Mission came to an Old Etonian in its midst was F.H. Drew, a bank clerk son of an Eton science master.[60] One recruit who approached Wilson's ideal was Guy Bury, a young Oxford graduate, who in 1911 went to Melanesia from his curacy at Reading in the spirit of a grand adventure and rattled off his naïve impressions of people and places in the characteristic idiom of his class. "I have quite fallen in love with the Melanesians already—they seem excessively pleased to see one," he wrote to his family on arriving at Norfolk Island; and on reaching Santa Cruz:

> ... I have no use for the Southern Melanesian. He is no gent; and these people up here most certainly are and real sportsmen. Only a short time ago one of our teachers shot a man for not coming to school regularly; and if that does not show right feeling, I should like to know what does![61]

He died three months later of blood poisoning, having in ignorance applied an excess of iodine to malignant sores.

These were of the élite: self-confident Englishmen from the upper-middle-class, educated for leadership at public school and university, and keen on cricket. Yet despite their influence in the Melanesian Mission, they were not a majority. During this period, an equal number of clerical missionaries came from backgrounds that were less privileged. Between 1911 and 1915, the Mission gained four recruits—R.J.A. Simmons, W.F. Long, Albert Mason and Reginald Hodgson—three of them sons of "splendid" working men, from one church in Leeds.[62] H.N. Drummond and D.E. Graves had been employed as mining engineers. W.H. Edgell had assisted in his father's solicitor's office. Rudolph Sprott had worked for a London publishing firm. Charles Godden was a farm labourer from Victoria who came under the influence of his vicar and put himself through theological college. While curate of a Sydney city parish, he volunteered for missionary work after hearing a sermon on Melanesia by Bishop Wilson. Many English recruits, similarly inspired to join the Melanesian Mission because of a visiting missionary speaker or some other personal contact, came directly from a three-year training course for non-graduates (in some cases, their fees being subsidized by the English Committee) in one of the Church of England missionary theological colleges: usually St Augustine's College, Canterbury, or St Boniface College, Warminster. A few were ordained in Melanesia after failing their theological examinations at home.

Until 1907, when W.G. Ivens compiled a handbook of advice, newcomers were commonly left by themselves in their island districts, without specific guidance concerning their itinerating life, food and diet, medicine, clothing, learning a Melanesian language or relations with the local people. The emphasis was on amateurism and the virtues of spartan simplicity. "When I first went to Melanesia", said Bishop Wilson, "we were rather discouraged from sleeping under mosquito nets; it was thought effeminate so we allowed ourselves to be bitten rather than appear effeminate."[63] Older missionaries, who themselves had absorbed much practical knowledge in their summers at Norfolk Island, held doggedly to the "school of hard knocks" view, that it was best to let a man learn everything on the spot by experience, whether it was the management of a 9-metre whaleboat or learning the complex language of his particular district.

Everyone began by learning Mota, the language of St Barnabas' at Norfolk Island and the teachers who were trained there, which was relatively easy because of a Mota dictionary, a grammar and a small number of translated works. The Mota Bible, completed by Codrington, was printed in England by the S.P.C.K. in 1912. Mota thus retained its predominance as the basis for all other translations and as the language of church services wherever the Prayer Book had not been translated into a local vernacular. It was "*the* language", wrote Ivens, "and the enlightenment or the importance of a place was measured at times by the ability or otherwise of its people to speak Mota".[64] Other languages, more difficult to master without the equivalent tools or years of experience, were pushed into the background, their usefulness deprecated. With the notable exception of the New Testament translations by Henry Welchman into Bugotu and by W.G. Ivens into Sa'a and Ulawa (and later into Lau), and the Gospels by C.E. Fox into Arosi, printed translations since Codrington's day were said to be "little and poor", and each year less was being done.

Did the new conditions of work make the task of a white missionary easier? Some thought not. Of all the missionaries in Melanesia, the Anglicans were said to suffer most from overwork and inadequate equipment. One-third of the income of the Melanesian Mission was swallowed up in running *Southern Cross V*. Salaries were low by clerical standards of the time— between £100 and £150 per annum, depending on length of service. (The bishop received an annual income of £600 from the Melanesian Mission Trust.) By contrast, L.M.S. men were paid £200, Presbyterians £240 and Anglican clergymen in Australia or New Zealand could expect a minimum stipend of

£200 in an established parish. Furlough was unsubsidized and infrequent, no more than once every five years. Intending recruits were warned of the trials of loneliness: that they would be working alone and might spend months without opportunity of "meeting a white man of like mind with themselves". This was a new preoccupation, which Codrington, with other missionaries of his generation, privately deplored from their retirement in England as "the very important difference between the modern men and the ancient".[65] The Mission discouraged marriage, though for economic and practical rather than doctrinal reasons, for it was easier to keep a single man in discomfort in the field than a married couple. Unlike the principal Roman Catholic and Protestant stations, which became oases of modest domestic comfort, Anglican mission houses were typically small and barely furnished. Everywhere the area under the responsibility of a single missionary was huge in size. In 1913, each "district" (or parish) in the Solomons was said to have an average of twenty-six schools, scattered over some 300 kilometres of coastline.[66]

"We are doctors & judges, as well as missionaries": so J.W. Blencowe described his work at Sánta Cruz.[67] The ideal was to visit each school village for one or two days each quarter, to celebrate Holy Communion, advise the teacher, exclude notorious sinners from the church and receive back penitents, conduct baptisms and weddings, examine candidates for baptism and confirmation, dress sores, settle disputes and inspect the school. "Insist on a Teacher keeping a Register, but do not put too much dependance on it," new missionaries were told. "Teachers have been known to fill up a Register for months ahead, supposing that what you wanted was a well filled book."[68]

Inevitably, therefore, it was a life of continuous itineration under rough conditions: by foot through the bush, or around the coast for six or eight weeks on end by whaleboat, manned by a volunteer crew, who were paid sixpence each per day. (The first district launch was not supplied until 1913.) Each year, Hopkins travelled 3400 kilometres by whaleboat around north Malaita, mostly by night to avoid the heat. After one of his own whaleboat visitations, Ivens recalled visiting a man-of-war "looking rather like a beachcomber than a mission priest":

> a battered straw hat, no coat, shirt torn, skin burned as brown as any native's, white trousers the worse for wear, and no boots on

Mission-house at Loh, Torres Islands, 1906. W.J. Durrad and the people of Vipaka village (From the Beattie Collection: Permission Auckland Institute and Museum)

On board *Southern Cross V* at Vella Lavella, 1906, Captain Sinker *(left)* and Bishop Wilson *(right)* (From the Beattie Collection: Permission Auckland Institute and Museum)

simply because there were none to put on; all were worn out with the rough travelling.⁶⁹

On San Cristobal, C.E. Fox would live for a month at a time in pagan bush villages—"barefoot and bareheaded, wearing a loin-cloth and singlet, and taking nothing except a small native bag slung on my shoulder, in which were my pipe and one book for solid reading".⁷⁰

Overwork, inexperience, poor housing, faulty diet, coupled with disabling attacks of malaria and other tropical infections, led to physical breakdowns and in seven cases to a premature death. In 1916, Woodford caused a stir by accusing the Mission on its own London platform of culpable negligence:

> I have known instances where missionaries of your Mission have not had the necessary comforts that, in my opinion, they should have had, and have lived in circumstances of the greatest discomfort, and I fear that some of the losses in men may have been preventible.⁷¹

Not surprisingly, there was a high turnover of staff. Of those who joined the Mission between 1900 and 1920, one-third (twenty-three) stayed for less than three years. On Guadalcanal, there were eight successive missionaries in thirteen years.

Another innovation in the internal organization of the Mission was the sending of unmarried women missionaries to the islands. In the days of Patteson and John Selwyn, the question was never raised; the island work was a masculine preserve. Wives of missionaries and a few single women, led by the formidable Mrs Elizabeth Colenso, estranged wife of an early C.M.S. missionary-printer in New Zealand, lived at Norfolk Island and undertook the "training" of those girls who were taken there, usually for three years, in preparation for their marriage to one of the older scholars. Their number was never large, about forty in the 1890s, for in many places, the islanders refused to allow a single girl to leave her home. Those who did come, their teachers complained, were usually too old or too ignorant to learn much in so short a time.

The training they received owed little to the realities of life in the islands. Whereas the work of Melanesian women was centred on their food gardens and the upbringing of children, girls at Norfolk Island were kept under continuous and often repressive supervision, to be taught Scripture, the Prayer Book Catechism, reading and writing, sewing and the domestic arts of cooking, washing, starching and ironing. Indeed, "women's work" was essentially a euphemism for the school's clothing factory, where, for three hours or more daily, prospective Christian wives cut out, sewed and patched up to 1600 garments annually for the 160 schoolboys and for themselves. When they later returned to their own districts married to a teacher, they were encouraged to reproduce the polite habits they had learned. Sarawia's wife, for example, had made her own starch out of native arrowroot. Travelling missionaries found themselves served afternoon-tea promptly at four o'clock. "She entertained me in regal splendour," Bice reported to Mrs Colenso of one of her former pupils on Maewo. "She is a credit to your establishment and your good and patient teaching ... White & clean linen were the order of the day and I even heard of starching & ironing."[72] Such customs, however, did not impress the girls' relatives, who complained bitterly that Norfolk Island schooling had made them unfit for garden work, nor would they "listen to their husbands".[73] As a method of influencing that half of the population of Melanesia who were women, Mrs Colenso's class was rightly suspected of being exceedingly limited. Yet high-minded men could envisage no alternative.

The position traditionally occupied by women in island society fascinated and depressed European missionary observers. The orthodox opinion was that the Melanesian women led lives of degradation, drudgery and fear, and were regarded as "little better than the pigs".[74] Such a judgement was superficial, based on an inadequate understanding of the significance of much traditional behaviour. Brooke was one of the few missionaries to perceive that Nggela women, for example, occupied an influential social role in village affairs, as messengers, mediators between enemies, and negotiators of loans. Nevertheless, the customary exclusion of women from certain religious and social activities, and the fact that all the teachers of Christianity were male, effectively ensured that women inhabitants of school villages were as a rule much less affected than the men by the new teaching. According to Wilson, it was a common sight for one side of the church to be filled with forty or fifty men, while on the opposite side, there were but four or five women, who "stood during the service, with their faces turned towards the wall, from shame at being in a house with men".[75]

Encouraged by the examples of the C.M.S., the Methodist missions in Papua and New Britain, and the (Anglican) New Guinea Mission, which had already begun to employ single women for village teaching and nursing, and by the French nuns associated with the Roman Catholic missions in the Pacific, Wilson decided to send women missionaries to the islands, in groups of two or three, to Christian districts where their safety would be assured. The first women's stations were established at Nggela in 1905, at Lamalanga on Pentecost in 1906, Mota in 1909 and Maravovo in 1913. At home, their initial occupants would have been devoted Sunday School teachers of poor children, but in Melanesia, they were limited in what they could do by their own genteel background and by the conventions of the day. As at Norfolk Island, there was no attempt to relate the activities of the stations to the daily life of the women around. There was also a communication difficulty, for the Englishwomen for a long time spoke only Mota, which the local women did not understand. The goals were moralistic: to teach the virtues of obedience, cleanliness, thoroughness and good manners, by which path Melanesian women could rise to the position that God had intended for them. They taught writing, reading, singing and Bible stories, gave out simple medical treatments, and on two or three mornings each week, held sewing classes for women and girls from nearby villages, who were taught to make skirts and jackets for themselves—a popular but exotic exercise, which drew the full blast of Welchman's notorious sarcasm. In the evenings, there were hymns around a portable harmonium. At Christmas, they distributed presents of beads, knives, garments, dressed dolls and toys supplied by well-meaning friends. Regularly, a few of them wrote shocked accounts of the filth and ignorance they saw around:

> Oh! how these women yell and scream after a relation or friend has died! You have no idea how awful it is. I have spoken very much to them about it, and they were really quieter, though I expect they saw us coming ... Of course, it is trying, as they do press so close, and, oh, the dirt! to say nothing of skin diseases ...[76]

Everywhere, the women's work was reported to be "very slow"; optimists were easily discouraged. It was not until 1916

Girls' sewing-room, St. Barnabas' College, Norfolk Island, 1906 (From the Beattie Collection: Permission Auckland Institute and Museum)

Women's mission-station at Honggo, Nggela, 1906 (From the Beattie Collection: Permission Auckland Institute and Museum)

that the Nggela station escaped this artificial strait-jacket to become a girl's boarding-school, but the then bishop, Cecil Wood, regarded it as a doubtful experiment, for which the women in charge, Ida Wench and Gwendolen Child, were compelled to supply the extra expenses themselves.

The multiplication of white staff and their permanent residence in the islands helped to alter the shape and orientation of the Mission. Whereas in 1894, the Melanesian clergy had slightly outnumbered the European, by 1911, there were twenty-one European clergymen, together with sixteen men and women lay workers, compared with thirteen (mainly elderly) Melanesians. Almost everywhere in the island church, therefore, resident missionaries had a new opportunity to assume supreme control, exercising powers of veto and taking decisions on matters that previously would have been left to the Melanesian Christians alone. "Insisted that in future all cases for judgement be submitted to me *at once* if I am anywhere near the village concerned or on first opportunity within a month if I am expected in the neighbourhood during that time," commanded Edgell at Pentecost in 1901; and his successor, H.N. Drummond, was equally authoritarian: "I stopped a death dance at Anarunqoe; refused to pay two teachers for their indolence; interfered with a teacher's wife officiating in the Church; and swept out two churches myself."[77] A degree of efficiency and uniformity was thus achieved, but at the expense of indigenous autonomy.

Reflecting the same trend, the Melanesian ministry was downgraded in importance. The original vision of an autonomous Melanesian church never entirely disappeared, and there was as much talk as ever of the black net with the white corks, but the focus had become blurred. Although Wilson warned of the dangers of a debilitating dependence on the English clergy, in the same breath, he admitted his belief that Melanesian teachers would "never attain to that complete independence for which Bishop Selwyn, our founder, used to hope".[78] A self-governing "Church of Melanesia" is "impossible now and will be impracticable for many years", wrote W.A. Uthwatt, Archdeacon of the Solomon Islands. "At present, as the work increases, so too does the necessity for the white man."[79] A few teachers were thought to be worthy of the diaconate; "very few indeed for the much graver responsibility of the priesthood". In seventeen years, Wilson ordained only three Melanesian priests.

A primary reason for this new caution was a sense of dissatisfaction with the quality of Christian converts. Among the younger missionaries who flooded into the Mission under Wilson, there was a suspicion that the islanders' acceptance of Christianity had been only superficial. They were still children in the faith, without deep sense of God or sin or holiness. Wherever Melanesian clergy and teachers had been left for long by themselves, it was alleged—and everyone pointed to the church on Mota—the work had visibly languished. Therefore, without the watchful oversight of a "white father", Melanesian Christians would either backslide into paganism or become slack in church attendance, school and other religious duties. The cautious prediction of Ivens was more optimistic than many of his co-workers would have allowed:

> If the white teachers were removed from Melanesia to-day the probability is that, though the daily services and daily school would still be held in most of the villages, yet there would be no advance and no enlargement of the work, no widening of the borders, and in such places as were manned by less able teachers it is doubtful whether the past gains of the Mission would be consolidated.[80]

In addition, there was a deep fear that Melanesians were too often proved to be morally unworthy of positions of responsibility in the church. The risk was too great. It was a common opinion among missionaries that sexual impurity was "one of the greatest, if not the greatest Melanesian failing";[81] and when they talked of "sin" among the islanders, they invariably meant adultery or fornication. They justified their claim by the numerous accusations of misconduct brought against village teachers and clergy (Wilson suspended thirteen teachers in 1899 alone), and in particular by the sensational "falls" of the two most trusted Melanesian priests: Henry Tagalad, who was buried in 1901 without Christian prayers because he was still under sentence of excommunication, and Clement Marau, who was degraded from office and excommunicated in 1907. Disappointed idealists felt that their confidence had been betrayed. "We might, perhaps, have averted his fall if we had not trusted him so much," lamented Selwyn in 1888, after Maros threw up his work as deacon at

Santa Maria and took a pagan wife.[82] In fact, their moralism had a double standard, for the dismissal of three missionaries within eight years after horrified discovery of their homosexual friendships with Melanesian schoolboys—adolescent homosexuality having been "rampant" at St Barnabas' during the 1890s—was not taken to invalidate the call for an increased white staff.[83]

Waning European belief in Melanesian capacity was reflected in lower wages. These were reduced from the generous scales laid down in the 1870s to £3 per annum, usually paid in trade goods, as the standard "present" for a "first-class" village teacher, and £15 for a priest. An indigenous ministry was justified less on grounds of theological principle, as the cornerstone of an autonomous church, than from reasons of economy, convenience and utility. Melanesian priests were required, it was declared in 1913, "to administer the Sacraments in districts where our white staff is weak"[84]—which neatly illustrated the reversal that had occurred in the priorities upon which the Melanesian Mission had originally been founded.

The shift in emphasis was not confined to the Melanesian Mission. Anglican policies on "native church organization" were far from unanimous, as illustrated by the report of an influential English subcommittee on the subject set up in 1899 by the United Boards of Missions. Having considered replies to a series of questions sent to societies, bishops and "specialists", it concluded rather lamely that there was general agreement regarding the desirable goal of a self-governing indigenous church, but "much difference of opinion" as to whether the time had yet come for the transference of controlling authority to non-Europeans.[85] For just as supreme rule in the Empire was retained in British hands, declared Bishop Ridding of Southwell at the 1894 Anglican Missionary Conference, so in church government even the "grandchildren of heathen savages could scarcely be left to themselves with no danger of lapsing from the truth".[86] The most famous example of reaction in the Anglican mission field was in West Africa, where Henry Venn's radical experiment of 1864, of evangelizing the Niger by means of an African agency under the African missionary bishop Samuel Crowther, was pronounced a failure and abandoned in the early 1890s under pressure from a new and arrogant generation of C.M.S. missionaries from England. Crowther thus became "not only the symbol of the failure of the Black race but of all non-whites the world over—the *raison d'être* for the all-white episcopacy in the Anglican Church".[87] In Melanesia, where the Niger experiment had always been followed with interest, it is unlikely that its collapse was forgotten.

Missionary attitudes were also influenced by the prevailing conviction in the South Pacific that the Melanesian peoples as a whole were doomed to dwindle away. With increasing outside contact, regular shipping services and the growth of commercial and planting interests came pulmonary and epidemic diseases against which the islanders had no immunity. Colds and influenza, often with dysentery and whooping cough, swept through the region almost every year, with disastrous consequences. One of the principal diseases carriers was the *Southern Cross*, which for years had left a trail of infection wherever it went. "A fortnight after its visit everyone is ill," wrote W.J. Durrad from the Banks Islands in 1917. "The fact is well known to the people and has become a subject of bitter and grim jest."[88] In 1910, he himself had witnessed at Tikopia the death of forty people from influenza, which led to pneumonia. Most scandalous of all was the bringing of a virulent strand of influenza to Malaita in 1931, which took 1100 lives.[89] Few missionaries, however, thought the role of their ship to have been a serious matter.

In Nggela, the population level seemed to remain constant, but in San Cristobal, Pentecost, Maewo and the Banks Islands, it visibly declined; large villages were reduced to small hamlets; missionaries reported "much sickness" and "many deaths" and discussed the serious possibility of extinction. Each year, a thousand converts or more were baptized throughout the diocese, but the number of living baptized Christians rose very slowly, from 8900 in 1894 to 12,700 ten years later. In the Banks group, despite hundreds of baptisms and many new schools, the Christian population had fallen by 504, partly from labour migration, but mainly due to disease. Mota itself had declined from 770 to 380.[90]

British colonial officials concluded that the decline they witnessed in Fiji and elsewhere in Melanesia was both universal and inevitable, perhaps due to the working of a hidden natural law. In 1909, Woodford had declared that nothing in the way of the most paternal legislation or fostering care, carried out at any expense whatever, can prevent the eventual extinction of the Melanesian race in the Pacific. This I look upon as a fundamental fact and as certain as the rising and setting of the sun.[91]

Most missionaries—though not all—did not dispute the general verdict. Wilson regretfully compared the Mission to a doctor treating a sick child:

> They have but a short time to live, and all that can be done is done for them, that their short lives may be brightened. A dying race should not promote contempt, but sympathy, and ... help ... We are placed then by GOD in His infirmary, to work amongst a dying race; but a race which will certainly die a Christian death.[92]

The fact of depopulation encouraged officials of the Western Pacific High Commission to propose the importation of Indian labourers to work on Solomons plantations, thereby relegating the interests of their island subjects to the background in the sacred name of economic development as an imperial duty. It had a parallel effect on thinking within the Melanesian Mission, by apparently dislodging the essential prerequisite for the goal of an indigenous leadership. For what need to prepare for a self-governing Melanesian church if the Melanesians themselves were destined to dwindle away to a mere historical curiosity?

NOTES AND REFERENCES

1. *Colonial Church Chronicle* 26 (1872): 431-37.
2. *Guardian* (London), 24 December 1872, p. 1612. On the results of the Day of Intercession, see W.T. Bullock in Church of England, *Authorised Report of the Second Missionary Conference ... 1877*, pp. 181-85.
3. H.W. Tucker, *The English Church in Other Lands, or the Spiritual Expansion of England* (London, 1886), p. 203; United Boards of Missions of the Provinces of Canterbury and York, *First Annual Review of the Foreign Missions of the Church ... 1908* (Teddington, 1907), pp. 58-60.
4. J.O.F. Murray, "The Story of the Central Board of Missions", *Chronicle of the Central Board of Missions of the Church of England*, n.s. 2 (1921): 58-63.
5. Church of England, *Conference of Bishops of the Anglican Communion holden at Lambeth Palace, July 6 to August 5, 1908* (London, 1908), Report no. 4; R.S. Copleston, "Lambeth and Missions Overseas,

1867-1920" *Chronicle of the Central Board of Missions of the Church of England*, n.s. 1 (1920): 14-17; 2 (1921): 10-14, 27-30.
6. Tucker, *English Church*, pp. 211-12; World Missionary Conference, 1910, *Report of Commission I*, pt 1; Owen Chadwick, *The Victorian Church*, pt 2, pp. 223-24.
7. Eugene Stock, "Thirty Years' Work in the Non-Christian World ... 1872 to 1902", *The East and the West* 1 (1903): 438-62.
8. J.R. Selwyn, *Pastoral Work in the Colonies and the Mission Field*, p. 28. See also John Ellison and G.H.S. Walpole, eds., *Church and Empire: A Series of Essays on the Responsibilities of Empire* (London: Longmans, 1907); and Church of England, United Boards of Missions, *The Official Report of the Missionary Conference of the Anglican Communion ... 1894*, pp. 2-9.
9. M.R. Neligan, "New Zealand: An Ill-Constructed Quadrilateral", in *Church and Empire*, eds. Ellison and Walpole, p. 173.
10. Church of England, United Boards of Missions, *Reports of the Boards of Missions of the Provinces of Canterbury and York on the Mission Field*, p. 10; H.W. Tucker, *Under His Banner: Papers on the Missionary Work of Modern Times* (London: S.P.C.K., 8th edn, 1904), pp. 97-98, 401.
11. Church of England, *Report of the Second Missionary Conference ... 1877*, pp. iii, 178.
12. *S.C.L.E.*, December 1908, p. 371.
13. Chadwick, *Victorian Church*, pt 2, pp. 247-51; H.H. Montgomery, *Foreign Missions* (London: Longmans, Green, 1904), p. 19.
14. Eton Association of the Melanesian Mission, *Annual Report*, 1907, p. 5.
15. Charles E. Fox, *Lord of the Southern Isles*, p. ix; David Neave, "Aspects of the History of the Universities' Mission to Central Africa, 1858-1900" (M. Phil. thesis, University of York, 1974), ch. 3.
16. Tucker, *Under His Banner*, pp. 396-97. See also *Guardian* (London), 22 July 1908, p. 1248.
17. *Church Times*, 28 May 1920, p. 528.
18. Robert Needham Cust, *The Gospel Message: Or Essays, Addresses, Suggestions, and Warnings on the Different Aspects of Christian Missions to Non-Christian Races and Peoples* (London, 1896), pp. 380-81.
19. E. Jacob to J.R. Selwyn, 4 December 1893; Jacob to Archbishop E.W. Benson, 4 January 1894, Benson Papers, 1893 Foreign, Lambeth Palace Library.
20. *M.M.R. & I.V.*, 1893, p. 1. As late as 1910, the Eton Association's annual St Barnabas' Day meeting at Eton College included a few of those who had heard Bishop G.A. Selwyn preach in the college chapel in 1854.
21. Church of the Province of New Zealand, *Proceedings of General Synod*, 1898, pp. 68-69; 1901, p. 47; 1904, p. 38; 1907, pp. 21, 47-48, 170-72. New Zealand Anglicans were not generous. In the late 1890s, though they comprised about 40 per cent of a total population of 700,000, subscriptions for Melanesia averaged £2600 per annum—equivalent to two shillings from each adult communicant member.
22. Melanesian Mission, *Occasional Paper*, Christmas 1894, p. 7.

23. ibid., p. 8.
24. ibid., August 1895, p. 4.
25. C. Wilson to Premier of Queensland, 23 May 1895, in Great Britain, *Parliamentary Papers*, vol. 70, 1895 [C.7912], pp. 309-10.
26. C. Wilson to H.H. Montgomery, 18 February 1896, Wilson-Montgomery Correspondence, U.S.P.G. Archives.
27. *Missionary Notes of the Australian Board of Missions*, 15 March 1895, pp. 20-21.
28. *I.V.*, 1879, pp. 27-29.
29. *S.C.L.*, January 1896, p. 2; Cecil Wilson, *The Wake of the Southern Cross*, p. 167.
30. Melanesian Mission, *Occasional Paper*, March 1896, p. 9.
31. J. Thurston, Diary, 3 September 1894, Thurston Papers, N.L.A.; *M.M.R.*, 1911, pp. 26-28; 1912, p. 27.
32. Sir John Thurston to Lord Ripon, 28 February 1895, C.O. 225/47, P.R.O. Woodford's administration is described by Deryck Scarr in *Fragments of Empire*, pp. 262-70.
33. C.M. Woodford to Sir John Thurston, 7 September 1896, C.O. 225/50, P.R.O.
34. The 1898 code is enclosed in C.M. Woodford to Sir George O'Brien, 1 March 1898, W.P.A., file no. W.P.H.C. 146/1898. However, government complaints about the political influence of mission teachers did not abate: see W.P.H.C. 1239/1916.
35. W.H. Edgell, Diary, 2 September 1900, in possession of Mrs R. Rowland; Cecil Wilson, Diary, 5 August 1903, in possession of Mrs Qona Clifton.
36. Henry Welchman, Diary, 10 January 1899, Melanesian Mission English Committee Office.
37. R.B. Joyce, *Sir William MacGregor* (Melbourne: Oxford University Press, 1971), pp. 167-80; J.H.P. Murray, *Papua or British New Guinea* (London: T. Fisher Unwin, 1912), p. 8; and *Papua of To-day* (London: P.S. King, 1925), pp. 246-50. On the British Solomon Islands, see David Hilliard, "Colonialism and Christianity: The Melanesian Mission in the Solomon Islands", *Journal of Pacific History* 9 (1974): 93-116.
38. For historical accounts of these missions, see Florence S.H. Young, *Pearls from the Pacific*; James E. Cormack, *Isles of Solomon* (Washington: Review & Herald Publishing Co., 1944); C.T.J. Luxton, *Isles of Solomon: A Tale of Missionary Adventure* (Auckland: Methodist Foreign Missionary Society of New Zealand, 1955); D.L. Hilliard, "Protestant Missions in the Solomon Islands, 1849-1942" (Ph.D. thesis), chs. 6-8; and id., "The South Sea Evangelical Mission in the Solomon Islands: The Foundation Years", *Journal of Pacific History* 4 (1969): 41-64; Ronald G. Williams, *The United Church in Papua, New Guinea, and the Solomon Islands* (Rabaul: Trinity Press, 1972), ch. 6; Hugh M. Laracy, *Marists and Melanesians*.
39. F.J. Barnett to all people of San Cristobal, 1 January 1916, quoted in Laracy, *Marists*, p. 47.
40. P.T. Williams in *S.C.L.E.*, December 1908, p. 365; *M.M.R. & I.V.*, 1902, p. 10.

41. H.H. Montgomery, "The Anglican Church in the South Pacific", *The East and the West* 1 (1903): 408, and his *Foreign Missions*, p. 134; *S.C.L.*, December 1899, pp. 5-6.
42. C. Bice, "The Church's Duty to the Heathen—(1) In Australasia—(2) In Other Lands", in *The Official Report of the Church Congress held at Hobart ... 1894*, p. 274.
43. Montgomery, "Anglican Church ...", p. 404.
44. Quoted in Luxton, *Isles of Solomon*, p. 17.
45. *Minutes of the Ninth General Conference of the Australasian Wesleyan Methodist Church ... Brisbane ... 1901* (Sydney, 1901), p. 47. On Bishop Willis's entry into Wesleyan Tonga, see W.P. Morrell, *The Anglican Church in New Zealand*, pp.209-12; Montgomery, "Anglican Church ...", pp. 409-11.
46. Wilson, Diary, 23 January 1902; Methodist Church of Australasia, Board of Missions, Minutes, 9 April 1902, Methodist Overseas Missions Records, M.L.
47. C. Wilson to H.H. Montgomery, 14 April 1905, S.P.G. Letters Received, U.S.P.G. Archives.
48. Welchman, Diary, 8 October 1907.
49. Laracy, *Marists*, pp. 41-45.
50. W.A. Uthwatt, "The Melanesian Mission in the Solomons", *Australasian Church Quarterly Review* 1 (1910-11): 241.
51. Edgell, Diary, 8 September 1898.
52. Welchman, Diary, 18 May 1900.
53. New Hebrides Presbyterian Mission, Synod Minutes, 25 June 1902, 20 June 1903, microfilm, Pacific Manuscripts Bureau, A.N.U.
54. Edgell, Diary, 13 October 1899, 26 February 1900; *M.M.R.*, 1905, p. 40; A.I. Hopkins, Autobiography, pp. 109, 114-15, 127-28, Church of Melanesia Archives. On the friendship between the Anglican C.E. Fox and the Marist Emile Babonneau on San Cristobal, see Laracy, *Marists*, pp. 46-47.
55. A.I. Hopkins, "Native Life in the South-West Pacific: From Two Points of View", *International Review of Missions* 17 (1928): 549.
56. *S.C.L.*, December 1899, p. 6.
57. Montgomery, "Anglican Church ...", pp. 405-6.
58. *S.C.L.*, September 1903, p. 59.
59. ibid., February 1913, p. 136.
60. Eton Association of the Melanesian Mission, *Annual Report*, 1902, pp. 8-9; 1904, p. 7. Drew's work on San Cristobal is described by Joseph H.C. Dickinson, *A Trader in the Savage Solomons: A Record of Romance and Adventure* (London: H.F. & G. Witherby, 1927), pp. 198-205.
61. G.F. Bury, "Home Letters", pp. 8, 18, Blencowe Papers, in possession of Mrs M. Blencowe.
62. Samuel Bickersteth, "The Home Ministry and Foreign Missions: From a Yorkshire Vicar", *International Review of Missions* 4 (1915): 124-25.
63. *S.C.L.E.*, December 1908, p. 371.
64. W.G. Ivens, "Some Historical Notes concerning the Melanesian Mission", in Appendix to *Dictionary and Grammar of the Language of Sa'a and*

Ulawa ..., p. 206. On the Mission's linguistic work generally, see *S.C.L.*, July 1923, pp. 15-20.
65. *S.C.L.E.*, December 1910, p. 770; R.H. Codrington to C.H. Brooke [21 December] 1911, Brooke to Codrington, 25 August 1922, Codrington Papers, Rhodes House Library.
66. *A.B.M. Review* 3 (1913): 197-98.
67. J.W. Blencowe to his mother, 16 May 1910, Blencowe Papers.
68. J.M. Steward, *Hints on District Work*, p. 8.
69. Ivens, " 'Yachting' in Melanesia", in Appendix to *Dictionary ... of Sa'a and Ulawa* ..., p. 212.
70. Charles E. Fox, *Kakamora*, pp. 102-3.
71. *S.C.L.E.*, December 1916, p. 184. Those who died during these years were: H. Welchman, 1908; F. Bollen, 1909; G. Bury, 1911; G.H. Andrews, 1912; F.H. Drew, 1915; Sarah Jeffrey, 1917; N. Dixon, 1921. Two others were drowned: C.C. Sage, 1913; W.F. Long, 1915.
72. C. Bice to Mrs Elizabeth Colenso, 27 August 1883, Codrington Papers.
73. Julia Farr, Diary, 15 November 1894, in possession of Mrs Mary Clift. The "women's work" at Norfolk Island is described in *S.C.L.*, May 1895, pp. 6-7; June 1895, pp. 5-6; July 1895, pp. 7-8.
74. See, e.g., Cecil Wilson, *Women of Melanesia* (reprinted from *S.C.L.*, October 1904, pp. 6-10); Florence Coombe, *Islands of Enchantment*, pp. 123, 182-83, 252. Cf. C.H. Brooke in *Mission Life*, n.s. 6 (1875): 172.
75. Wilson, *Women of Melanesia* (pages unnumbered).
76. *S.C.L.E.*, April 1907, p. 47. Cf. Dickinson, *A Trader*, pp. 38-39.
77. Edgell, Diary, 8 April 1901; *M.M.R.*, 1905, p. 16.
78. *M.M.R. & I.V.*, 1902, p. 8.
79. Uthwatt, "Melanesian Mission ...", p. 238.
80. Ivens, "Melanesia and its People", in Appendix to *Dictionary ... of Sa'a and Ulawa* ..., p. 192.
81. R.E. Tempest, "Memories", p. 13, Melanesian Mission English Committee Office.
82. *M.M.R.*, 1888, p. 5. Cf. *I.V.*, 1881, pp. 51-52. On Clement Marau's "fall", see below, p. 173.
83. The missionaries dismissed were A.E.C. Forrest, Arthur Brittain and C.G.D. Browne: Wilson, Diary, 25 April 1896, 4 September 1896, 18 May 1897, 12 November 1904; Wilson to Montgomery, 24 August 1896, Wilson-Montgomery Correspondence; Frederick Temple Papers, 1897 Home, ff. 13-40, Lambeth Palace Library. On Forrest, see below, pp. 185-86.
84. *M.M.R.*, 1913, p. 4.
85. Church of England, United Boards of Missions, *A Study of Some Missionary Problems: Being a Report issued by the United Boards of Missions of the Provinces of Canterbury and York*. See also Davidson Papers, 1901 M6, Lambeth Palace Library. The subcommittee included among its members: R.H. Codrington, then a Prebendary of Chichester Cathedral; Eugene Stock of the C.M.S.; and Lord Stanmore, who as Sir Arthur Gordon had been first Governor of Fiji and High Commissioner for the Western Pacific.

86. Church of England, United Boards of Missions, *Official Report of the Missionary Conference of the Anglican Communion ... 1894*, p. 511. For a similar view, see *Guardian* (London), 24 June 1908, p. 1090.
87. James Bertin Webster, *The African Churches among the Yoruba, 1888-1922* (Oxford: Clarendon Press, 1964), p. 41. See also J.F. Ade Ajayi, *Christian Missions in Nigeria, 1841-1891: The Making of a New Elite* (London: Longmans, Green, 1965), pp. 250-73.
88. W.J. Durrad, "The Decrease of the Population of Melanesia", p. 3, British and Foreign Anti-Slavery and Aborigines Protection Society Papers, G. 397, Rhodes House Library.
89. Malaita District Report, 1931, W.P.A., file no. W.P.H.C. 1214/1932.
90. *M.M.R.*, 1904, p. 5.
91. C.M. Woodford to Sir Everard im Thurn, 26 December, enclosure in im Thurn to C.O., 24 January 1910, C.O. 225/90, P.R.O.; Scarr, *Fragments of Empire*, pp. 293-97.
92. *M.M.R.*, 1904, p. 7.

6
The Tide Turns

At the turn of the century, despite the population decline in southern Melanesia, the dominant mood of the Melanesian Mission was one of optimism. After decades of slow growth or stagnation, inadequate income and failure to achieve its original goals, the possibility that Melanesian paganism would soon crumble in the face of a systematic and sustained Christian onslaught seemed to be a real one. Given twelve more white missionaries, Wilson had predicted in 1899, most of Melanesia would be Christian in twelve years. In 1901, 1800 islanders were baptized, which was the highest number ever recorded for a single year. Especially in the Solomons, the attitude of the Melanesians towards Christianity seemed to be undergoing a change. Whereas in the past, wrote Archdeacon Uthwatt in 1911, the impetus had often come from the missionary who actively sought out opportunities for placing his teachers,

> now the natives themselves are pleading that we may send them men. Where there are heathen, the man in charge of the district frequently receives deputations asking for teachers. They will build a school and a house for the teacher, will provide him with food, will come regularly to the daily services, and will send their children to school, if only we will give them a man. They want to be Christian. We cannot meet this demand ... Never in the history of the Mission has the desire been so urgent or so general.[1]

Mission statistics published in the annual reports showed growth, though it was neither continuous nor consistent. Between the years 1894 and 1904, the number of baptized Melanesians in the diocese rose from 8929 to 12,690. The pace then visibly slackened. In 1908, Woodford described the Melanesian Mission in the Solomons as largely "moribund", and two years later, J.W. Blencowe was depressed by the number of former Norfolk

Island scholars who were "doing nothing" and by "what a very little we have to show for our work".[2] In 1912, the baptized totalled 14,333; in 1918, 14,194. These figures were paralleled by a rise and levelling off in the number of school villages: 1894, 122; 1904, 253; 1912, 329; 1918, 318.

From the statistics for each island, the following inferences are possible:

The Melanesian Mission made its greatest advances in the decade after 1894 in Santa Isabel, south Malaita, Ulawa, Pentecost and the sparsely peopled Torres Islands.

The first substantial Christian success on Malaita and Pentecost coincided with the return of Christianized labourers from Queensland and Fiji, at the end of the labour trade.

From about 1908 onwards, while other missions in the region expanded—so that by 1918, Roman Catholics claimed 3000 baptized converts, mainly on Guadalcanal, and the Methodists claimed a similar number in the western Solomons—the Melanesian Mission stagnated everywhere, except in San Cristobal and north Malaita.

Although there are no accurate population statistics, it is certain that in the Banks and Torres Islands, the annual gains through baptism were more than counterbalanced by depopulation caused by inter-island labour recruiting and epidemic disease.

In 1918, as in 1894, the largest Anglican communities were in the Banks Islands, Nggela and Santa Isabel, where virtually the entire population had by this time been baptized and where alone the Melanesian Mission had succeeded in retaining its monopoly.

The centre of gravity of the Mission moved northwards. Whereas in 1894, one half of its baptized converts were Solomon Islanders, by 1911, the proportion was almost three-fifths. Moreover, it was in the thickly populated islands of the Solomons that there existed the greatest opportunities for future growth.

What did Melanesians expect from a Christian school, and in particular, from a school of the Melanesian Mission? How did the Anglicans demonstrate and establish that the religion they taught was true? The latter question was rarely tackled directly, for missionaries generally preferred to proceed by assertion rather than by argument. One of the first difficulties, in Comins' experience, was to persuade pagans of a universal religious truth: that there was but one supreme non-ancestral God, and that "God is *their* God as much as the white man's".[3] Would the Christian God "understand the language of Boli?", Brooke was asked at Nggela: " 'If we only knew the language of *Sydney*!' Touching my tongue, I told them that He who made the tongue knew all languages, and did I not pray daily in Boli words?"[4]

A more fundamental encounter was between a religion based on written documents that claimed to proclaim an inflexible truth and one that was not defined by theological statements. "The [religious] ideas of the natives are not clear upon many points," observed Codrington, "they are not accustomed to present them in any systematic form among themselves."[5] Missionaries of the first generation seized upon this aspect of Melanesian paganism in order to impress their listeners with the certainty of Christianity, which came direct from the "great God" through Jesus Christ and the divinely-inspired Bible.

> Their religion was a matter of mere hearsay and conjecture, and had been handed on from mouth to mouth, and had grown as it came down after the manner of mere verbal testimony. There could be no doubt with us because we have the living testimony of Christ's own words which never pass away. Their religion came from nowhere and no one knew of its beginning; of ours at all events we were sure.[6]

It was a religious apologetic which Melanesian pagans found unconvincing. Their own religious system was concerned primarily with the satisfying of social and economic needs in the present. They used religious ritual to guarantee success in important undertakings and for protection against ill-fortune, and from the first, they had evaluated Christianity similarly, in terms of its tangible results.

Twentieth-century missionaries were less embarrassed than their predecessors by the overriding interest of the Melanesians in the material benefits that they expected to follow from a Christian school. Despite the inferiority of the Melanesian Mission to traders and recruiters as a supplier of European manufactured goods, the desire for trade had lost none of its force. Boys still went to Norfolk Island in the expectation of instant wealth. Teachers were paid partly in the form of calico, axes, knives, tinned meat, soap, pipes, tobacco, hurricane-lamps, kerosene and other such articles, much of which eventually ended up with the people they taught. The acquisition of literacy was not the only motive for attending school. Those who came regularly expected also to receive at least a fish-hook each week, with something more substantial when the missionary made his annual inspection. As late as 1925, the people of Santa Catalina, San Cristobal, announced that their acceptance of a school was conditional upon gifts of tobacco and calico.

Even more desirable was a white missionary, who always carried a large stock of trade articles, which he distributed as presents—twist tobacco, clay pipes, matches, beads, blue and red cloth, fish-hooks, Jew's harps, penny whistles, axes and knives —in each village he visited. For himself, he had tins of delicious food, boxes of clothes, and wonderful mechanisms such as a pocket-watch, a magic-lantern or a camera. When Hopkins took up residence at Ngorefou in north Malaita in 1902, there was high excitement among the local people: "The white man meant to some great vague hopes of money, trade, of Government support, of prestige that would make their foes look small."[7]

However, the economic benefit anticipated to flow from a Christian school was only one of the advantages that the Christian religion seemed to offer a pagan Melanesian in the years after the turn of the century. "Peace, union, the presence of a white man, communion with the outer world, a chance of getting some of the white man's things", observed Ivens, "—these are factors that must tell on his mind and predispose him towards Christianity."[8] Some asked for a school out of curiosity. Local leaders began to look upon schools in a new light, as a status symbol without which their village was not complete. Changed circumstances gave Christianity a new prestige, which previously it had lacked.

"The civilised world has broken in upon us," observed the Mission's annual report for 1909.[9] In the decade before the First World War, coastal New Guinea and the Melanesian islands were being "opened up" as one of the world's last frontiers of European settlement and commercial development. In the British Solomon Islands, as Woodford's administration extended its control, planters and traders multiplied. Aggressive missions competing for converts deployed their agents into every island

and language district. Thousands of hectares of coastal bush were cleared and planted in coconut trees; applications for land poured in. By 1912, the white population of the protectorate exceeded five hundred and there were fifty planters on the coastal plain of northern Guadalcanal. More than 4500 Solomon Islanders were employed as labourers on local plantations. In a single week of 1911, eight steamers—two warships, five trading vessels and a mission-ship—anchored at Tulagi and Gavutu.

To the inhabitants of coastal societies, a new way of living was demanding their acceptance. There was an expectation of change, which Christianity—known as the "New Way" or the "New Law"—promised to fulfil. In many instances, therefore, it was discussed and absorbed, along with everything else that came with the white man, because in one way or another, it seemed to be a religion of more practical validity in the new contact situation. But novelty and foreign origin could still be a hindrance and a reason for polite rejection. Malaita pagans evaded Hopkins by promising that they would come to school "bye and bye" or "when I have fulfilled my vow" or "when my father dies", and remarks thus recorded can only be a fraction of the whole. If the missionaries had "only appeared earlier", said the old men of Pentecost, "it would have been different".[10] Writing in 1908, Durrad regretted that Christianity had "not yet laid hold of the spirit and genius of the race". It was "still largely an exotic", he believed, and the notion that Christ was a white man, "perhaps even a sort of Englishman", was deeply rooted in Melanesian thinking.[11]

The influence of the Solomons government, which ended head-hunting and fighting by the threat of force, generally worked to the advantage of Christianity. The old belief in a working alliance between the Melanesian Mission and British men-of-war, which attributed to Anglican missionaries or teachers the power of conjuring up at will a warship to destroy a pagan village or to bring the people into line, survived into the second decade of the twentieth century. In areas under administrative control, villagers were often encouraged by District Officers to accept schools. In remote places, where visits from government officials were few and perfunctory and a knowledge of the administration was inevitably vague, it was easily assumed that English-speaking mission and British government, symbolized by "the

Christian "school people" and the village church at Fagani, San Cristobal, 1906 (From the Beattie Collection: Permission Auckland Institute and Museum)

Bishop and the Governor", were merely different voices of the same all-powerful authority. Some colonial subjects therefore thought it safer to follow the religion of the government, as was demonstrated by a warrior leader at Kia, Santa Isabel, who accepted a school believing that if he "belonged to the Bishop" he would receive some special protection or favour.[12]

New diseases brought by the foreigners, against which traditional medicines, sacrifices and magic failed to work a cure, sometimes encouraged helpless pagans to move to a school village or to ask for a teacher for themselves, in the hope that the foreigners' God would supply protection. Declining population and the sight of deserted settlements discouraged confidence in the old order, just as the reputation of missionaries with amateur medical knowledge for being "able to cure all diseases instantly" encouraged confidence in the new.[13]

But disease could equally have a deterrent effect, for it was seen to be true that the adoption of Christianity did not automatically ensure temporal prosperity. Perhaps the Christian God was responsible for sending new diseases? In 1912, it was reported from San Cristobal, for example, that a pagan village had hesitated over accepting a Christian school because "they thought that the white men's religion would mean the introduction of white men's sicknesses, such as measles and influenza".[14] In places where a school had only recently been accepted and sickness was rife, missionaries were haunted by the fear that the islanders should "attribute to Christianity or at least to the Mission the pestilence that is attacking them". It was a common enough accusation, leading sometimes to violent revenge. In Christian Nggela, there was a panic in 1902, when a number of elderly people who had been confirmed by the bishop in the previous year died in an epidemic. The number of communicants was "much decreased", and teachers reported that it would be years before anyone else could be persuaded to offer for confirmation.[15]

The visible association between Christianity and peace was increasingly an attractive one. The forms and conventions that had limited traditional warfare were disturbed by European contact. By the 1890s, the widespread use of rifles, the annihilation of whole communities by head-hunters and, in the Solomons after 1896, the possibility of armed retribution by government forces, made warfare a burdensome activity, the gains of which were outweighed by its disadvantages. Wherever there was a teacher, on the other hand, it seemed that a village could live in a state of peace. The acceptance of Christianity as the "gospel of peace" thus offered a convenient rationale for the termination of conflict. "What will it cost us to buy this new teaching which gives peace, for we are tired of fighting?" asked the chief of a bush village on Santa Isabel, and the same appeal was heard elsewhere.[16] At Fenualoa in the Reef Islands, in 1906, the people of every village begged for teachers: "They said they were being killed out through the fighting, and the Good Religion which we had would stop it as nothing else could."[17] As missionaries found the islanders receptive to the idea of peace, so they stressed the prospect of relief from a life of violence and insecurity as an inducement to receive a school.

Social environment was important in disposing the Melanesians to try the foreigners' religion. But that does not deny the weight that should also be given to spiritual or emotional experiences beyond the historian's measuring scale, or to personal encounters that attracted the islanders to Christianity. A missionary who had an air of authority or one who through his friendliness, open-handed generosity or fluency in the local language established a rapport with the inhabitants of his district, would naturally arouse interest in Christianity. Through the force of his personality, he would obtain openings for schools, while a missionary who lacked these qualities might encounter opposition or make little headway. "You stayed with the people," recalled Fox of his own successful years in charge of San Cristobal (1915-24); "if they liked you they would accept a school."[18] But it was not so with Rudolph Sprott, for example, who in 1910, had to be removed from San Cristobal because the local people resented him for his bad temper and had pillaged his house.

Europeans could thus be important in determining the form in which Christianity was presented to Melanesian pagans, but overall they were less important than the Melanesian teachers and the observable quality of life in existing school villages. One teacher wrote of his own experience:

> I always notice one thing that seems to hinder people from accepting Christianity readily, and that is a loud, scolding manner, as if you

are coming down heavily on a man. Where a person is already enlightened that may be all right. But if he is still ignorant, and you scold him hard, why, that tends to drive him away.[19]

As an interpreter of Christianity and organizer of an indigenous church, the Melanesian clergyman who came closest to the European missionaries' ideal was the Banks Islander, Clement Marau—"probably the ablest Melanesian to work in the Mission".[20] Outside the Mission, he had already acquired a modest fame for his recollections of schooling with Patteson at Norfolk Island and first years as a teacher in the Solomons, which had been translated from Mota by Codrington and published in London in 1894 as the *Story of a Melanesian Deacon*. When ordained a priest in 1903, after twenty-two years at Ulawa as teacher and deacon, he was at the peak of his influence. He had married a local woman, and the teachers gave him the respect and deference that they normally accorded only to Europeans. He played the harmonium, composing his own hymns and music. He was also a natural orator, whose skill in the illustration of Christian doctrine by native metaphors and idiom were unsurpassed: "On a hot day you see the heat rising ... and getting hotter and hotter until you expect soon to see flame; so the Presence of God in the Old Testament grew hotter and hotter, until at last it became visible in Christ."[21]

Through Marau's forceful leadership and uncompromising tactics, over half of Ulawa's 1200 inhabitants were by this time either baptized or attending school. "It is in a state of earthly peace," he reported, "but not yet of spiritual peace ... The powers of Christianity and heathenism are still at war here."[22] In the large village of Mwadjo'a, he was the acknowledged leader in temporal as well as religious affairs. Corporate village life was regulated daily, in accordance with his version of a truly Christian society:

> A bell rings at nine o'clock each night, sending everybody to their homes; no one being permitted to loiter about after that bell has rung. On Sundays the people meet for a social meal at mid-day. The fish is caught, and all the food prepared, on the Saturday. Young and old, Chiefs, Teachers and people here all meet together. In large bowls the food is brought in, and divided out to all alike. If there have been any quarrels among the people, coming to the social meal is a sign that such are ended. Conversely, if any stop away, it is

172 *God's Gentlemen*

Clement Marau, 1906 (From the Beattie Collection: Permission Auckland Institute and Museum)

a sign that the offence is not forgiven, and that something yet remains to be done.[23]

Clement Marau's prestige was further enhanced by the construction at Mwadjo'a of a splendid church of coral-rock and limestone, 24 metres long by 10 metres wide, with walls 3 metres high and an expensive corrugated-iron roof, which had been his special ambition. The church furniture was inlaid with pearl-shell. When completed in 1901, after seven years' work by the people of the village, it was the first building of its kind in the Solomons and the most elaborate yet built in the island diocese. Like the Patteson memorial chapel at Norfolk Island, it had a semi-circular apse and was dedicated to St Barnabas. Its fame spread throughout the south-east Solomons, and its example was followed by Christian communities elsewhere in Ulawa and south Malaita. But in the aftermath of Marau's sensational fall from grace in 1907, when investigation revealed that he had been using his supreme position to visit women at night after the evening bell had rung and to punish those who knew of his adulteries, the once-flourishing Ulawa church almost disintegrated in a resurgence of pagan customs and religious rites.[24] Although its excommunicated priest was eventually readmitted to communion, he remained a centre of disturbance and the object of pagan hostility, and in 1914, he was compelled by Woodford to return to his home at Mere Lava. His son, Martin Marau, ordained deacon in 1919, succeeded as leader of the Ulawa church.

By common consent, the most dedicated and the most successful, if not the most loved, of the Anglican missionaries of this period was Dr Henry Welchman of Santa Isabel. It was through the influence of Welchman, in partnership with Soga's passionate advocacy of Christianity, that the Mission had become securely established in Bugotu. Soga died in 1898, on his deathbed exhorting his followers to "Stick to the Church and the School and to what the Bishop and the Doctor say, for they are our friends and will tell you what is right".[25] However, the absence of a strong successor and the suppression of New Georgia headhunting by the protectorate government in 1900 led to a collapse of centralized political authority in Bugotu. Individual "bigmen", whose activities had previously been checked by Soga, asserted their own claims to independence and those people who had moved to Bugotu to be under Soga's protection returned to their original homes. To end the confusion and unsettlement, Welchman called a meeting of leading men in 1900, to decide who should be the supreme leader and judge of Bugotu. They chose Eric Notere, who was later confirmed by Woodford as official head-man, but his prestige never approached that of Soga.

Embittered by the harrowing death of his young wife at Siota in 1897, emotionally frustrated and each year "still restless and disquieted",[26] Welchman threw himself without reserve into his life's work as architect of the Bugotu church. "He is an utterly devoted missionary," privately noted Wilson, "but a terror to work with."[27] He himself was upbraided by Welchman for allowing "flippancy" and a "godless" atmosphere on board the *Southern Cross*, on which travelling missionaries and secular visitors spent their days reading novels or in frivolous conversation instead of cultivating their souls and discussing the things of the spirit.[28] At the head of the Bugotu church, the puritan missionary, with his amazing medical skill, inspired increasing awe, even fear. "I don't know what has come over this people," he confided to his diary, "they are altogether different from old days."[29] Those who disobeyed his commands were scolded until they confessed their foolishness; candidates for baptism and confirmation whom he judged to be "parrot talkers" or insufficiently earnest were rejected by the score without hesitation; and to purge the infant church of "evil doers" and those who disobeyed ecclesiastical edicts, he used the extreme weapon of excommunication more than anyone else in the diocese. By 1908, when there were 119 Bugotu excommunicates, at least one in every ten adult converts was excluded from church services.

Welchman dreamed of a morally disciplined and totally indigenous church for Santa Isabel in which the islanders, enlightened by the new knowledge of sin and salvation, would retain their old customs and livelihood as independent fishermen and farmers, with minimal change. The idea of a link between Christianity and Western civilization, and especially the fashionable cause of industrial missions as the means of rescuing the Melanesians from idleness and extinction, he attacked with vehemence as unnecessary, impracticable and a dangerous first step along the path to amoral secularism. He refused always to live in a European-style house. "I believe", he said, "the steps up form a barrier between the white man and the people. I like a native house with a mud floor, where the men can come and sit about and feel at home."[30]

Welchman placed high value on the knowledge and efficiency of his village teachers. "He never spared reproof," wrote his

Dr. Henry Welchman at Mara na Tambu, Santa Isabel (From the Beattie Collection: Permission Auckland Institute and Museum)

Bishop Wilson dedicating a church at Pirihandi, Santa Isabel (From the Beattie Collection: Permission Auckland Institute and Museum)

admiring biographer.³¹ To maintain standards, he visited schools for half of each year, going around the coast by canoe or on his own schooner *Ruth*, or by foot into the rugged interior. Alone in the Mission, he held regular teachers' meetings—from 1905, every two months at his headquarters on the islet of Mara na Tambu. Teachers from every district assembled there in batches for theological lectures on the Thirty-nine Articles and other doctrines of the Church of England, and to receive directives for the conduct of school classes and church services. In addition, they were occasions for the reception of church collections and the distribution of vernacular scriptures, medicines, marriage licences and kerosene for church lamps. Welchman's last diary entry in November 1908, two days before his solitary death as the result of prolonged illness and overwork, captures something of the mood of his restless last years:

> At Matins preached on the election of Matthias. School followed & they were very stupid & inattentive. Then sat with the Catechumens. Translated more Samuel. Had more Catechumens later. Ellison [Ellison Gito, a senior teacher] called on his way to Kia & I arranged to visit them early in December. Held the class for Catechumens, before Evensong, preached on "Christ taking away the sins of the world". Class for Confirmation candidates afterwards. Sat out after supper & talked of gas & electricity. Told them the tale of St Patrick & the old snake.³²

When the news of his death was received, government officials paid heartfelt tribute to his life and work. The traders and planters of the Solomons, whose injuries he had often sailed a hundred kilometres by open boat to treat, erected in gratitude a memorial at Tulagi, while the Mission collected funds for a Welchman Memorial Hospital at Maravovo. He had worked at Santa Isabel with few breaks for nearly twenty years, and when he died, there was no village in the Bugotu district without its own church, school and teacher. Even after his death, his influence was unsurpassed, and the rules he had instituted were regarded almost as sacred: "The Doctor forbade that" or "The Doctor laid down this rule" were phrases in constant use.³³ With thirty school villages, 1600 baptized and its own clergyman (Hugo Hembala), Santa Isabel was regarded as the "best district" in the Mission.³⁴

On those islands that had been the principal sources of labour recruits, missionaries attributed the changed attitude to Christianity mainly to the religious zeal of converted labourers. This influence climaxed in the huge repatriation of Pacific Islanders from Queensland between 1906 and 1908, when under the 1901 "White Australia" legislation of the first Commonwealth Parliament, some 4300 islanders were deported to their homes.[35] About three-quarters of these were from the Solomons; two-fifths were from Malaita. "God has never till now given the opportunity as He is doing now," was Hopkins' reply to those who asked why his mission had not previously "opened up" Malaita, Guadalcanal and San Cristobal.[36] Yet in practice, a missionary-anthropologist has observed, Anglican methods were ill-adapted to a populous and culturally segmented island such as Malaita, in which the new openness to Christianity was "on a basis of culture contact rather than social structure", as had been the case in Nggela and Santa Isabel.[37] A "dramatic deployment" of European staff and teachers was required, but never carried out. Moreover, Anglican influence on the Queensland plantations had been weak and unco-ordinated, so that only a minority of the Christian repatriates willingly associated themselves with the Melanesian Mission on returning to the islands.

The *Southern Cross* had already made a series of visits to north Malaita in the 1890s, but its attempts to obtain boys for Norfolk Island were rebuffed by sophisticated coastal people and artificial island dwellers of the Lau Lagoon, who had long been familiar with labour recruiters. Because of the deep hostility of Malaita bushmen to those who followed an alien religion and violated customary taboos, it was impossible for Christian labourers who wished to remain Christians to return to their original homes. For mutual protection, they were therefore compelled to huddle together in new settlements along the coastal strip, separated from the pagan communities. The first such Anglican villages were founded in 1898 by George Limai and James Dausuke, who had been taken in 1894 from a church school in Suva for training at Norfolk Island. They returned to Malaita with some of their Fiji fellow-converts, to form small settlements at Fiu, a passage on the west coast, north of the Langalanga Lagoon, and at Ata'a Cove on the north-east coast.

These were not the first Christian settlements in north

Malaita. A band of Christian labourers had already congregated at Malu'u, under the leadership of Peter Ambuofa, who had returned to his home in 1894 as a convert of the Queensland Kanaka Mission. The Malu'u Christians were attached to their own ways. When Hopkins arrived in the area in 1902, he found it impossible to assimilate his own sober vernacular services read from the Book of Common Prayer with Ambuofa's enthusiastic Moody-and-Sankey Pidgin English fundamentalism. It was in response to Ambuofa's continued appeals for help that Florence Young and her co-workers of the Q.K.M. decided in 1904 to establish a Solomon Islands branch, thereby breaking the tenuous links between the ex-Queenslanders at Malu'u and the Melanesian Mission. Because most of the returning Christian Malaitans were converts of the Q.K.M., they naturally attached themselves to the S.S.E.M., its successor, which enjoyed great success. By 1908, there were forty-four S.S.E.M. schools on Malaita, in every coastal district, whereas the Anglicans could claim only twenty-six.[38]

The announcement of the end of the labour trade brought forth from the Melanesian Mission its first unequivocal verdict on labour recruitment since Codrington's denunciations of the 1870s. The trade had "hung like a curse" on the islands, declared the 1906 mission report, and the number of those who really benefited from it was "infinitesimal" compared with those who had suffered irremediably. In its end, the "Hand of God" could be seen.[39] Nevertheless, there were fears of injustice and inhumanity inherent in the existing repatriation legislation, and in 1906, Hopkins went to Australia to lay the Mission's views before federal government authorities. At the same time, a Royal Commission was investigating the likely effects of the deportation on the Queensland sugar industry. Having heard evidence from (among others) Charles Sage, who had succeeded Mrs Robinson in charge of the Selwyn Mission at Mackay, Miss Young of the Q.K.M., and Bishop Frodsham of North Queensland, it recommended revision of the 1901 Act, to widen the category of those eligible for exemption from deportation. While in Queensland, Hopkins visited those islanders awaiting repatriation, to obtain teachers for his own Malaita schools. It was too late. Enthusiasm had cooled, and most converts of the Selwyn Mission had dispersed before they could be persuaded to return as a body to Malaita, to build up a strong Anglican colony at Fiu. Hopkins returned with ten teachers. Sixteen of the "best boys", however, had already volunteered for service in the New Guinea Mission. From the depleted ranks of the other Anglican plantation schools, he obtained no teachers at all. It was no surprising conclusion to nearly forty years of official Anglican apathy towards the Queensland labourers.[40]

The consequences for the Melanesian Mission of the repatriation were mixed. Missionaries who had feared a great unsettlement of conditions, especially on Malaita, were greatly surprised by the absence of violent disruption.

> In a few months Messrs. Burns, Philp's steamers finished their work, and the face of the Islands was temporarily changed. Everywhere were seen men and women in European clothes, the men with thick boots, black hats, and blue serge clothing, the women with gorgeous head decorations, and dainty shoes, very unsuitable for reef-walking.[41]

Everywhere, the old authority of the Mota-speaking teachers was challenged by the influx of vocal and self-assertive ex-Queenslanders, who spoke Pidgin English, wore new clothes and felt superior in knowledge and experience. Wilson found two returned labourers in the Banks Islands claiming to have been ordained in Queensland, therefore with the right to officiate at services. One of them prophesied a flood that would destroy everyone on Vanua Lava, and that "the Americans" were coming to turn the Britishers out of Australia and the islands—which must be among the earliest occasions in Melanesia that Americans were invoked as saviours.[42] Many of those who returned to Christian villages resisted pressure to conform to an unfamiliar round of religious worship and absented themselves altogether. "Daily Prayers in Church did not meet with the approval of the Queenslanders, nor did prayer in their own languages," Wilson reported: "Even boys from Church schools in Queensland were anxious at first to build churches where they could use the English Prayer-book instead of their own."[43] At Fiu, there was dissension when a band of Q.K.M. converts rejected the Prayer Book altogether and insisted on extempore prayer.

European observers agreed that a new spirit was abroad. Two phrases were said to be in common use: "White man no good" and "country belong us". Missionaries shook their heads over the loss of the "beauty of humility" and at the spectacle of lapsed Christians and sophisticated pagans who challenged the existing order and stirred up "strife and hatred and contempt".[44] Throughout the islands, money was said to be the one recurring topic of conversation. Questions were asked as to the price paid by the white man for land in the islands: "the Brisbane land fetched so much a foot; had they here received as much?"[45] In the Torres Islands, Durrad's attempt to buy ½ hectare of land for a school on Hiu was frustrated by its ex-Queensland owner, who demanded £300 or an annual rent of £20, because the Mission was wealthy and could afford this price, if it really wanted the land. Pay demands were described by missionaries as "exorbitant". A few sticks of tobacco in payment to a boat's crew for a few days' work, or 2/6d. per week, was no longer sufficient. On Nggela, where there was a large contingent of returned labourers, the teachers were persuaded that their annual "present" of £3 from the Mission was exploitation by Queensland standards. In 1908, they combined in strike, demanding £12 per annum, or £15 if they went to another island to teach, but their resistance collapsed when angry missionaries refused to countenance their claims.[46]

Nevertheless, it was estimated in 1908 that three-quarters of the schools recently started throughout the diocese were due directly to returned labourers. In north Malaita, the Mission had gained a total of nineteen teachers from Queensland and Fiji. The most notable of these was Jack Talofuila, a native of the artificial island of Sulufou in the Lau Lagoon and a nephew of Kwaisulia, an influential "passage master" of nearby Ada Gege. After sixteen years in Queensland, where he had been converted at Mrs Robinson's school and later became one of her teachers, he returned to Malaita in 1904, to begin a school at Fou'ia, on the shore opposite his home. While Sulufou itself remained strongly pagan for another forty years, those few of its inhabitants who wished to become Christians took up residence in Talofuila's community. Fou'ia thus became the Christian headquarters of the Lau district, despite the opposition of Kwaisulia, who until his death in 1909, obstructed the work of Talofuila's and other schools as much as possible.[47]

Everywhere in north Malaita, conflict between pagans and

Christians was continuous and intense. Each party ridiculed the beliefs of the other. Christians desecrated pagan shrines and sacred places, while bush pagans resisted the Christian invasion with demands for fines, pig-stealing, the destruction of gardens and killing—confident that their opponents would not retaliate. Violence was further aggravated by the smuggling of rifles and ammunition ashore by repatriates. Of the recorded murders, Arthur Ako, leader of the Fiu Christian village, was killed in his garden in 1904; James Ivo, a teacher from Nggela, was shot at Ngorefou in 1906; and James Sili, accused of sorcery, was shot on the verandah of Hopkins' mission-house in 1910. It was only after 1909, with the extension of government influence from the station newly established at Auki, that a degree of peace was attained in the coastal districts.

The teaching of Christian labourers returned from Queensland and Fiji was a principal reason for the Mission's striking success on Pentecost in the New Hebrides. The number of school villages, 3 in 1891, rose to 26 in 1898, 42 in 1900 and 61 in 1902. From 1897, W.H. Edgell tramped enthusiastically through the bush from village to village, to visit scattered schools and establish new ones. But the movement towards Christianity had already begun in 1893, independent of European direction, in north Pentecost, led by the pioneer teachers Louis Tariliu, Thomas Ulgau and Peter Moltata. News of the new religion was passed from mouth to mouth when people from the north Pentecost villages gathered together for feasts and dances.[48]

In central Pentecost, the turning-point came later in the 1890s, when the first of a steady stream of Queensland labourers began returning to their homes, with the intention of beginning Christian schools. Edgell admired their fervour, but as an Anglo-Catholic, committed to the use of the Book of Common Prayer in the vernacular, he admitted a prejudice against their "schismatic" form of worship—"à la Salvation Army":

> 4 Sankey & Moody hymns of the ranting style. 2 short anthems (?) during sermon. Groanings & exclamations during the 3 extempory prayers which nearly made me seriously ill.[49]

He nevertheless consented to use returned labourers as teachers, provided they conformed to Anglican usage. It was not a time for rigidity. Because of the unprecedented demand for schools and the tiny supply of competent Mota-educated men from Norfolk Island or elsewhere, he was compelled to install as teachers almost anyone who was willing to take on the task, whether Pidgin English-speaking ex-labourers or earnest youths plucked from existing schools.

Numerically, the progress was impressive. In 1901, Edgell baptized 639 adults and infants on Pentecost, which was the largest number yet recorded for one mission district, and when he left in 1903, 2000 people—one-third of the island's population—were either baptized or attending school. H.N. Drummond, who followed him, thought the success to be largely illusory:

> The island has been opened up much too quickly, and besides, most incompetent teachers having been appointed, the people have been baptized almost indiscriminately. When a hundred natives are baptized in a day without previous examination, the natural consequence is an undervaluation of the sacrament and Church membership. Natives easily leave the Church they have been easily admitted to, and I was scarcely surprised to find on going into the matter that fifty per cent of those baptized on one such occasion now never enter a place of worship or attend school.[50]

To encourage efficient teaching, Drummond organized the Pentecost church along the lines already demonstrated by Welchman on Santa Isabel, and with similar success. He enforced stricter church discipline, campaigned against funeral feasts and excessive kava drinking, translated hymns and Prayer Book into the vernacular, held regular teachers' classes and pressed small villages with weak schools to amalgamate into larger settlements. The church also became the sponsor of new communal activities. A big gathering for dances, games, feasting and church services, attended by a thousand people, was held each Christmas Day at the women's station at Lamalanga. In north Pentecost, Anglican converts gave £100 towards a central church for the district, built in wood of European design, where every village within walking distance gathered for Sunday services.[51]

On the neighbouring island of Omba, "after 30 years of lethargy and indifference", a parallel movement to Christianity with a different outcome began in the late 1890s with a spate of new schools commenced by Queensland returns.[52] Charles Godden went there from Sydney in 1901, the first European missionary since Bice's departure ten years previously, and established a new headquarters station at Lolowai Bay at the easternmost tip of the island.

Godden was one of the very few Evangelical clergymen in the Melanesian Mission—"very distinctly low church à la Australia", had been Edgell's private verdict on their first meeting. His sincerity was attractive, and among islanders and traders he was known simply as "Charlie".[53] In organization, he was more cautious than Edgell, refusing to begin new schools without capable teachers, yet by 1905, he reported that one-third of Omba's 4000 people were under some degree of Christian influence. His missionary career and recent marriage were suddenly ended in October 1906, when a newly returned Queensland labourer named Alamemea killed him by rifle shot and tomahawk. Unlike the death of Patteson, however, there was no mystery as to the cause. Alamemea had been imprisoned in Queensland on a charge of attempted murder: "he was punished in Queensland by three years' imprisonment and he promised himself that when he returned home he would murder the first white man he saw".[54] Godden had been warned of the danger. Alamemea was captured soon afterward and handed over to a French warship, which took him to Fiji for life imprisonment.

"History repeats itself," announced the *Southern Cross Log*.[55] As with Patteson's martyrdom thirty-five years earlier, the labour trade was held to be responsible: the enforced repatriation of Pacific Islanders from Queensland, their "hearts full of soreness and bitterness", had inevitably led to the death of an innocent man. The explanation was dramatic, but untrue. The response of the religious public to the news faintly echoed the reactions of 1871. There were resolutions of sympathy, memorial services, a memorial fund, and a slight revival of Australian interest in the Melanesian Mission. Even in a "safe" Pacific island, it had been proudly demonstrated, missionary work still had its posts of danger. Wilson dreamed of a "tidal-wave of Christian enthusiasm, and desire for Christian revenge, which shall first overwhelm [Omba] and the New Hebrides, and pass far on into the further islands of Melanesia".[56] There was instead a brief flurry of offers for missionary service, mainly from laymen, and one of Godden's fellow theological students volunteered to take his place.

At Godden's death, the momentum of the Anglican advance

on Omba was halted. His immediate successors lacked his personal qualities. For nearly three years from 1913, there was no Anglican missionary on the island, whereas the Roman Catholic and Churches of Christ missions were expanding their activities; nor were there strong teachers to assume local leadership. Schools and congregations stagnated, buildings fell into disrepair and were deserted. In 1909, there were thirty-five schools with 550 baptized; in 1918, the numbers were twenty and 350. The Omba mission logbook reported "many deaths and failures".[57] "Had Mr. Godden been permitted to continue his work here," reported a dejected missionary, "one ventures to think the position of the Church in this island would have been vastly different to what it is now."[58]

Some pagan islands were apparently impervious to Christian influence. None was more so than those of the Santa Cruz group, comprising Santa Cruz Island (or Ndeni) and the scattered Reef Islands archipelago, fifty kilometres to the north, which everyone admitted was the "weakest part of the whole Mission".[59] It had been Patteson's intention to use the extensive trading contacts of the Reef Islanders as an entrance to the mainland, but both places acquired a uniquely sinister reputation through his own murder in 1871 and the killing of Commodore Goodenough at Santa Cruz Island four years later. The rescue by missionaries of a castaway canoe voyager, who had ended up at Port Adam in south Malaita in 1877, enabled a friendly contact with Nupani and Nifiloli in the Reefs, through which Mano Wadrokal was able to settle in 1880 at Nelua on the north coast of Santa Cruz Island. In 1882 and each year thereafter, a missionary spent six weeks or more there, which was the first sustained European contact with the Santa Cruz people since the ill-fated colony of the Spanish explorer Mendaña at Graciosa Bay in 1595. Schools were commenced at Nelua, under the wavering protection of the local chief Natei, and at Te Motu; boys were taken to Norfolk Island; and in 1890, the first converts were baptized.

However, those conventional methods, which elsewhere eventually evoked some degree of success, were a total failure in Santa Cruz, despite the absence of rival European influences. It proved almost impossible to train effective teachers from among the islanders themselves. Just as labour recruiters had found recruits from the Santa Cruz group to be physically unsatisfactory, so the Mission discovered that local youths taken to Norfolk Island were more prone than others to sickness, and especially to pulmonary diseases. They were "always the first to fall ill", wrote Ivens, "and during any epidemic they were a constant source of anxiety".[60] In one epidemic, five Santa Cruz scholars died within a few days. Others had to be returned home prematurely. In addition, because the separation of the sexes was more closely observed on Santa Cruz Island than elsewhere, women could only be taught in separate classes by women teachers. The language posed a uniquely formidable problem. Unlike the languages spoken elsewhere in the Mission's field, which were of the Austronesian group, the languages of Santa Cruz Island were basically non-Austronesian in structure and unusually difficult to acquire. There were scarcely any translations, yet without books poorly trained Santa Cruz teachers who knew little Mota had nothing to teach in their schools. Banks Islands teachers were afraid of the excitable and quarrelsome Santa Cruz people, whose customs were so different from their own, and refused to stay. Moreover, the isolation of the group, 400 kilometres east of the south-east Solomons, and the scarcity of food and fresh water in the Reef Islands, made the post as unattractive for missionaries as for traders.

A.E.C. Forrest, who was the one missionary who stayed long enough to learn the language, was dismissed in 1896, after nine years of excellent service, following the discovery of his sexual relationships with devoted male converts. It was "a terrible blow to the mission", wrote Wilson, in private distress.

> He has led some of our best boys into indecent offences with himself, & has gone on doing so for more than 2 years at least. The headteacher at [Santa Cruz], & many others I fear have been led into beastliness, & it would almost seem as though all was ruined for a time ... He says that they do not think much of his offence; if so, his work during the 9 years he has been here has been worth nothing.[61]

Instead of disappearing into penitent obscurity, however, Forrest outraged his former colleagues by remaining at Santa Cruz as an independent trader, while exaggerated rumours circulated among the European community in the Solomons of his heavy drinking, hard swearing, large debts and embittered boasts that he had destroyed the Mission. Arrested in 1901 by an agent of Woodford on a charge of gross indecency, he escaped custody in Sydney and re-established himself at Tegua in the Torres Islands, the northernmost group of the New Hebrides chain, beyond the jurisdiction of the Solomon Islands administration. He committed suicide by taking poison in 1908, afterwards to become the subject of colourful traders' tales of the fallen gentleman of "artistic temperament" who had been hounded to death by vindictive Christians.[62]

"The conquest of Santa Cruz has begun," was Montgomery's confident assertion, following his visit in 1892.[63] But ten years later, all reports were uniformly gloomy. As a result of Forrest's departure, the lapses of two senior teachers from the Christian sexual code, and the defection of others to paganism, the few surviving schools were poorly taught and scantily attended. There seemed to be no interest in Christianity. Although the Solomons protectorate had been extended there in 1898, there was no government station in the group (the first was established at Vanikolo in 1923), and rival communities engaged in warfare without interruption. At Nelua, pigs slept inside the ruined church. In the Polynesian-language Reef Islands, the only continuous school was at Matema (population: 40) under Ben Teilo, from where knowledge of Christianity spread to the distant islands of Utupua and Vanikolo. Schools were begun elsewhere in the Reefs—in 1904 at Nukapu, where Patteson had been killed —only to be abandoned under the impact of introduced epidemic disease, the opposition of hostile pagans, or as teachers fell into disgrace or went off with their pupils on seasonal trading expeditions.

In 1910, after thirty years of contact, only one per cent of the group's 8000 inhabitants was thought to be under Christian influence. The cry was for a dramatic new method, adapted to the special circumstances of the Santa Cruz and Reefs peoples.[64] A "Santa Cruz Brotherhood" was planned, on the lines of the quasi-monastic missionary brotherhoods of unmarried clergymen springing up elsewhere in the Anglican Church for special work in urban or missionary situations. Three or four missionaries would itinerate from a common headquarters and operate a central school for training indigenous teachers within the group.

The Brotherhood began work in 1910, in an atmosphere of high expectation, but lasted for only eighteen months. One member (Guy Bury) died; two others were withdrawn to fill vacant posts elsewhere. After Blencowe returned to England in 1911, schools and church services on Santa Cruz Island ceased altogether. Norfolk Island scholars and overseas supporters of the mission were urged to pray "that the reproach of Santa Cruz may be wiped away".[65] It was easier to pray than to act. No missionary was sent to the group until 1925. There was then only one tiny school on the mainland and the Santa Cruz people as a whole saw no valid reason why they should accept a foreign religion.

Elsewhere in the Anglican field, despite regular reverses, the missionaries had no doubt that the first two decades of the twentieth century had been a turning-point in the spread of Christianity. Whereas a generation earlier, R.E. Tempest observed, island Melanesia had been "largely heathen" and Christians had been a small minority, the religious picture in 1919 presented a dramatic contrast. Malaita and Guadalcanal, "the last strongholds of heathenism", were encircled with Christian schools, while on most smaller islands in the Solomons and northern New Hebrides there were few unbaptized pagans left. Already, it seemed, Melanesia was "largely Christian".[66]

NOTES AND REFERENCES

1. W.A. Uthwatt, "The Melanesian Mission in the Solomons", *Australasian Church Quarterly Review* 1 (1910–11): 239.
2. C.M. Woodford to Sir Everard im Thurn, 16 January 1908, W.P.A., file no. W.P.H.C. 89/1907; J.W. Blencowe to his father, 19 June 1910, Blencowe Papers, in possession of Mrs M. Blencowe. See also the comments of the Assistant Resident Commissioner, Arthur Mahaffy, in "The Solomon Islands", *Empire Review* 4 (1902): 195.
3. *I.V.*, 1883, p. 84.
4. *Mission Life*, n.s. 5 (1874): 263.
5. R.H. Codrington, *The Melanesians*, p. 116.
6. C. Bice and A. Brittain, *Journal of Residence in the New Hebrides, S.W. Pacific Ocean ... 1886*, p. 34. For a similar approach, see J.C. Patteson, journal-letter, 4 June 1860, entry, 18 September, Patteson Papers, U.S.P.G. Archives.
7. A.I. Hopkins, Autobiography, p. 29, Church of Melanesia Archives. Cf. Hugh M. Laracy, *Marists and Melanesians*, pp. 71–72.
8. *S.C.L.*, September 1901, p. 105.

9. *M.M.R.*, 1909, p. 14.
10. Hopkins, Autobiography, p. 65; *I.V.*, 1887, p. 13.
11. *M.M.R.*, 1908, p. 33; *S.C.L.*, July 1912, p. 25.
12. *S.C.L.E.*, September 1908, p. 313; November 1926, p. 165. Cf. Laracy, *Marists*, pp. 78-81.
13. R.E. Tempest, "Melanesia, 1877-1919", p. 6, Melanesian Mission English Committee Office. For an example, from Guadalcanal in 1912, see H. Ian Hogbin, *A Guadalcanal Society*, pp. 90-91. See also Laracy, *Marists*, pp. 77-78.
14. *S.C.L.*, November 1912, p. 102.
15. Melanesian Mission, *Occasional Paper*, March 1896, p.17; *M.M.R. & I.V.*, p. 26.
16. Cecil Wilson, *The Wake of the Southern Cross*, pp. 235, 239-40; *S.C.L.*, October 1895, p. 2.
17. *S.C.L.*, June 1907, p. 11.
18. Interview with Rev. Dr C.E. Fox, Taroaniara, April 1965.
19. *A.B.M. Review* 9 (1918): 74.
20. Charles E. Fox, *Lord of the Southern Isles*, p. 163.
21. *M.M.R. & I.V.*, 1902, p. 7.
22. *M.M.R.*, 1905, p. 33.
23. ibid., p. 32.
24. Cecil Wilson, Diary, 30 September 1907, in possession of Mrs Qona Clifton.
25. Ellen Wilson, *Dr Welchman of Bugotu*, p. 40.
26. Henry Welchman, Diary, 12 January 1905, Melanesian Mission English Committee Office.
27. Wilson, Diary, 7 October 1905.
28. Welchman, Diary, 11-13 October 1907.
29. ibid., 27 September 1907.
30. Wilson, *Dr Welchman*, p. 59.
31. ibid., p. 101.
32. Welchman, Diary, 10 November 1908.
33. *S.C.L.*, June 1911, p. 12.
34. *M.M.R.*, 1909, p. 12.
35. On the repatriation generally, see Peter Corris, *Passage, Port and Plantation*, ch. 8; and id., " 'White Australia' in Action: The Repatriation of Pacific Islanders from Queensland", *Historical Studies*, 15, no. 58 (1972): 237-50.
36. *M.M.R.*, 1909, p. 48.
37. A.R. Tippett, *Solomon Islands Christianity*, p. 48.
38. David Hilliard, "The South Sea Evangelical Mission in the Solomon Islands: The Foundation Years", *Journal of Pacific History* 4 (1969): 45-49; Corris, *Passage*, pp. 123-24.
39. *M.M.R.*, 1906, p. 129.
40. Hopkins, Autobiography, pp. 155-59; *S.C.L.*, March 1907, pp. 113-14; "Sugar Industry Labour Commission. Minutes of Evidence taken before the Royal Commission ...", Queensland, *Parliamentary Papers*, vol. 2,

1906, pp. 51-55, 169-71, 386-92; David Wetherell, *Reluctant Mission*, pp. 114-16.
41. *M.M.R*, 1907, pp. 3-4.
42. ibid., p. 5.
43. ibid., p. 4.
44. *S.C.L.E.*, June 1908, pp. 274-75; December 1908, pp. 366-67.
45. *M.M.R.*, 1907, p. 4.
46. *M.M.R.*, 1909, p. 10.
47. On Talofuila and Kwaisulia, see A.I. Hopkins, *From Heathen Boy to Christian Priest*; and Peter Corris, "Kwaisulia of Ada Gege", in *Pacific Islands Portraits*, eds. J.W. Davidson and Deryck Scarr, pp. 263-64.
48. Michael Henry Tavoa, "Church on Raga and Short Account of Selwyn and Patteson and their Melanesian Mission" (Dip.Theol. essay).
49. W.H. Edgell, Diary, 26 February 1901, in possession of Mrs R. Rowland.
50. *M.M.R.*, 1906, p. 136.
51. For a further account of Drummond's work on Pentecost, see Fox, *Lord of the Southern Isles*, pp. 108-110.
52. Edgell, Diary, 5 October 1898.
53. ibid., 24 April 1901. His life is recounted by his daughter, Ruth Godden, in *Lolowai: The Story of Charles Godden and the Western Pacific*.
54. Captain E. Rason to Sir Everard im Thurn, 25 October 1906, W.P.A., file no. W.P.H.C. 264/1906; *Sydney Morning Herald*, 5, 6 and 9 November 1906.
55. *S.C.L.*, December 1906, p. 73.
56. *M.M.R.*, 1906, pp. 121-22.
57. A.S. Webb, "Aoba Logbook", 19 September 1919, Lolowai Mission Records, microfilm, Pacific Manuscripts Bureau, A.N.U.
58. *A.B.M. Review* 9 (1918): 53.
59. *M.M.R.*, 1905, p. 7.
60. W.G. Ivens, "Santa Cruz", in Appendix to *Dictionary and Grammar of the Language of Sa'a and Ulawa ...*, p. 239.
61. C. Wilson to H.H. Montgomery, 11 May 1896, Wilson-Montgomery Correspondence, U.S.P.G. Archives.
62. Wilson, Diary, 13 November 1902; Bohun Lynch, ed., *Iles of Illusion: Letters from the South Seas* (London: Constable, 1923), pp. 43-45; W.J. Durrad in *S.C.L.*, April 1950, pp. 38-43. On the Forrest case—described by the High Commissioner for the Western Pacific, Sir Everard im Thurn, "among the most puzzling of any that I have had in these seas"—see W.P.A., file nos. W.P.H.C. 336/1898, 121/1908 Confidential.
63. H.H. Montgomery, *The Light of Melanesia*, p. 139.
64. *A.B.M. Review* 1 (1910): 18-19.
65. Ivens, "Santa Cruz", p. 249. On the subsequent Christianization of Santa Cruz, see Fox, *Lord of the Southern Isles*, pp. 206-7.
66. Tempest, "Melanesia, 1877-1919", pp. 1-3.

7
Towards a Melanesian Christianity

The extended encounter between Anglican Christianity and Melanesian paganism during the first two decades of the twentieth century compelled missionaries to define more precisely their attitudes towards the indigenous religious system. Along with all other missionaries in the Solomon Islands and New Hebrides, the Anglicans shared the assumption that their own religion was totally and objectively true, and that no people were inherently incapable of receiving it. They differed from Evangelicals on one side and Roman Catholics on the other, in that they were slightly less dogmatic, less preoccupied with spiritual warfare and inclined to agnosticism on the question of the salvation of unbaptized pagans. "I hope and believe", wrote John Selwyn in 1884, "that God presents himself in another life to those who have rejected Him here, and does all He can, short of compulsion, to win them;" and among missionaries of the next generation, it was widely believed that pagans would be judged at death according to the Light they had already received.[1] In addition, men with a university education were more open to influence from the intellectual currents of the time, therefore better equipped than others to undertake systematic ethnographical studies of the people amongst whom they worked.

George Augustus Selwyn and Patteson had together created a climate of thought in the Melanesian Mission that rejected the popular missionary stereotypes of "poor heathen" and "perishing savages".[2] Although convinced of the superiority of European culture, Patteson himself had stressed the innate intelligence of the Melanesians and the need to retain their distinctive social customs within a civilized Christian community. However, his own scholarly interests were in philology rather than ethnology, and there was little that was positive in his estimate of indigenous religious beliefs, apart from the recognition of an "instinct of faith".

More than anyone else, it was Codrington, the urbane Oxford scholar, who implanted in the continuing tradition of the Mission the idea that no religion was wholly false, that "heathen" beliefs should always be approached with sympathy and respect. He himself believed in a shared human religious experience: "the common foundation ... which lies in human nature itself, ready for the superstructure of the Gospel".[3] On the positive relationship between Christianity and Melanesian religions, his mature thinking was cautious. Reflecting a typically late-Victorian preoccupation, he doubted the moral value of a system in which there was no prospect of reward or punishment in another world to encourage virtue and to deter from vice, and he reassured anxious Christian audiences of the "cruelty", "superstitions" and "abominations" that threw dark shadows over even the brightest portions of his picture. Nevertheless, he welcomed the universal Melanesian belief that a man had a soul, "in a different sense from that which can be applied to a brute", that death was but a change of existence and that there was a "bond of fellowship" between the living and the dead. Because the islanders believed in a "moral voice", they had a sense of a difference between right and wrong. Through sacrifices, prayer and magic, they expressed their dependence upon unseen powers superior to their own. All these were secure foundations or preparations for Christian teaching. The gospel was new to the Melanesians, but not alien to their existing religious conceptions; they passed "naturally" out of the old into the new.[4]

Among Anglican and Protestant missionaries of the next generation, similar opinions gained wide though by no means universal acceptance. At the first World Missionary Conference at Edinburgh in 1910, a majority of its correspondents and delegates upheld the view that "animistic religions" contained a modicum of truth, which supplied "points of contact" for Christianity.[5] In Melanesia, some missionaries of the Church of England pondered the possibility of a primitive revelation of divine truth and extended the contiguous elements in indigenous religion to embrace taboos, the outpouring of blood by the sacrifice of pigs and the acquisition of *mana* by set rituals and forms of words.[6] After the death of Frank Bollen in 1909, Wilson discovered among his possessions a collection of notes on the pagan religion of Guadalcanal.

> Some may suppose that these scraps about the old religion are useless, and had better be treated as things to be forgotten by the missionary. But this is not the case. He is dealing with men who had been feeling after GOD, and had not found Him, but had satisfied the religious instincts GOD had given them with these gods. Far better that they should believe these than nothing at all.[7]

Anthropological enquiry in the Melanesian Mission was boosted by the Cambridge anthropologist W.H.R. Rivers, who in 1908 travelled to and from the Solomon Islands on the *Southern Cross*. By interviews with Christian teachers and converts during the voyage, he accumulated much of the material for his diffusionist *History of Melanesian Society*, published in 1914. Invited to speak at the Mission's annual meeting in London in 1909—the first and last secular anthropologist to do so—he warmly praised its policy of endeavouring "to keep what is good and to build up the new faith on that foundation". He stressed the value to missionaries of the new science of anthropology and urged the Mission to lead the way by requiring its recruits to have taken a university lecture course in the subject.[8]

To influence Melanesians, Rivers had told those missionaries he met on the *Southern Cross*, a European must be able to see things as they (the Melanesians) saw them. This could only be achieved through accurate knowledge of their beliefs, customs and languages. It was under Rivers' influence that the young New Zealander C.E. Fox embarked upon a scientific investigation of Melanesian culture. His important pioneer study of San Cristobal, *The Threshold of the Pacific*, appeared in 1924, two years after Rivers' death. In England, it had been prepared for publication by Grafton Elliot Smith, an anatomist and anthropologist of the University of London and the principal apostle of the then fashionable doctrine of cultural diffusionism.[9] In the tradition of Codrington, Fox sought to anchor Christian doctrines in indigenous concepts. He challenged the common European notion that the "Melanesian mind" was an obscure and mysterious world, which could be neither penetrated nor comprehended by a civilized Englishman. Between white and black, there were no innate differences, no impassable barriers: "It is not the savage's mind, but his environment and history that are different ... I do not believe their minds are 'different' in some mysterious way; we only think so because of our complete ignorance of their life."[10]

But anthropological learning and linguistic skills did not necessarily produce a personal affinity with the subjects of investigation. Fox himself held the Melanesian peoples, their religion and customs in high esteem. This was less obvious in the case of his contemporary, W.G. Ivens, a brilliant linguist, who later published two major studies of Solomons societies: *Melanesians of the South-east Solomon Islands* (1927), based on material he had begun collecting while based at Sa'a and Ulawa between 1895 and 1909, and *The Island Builders of the Pacific* (1930), on the people of the Lau Lagoon, north-east Malaita. Ivens' field studies, dictionaries and grammars were permanent contributions to Pacific scholarship. His personal attitude towards the Melanesians he studied, however, was not conscicuously sympathetic. "Never be familiar," he instructed new missionaries. Instead, they were advised to remember that the "ordinary Heathen person is plausible, and one may say quite correctly that he has no knowledge of truth ... His life is a life of suspicion and he is servile in his belief in the ghosts and spirits of his ancestors, and in his fear of others." For these "benighted people", who knew nothing of "the high virtues, of justice or mercy or love", to give up their traditional religion was no loss; only through accepting Christianity would they acquire sufficient individual and social vigour to save themselves from extinction.[11]

Outside the Melanesian Mission, very few missionaries in the Solomon Islands and New Hebrides undertook the systematic recording of traditional social customs and cultures or showed more than a casual interest in anthropological literature. The Marists were with few exceptions "strikingly indifferent"; "Studying the native cultures was a hobby, a foible individuals might indulge if they chose."[12] In the non-Anglican Protestant missions, a similar attitude was paramount. Individual missionaries contributed notably to linguistic knowledge through their recording of local languages, but they produced no ethnographical studies comparable in depth with those of the Methodist George Brown on New Britain or J.H. Holmes of the L.M.S. on the peoples of the Papuan Gulf.[13]

In their approach to the indigenous culture, the Anglicans were unique. The Marists showed pragmatic tolerance; the Solomon Islands Methodist mission under J.F. Goldie was preoccupied with Western-style material progress; the S.S.E.M., the Presbyterians and the Seventh-day Adventists abhorred anything that savoured of paganism. By contrast, the proud self-image of the Melanesian Mission was that of a tolerant bearer of Christianity to the Melanesians, whose object was to conserve as much as possible of the traditional social and cultural order as the basis of a Melanesian Christian church. Sympathetic observers, such as the New Hebrides lawyer Edward Jacomb, praised the Anglican missionaries for their enlightened efforts "to understand and appreciate the native mode of thought", a verdict that was echoed a decade later by the anthropologist Raymond Firth—though in the disapproving eyes of the S.S.E.M., the Melanesian Mission "went too far".[14]

Anglican missionaries of the early twentieth century were more reluctant than their nineteenth-century predecessors to regard civilization as an inseparable accompaniment of Christianity and were repelled by what they saw of assertive, semi-sophisticated ex-Queensland labourers—"third-rate white men". Rather, they sought to protect their converts from the social confusion caused by "over-stimulation" and "unnaturally rapid" change. "As far as possible", said the *Southern Cross Log* in 1914, "we encourage the old habits so long as they are not wrong. The Melanesian Mission is there to give Christianity to the natives, and not to give them a twentieth century civilisation, or what is worse, a veneer of it."[15] It was a sign of the new doctrine of Christianity-without-social-change that the wearing of European clothing, encouraged by earlier missionaries as an aspect of the Christian civilizing mission, was actively discouraged from about 1910 onwards, as a source of disease and unsuitable for the "natural" island environment.[16]

Parallel missionary policies were being pursued at the same time in other High Church missions in Africa and the Pacific, notably in the U.M.C.A. and the New Guinea Mission. The object of missions, declared the editor of an Australian Anglican missionary journal in 1927, "is not to make the native Christian something quite different in every respect to what he was as a heathen", but "to help the convert to be a better aboriginal or

Papuan or Bantu than he was before; not to become a half-baked European".[17] Missionaries in Africa were saying the same: "We want our people to be good Christian Africans, not imitation Europeans."[18] Intellectually, it was an outlook distilled from a university-bred appreciation of anthropological scholarship, a wistful admiration for a stable village life lived in accordance with tradition and the round of nature, a Catholic vision of the Church as an organization visibly embracing people of all races and customs, and an inherent distaste for harsh Calvinist teaching on man's natural depravity. Instead of natural depravity, Anglican missionaries were fond of saying, pagan Melanesians combined their share of human original sin with the qualities of gentlemen and many vestiges of "natural goodness". Traditional Solomon Islands culture, affirmed Hopkins in *In the Isles of King Solomon* (1928), had "a dignity and beauty peculiar to itself", and elsewhere he wrote with affection of the "natural virtues" of the Melanesians—kindness, gentleness, simplicity, dignity, cheerfulness, loyalty and generosity. From these qualities could emerge a unique Christian personality, demonstrating to the white man "aspects of the full Christian character from which he himself is yet far off".[19]

Only Fox went beyond verbal magnanimity to experience Melanesian society from within. In January 1920, he performed *ha'imarahuda* with Martin Takibaina, a San Cristobal teacher. By this act, the two men exchanged names, together with possessions, rights and obligations, and Fox was thus adopted by Takibaina's relatives as one of themselves. He took to his new life with enthusiasm:

> ... I lived entirely on native food, never wore hat or shoes, smoked village tobacco when I could get it & so on. One month I spent as cook on a plantation living with the boys, same food and conditions ... I have never in all my life been so happy as I often have been in these months. I have been treated by Melanesians as a Melanesian and learnt many things.[20]

The various sections of the European community in the Solomons reacted predictably. The S.S.E.M. missionary on San Cristobal, shocked by the descent into savagery, sent a scathing letter full of texts. Fox's bishop was sympathetic; a French priest wrote "a loving letter"; the local traders and District Officer laughed at his "eccentricity", but placed no obstacles in his way. The venture came to an end after six months, when Fox was forced to return to a semi-European diet. The adoption, however, was a permanent relationship with the Arosi people, which survived Takibaina's death in April 1921.

What did the more permissive attitude of the Anglicans towards the Melanesian past mean in practice? Unlike missions in the austere Evangelical tradition, there was no blanket prohibition of betel-nut chewing, smoking, traditional dancing, mourning rites, Christian attendance at pagan feasts or bride price—though some missionaries did campaign without much success to reduce bridal payments to a uniform low level.[21] More than in other missions some encouragement was given to the retention of native handcrafts and their use in the decoration of village churches. The finest results were to be seen mainly in the solidly Anglican communities of Nggela and Santa Isabel, where many churches possessed richly ornamented lecterns, altars and crosses, like the one at Wango, San Cristobal, described by Wilson as

> wonderful outside with its dog-tooth pattern in red, white and black, and two doors side by side at the west end with large crosses on them in relief ... The inside was still more wonderful; a decorated painted font; well-made seats, placed College-chapel wise, and book-desks resting on the tails of carved bonito fish; a bark floor, and cement altar steps.[22]

The Christian worship held inside such churches nevertheless contained few adaptations to the needs of the Melanesian village congregations. Traditional music was ignored; hymns were translations of English verses sung to English tunes. Reflecting the liturgical conservatism of Anglicanism in the missionaries' homelands, daily church services were invariably conducted according to the Book of Common Prayer. "We know it and love it," was Drummond's justification, "and being Englishmen we think it the best possible thing for others to learn. And beyond this we find here something wherewith to bind together the whole Anglican Communion throughout the world."[23] For special occasions, however, some attempts were made to "baptize" certain Melanesian religious ceremonies, with Christian prayers taking the place of traditional spells and rituals. Alone of the

Interior of St. Paul's Church at Heuru, San Cristobal, 1906 (From the Beattie Collection: Permission Auckland Institute and Museum)

missions in the region, the Melanesian Mission made explicit provision for the Christian blessing of canoes, nets, houses, gardens or "whatever was the custom of the people in their heathen state".[24] Anglican Melanesians were also encouraged to continue the traditional practice of "first fruits", by placing the first of their nuts, yams and taro in church, instead of offering them to the spirits as formerly. At Port Adam, south Malaita, where porpoise drives had hitherto been interwoven with pagan religious rituals, Ivens encouraged the people in 1902 to hold a Christian porpoise hunt. For this, he dedicated six canoes and a new canoe-house and composed special prayers for starting, finding and driving "the game", while the Christian fishermen prepared themselves by seclusion, fasting and prayer.[25] In 1925, on a return visit to the district, he inaugurated an "opening of the sea" ceremony to mark the December beginning of the bonito fishing season. During the 1930s, the "blessing of the porpoise" was revived as an annual ceremony at the fishing-grounds on south Malaita and in north Malaita at Bitama harbour.

But toleration by foreigners was by itself not enough to preserve the past. Even without pressure from missionaries, the acceptance of Christianity had the effect of bringing about the decline or rejection of traditional economic and social activities not directly incompatible with belief in the Christian God. "There is no doubt", conceded Durrad, writing in 1917, "that social life as a whole is a more drab affair now than it used to be."[26] Three examples may be drawn from San Cristobal. As early as 1892, the Christians of Fagani, who had a reputation as "great singers and dancers", gave up their travelling dancing parties because they felt it to be "inconsistent with a Christian profession that they should keep up what belonged to their heathenism". A generation later, Fox concluded a description of a spectacular dance he had witnessed in a pagan bush village with the gloomy prediction that when the the village became Christian, this ceremony—which was "probably less heathen than the Maypole and the Christmas-tree"—would be performed no more; and "whatever we may have intended, the practical result of our own Mission work has been to sweep away any number of similar things". One such was the cessation of the manufacture of shell ornaments by the people of Hounihu village, which was attributed by the anthropologist C.S. Belshaw partly to the villagers' loss of faith in their ability to do the work as Christians and also to the new demands on their time by (Anglican) mission and government, which made it difficult to acquire the necessary specialized skills.[27]

In relation to one important Melanesian social institution, the attitude of the Mission passed from early toleration to active interference. This was over the *tamate* secret societies and the *sukwe* (public graded society) of the Banks Islands. Throughout the northern New Hebrides, where there was no hereditary chieftainship, a man achieved political authority and social standing through his rank in a graded hierarchy, in which he advanced from one grade to another through sacrifices and the ceremonial provision of shell money, pigs and food for feasting. Societies throughout the group combined many common features with special local characteristics. Every settlement in the Banks Islands had its own *gamal* (*sukwe* club-house) and *salagoro* (*tamate* lodge or sacred meeting-place). The *Tamate Liwoa* centred on Mota, drawn only from those older men who had achieved high rank in the *sukwe*, was the principal secret society of the whole Banks group.[28]

Patteson had disapproved of aspects of the ceremonies he had witnessed on Mota in the 1860s. However, he refused to legislate for his converts, in the idealistic expectation that when they had become enlightened by a full understanding of the Christian faith, so they would voluntarily discard any customs that they recognized to be inconsistent with their new religion. Successive missionaries in the Banks, fluent in the Mota language but never resident in the group for more than a few consecutive months annually, maintained the policy of qualified toleration. There were periodic attempts by teachers and missionaries to reduce the period of *salagoro* enclosure, with its associated taboos, from a hundred days at a time to ten or even three. But as Simon Kwalges discovered at Ureparapara, the obstacles to change were considerable.

> I ordered them to come out on the tenth day, but they did not like it. Mr Cullwick [T.C. Cullwick, the district missionary] came to me at that time, and saw for himself, and we told them to come out, but they did not care to, for they said if they came out they would die, and they were also afraid of the people of the neighbourhood who would be angry with him. Therefore they did not want to come out; but we spoke again to them, and they came out on the Saturday. Mr Cullwick told them to come on Sunday, and on Sunday morning he and I waited for them, but waited in vain. We rang the bell for prayers to bring them, but they did not come.[29]

There was as yet no question of absolute prohibition. Island missionaries, led by Palmer, were inclined to regard the practices of secret initiation and rank-taking as essentially harmless equivalents of Freemasonry. "All supernatural character has probably now disappeared at Mota," was Codrington's comfortable verdict, "and the societies are maintained for the pleasure of the thing, from old associations, and the conveniences of a club at the *Salagoro*."[30]

The central position occupied by *sukwe* and *tamate* in Banks Islands society did not fully come to light until the missionaries began living in the group all year round. This was because, unknown to their European teachers, the islanders had hitherto postponed their principal ceremonies until the end of each year

Robert Pantutun, 1906 (From the Beattie Collection: Permission Auckland Institute and Museum)

when the missionaries were absent at Norfolk Island. During visits from the *Southern Cross*, ritual taboos were lifted. Accordingly, when H.V. Adams went to stay permanently at Mota Lava and Mota in 1900, he found to his surprise that his continued presence was unwelcome. The listless state of the Mota church, where church services were found to be sparsely attended, children untaught and Sunday no longer observed as a holy day, presented a gloomy contrast to the continuous enthusiasm with which the islanders carried on their traditional death feasts, *tamate* initiations and the lengthy communal ceremonies by which a man took rank in the *sukwe*. It was found that the prestige of George Sarawia, who had died in 1901, had rested not so much on his office as a Christian priest as upon his high rank in the Mota *sukwe*, in which he was a head-man. The only solution, Adams argued, was to abolish *sukwe*, or at least to curtail its "abuses". A compromise arranged in 1904, by which the bishop permitted *sukwe* ceremonies to continue on condition that they were compressed into one day at a time, so as not to interfere with church and school, was a dead letter from the first.[31]

By 1910, Wilson had convinced himself that *sukwe* could be neither Christianized nor regulated and that Christianity in the Banks Islands was in danger of being smothered by a social manifestation of evil. He was particularly disturbed by the death-bed confession of the elderly deacon Robert Pantutun—that *sukwe*, because of its inherent association with pagan beliefs, was the fundamental cause of the falling away from Christianity on Mota.

> [Pantutun] said that in order to gain rank in it money was needed, and to get it sacrifices were offered as in old days. Rain, wind, sunshine, health, and sickness were all bought from those who had power over these things. He said that he had spoken in every *gamal* ... and *salagoro* ... repeatedly, and with tears, against this practice of heathenism, but his voice had fallen on deaf ears.[32]

However, the chief objection to *sukwe* made by Banks teachers and clergy was not that it led to paganism or immorality, but that it "prevents people going to prayers".

> What prevent church going are the occupations of the people in preparing for the Suqe [*sukwe*] ceremonies, the seclusion practised by candidates and the general excitement of everyone, which makes a sober church service and the discipline of school almost distasteful.[33]

Wilson therefore launched a crusade of purification. On every ground, he proclaimed, *sukwe* was a moral challenge to the supreme influence of the Church. It was *nalinan Satan*—an "utterly vile thing"—which Christians must renounce completely. Anyone participating in "heathen customs" would be excommunicated for three months.

It was a controversial ruling. Some of the mission staff deplored the readiness to embark on destruction of an institution of fundamental economic and social significance, whose ritual and colour contributed to the vitality of the community. It was one thing to disapprove of *sukwe* within an ideal Christian society; it was quite another to ban it outright and to persecute its practitioners. Throughout the Banks Islands, the reaction to the Mission's campaign against the *sukwe* was, understandably, one of bitter resentment: "They themselves do not in the least realise that we consider the *suqe* a stumbling-block to *them*," wrote Durrad. "They think of it only as an offence to *us*."[34] The battle-lines were drawn. Native teachers and clergymen moved from compromise to wholehearted opposition. Twenty years later, however, *sukwe* was by no means dead (it survived in a modified form until the 1950s), still the object of missionary denunciations because of its "crippling system of debts". Debt was also the justification for an episcopal prohibition of the *hunggwe* graded societies of Pentecost and Omba in 1934, though here too the older men who had themselves achieved high rank refused to submit. Missionary attitudes mellowed. In the 1970s, *hunggwe* ceremonies, accompanied by large-scale pig-killing, were enjoying a resurgence in some districts of Omba, with the sanction of the Church and accompanied by Christian prayers.[35]

Some of the problems that had arisen during the creation of an Anglican Melanesian community in the 1900s were reflected in the resolutions passed by a conference of the white staff of the Mission held at Bungana school, Nggela, in June 1911, at the close of Wilson's episcopate, and at a meeting of Solomons clergy and teachers at Pamua, San Cristobal, six months later. The Bungana conference was in itself significant as the first breach in the episcopal autocracy, which had become further entrenched since the island missionaries ceased to return annually to Norfolk Island. Isolated missionaries were no longer content to be governed solely by the bishop acting alone, and had pressed for some kind of formal representation in the shaping of policy. The conference also revealed vividly the changing nature of race relations within the Mission, for it was the opinions of the European workers—laymen as well as clergy—that were sought, whereas the consultation of "selected" Melanesian clergy and head teachers was intended to be a separate process.

At the Pamua conference, fifteen Melanesians and three Europeans shared equally in discussion through the medium of Mota—evidence enough that the old tradition of a rough equality between the races had not disappeared altogether. Most of its attention was devoted to codifying the duties of village teachers.[36] It was declared that they had no power to excommunicate; they should instruct their people in the Catechism every Tuesday and Thursday, and in the duty of keeping Sunday as a holy day; they should make full enquiries before marrying a couple in church; they were to encourage their people to help the Church by serving as their district missionary's boat-crew. A bell was to be rung in the early morning for private prayer before Mattins and in the evening before Evensong. Almsgiving in money and copra for the work of the Church was to be encouraged. Teachers were to direct "only such things as concern the Church", were not to impose fines and should co-operate with the "chief", whose own duty it was to oversee the secular affairs of the village. It was desirable, moreover, for teachers to be on friendly terms with neighbouring pagans and to "talk to them about this way of life". The proper attitude of Christians to pagan feasts and dances was laid down for the first time:

> ... churchpeople shall dance only at Christmas, Easter, or the great Church Festivals. It is forbidden for churchpeople to take part in heathen dances. If churchpeople attend heathen feasts they are to eat only such food as has not been consecrated, and must not remain more than one day.[37]

The Bungana conference passed fifty-one resolutions, many of them concerned with minor matters of discipline and usage, hastily considered and never fully put into effect.[38] The only topic that aroused impassioned debate was that of the Mission's common teaching language. Expansion in the Solomon Islands, whose languages bore no great resemblance to Mota, and the diminishing contact between the district missionaries and the Mota-speaking head station at Norfolk Island, inevitably led to a demand for the substitution of mission-Mota by English, for English was the language of commerce and government, while Pidgin English was already spoken by thousands of returned labourers who were displacing mission teachers as the spokesmen and interpreters for their villages.

Before Wilson's time, no one had questioned the use of Mota as the Mission's *lingua franca*, but from 1911 onwards, the "language question", one missionary recalled, was "the problem which most exercised and divided the Mission".[39] There was strong resistance to change. The advocates of Mota wanted to preserve it within the Church as the living voice of the Melanesian past. Inherited from Patteson, there was a realistic appreciation of the fact that, because each language is the outcome of a different culture, Christian religious concepts could be effectively imparted to Melanesians only through a medium that expressed their own thought patterns and social values. "Christianity, when presented in English to the peoples," wrote Ivens, "suggests nothing to the heart and offers no solution of the problem of life."[40] It was claimed that English made the Church more foreign, whereas the use of Mota by Europeans, Melanesian clergy and teachers alike—fed by the bi-annual Mota newspaper *O Sala Ususur*—visibly united the Mission across the boundaries of colour and culture. And if Mota was incompatible with progress, this was no great loss, for Melanesia was a backward corner of the world, its people "intellectually sluggish", without need of advanced teaching.[41]

The modernizers were an alliance of pragmatists, who could not speak Mota, and visionaries. They were led by R.P. Wilson, in every other respect a deep-dyed conservative, who deplored the intellectual restrictions imposed by the paucity of Mota translations and the air of stagnation that consequently hung over village schools. Young Melanesians were yearning for Western education as a means to social and economic equality: "Are we always going to be like this?" "Are we never going to rise and learn, and live more like the rest of the world?"[42] Accordingly, he stressed the "obvious duty" of the Mission to open up to its converts through English the path to secular knowledge and advanced education overseas:

> ... I am convinced that unless English be introduced and a higher education (Mota leads to nothing—no literature) the natives will go to the wall, owing to the advance of whites, Chinese, Japanese & perhaps West Indians.[43]

He was among the first members of the European staff in the twentieth century to envisage a future for the Melanesians that was neither one of ultimate extinction nor that of tradition-oriented village dwellers in an isolated world backwater, but one in which an English-educated élite would participate in government and commerce on an equal footing with Europeans.

Mission policy see-sawed between the use of Mota and English according to the relative strength of each party and the views of the bishop of the day. No one throught it possible to teach both languages at once. English had first been taught at the short-lived school at Siota. R.P. Wilson introduced it into his boys' school at Bungana in 1910, and its experimental use there, though nowhere else, was permitted by the 1911 conference. Cecil Wilson's successor as bishop, Cecil Wood, initially reimposed Mota to enable Bungana boys to proceed without difficulty to St Barnabas', then swung around to favour English—a decision prompted largely by his own failure to become fluent in a Melanesian language. Accordingly, at a second missionary conference at Maravovo in 1916, it was resolved, with much dissension, that "English be adopted as the medium of instruction at the local Central Schools and at Norfolk Island".[44] In 1918, at a third conference, the decision was reversed and Mota enthroned once more. The question was not to be finally settled for another thirteen years.

The bastion of the Mota language, as of all the Mission's traditions, was the training-school at Norfolk Island. Over St Barnabas' College still hovered the presence of the martyred Patteson. Each year, on 20 September, there was a commemoration of his death. In the house he had occupied, the study was kept for almost half a century just as he had left it in 1871, so that in 1909, the newly arrived missionary, J.W. Blencowe, could write letters sitting at the bishop's desk, surrounded by his books and diaries.[45] Visitors and newcomers to the staff invariably remembered their first awestruck impression of the memorial chapel. It was "the cathedral of the Kanaka", declared Jacomb.

> It is hallowed by the past. It is a holy place. It is a place which generations of Kanakas and Missionaries look back upon just as a 'Varsity man looks back upon his college.[46]

"The biography of the Bishop had thrilled me when I first read it," wrote Durrad many years later, "and here I seemed nearer to realising the power of his sacrifice than I had felt before."⁴⁷

But changes in the internal organization of the Mission, coupled with those external political and social developments that together seemed to make Mota a dead language, also undermined the hitherto unchallenged position of Norfolk Island as the pivot of Melanesian Anglicanism.The issue was less contentious than the language question, which had involved the very transmission of religious truth. Among missionaries permanently resident in the islands, there was by 1910 a unanimous opinion that the location of the Mission's headquarters and training-school 1400 kilometres south of its southernmost schools, linked only by the *Southern Cross*, was an anachronism. Those practical arguments that had justified the original choice were no longer valid. Convenience, economy, the expansion of white settlement and missionary activity in the Solomons, and the example of other missions that maintained successful training institutions in the midst of their respective fields: all demanded that the bishop should in future reside amongst his staff. The educational work would best be carried on by a number of central schools in the principal island groups. Some thought it might be possible to dispense altogether with the expensive *Southern Cross*, to rely on small boats and commercial shipping services. The minority opposition was led by the aged R.B. Comins and T.C. Cullwick, headmaster of St Barnabas', who conceded the need for an island headquarters, yet clung to the principle of a senior training institution in a temperate climate at Norfolk Island and stressed its sacred associations with the past.⁴⁸

Prompted by Woodford and Bishop Montgomery, Wilson himself reluctantly came to the conclusion that to move the episcopal headquarters from Norfolk Island was both inevitable and desirable. But it was not for him to lead the way. After seventeen years as bishop—"only 17 runs ... but they were scored on a very difficult wicket"—he was tired, depressed by clashes with some of his staff, and secretly yearning for a quiet parish where he could settle with his devoted wife and five children. He resigned in July 1911, to enable the transference to be accomplished by a successor without family ties.⁴⁹

The vacant see of Melanesia, despite its fame among Anglican

Towards a Melanesian Christianity 207

Melanesian schoolgirls at Archdeacon Comins' house, St. Barnabas' College, Norfolk Island, 1906 (From the Beattie Collection: Permission Auckland Institute and Museum)

missionary dioceses, was no easy post to fill. The staff at Norfolk Island, without consulting the island missionaries, delegated the Mission's right of nomination to Archbishop Davidson of Canterbury and two other trusted English ecclesiastics.[50] The litany of qualities required for Melanesia, as recited by the nominators, was by this time familiar enough. The ideal man would be young, unmarried, "missionary hearted", strong in character and physique, a "firm Anglican" and no stiff extremist, an Oxford or Cambridge graduate who could gather around him a band of university men: in short "a really first class man", to maintain the Selwyn-Patteson tradition. Potential candidates were sounded out, only to decline the offer. The archbishop became disheartened: "It is a strange outcome of our talk about missionary zeal and enthusiasm that we literally cannot find leaders for our greatest Missionary posts."[51] After eight months, an apparently suitable candidate was found in Cecil Wood, senior curate of a London suburban parish, who already had a reputation as an effective administrator and a keen student of missionary theory.

The appointment was an unhappy one. Wood turned out to be a tactless, ivory-tower theologian, who displayed no particular liking for missionary life as it was actually lived. Missionaries resented that he lectured them on the theory of missions, but failed to "throw himself heart and soul into the district work", thus learning from practical experience.[52] In his theological views, he was an Anglo-Catholic—the first Bishop of Melanesia to be thus identified and the first to wear a cope and mitre. At his enthronement at Norfolk Island, in August 1912, when the door of the chapel was thrown open to admit him ceremonially as bishop, the Melanesian scholars lined up inside were "so amazed" by the unfamiliar sight of episcopal magnificence that they "could not sing a word" of their hymn of welcome.[53] Wood's innovations in worship and ritual were accepted without fuss. But these were not the priorities of the island missionaries, who were angered by the bishop's eccentric administration and by his refusal to commit himself to a final decision on the burning practical questions of Mota versus English and the future of the Norfolk Island headquarters.

Under leadership that failed to adapt to Melanesian conditions, the pace of the Mission faltered. Almost everywhere in the diocese, the number of adherents remained static or declined, while rival missions displayed all the visible signs of progress. The First World War almost dried up the English sources of missionary recruits at a time of many losses by resignation or death. By 1918, there were five fewer on the European staff than ten years previously (30 : 35), and most of these were permanently teaching in schools. Seven district stations were vacant.

Towards a Melanesian Christianity 209

Cecil John Wood (From the Beattie Collection: Permission Auckland Institute and Museum)

Nor was the pastoral oversight of island districts being entrusted to Melanesians, for the number of active Melanesian clergy had been increased by only two, to fifteen.

The mood among clergymen of otherwise conservative disposition became openly rebellious. Finally in October 1918, they mutinied. Eighteen clergy and lay workers met at Maravovo to pass a unanimous vote of "dissatisfaction at the present working of the Mission", with a demand that the bishop should in future act on the advice of two counsellors, to be chosen from the staff. Wood, who was already wondering whether he should continue in office, promptly resigned.[54]

In ecclesiastical circles, the enforced resignation of the Bishop of Melanesia was a scandal. In New Zealand, the missionaries were thought of as Bolshevik sympathizers in mindless revolt against legitimate authority. The octogenarian primate, Bishop Nevill of Dunedin, was outraged: "I never in my life heard of such a course being taken & regard it as a novelty in Ecclesiastical History & a dangerous precedent."[55] The air was not cleared until a special select committee of the General Synod of 1919 reported that the staff had in fact "adopted the only course open to them to obtain an adjustment of their legitimate grievances".[56]

Within the Mission, there was little rejoicing. Morale was low. Wood's six-year episcopate had been a "terrible failure" and the optimism of the early 1900s had evaporated. Since 1911, grumbled the English Committee, no "forward advance" had been made anywhere. From the Close of Chichester Cathedral, Codrington—nearing his ninetieth year, but still writing to former Norfolk Island pupils—confessed to Brooke his sorrow that the "present condition of the Mission makes me think that my little labours came to nothing".[57]

NOTES AND REFERENCES

1. J.R. Selwyn, "Letters from the Right Reverend the Lord Bishop of Melanesia", *Australasian Month* 1 (1884): 346; [C.H. Brooke], *Percy Pomo*, p. 264. Interview with Rev. Dr C.E. Fox, Taroaniara, April 1965.
2. E.g., H.W. Tucker, *Memoir of the Life and Episcopate of George Augustus Selwyn*, vol. 1, p. 329; J.C. Patteson, *The Melanesian Mission* (address, 2 April 1864).
3. R.H. Codrington, "Religious Beliefs and Practices in Melanesia", *Journal of the Anthropological Institute* 10 (1880-81): 312.
4. ibid., pp. 312-13; "The Gospel as presented to Savage Peoples", Chichester Cathedral Wittering Lectures, 1902, Codrington Papers, Rhodes House Library; "Various Forms of Paganism", in *The Official Report of the Missionary Conference of the Anglican Communion ... 1894*, pp. 112-16.
5. World Missionary Conference, 1910, *Report of Commission IV*, ch. 2.
6. E.g., Cecil W. Howard, "The Islands of Melanesia", *The East and the West* 6 (1908): 288-89; *S.C.L.*, May 1913, pp. 150-51.

7. *S.C.L.*, October 1909, p. 70.
8. ibid., February 1910, pp. 140-44. C.E. Fox reviewed Rivers' *History* in *S.C.L.*, January 1917, pp. 19-23.
9. On the diffusionism of Rivers and Elliot Smith, see Annemarie de Waal Malefijt, *Images of Man: A History of Anthropological Thought* (New York: Knopf, 1973), ch. 9.
10. Charles E. Fox, *The Threshold of the Pacific*, pp. 250-51.
11. W.G. Ivens, *Hints to Missionaries to Melanesia*, pp. 24-25. See also Ivens in *S.C.L.*, January 1910, p. 114; and his "Melanesia and its People", in Appendix to *Dictionary and Grammar of the Language of Sa'a and Ulawa* ..., pp. 188-89. On the anthropological and linguistic work of Ivens, see the obituary by A. Capell, *Oceania* 11 (1940-41): 205.
12. Hugh M. Laracy, *Marists and Melanesians*, p. 70.
13. See George Brown, *Melanesians and Polynesians: Their Life-histories Described and Compared* (London: Macmillan, 1910); J.H. Holmes, *In Primitive New Guinea* (London: Seeley, Service, 1924). Both men corresponded with leading scientists of the day and published numerous articles in learned journals. The Evangelical ethnologists are discussed by W.N. Gunson, "Victorian Christianity in the South Seas: A Survey", *Journal of Religious History* 8 (1974-75): 191-93.
14. Edward Jacomb, *The Future of the Kanaka*, pp. 150-52, 178-82; *S.C.L.* January 1930, pp. 19-20. Interview with N.C. Deck, Sydney, July 1963.
15. *S.C.L.*, June 1914, p. 348. See also C.W. Browning in Melanesian Mission English Committee, *Annual Report*, 1899, pp. 51-52.
16. On the new attitude to European dress, see W.J. Durrad, "The Depopulation of Melanesia", in *Essays on the Depopulation of Melanesia*, ed. W.H.R. Rivers, pp. 3-24.
17. *A.B.M. Review* 14 (1927): 8. Cf. David Wetherell, *Reluctant Mission*, ch. 4; Melanesian Mission, *A Handbook of the Melanesian Mission* (1926), p. 4: "We are here not to make them into copies of Europeans but to help them to become truer Melanesians."
18. Gerald Broomfield, "Commerce and Christianity or Back to Livingstone", in *The Mission of the Anglican Communion*, eds. E.R. Morgan and Roger Lloyd (London: S.P.C.K. and S.P.G., 1948), pp. 66-70. See also H.A.C. Cairns, *Prelude to Imperialism: British Reactions to Central African Society, 1840-1890* (London: Routledge & Kegan Paul, 1965), pp. 218-22.
19. *S.C.L.*, September 1912, pp. 64-67; A.I. Hopkins, *In the Isles of King Solomon*, p. 36. Cf. M.J. Stone-Wigg (Anglican Bishop of New Guinea), "The Papuans, a People of the South Pacific", in *Mankind and the Church: Being an Attempt to Estimate the Contribution of Great Races to the Fulness of the Church of God*, ed. H.H. Montgomery (London: Longmans, Green, 1907), pp. 3-69.
20. Fox to Durrad, 8 July 1920, in W.J. Durrad's Introduction to C.E. Fox, "A Missionary in Melanesia", Durrad Papers, Alexander Turnbull Library. See also Fox, *Kakamora*, pp. 48-50, and (for the traders' version) S.M. Lambert, *A Doctor in Paradise* (London and Melbourne: Dent, 1942), p. 345.

21. For a comparison of the policies of missions in the Solomons, see D.L. Hilliard, "Protestant Missions in the Solomon Islands, 1849-1942" (Ph.D. thesis), pp. 501-19.
22. *S.C.L.*, November 1909, p. 95.
23. ibid., January 1910, p. 124.
24. Melanesian Mission, *The Constitutions, Canons and Regulations of the Missionary Diocese of Melanesia*, p. 14.
25. *S.C.L.*, January 1902, p. 165; July 1902, pp. 21-22.
26. Durrad, "The Depopulation of Melanesia", in *Essays on the Depopulation of Melanesia*, ed. Rivers, p. 12.
27. *M.M.R. & I.V.*, 1891, p. 93; *S.C.L.E.*, December 1922, p. 143; Cyril S. Belshaw, "Changes in Heirloom Jewellery in the Central Solomons", *Oceania* 20 (1949-50): 178-79.
28. For accounts of the men's societies of the Banks Islands, see R.H. Codrington, *The Melanesians*, ch. 5; M.R. Allen, *Male Cults and Secret Initiations in Melanesia* (Carlton: Melbourne University Press, 1967), ch. 6; Richard Maitland Bradfield, *A Natural History of Associations: A Study in the Meaning of Community* (London: Duckworth, 1973), vol. 1, ch. 8.
29. *S.C.L.*, March 1896, p. 6.
30. Codrington, "Religious Beliefs and Practices in Melanesia", p. 288.
31. *M.M.R. & I.V.*, 1901, pp. 20-21; *S.C.L.*, November 1904, pp. 5-8; April 1905, pp. 29-37, pp. 147-49; W.J. Durrad, *The Attitude of the Church to the Suqe*, pp. 1-4, 18.
32. *S.C.L.*, April 1911, p. 150.
33. Durrad, *Attitude of the Church*, p. 17.
34. *S.C.L.*, May 1912, p. 342.
35. See Report of British District Agent on Visit to Torres and Banks Islands, 10 October 1929, G.E. Fermor Leggatt to British Resident Commissioner, 16 March 1930, W.P.A., file no. N.H. 276/1929; "Account of Huqe of Duidui, Aoba", in Lolowai Mission Records, microfilm, Pacific Manuscripts Bureau, A.N.U.; *S.C.L.*, October 1934, pp. 9-10; April 1937, pp. 34-35. Personal communication, Bishop D.A. Rawcliffe, August 1975.
36. *S.C.L.*, February 1912, pp. 284-88.
37. ibid., p. 287.
38. *S.C.L.*, August 1911, pp. 202-4; September 1911, pp. 219-24.
39. R.E. Tempest, "Memories", p. 6, Melanesian Mission English Committee Office.
40. *S.C.L.*, November 1909, p. 86.
41. *S.C.L.E.*, November 1917, pp. 142-47.
42. ibid., August 1918, pp. 93-95.
43. R.P. Wilson to H.H. Montgomery, 13 June 1918, S.P.G. Letters Received, U.S.P.G. Archives.
44. *S.C.L.E.*, January 1917, p. 14.
45. J.W. Blencowe to his mother, 30 April 1909, Blencowe Papers, in possession of Mrs M. Blencowe.
46. Jacomb, *Future of the Kanaka*, p. 162.
47. W.J. Durrad, Introduction to Fox, "A Missionary in Melanesia", Durrad

Papers; also Ellen Wilson, *Dr Welchman of Bugotu*, p. 3.
48. *S.C.L.*, December 1910, pp. 94–95; *M.M.R.*, 1910, pp. 8–10.
49. *A.B.M. Review* 2 (1911): 77. In 1917, he was elected Bishop of Bunbury, Western Australia. His obituary appeared in *The Times*, 29 January 1941.
50. They were Bishop Jacob of St Albans, chairman of the English Committee, who in 1894 had recommended Cecil Wilson, and Canon John Still, who as a young man had gone to Melanesia with John Selwyn.
51. Davidson to Bishop of Southampton, 2 December 1911, Davidson Papers 1911 M8, Lambeth Palace Library.
52. R.P. Wilson to C.J. Wood, 5 June 1918, Church of the Province of New Zealand Records, 7/3, National Archives of New Zealand.
53. R.H. Codrington to C.H. Brooke, 22 November 1912, Codrington Papers.
54. R.P. Wilson to Primate of New Zealand, 25 October 1918, Church of the Province of New Zealand Records, 7/3; C.J. Wood to Archbishop of Canterbury, 3 March 1919, ibid.; *S.C.L.*, February 1919, pp. 1–2.
55. Primate to New Zealand bishops, 16 December 1918 (draft), Church of the Province of New Zealand Records, 7/3.
56. Church of the Province of New Zealand, *Proceedings of General Synod*, 1919, p. 67.
57. Melanesian Mission English Committee, *Memorandum on the Future of the Melanesian Mission*, p. 4; A.E. Corner to H.H. Montgomery, 23 October 1918, S.P.G. Letters Received; Codrington to Brooke, 11 September 1919, Codrington Papers.

8
Dreams and Disenchantment

Inherent in every church is a natural tension between otherworldly vision and worldly business, between those who dream dreams and those who are called upon to implement them. In the Melanesian Mission during the 1920s, the tension between the two was sharper than ever before as missionaries, full of optimism after the sterility of the previous decade, debated among themselves the goals and shape of their ideal "Church of Melanesia".

On both levels, the visionary and the mundane, mission fortunes were at a low ebb at the end of 1918. Among the white staff, there was a feeling of crisis—a belief that the Mission had come to a turning-point in its history. There was a demand for "a leader who knows us, and whom we know, and who knows what our life and work out here really are"—"a Melanesian Bishop, and not merely a Bishop of Melanesia".[1] Frustration exploded at a meeting of English and Melanesian clergymen at Norfolk Island early in 1919. Almost unanimously, they decided against following the established practice of delegating the right of episcopal nomination to outsiders—which inevitably would have meant the appointment of a man direct from England—and instead chose John Steward, then in charge of a small training college at Maravovo, who had worked as a district missionary in the Solomon Islands since 1902. The recommendation of an internal candidate (and one of the leaders in the revolt against Wood) was reluctantly approved by the New Zealand bishops and Steward took up office in September 1919.

From the standpoint of the Mission, there was much to be said for the appointment and little against it. Steward never lost the manner and style of a wealthy English gentleman, which he was. Bishop Wilson had privately criticized his early work on Nggela as evidence of inefficiency and indolence. After sixteen years in the Solomons, however, Steward's first-hand knowledge of Melanesia and the routine of mission life was equalled by few others. In appearance, he was stout and jolly, and his lofty sense of the episcopal office was tempered by an unpretentious delight in the absurd. His personal religion was strongly supernaturalist. He advocated the practice of exorcism and the laying on of hands for treatment of the sick, and believed that Melanesian Christians should be encouraged to trust in angels as benevolent agents of God who could be called upon to overcome the influence of evil spirits. An unashamed romantic, his head was full of imaginative but often impractical schemes. It was characteristic that almost his first official act on returning to Melanesia as bishop was to set out on a dramatic "Primary Visitation". This comprised an 850-kilometre seven months' journey around the central and eastern Solomons by whaleboat, during which, his biographer records, he passed time singing music-hall songs with his chaplain and solicitously dosed his tired crew with port wine and quinine, in the same spirit in which his old public school rowing coach, " 'Buffy' Evans used to cosset a Radley Eight with champagne when it seemed to him that they shewed sign of staleness".[2] It is hard to imagine any other mission leader in the Solomons or New Hebrides doing the same.

Steward lost no time in making the long-discussed break with Norfolk Island. At the end of 1919, St Barnabas' College was closed; most of its wooden buildings were dismantled and reassembled at various island stations. The new headquarters of the Mission were fixed in the Solomon Islands at Siota, a site neglected for twenty years, but within easy reach of Tulagi and a comforting symbol of continuity. "It was not starting in a new place; it had been a school before and everybody felt that we should pick up the work where it had been put down in the past and carry on in the Solomons all the traditions of Norfolk Island."[3] The Patteson memorial chapel, which it was impossible to rebuild elsewhere, remained at Norfolk Island as the outstanding relic of the island's half-century connection with the Melanesian Mission.

Everyone agreed that the organization of the Church should be made more Melanesian. Missionaries who were respected among

John Manwaring Steward (From the Melanesian Mission English Committee *Annual Report*, 1924)

their colleagues criticized the "excessive care" hitherto taken in advancing senior teachers beyond the diaconate to the priesthood and urged that the "native priesthood" might be rapidly increased "without due risk". Their stated reasons were frankly practical. Without the sacraments, there could be no living church; yet because there were not enough white priests to administer Holy Communion regularly to congregations scattered over thirty-six islands, four thousand Melanesian communicants were being deprived of access to their heavenly food. Therefore, Melanesian priests were needed to fill the gaps.[4]

Steward needed no persuading. He had been one of the three delegates from the Melanesian Mission to the 1910 Edinburgh Missionary Conference, where confident discussions had ranged widely over every aspect of received missionary strategy and theology. By the 1920s, moreover, in many places in Asia and Africa, the existence of "younger churches" under indigenous leadership could be seen to be no longer a goal but a fact. Thus influenced by the new "church-centric" currents in international missionary thinking, Steward dreamed of a future self-governing Melanesian church, which would be no foreign importation, but a "native Church of the people", and this could come only through a "really strong native ministry". On the ordination of Melanesians, he described his policy as "bold but not unduly so, cautious but not fearful", aimed at providing a priest for every three or four large villages.[5] From being a rare exception, hedged about with qualifications and confined mainly to older men, the creation of an indigenous ministry again became an integral part of Anglican policy. The number of Melanesian clergy rose from 15 (10 deacons, 5 priests) in 1919 to 28 (14 deacons, 14 priests) in 1928. (In 1928, there were 20 European priests in the Mission). Regular two-year ordination courses were inaugurated at Siota in 1921 for the Solomons and at Lolowai in 1927 for the New Hebrides. In theory, despite different rates of pay, there was no ecclesiastical colour-bar. In performing their sacramental functions, the island clergy were not subordinate to their English and colonial counterparts, and when Steward constituted his triennial Sacred Synod of the diocese, at Siota in 1921, the criterion for admission to its discussions was the order of priesthood, without distinction of race.[6]

In other missions, the practice was different. British Protestants, who did not share the sacramental theology of the Anglicans, did not see the ordination of Melanesians in the same light as a practical necessity, while in the Roman Catholic Church, the rigid insistence on a Latin-educated and celibate priesthood effectively prevented the early admission of Melanesians to the priestly office. The first New Hebridean Presbyterian pastors were ordained in 1897 and 1900, but forty years later they numbered only ten and their ecclesiastical status was inferior to that of European ministers. "Many theorisers think that these natives can be trained to be good teachers and preachers," wrote a senior missionary in 1918. "One in a thousand may, but the ordinary native of the New Hebrides never will."[7] In the British Solomon Islands, the first indigenous Seventh-day Adventist pastors were ordained in 1935, the first Methodist minister in 1938 and the first Roman Catholic priest in 1966.[8]

The Melanesian Anglican clergy enjoyed considerable influence and prestige within their own communities. Continual shortage of English and colonial recruits, which meant fewer district missionaries, gave them in many places a new freedom of action to show what they could do, though in such cases, R.E. Tempest remembered, "it was always felt, especially by the older missionaries, that the position was unsatisfactory and that there ought to be a white man in charge".[9] Nevertheless, by the 1920s, it was clear that Matthias Tarileo on Pentecost, Martin Marau on Ulawa, and Hugo Hembala and Ben Hageria on Santa Isabel, for example, were undisputed leaders of the church on their own islands. When William Vaget, the priest at Mere Lava, died in 1916, the *Southern Cross Log* conceded that "although his mental ability and teaching powers were by no means brilliant", he had acquired "a wonderful influence ... over his people" and had made the island "an active centre of religious life".[10] Men such as these, Steward recognized, neither needed nor wanted a foreign clergyman at their side for support.

> Many years ago, the Native Priest in a District where they were expecting a new District Missionary, said to me, "Oh, I DO hope they will not send us a boy." It is very galling for an old man to be disregarded and "bossed about" by a much younger man, just because the latter is a Foreigner and a novice.[11]

When Tempest first visited Mere Lava in 1918, he was immediately asked by Clement Marau to make a Mota translation of the Athanasian Creed, which was not included in the Mota Prayer Book. "I was told afterwards", Tempest wrote, "that this was a favourite trick of his to test the quality of new Missionaries."[12]

The acknowledged leader of the Melanesian clergy until his death in 1931 was Hugo Hembala. As their spokesman in synod, he was an impressive figure—"a big man, with great natural dignity"—who was listened to by Europeans with respect. In Bugotu, where he was called *Tamanina* ("Our Father"), he held the same paramount position as had previously been occupied by Soga and Welchman. Representing the *mana* of the Church, he undertook a vigorous campaign against the continuance of pagan sorcery on Santa Isabel.

> This last year [he wrote in 1925] I determined hotly within myself to make a thorough search amongst all the people for every old heathen thing that still remained hidden in their hearts, to get rid of them entirely ... And they all made full confession of everything, great or small, not one thing of any kind could they keep hidden in their breasts; and all of them in every village promised earnestly to renounce entirely those bad things of olden days, and to cleave with all their might to the teaching of Jesus Christ the only Saviour.[13]

He himself was attributed with minor miracles, and when he found travelling difficult because of advancing age, his devoted congregations contributed £400 to buy him a launch.

Nevertheless, the increased number of Melanesian clergy did little to change the distribution of power in the Mission, which in ethos and structure remained thoroughly paternalistic. New missionaries, enjoined by Steward to be "friendly to all, familiar with none", fitted easily into the pre-cast role of white guardian and guide of an affectionate brown flock.[14] Despite the establishment of a quasi-parliamentary diocesan synod, many higher policy decisions were made by Europeans alone in their staff conferences, while the all-important area of finance remained firmly in the hands of the bishop. Village congregations, exhorted by missionaries to produce copra for church collections (*alena*) as a means to becoming a "self-supporting native church", saw the money they raised disappear into general mission funds and quickly lost interest. For pastoral work, no one doubted that

Hugo Hembala, 1906 (From the Beattie Collection: Permission Auckland Institute and Museum)

white supervision would be needed "for many years", until Melanesian priests became qualified by experience and education to assume controlling authority. Indeed, as fast as islanders were ordained, so Steward called louder than ever for more white missionaries—"public school boys or university men", "Gentleman-adventurers for Christ", the "very best" priests that England could provide—for itinerant administration of island districts and the "supervision" and "guidance" of the indigenous clergy.[15] Roland Allen, who was regarded as something of an *enfant terrible* among English mission theorists for his radical advocacy of the church-building methods demonstrated in the New Testament, urged Steward to rethink his strategy, to rely entirely on the leadership resources of the indigenous Christian community and "cut out this sort of appeal altogether".

> When the Apostles went out into the world the converts were before them, the priests before them, the Church before them. They set their faces steadily forward and never looked behind them for supplies of men and money. That way has hope ... There is a great difference between going to people with the power of Christ to say to them "Rise up and walk in the Name of Christ", and going to them with the message that you hope one day to find a man in England to hold them up, if you have any luck in the next scramble for men.[16]

But for another generation, there was no way by which Melanesians could equip themselves to replace the foreigners in the leadership of a Melanesian Anglican church. Nor was there a formal machinery for self-government in the Church at either the village or the district level. Indigenous clergy were ordained specifically for a village pastoral ministry, with no more than eight years of elementary schooling in the Mota language behind them, and (far behind the practice of C.M.S. and U.M.C.A. missions in Africa) it was not until the 1940s that a few carefully selected Melanesian ordinands were sent overseas, to Australia or New Zealand, to receive a theological training equivalent to that of their white counterparts. Much later, in 1963, two New Zealand-educated Solomon Islanders, Leonard Alufurai and Dudley Tuti, were raised to the episcopate as assistants to the ninth English-born diocesan bishop.

The reluctance of the Anglicans to create an educated clerical élite followed naturally from the missionary vision of the

Melanesian church of the future as essentially a network of tradition-based Mota-reading village congregations, shepherded by their own village priests. Mission policy was also conditioned by the then almost universal belief among the white population in the south-west Pacific that Melanesians had less innate intelligence than Europeans and that an academic education was beyond their capacity. In Melanesian colonial territories before the Second World War, this attitude was a primary reason for the extremely low priority given by governments to "native education". In the Solomon Islands, the British administration operated no schools of its own until the 1950s, and during the 'twenties and 'thirties, it spent no more than £200 per annum, in the form of subsidies to those three or four mission schools that gave technical instruction. As a percentage of total government expenditure (0.3 per cent), this was among the very lowest expenditures on education of any colonial territory under British rule.[17]

Similarly, in the Melanesian Mission, the original emphasis of Patteson and Codrington on systematic teaching and thorough intellectual comprehension was gradually whittled away. "We do not aim at producing the highly educated teacher that we might produce with the material at our disposal," wrote a disappointed Bishop Wilson in 1895, soon after his arrival at Norfolk Island. A few missionaries began to urge that because Melanesians were "capable of higher things", they should be taught literacy in English as the means to advancement.[18] But more common was the claim that it was virtually impossible to train "the Melanesian mind" to the point of rapid comprehension. If island children were subjected to "normal European school hours", predicted Florence Coombe, a teacher at Norfolk Island, in 1909, "they would soon be laid low with brain-fever". Durrad, who was among the most sensitive missionaries of his generation, believed that "the idea of an *intellectual* test for advancement" was incomprehensible to Melanesians. H.N. Drummond, the last headmaster of St Barnabas' College, advised: "It is of the greatest importance in teaching to remember that there are, intellectually, no men and women in the class-room, but that all are children, boys and girls."[19]

Such opinions produced an approach to class-room instruction at every level that was minimal, intellectually undemanding, and in which "character", "Christian life" and the obedient repetition of simple dogmatic truths counted alone as virtue. A "religious education—i.e., spiritual enlightenment—is the purpose of the Mission's efforts", declared a 1930 report on the Anglican schools in the New Hebrides, "and since to attain this, the 'whole man' must be raised to a higher level, a general education as far as possible is given; but unaided, and with very limited means, this can only be of an elementary nature."[20] It was. In no boarding-school did class-room work occupy more than three and a half hours on weekdays during term, with extra holidays freely granted for saint's days and many other reasons: about five hundred hours' teaching each year. While Mota was retained as the principal language of instruction, however, there was no incentive to attempt more; nor was there a demand from government or planters for Mota-educated employees.

At the senior training institutions at Siota and Lolowai, the situation was little different. Classroom instruction was given by one hard-pressed teacher for three hours daily; the only Mota textbooks were the Bible, the Book of Common Prayer, a catechism, Codrington's "Lessons on the Parables of our Lord", and a few other printed translations on biblical and devotional topics. The syllabus for teachers in training at Siota in 1926 comprised the Gospels, one of the Epistles, instruction on how to prepare candidates for confirmation, portions of the Old Testament, church history and "general knowledge". Ten years later, it had hardly altered, nor had there been any more major translations into Mota. "The devotional standard is, I think, high," reported the warden; "the intellectual, considering all the handicaps, not low, except in one or two cases."[21] For teachers on refresher courses, it was thought to be more important to "reinspire" than to re-educate. Hopkins, who was warden from 1919 to 1925, thought it "useless to attempt to add much to their little stock of learning",

> but I aimed at stimulating their intelligence and getting their minds to work not by pouring knowledge in, but by giving them visions. So they filled notebooks joyfully with all sorts of outlines of various subjects sacred and secular, little bits of geography, astronomy, Church History, doctrine, a good deal on the lines of Bible Helps. Their notebooks were their only library for future reference.[22]

The institution that the Anglicans pointed to with pride as the most effective demonstration of their educational ideals was the senior boys' school for the Solomons—All Hallows, at Pawa on Uki. The Pawa school enrolled up to 120 boys, most of them aged between fifteen and twenty. They were divided into four classes, each representing a year of work. Under Fox, who was headmaster for eight years from 1924—who himself had taught at the old St Barnabas'—a conscious attempt was made to perpetuate the Norfolk Island blend of moderate Anglicanism, English public school organization and discipline, and respect for the Melanesian past. In the Solomon Islands context, Pawa was a unique synthesis. A District Officer who visited in 1937 remembered it as "run on public school lines", the staff "very hearty and jolly".[23] The pupils grew most of their own food, cooked copra and dived for trochus-shell to raise the school's income beyond the Mission's meagre annual subsidy of £5 per student. Each week there was traditional dancing. As at Norfolk Island, there was regular community singing in Mota of popular English rounds and ditties: songs such as "John Peel", "Auld Lang Syne" and "For He's a Jolly Good Fellow". The lofty school chapel had an altar of ebony, inlaid with mother-of-pearl, a roof of sago palm and a square battlemented tower, which when weathered looked like an old stone church. There was a drum-and-fife band, a school choir and a carpenter's shop. To encourage new loyalties and to keep youthful aggression within harmless bounds, boys from different islands were divided into five "houses", ruled by prefects, which competed for trophies in weekly matches of football and cricket. Fox later wrote: "It seemed to me that the boys needed something to replace the excitement of the fighting which was the spice of life to their fathers, and in which many of them had taken part ..."[24]

The atmosphere at Pawa was devout. The idea of becoming a teacher, perhaps a priest, was continually put before the pupils, so that most were accustomed to take for granted that this would be their life's work. Of those who passed through in Fox's time, more than forty were subsequently ordained.

A different emphasis was attempted at Maravovo, where for fifteen years there was talk of making a beginning in industrial education. Industrial missions were a popular cause in Protestant circles throughout the world from the 1880s onwards. In essence, they were another expression of the mid-nineteenth-century doctrine of Christian civilization, but among enthusiasts the notion that missions should seek to lead their converts to material prosperity through commercial and vocational enterprises was propagated as a new gospel of "practical Christianity". In 1900, there were 179 recognized mission-sponsored industrial training institutions, compared with 29 in 1880.[25] In Melanesia during the 1900s, the need for industrial missions seemed to be justified by the newly popular theory that the observed population decline was due mainly to indolence and loss of interest in life, caused by the disruption of native culture by European contact and the enforced abandonment of warfare, head-hunting and pagan feasting. Optimistic Christians, like Charles Abel of the L.M.S. in Papua, countered neo-Darwinian racial pessimists who argued that Melanesians were irreversibly doomed to extinction with the claim that the disastrous social void could be filled and "zest" (a favourite word) restored through the satisfying values and incentives of a virile Christian civilization. Christian converts should therefore be encouraged to improve their physical and economic status through plantation labour, improved village agriculture and new occupations such as carpentry, boat-building and simple manufactures for the European market.[26]

Throughout northern Melanesia, L.M.S. and Methodist missionaries took up with enthusiasm the cause of racial salvation through economic development and self-help. Australian businessmen connected with the S.S.E.M. founded the Malayta Company in 1909 as a self-consciously Christian trading and planting venture. The Churches of Christ mission at Omba had its origin in a trading-station. But most Anglicans found little to admire in these industrial enterprises. Far from Patteson's original goal of creating a civilized (though not Anglicized) social and economic context for Christianity in the islands, the emphasis of the 1900s was on preserving Melanesian village life from the taint of an alien civilization rather than changing it. Welchman, whose views swayed many of his contemporaries, poured scorn on the whole concept of industrial missions as a foolish and unspiritual distraction from the essential task of creating a Christian civilization of the heart; Melanesians had already created an industrious way of life admirably suited to their wants and environment, which needed no substantial change after their conversion to Christianity.[27] Less high-minded motives were also at work. English gentlemen of genteel background and private income whose thinking dominated the Mission were detached from the world of trade and commercial agriculture. Durrad remembered:

> It seemed beneath us. Lesser men as we were, we still breathed the atmosphere of the Etonian and Oxford aristocracy in which the early days of the Mission had been passed. We watched the founding of another mission of quite a different type from our own, and listened with amused contempt to the stray yarns of missionaries whose evangelical fervour seemed curiously mixed up with tobacco and copra. But they made us think.[28]

The Anglicans took a first reluctant step in this same direction in 1911, when Bishop Wilson bought 320 hectares around Maravovo for a plantation, with the intention of providing the local people with opportunity of employment under Christian auspices (there was vague talk about founding a "Church Company" to work the land) and assisting the Mission towards financial self-support. By 1914, over forty hectares had been planted and twenty-five labourers from other islands were employed there. Wood arrived full of ideas on the need to encourage industrial work to fill the supposed "gap" in Melanesian village life, but his theories remained on paper. No "trace of the industrial Mission can be found in the Melanesian Mission system", observed Jacomb in 1919. Such neglect of education in "the practical side of life" was to be deplored, he argued, on the ground that the "raising of the standard of civilization is the test by which a tribe's conversion must be measured".[29] Within the Mission, similar if less stark ideas were gaining ground. Rivers, whose views as a sympathetic anthropologist carried weight in Anglican circles, was a strong advocate of vigorous Christianity and new village occupations, to prevent the social malaise of *tedium vitae*, and the *Essays on the Depopulation of Melanesia* (1922) that he edited (which grew out of papers on the subject commissioned by the English Committee) contained an influential exposition of his views. Steward himself became a half-hearted convert to the cause.

But the ethos of the Mission was not congenial. The vision of the 1920s remained other-worldly: conversion was one thing, social reconstruction and modernization were another. When technical instructors were not forthcoming, enthusiasm for Christian industry quickly melted away. By 1925, Maravovo had become a large (200-pupil) central boys' school, intended to be preparatory to Pawa and run on similar public-school lines. Industrial education in the Melanesian Mission, a popular booklet on its work tacitly conceded in 1927, was in the realm of future hope rather than of present achievement. The assertion by a foolish and superficial travel writer that the Anglican mission actually engaged in trade was regarded as a monstrous libel; a public retraction was demanded and obtained.[30]

The most important organization of the Melanesian church of the 1920s owed nothing to theological college or to synod. This was the Melanesian Brotherhood, which a remarkable man named Ini Kopuria founded in 1926. He was born at the turn of the century near Maravovo, where he was baptized (being given the name of an Anglo-Saxon Christian king) and was sent away to school, first to Pamua and later to Norfolk Island. Among contemporaries, Ini stood out for his independence and originality. Instead of becoming a village teacher, as his mentors had planned, he sought adventure by joining the protectorate's Native Armed Constabulary, stationed on his native Guadalcanal. In 1924, following an accident and illness, he underwent an intense religious experience and decided to form a brotherhood of young men vowed to take Christianity to the pagan villages of Guadalcanal, where he had worked as a policeman. "I have visited all the villages as a police sergeant," he said, "and they all know me: why not go to them now as a missionary?"[31]

The idea for the Brotherhood grew out of a complex of influences. The tradition of the Mission was sympathetic to a Melanesian variant of a religious order. Steward himself had once dreamed of founding a semi-monastic brotherhood of twelve priests to convert Malaita. While Ini was at Pamua, in 1916, Fox had formed a band of young men into a Brotherhood of St Aidan, to start new schools in the pagan bush villages of San Cristobal. (It lasted for four years.) At Norfolk Island, Hopkins had told Ini and other pupils about the English monks who evangelized Germany and the significance of the threefold monastic vow. There was something in it of a nostalgic desire

Ini Kopuria, founder of the Melanesian Brotherhood (Permission New Zealand Anglican Board of Missions)

Bishop Steward with the original seven members of the Melanesian Brotherhood, 1926 (Permission New Zealand Anglican Board of Missions)

to recreate the happy companionship of earlier schooldays. But fundamentally, it was an expression of a Melanesian aspiration for an indigenous vehicle for Christianity outside the European-dominated framework of the Mission.

Steward was sympathetic. He recognized Ini's religious earnestness and helped him to draw up a rule. As the Brotherhood was eventually constituted, there was little in its organization or its theology to which the most orthodox Anglican could object. The Brothers were to promise to remain unmarried, to take no payment and to obey those in authority. They were to work always in pairs, and would be organized in "Households", with no more than twelve members in each, headed by a *Moemera* ("Elder Brother"). The "Father" of the Brotherhood was the bishop, whose decision in disputes was final. On 28 October 1925, St Simon and St Jude's Day, the former policeman made a formal renunciation of possessions, marriage and freedom of action. In the following year *Ira Retatasiu*, or the Company of Brothers, was founded, with Ini as Head Brother and six new members from Santa Isabel, Guadalcanal and the Russell Islands, whom he had persuaded to join him.[32]

The purpose of the Brotherhood was evangelistic: "to declare the way of Jesus Christ among the heathen, not to minister to those who have already received the law".³³ It was not a religious order of the traditional Western type, with its members committed to life vows, but a looser association on lines unique to Melanesia. Promises were to be taken for only one year at a time. At the annual meeting held about 28 October on Ini's land at Tambalia (given by him to the Brotherhood), each Brother had the choice of either withdrawing or remaining for a further year. The ordinary dress was a black loin-cloth and white sash; on Sundays and saints' days, it was a white loin-cloth with black sash.

The Brotherhood's first year was unspectacular. A few new schools were commenced in Guadalcanal villages near Aola and at Marau Sound, where the tradition of Patteson's visits sixty years previously still lingered. In 1927, it was decided to go further afield. A second Household was sent to Santa Cruz, where nothing had been done for more than a decade. Others later went to north and central Malaita, to the Polynesian outliers of Sikaiana (1929) and Ontong Java (1933), to Tulagi to work among the hundreds of dock-workers, boats' crews and labourers employed in the area, and beyond the Solomons to Omba and Pentecost in the New Hebrides, to New Britain and to the descendants of Solomons labourers in Fiji.

The idea worked because it met a social need. For young men in their late teens or early twenties who had just left a mission boarding-school, having little or no knowledge of English, too young to marry and settle down, yet motivated to work for a few years in the context of the Mission, there had hitherto been no alternative to returning home to the humdrum life of an assistant teacher. Some, like Ini, had sought to experience the wider world by joining the government police or by taking employment on a trading vessel or as a plantation labourer. Attracted by the *esprit de corps* of the Brotherhood, the opportunity to work with old school-friends, the romance of the life of an itinerant evangelist on foreign islands and Ini's magnetic personality, young men flocked into the Brotherhood. Contrary to Steward's cautious expectations (he had doubted whether the total would ever exceed twenty), the numbers jumped from 15 in 1928 to 128 seven years later. After the initial glamour wore off, however, it was those islands that had been Christianized the longest that supplied the fewest recruits. In 1935, there were none from the Banks, 4 from Nggela and 13 from Santa Isabel; but there were 45 members from Malaita and 22 from Pentecost, mostly men with little or no education from villages only recently converted.³⁴

Few Europeans gave much weight to the concept of a Melanesian religious order. Fox joined in 1932—the only foreigner ever to do so—and as Tasiu Charles, remained a member for eleven years until compelled by a later bishop to withdraw. Ini himself, because he resisted the European assumption that "*every* Melanesian, because of his colour, should be inferior to *every* white man because of his colour", was seen by many missionaries as conceited; while a band of young men under obedience was regarded as a convenient supply of labour for odd jobs—rebuilding a church or acting as caretakers of a mission-station.³⁵ As members of an indigenous religious organization, however, the Brothers acquired unique prestige among island Christians. "Now their *mana* is great, that of the Brothers and of the Bishop," emphasized a Tikopia village teacher. Their work could be dangerous. Stories were told of their healings of the sick, by combining Christian prayers with traditional medicines; of their victorious encounters with hostile pagans; of the visible signs that they carried with them God's special protection.³⁶

The early success of the Brotherhood nevertheless contained the seeds of a subsequent decline, which was arrested only in the 1960s. The rule that it should concentrate on work among heathen, though later modified to permit revival work, meant that many of its early gains were nullified by the inability of local clergy and missionaries to follow them up by supplying teachers for a regular school. In at least thirty places, Fox claimed, mainly on Malaita, villages that were "opened" by the Brothers eventually accepted a teacher from the Roman Catholics or the S.S.E.M. The original system of annual vows meant a rapid turnover of members, few remaining longer than three years to give stability and assist in the training of novices. Much of its initial appeal, moreover, rested upon three factors, which did not survive the 1930s: the small range of secular occupations for young men outside their home villages; the assumption of missionaries that their male school pupils were morally obliged to work for the Church; and the unchallenged leadership of the founder himself. Ini remained as Head Brother until 1940, when he was dispensed by the bishop from his vow of celibacy and then married. Until his death in 1945, he worked, unhappily, as a village deacon on Guadalcanal.

The most visible expression of the ecclesiastical romanticism of the 1920s was the triumph of Anglo-Catholicism as the dominant religious ideology of the Mission. The religious atmosphere had hitherto been of the moderate High Church variety as implanted by Selwyn and Patteson, though a few missionaries were Evangelical in sympathy and many others would have regarded themselves as neither High nor Low. From the mid-1890s, however, as the Anglo-Catholic successors of the Tractarians began attaining their peak of influence in the Church of England, some of Bishop Wilson's English recruits introduced coloured stoles and the eastward position of the priest facing the altar in celebrating Holy Communion (instead of the traditional "north-end"), along with Catholic devotional practices, such as making the sign of the cross. The older missionaries were discomforted. Welchman warned his Bugotu teachers that the ceremonial newly introduced at Norfolk Island "might prove a snare to them" and urged the bishop to stop it.[37] The Melanesian Mission belonged to no church party, Wilson publicly affirmed in 1907, against those at home who were suggesting otherwise, "unless being loyal to the Prayer-book, and wide as the Prayer-book, makes us so".[38] And to prove his point, he encouraged the Church Missionary Association of New Zealand to pay the stipends of missionaries who were known to be "sound Evangelical Churchmen". Ten missionaries were thus supported at various times between 1895 and 1919, when Steward brought the co-operation scheme to an end.[39]

The theological currents within Anglicanism were flowing in the opposite direction. In England, the Anglo-Catholic movement was leaving the defensive to become an enthusiastic and confident party within the national church, whose crusading zeal was to climax in the centenary celebrations of the Oxford Movement in 1933. From its late-Victorian mission field in the slums of English industrial cities, its influence expanded overseas. Young priests were urged by Anglo-Catholic missionary prelates to do service abroad, to plant the full Catholic faith of the English Church away from the stultifying atmosphere of the Establishment, in a clear air free of awkward congregations who objected to Romanizing ritual innovations or Protestant pressure-groups who threatened litigation. Thus attracted by the opportunity to create their ideal church, dedicated men answered the call to Central Africa, to join the ascetic U.M.C.A., which was acknowledged to be the principal Anglo-Catholic missionary society, or to sympathetic dioceses such as those of the West Indies or South Africa, to Accra or Korea.[40] A few Anglo-Catholics went to Melanesia. In 1912, Wood introduced sacramental confession and a daily service of Holy Communion at Norfolk Island, which was then paralleled by very few Anglican churches in Australia or New Zealand.

In Melanesia, the visible spread of Anglo-Catholicism was assisted by the demands of the missionary situation. Because elaborate ritual was believed to stimulate the imaginations of simple people, it was justified as an important way to approach the islanders—which was the same argument as was used in England to defend the use of ritual in urban working-class parishes. Durrad, who in 1911 was the first missionary to begin regular sung celebrations of Holy Communion, argued that the time was ripe for drastic changes in worship:

> The staid and sober services of half a century ago, still to a certain extent in vogue here, seem to make no appeal to these emotional people, who are like Southern Europeans in love of colour and the dramatic element. We need to get rid of the drab from the picture and give some appeal to the imagination and the eye. These people are children. With them laughter and tears are close together, and they are as easily moved to the one as to the other.[41]

During the next fifteen years, through a handful of English missionary priests in strategic position, the religious complexion of the diocese changed dramatically. At Vureas school in the Banks under Durrad (1911-18) and H.L. Hart (1920-27) and in the Solomons at Maravovo school under George Warren (1920-38), Catholic ritual was progressively introduced and taken up with enthusiasm by impressionable schoolboys. From the schools, it filtered into the training colleges and the village churches. Private confession was "definitely taught, consistently encouraged, and regularly practised", reported Durrad from Vureas: "It has helped much in checking the spread of evil."[42] Accompanying Catholic sacramental doctrines came the terms

Mass and Eucharist, replacing Patteson's Mota word *ganarongo*, "holy feast". Melanesian priests in training were instructed in the Catholic priestly role—"Fathers in God"—and learnt to sing the psalms in plain-song. Faith was nurtured less on scripture, less on sermons, more on liturgy and the "teaching church". Episcopal authority was explained to schoolchildren in uncompromising terms:

> The Bishops take the place of the Apostles. They have the powers Jesus gave to the Apostles. They are the Rulers of the Catholic Church. Father Bishop is the Ruler of the Church in Melanesia.⁴³

Following pre-Reformation English precedent, there was a new stress on the public observance of church festivals, saints' days and the liturgical seasons, each with its distinctive ritual: processions with palms on Palm Sunday, Rogationtide processions through the village to bless houses, crops and cemetery, and in each church a special celebration of its patronal festival. The traditional eucharistic vestments replaced cassock and surplice for the celebrant at Holy Communion, and the use of incense (made from a local gum) at high festivals became a regular practice in the larger churches.

By the mid-1920s, many of the influential European clergy in the Mission were ardently Anglo-Catholic in doctrine and practice. As the tradition became established, the pressure was on the others, and newcomers, to fall into line. To avoid confusion, there was a call for ritual uniformity. Steward—who himself held mild Anglo-Catholic opinions—issued precise instructions on the ceremonial forms to be used throughout the diocese, with allowance for adaptation to the needs of particular village congregations. His directives would have been inconceivable twenty years earlier. A Solomons staff conference in 1926 deliberately identified itself with the Catholic wing of Anglicanism by resolving unanimously that in all schools the Holy Eucharist should be shown to be the principal service and that the "Catholic Faith be taught in its entirety throughout the Mission", though to avoid alienating Low Church supporters in New Zealand and elsewhere, the theological colour of the diocese was not publicly emphasized.⁴⁴

Another sign of the advance of Anglo-Catholicism during the 1920s was the foundation at Siota in 1929 of a small religious sisterhood called the Community of the Sisters of the Cross. Its founder and superior was Margaret Wilson ("Mother Margaret of the Cross"), daughter of J.M. Wilson, one-time headmaster of Clifton College and a prominent Broad Churchman, who had come to Melanesia with her companion Gwen Shaw from Bombay, where both women had been members of an English Anglo-Catholic sisterhood. In 1936, the four members of the new community took charge of the Mission's girls' school at Bungana, where they made imaginative changes to the curriculum, with a new emphasis on scientific food gardening, and attracted a cluster of Melanesian and Polynesian novices, called *Ta'ina*. Relations with the European mission staff, however, were often tense. As a self-contained and independent-minded group of women, the Sisters of the Cross were distrusted by many of their co-workers, and successive bishops doubted their filial submission to episcopal authority. In 1950, the community resolved its religious frustrations by joining the Roman Catholic Church. Angry Anglicans suspected Mother Margaret to be comparing herself with the great Cardinal Newman.[45]

To build an ideal Catholic Church required purity not only in doctrine and government but also in sexual habit. Although practically abandoned in the home churches, moral discipline by church law was defended in the mission field as a return to the practice of the early Church, and its use was well established in all Pacific Protestant missions. In Melanesia, it had predated Anglo-Catholic influence, but it received enthusiastic Anglo-Catholic support. In the early years of the Banks and Solomons Christian communities, exclusion from church was a voluntary gesture, in that those baptized Christians who lapsed from the Christian sexual code usually absented themselves from daily services until they were prepared publicly to confess their wrong-doing before the rest of the village congregation. There was no set form. During the 1890s, Welchman and other missionaries separately expanded this convention into a system of ecclesiastical law involving the formal sentence of excommunication for specific offences, by which baptized people were forbidden to attend church until public confession and absolution. On the islet of Rowa in the Banks group, William Kwasvarong, a deacon, started his own system of compulsory discipline. Each Saturday, all adults met at the church publicly to confess their occasions of ill-temper and other faults of the previous week, after which Kwasvarong meted out the appropriate penalties. "Strange to say," noted Wilson in surprise, "the people say they like it."[46] Edgell demanded not only exclusion from services for a set period, but also the provision of a bag of coconuts or its money equivalent (about five shillings) for church funds. In some places, public feeling against excommunicates ran so high that they were banished from their village until readmitted to church. "Christians are not to shake hands with them or eat with them," was Matthias Tarileo's rule for Pentecost, nor were they to attend their dances or to go into their houses or gardens; and if excommunicates died, they were to be buried as heathen.[47]

There was no uniform system of ecclesiastical discipline in the diocese until 1921, when during the first synod, all existing practice was codified into a common system of church law. No one objected that the method endorsed was discriminatory, for offending Europeans were not subject to formal discipline. It was also coercive, the avowed objective being to induce by public disgrace and social ostracism a sense of sin and shame. There were two grades of excommunication. The Lesser Excommunication, which suspended the offender from participation in all public services of the church, could be imposed by any priest, Melanesian or European, though a list of those "put out of church" in each district had to be reported to the bishop. It was the normal punishment for discovered adultery, fornication, theft, persistent failure to observe Sunday as a day of rest, marriage without a Christian service and religious behaviour that seemed to compromise a Christian profession—possession or use of "any harmful heathen charm", invocation of "heathen spirits" or reverence of "heathen powers or places". The most common reasons were adultery or remarriage after civil divorce. The length of sentence varied from a few weeks to two years, depending on the alleged seriousness of the offence. At the end of the set period, if the conduct and repentance of the sinner were judged to be satisfactory, he confessed; the excommunication was then publicly lifted and he was readmitted to church. The Greater Excommunication was reserved for "notorious evil livers" and could be pronounced by the bishop alone. It was seldom used.[48]

Missionary preoccupations were not wholly ecclesiastical. In their incursions into secular politics, the Anglicans uniquely combined the conviction of a religious establishment, that they had a moral responsibility for the whole of society, with the voice of conservative gentlemen who had no intention of sinking the British colonial boat. In Steward's view, the white missionary should be a mediator in the colonial order between governors and governed. Because their ministrations had made them more familiar with village society than transitory British officials, he claimed, missionaries were the "natural go-betweens", whose function was to uphold justice and prevent unnecessary friction by explaining to each party the views of the other with sympathy and without bias.[49]

When a nominated Advisory Council was set up in the British Solomons in 1921, Steward, as Lord Bishop of Melanesia, was automatically invited to take a seat as one of the four non-official members. Already he had criticized the Native Taxation Regulation of 1920, the only mission leader to do so. There was no explanation to the islanders of its purpose and limitations, he complained; no guarantee that the funds thus raised would be devoted to medical and other services, for the benefit of those who were being taxed. Yet it was only by such that the government would begin to dispel the distrust which its actions were arousing.

> We cannot shut our eyes to the fact that at present the native is very sceptical as to the disinterestedness of the White people who have come into these Islands, and although they are of too submissive a nature to shew by any violence their resentment of what they may consider injustice or oppression, none the less it is essential that they should be taught that at any rate the British Government has no ulterior motive in undertaking the Protectorate of their country.[50]

When a draft "Native Code" was put before the Advisory Council for discussion, Steward—as the only one of its members who even remotely understood its practical implications for Solomons villagers—led a successful attack on the more repressive clauses, such as the infliction of heavy fines for trivial breaches of regulations and the proposed prohibition of smoking and betel-chewing. In 1923, during the bishop's absence in England, four missionaries made an ultimately successful protest against a provision of the new Native Administration Regulation, which imposed fine or imprisonment on any (unemployed) islander absent from his home village for more than two months each year without written permission of his District Officer. It was an "un-British act of legislation", thundered Reginald Hodgson, first headmaster of Pawa school, "which makes one rather feel ashamed of one's nationality", and he persuaded the English Committee to take the matter up with the Colonial Office. In a similar vein, Anglican missionary support for legislation against adultery (enacted in 1924) was justified by the alleged demands of "native public opinion".[51]

The British Solomon Islands Protectorate in the 1920s was a repressive backwater of empire. Government officials regarded the place as a colonial "dead end" and even the High Commissioner, Sir Hunter Rodwell, confessed that he found the atmosphere "somewhat depressing".[52] On San Cristobal, Fox discovered, women were practising abortion because "they did not want their children to grow up in 'The White Man's Solomons' ".[53] The impression of maladministration appeared to be confirmed in October 1927, when the news emerged of the murder of W.R. Bell, the Malaita District Officer, with his party, while collecting the unpopular poll tax from conservative pagans at Kwaio. The English Committee leapt into action. On the motion of Sir Bickham Sweet-Escott, a vice-president and former High Commissioner of the Western Pacific, it recommended a "full enquiry" into the method of collecting and using the native tax and into the general administration of the protectorate. There was a "strong feeling" that the group should be elevated into a Crown Colony, independent of the High Commissioner in Fiji, as a means to more efficient government. This request "must come from the Solomon Islands, and especially from the Natives", naïvely urged the committee's secretary. "It would not be a difficult matter for the Bishop to get the Native Chiefs to send a petition to the King or the Imperial Govt." However, the campaign died when Steward objected, for he feared that the elected Legislative Council of a small Crown Colony would be dominated by "undesirable" whites whose commercial ambitions would override the interests of the islanders.[54]

Mediation between islanders and government excluded political confrontation. Unlike the vociferous Methodist chairman,

J.F. Goldie, the Anglicans were deeply reluctant to antagonize those in civil authority. Privately, the bishop might fume over the frequent incompetence of protectorate officialdom, but the language of communications was diplomatic, even obsequious. Clergy were likewise instructed to approach government officers with as much courtesy and tact as they could muster. Left-wing critics of imperialism who sought evidence of exploitation were given no ammunition: "The natives here are being well and carefully governed and looked after by an efficient Government who spares no pains to forward the welfare of the people."[55] Any tendency among Melanesians to regard government and mission as rival powers was always to be countered.

> Be very careful to give them no grounds for this idea. Try and explain to them that the Government really desires their well-being, and generally, act as a palliative rather than an irritant. Remember that, in the long run, the Government holds "all the high cards".[56]

Interpreting the actions of the government to Solomons village people thus usually meant little more than an exhortation to obey with "cheerful acceptance". That the truculent inhabitants of north Malaita accepted the poll tax without bloodshed has been attributed largely to the influence of Albert Mason, missionary at Fiu. By the 1930s, despite an official accusation that individual Anglicans, like other missionaries, were disseminating a "spirit of discontent" with government authority as a means of maintaining the loyalty of their followers, there were good grounds for the episcopal assertion that for nearly four decades the Melanesian Mission had done "a very great deal" to make the British administration "effective and acceptable to the native population".[57]

In the New Hebrides, where Britain did not rule alone, mission-government relations were less tranquil. Since the recognition of the group by an Anglo-French Convention in 1906 as a sphere of joint influence, the attitude of the Anglicans had become steadily more critical. In 1907, Wilson had been inclined to welcome the new Condominium administration as automatically preferable to the prospect of lawlessness, only to admit four years later that he was "greatly disappointed".[58] The anti-French Presbyterians, on the other hand, had no such high expectations, and when the two principal English-speaking missions joined forces in a concerted attack on the Condominium, as it was then constituted, the energy of the campaign was drawn mainly from the Presbyterian side.

Both organizations saw themselves in the highly moral role of champion of the voiceless New Hebrideans. Their spokesman protested against illegal grog-selling, enforced recruitment, plantation cruelty, fraudulent French land claims and the absence of bilingual officials and an effective machinery of justice. While British settlers were firmly subjected to the regulations by their national administration, it was "notorious" that French planters were, as a matter of French official policy, seldom inconvenienced by the strict demands of the law. Already the French settlers outnumbered the British by more than two to one (700 : 300) and they made no secret of their belief that it was the ultimate destiny of the New Hebrides to become part of France's colonial empire. "If the interests and power pass into the hands of the French," warned Charles Grunling, Anglican missionary at Omba, "judging by what one has heard and read, what hope is there for either native or missionary?"[59]

Both missions sought to secure the political changes they wanted by arousing public opinion outside the New Hebrides.[60] Prime Ministers and Cabinet ministers in Australia and New Zealand were lobbied by church representatives armed with examples of recruiting abuses, seeking public assurances that the New Hebrides would never be abandoned to the hell of French rule. In England, there were influential deputations representing the two missions and the Anti-Slavery Society to the Colonial Office (November 1911) and to the Foreign Office (June 1914). In the New Hebrides, there was a conference at Paama in June 1913 at which Presbyterian, Anglican and Churches of Christ representatives passed resolutions on the "deplorable" conditions under the Condominium and appealed to the "British people in all parts of the Empire" to demand either that the 1906 Convention be observed equally by both administrations or that the whole group be brought under the British flag.[61] Certainly, it was evidence supplied from mission sources that strengthened the hand of British delegates at a second Anglo-French conference on the New Hebrides held in mid-1914. The result was a series of amendments to the Convention, which removed some of the more obvious weaknesses, though the fundamental defects of divided authority, divergent purposes and inefficient administration remained.

During the post-war Peace Conference, as rumours circulated of imminent French annexation of the New Hebrides, there was another bout of mission-inspired agitation in Australia and New Zealand. But while Presbyterians still pressed for British rule, the Anglicans were vague. In 1920, the English Committee was urged by the Anti-Slavery Society to compile a memorial that could be presented to the League of Nations to justify the transference of the New Hebrides to the Mandates Commission. Nothing was done because Steward, who had no personal knowledge of conditions in the group, was reluctant to identify the Mission with any specific political solution; nor could the committee by itself collect sufficient up-to-date and unassailable evidence of maladministration to substantiate a decisive indictment. "I cannot say that we got much that is fresh from them," noted the Anti-Slavery secretary after a meeting with mission representatives.[62] Apart from priming a few sympathetic politicians to ask questions in Parliament on the perennial abuses, no one in England was quite clear what to aim for or how to go about it.[63]

The confusion surrounding the political future of the New Hebrides was not finally settled until 1922, when the revised Convention of 1914 was proclaimed. Thereafter, only the most optimistic of either nationality could envisage a practical alternative to the dual administration. Continued Presbyterian demands for transfer to British control received at best only nominal Anglican support.[64] Collectively, the Melanesian Mission saw its social role in the New Hebrides no longer as a political crusader, but as a rescue worker. What should the Church do?, asked Hopkins in 1926: "She can keep the question alive, report oppression and law-breaking, and from within do all she can to cheer the dejected souls of the dwindling brown folk."[65]

For the next fifteen years, Anglican representations on the administration of the New Hebrides assumed the character of a ritualized exchange in which every move was entirely predictable. Demands for further reform were not aggressive. "May I as a Cambridge man (a junior contemporary to yourself)", began a letter from Tempest to the Duke of Devonshire, Secretary of State for the Colonies

> ... appeal to you to interest yourself in a matter which though of small moment to the world at large is of vital importance to those of us who live in the New Hebrides and have the welfare of the native people at heart.[66]

In public statement and private correspondence, the Condominium system was attacked as a "lamentable failure", "weak and inefficient", a "disgrace", "obnoxious";[67] but protests were usually unspecific, easily dismissed by officials as typical missionary exaggerations based on a few incidents of the distant past. "The same alleged abuses have been going on as long as I can remember and the same protests by the Mission," sniffed a bored High Commission secretary.[68] Similarly, whenever complaints were submitted by missionaries to the British administration of irregular recruiting incidents—usually the recruitment of women by French planters without the consent of their husbands or relatives—no one had much confidence in the outcome of any investigation.[69] In the isolated Anglican islands of the northern New Hebrides, up to 500 kilometres from the capital at Vila, on Efate, a British official was seldom seen more than once a year. In some cases, the original complaint, based on inadequate hearsay, was found to be groundless; in other instances, the French Resident Commissioner or the Joint Court Prosecutor for some reason or other declined to act. "Your Reverence will well understand", wrote the Acting British Commissioner, G.A. Joy, to the Assistant Bishop, F.M. Molyneux, "that no advantage is to be gained by the presentation of alleged illegal acts to my Colleague, where the evidence is of such a nature that it is unlikely to produce any result ..."[70] On one celebrated occasion, at Lamalanga in August 1928, Molyneux took the law into his own hands; he boarded a French recruiting vessel to obtain the release of an illegally recruited woman and was beaten by a crew member in the process. British and French officials were mightily embarrassed, while the people of Pentecost were astounded that anyone should have presumed to strike a bishop.[71] It was an incident that symbolized the history of Anglican political intervention in the New Hebrides: a few sensational statements, protective gestures, but with very limited effect.

The Melanesian Mission and its overseas supporters were still haunted by the founder's sense of mission to the whole of northern Melanesia. In Anglican eyes, these islands were in a unique sense "ours", by long occupation, martyrdom and the labours of "great ancestors":

> What other people know these Islanders as we of the Melanesian Mission know them? Know them by tradition, know them by experience! What other body has such good machinery at hand for the conversion of these people?[72]

But in 1918, after seventy years of work, the Anglican mission was ingloriously outpaced by more recent arrivals and what it had was visibly stagnating. Melanesians were being converted to Christianity, but it was not to the faith of Selwyn and Patteson. With the ending of the war, and a vacancy in the see, everyone agreed that something had to be done. Many missionaries felt the diocese to be too large and unwieldy to be administered with efficiency or appropriate paternal care by one man. There was talk of dividing the existing diocese into two, three or four manageable portions, the whole work still to be called the Melanesian Mission. Steward himself advocated the early formation of an autonomous ecclesiastical province in the South Pacific, an "Oceanic Province" following ethnic and not political lines, embracing the subdivided diocese of Melanesia and the Fiji-based diocese of Polynesia (created in 1908), as essential for the future growth of Anglican influence in the region. However, this far-sighted but administratively unworkable scheme failed to gain the necessary support from the bishops of Australia and New Zealand, who suspected Steward of being not quite earthbound.[73]

There was much to be said for a well-publicized advance—a "great forward movement"—into populous territory, where quick results would revive both numbers and confidence. Success would breed success. Everything pointed to the northern Solomon Islands and the Bismarck Archipelago, formerly part of German New Guinea, which were brought under an Australian military administration in 1914, and from 1921 were governed by Australia as a "C"-class Mandate from the League of Nations. These islands offered a potentially "vast field for Christian work".[74] If the Melanesian Mission failed to seize the strategic opportunity presented by the political rearrangement of northern

Melanesia, the *Log* predicted darkly, it would "have to be content in future with a very inferior place among Missions".[75] Moreover, a northward extension of the Mission as far as New Guinea appealed to Anglican historic susceptibilities. G.A. Selwyn had certainly envisaged the possibility. After his Melanesian tour in 1892, Montgomery had urged the incorporation of the newly founded New Guinea Mission into an Anglican missionary chain stretching back to Norfolk Island, which would make the bishopric of Melanesia "one of the noblest and most inspiring posts in the world".[76]

The most fervent advocates of a "northern advance" were not to be found among the island staff of the Melanesian Mission, who were already spread thinly enough, but in England and Australia. The English Committee was encouraged by the unexpected windfall of a £33,000 legacy and undeterred by the ignominious failure of a Bishop Patteson Jubilee Memorial appeal in 1921, which asked English supporters for £25,000 for extension work and raised £1813. In Australia, where the acquisition of the former German possessions represented the fulfilment of a long-standing imperialist ambition, Anglican leaders spoke loftily of national responsibilities and the duty of the Commonwealth's largest church to fulfil its missionary obligations in the Pacific. The mandate system, it was declared, embodied the Christian principle of stewardship, but without church participation, the Australian trusteeship in New Guinea would be no more than an empty shell.

> ... we of the great Church of England must not shirk our responsibilities. The well-being of these people has been entrusted to our nation. Let us see that their spiritual welfare is not neglected by our National Church.[77]

Anglican leaders were easily moved by appeals to tradition, sacred obligation and national sentiment. The first official support for the principle of a new Melanesian diocese centred upon New Britain came in a resolution of the Australian Board of Missions in June 1919. In August 1919, a meeting of mission staff at Norfolk Island gave formal support to the idea of a bishop for the ex-German Solomons. In January 1920, the English Committee agreed to support a new northern diocese, provided that it remained within the Melanesian Mission. In July 1920, twenty-five bishops from the Australian and New Zealand church provinces, assembled in London for the Lambeth Conference, were called by the English Committee to a conference on "Pacific Missionary Problems". The conference was notable as the first co-ordinated attempt since 1850 to formulate a common Anglican missionary strategy for the South Pacific. Its weakness was that the Bishop of Melanesia, on whose diocese most of the discussion was centred, had not come to Lambeth. The bishops, supported by other church representatives, resolved that the time had come for the formation of a new diocese of the Melanesian Mission to include New Britain and the adjacent ex-German islands, whose "foundation, support and administration" should be the responsibility of the Australian church, working through the A.B.M., to be assisted by the English Committee.[78]

There followed eight years of leisurely negotiations, resolutions and inaction. The English Committee muttered restively about lost opportunities and the vagueness of A.B.M. policies and promises. No one apparently thought of founding a mission without a bishop at its head, for the idea that had been revolutionary in 1861, when Mackenzie had led his missionary band up the Zambesi, had by this time acquired the status of an Anglican orthodoxy. The A.B.M., embarrassed by an income that never kept pace with the demands of its primary fields in New Guinea and northern Australia, drew back from the formidable task of endowing a new missionary see from its own resources. Rather than found a separate diocese of the Mandated Territory, it was thought "expedient" for work there to be inaugurated by the existing diocese of Melanesia, whose territorial limits were conveniently undefined, under the local supervision of an assistant bishop. Australian recruits and contributions (£2000 per annum), which had hitherto been transmitted by the A.B.M. to "old Melanesia", would henceforward be assigned to the Mandated Territory, and no extra funds would be required. The "great forward movement" had become a mission on the cheap.

Under strong pressure to save the reputation of the A.B.M., Steward agreed in August 1925 to undertake personally the supervision of the proposed Australian Anglican mission in the Mandated Territory, and in November he visited Rabaul, to arrange with the administration for a suitable Anglican field.[79] By this time, the Methodists (arrived 1875) and Roman Catholics (1882) had extended their operations so widely that the only large area in the Bismarck Archipelago without a Christian mission was a 500-kilometre stretch of coastline in the Gasmata district, at the isolated south-western end of New Britain. This was accepted. In 1928, Canon E.N. Wilton of Bathurst, New South Wales, was chosen by the A.B.M. for appointment as Assistant Bishop of Melanesia, with the title of Northern Melanesia, to take charge of the new mission.

The early years of the much publicized "great adventure" were as inglorious as the prolonged inactivity that had preceded its birth. Since 1924, there had been an Anglican church in Rabaul, which was a jealously preserved religious centre of the colour-prejudiced white community. Wilton, whose qualifications for a senior missionary post were obscure, was clearly more attracted by the comforts of town life then the rigours of pioneering on the south coast. He wrote hopefully of extending the helping hand of the Church to the spiritually neglected planters around Rabaul:

> What is so little realised by those outside the actual sphere of missionary service is the paramount importance of giving for our own colour. Through the white man (a splendid fellow, for the most part, he is, too!) we shall in due time reach thousands of natives.[80]

In 1929, when he was compelled to resign following allegations of sexual misconduct ("utterly broken down in health", reported the church press),[81] the Anglican mission in the Mandated Territory comprised a parish clergyman in Rabaul and three inexperienced missionaries at the opposite end of the island, a schooner and no converts, 1000 kilometres from the Bishop of Melanesia's headquarters at Siota. Five years later the position was little different. No successor as bishop had yet been appointed, and the Administrator of the Territory of New Guinea was complaining that the Anglicans had been content to do no more than "scratch the ground".[82]

The Mandated Territory enterprise had come to grief because of two weaknesses inherent in Anglican missionary strategy: the fondness of bishops and senior churchmen for grandiose schemes that bore little relation to the likely supply of men and money, and the absence of the strong centralized machinery that alone could have enabled such a venture to draw upon the entire body of mission-conscious church-goers. During the 1920s, moreover, the financial supporting organization of the Melanesian Mission was at its weakest. Responsibility for policy and expenditure was vested in the bishop, who since 1919 had lived permanently in the islands, far away from bills and creditors, whereas income was administered separately by five unconnected and uncoordinated bodies: the New Zealand Anglican Board of Missions (set up by General Synod in 1922), the Melanesian Mission Trust Board, the reconstituted Australian Board of Missions (which in 1910 had absorbed Melanesia's separate fund-raising organization), an advisory committee of businessmen in Auckland and the English Committee.

Many churchmen thought it embarrassing that although the Melanesian missionary diocese was legally associated with the New Zealand ecclesiastical province—"the child of the New Zealand Church"—the mainstay of its financial support was not in Australasia but in England.[83] Until the 1930s, the English Committee supplied up to £14,000 annually, or more than half the Mission's total income, from individual and parish subscriptions and dividends from invested legacies. Legally, it was an independent society in its own right, beyond the control of the Bishop of Melanesia.

The organization of the Melanesian Mission English Committee was typical of many small Church of England missionary societies. Its four thousand listed subscribers were predominantly female and mostly from the south of England, from prosperous suburbs, watering-places and cathedral cities. During the 1920s, the committee was nominally headed by the Archbishop of Canterbury, who was president, and an array of vice-presidents with famous names from the Church, the Royal Navy and the Colonial Service.[84] The working head was the general secretary, A.E. Corner, a well-to-do clergyman, who managed the London office on a weekly visit from his home in Bournemouth. There was also a small children's organization, the Guild of Light-Hearts, whose special hymn contrasted the "Light-hearts" of happy Melanesian Christians with the "Dark-hearts" of pagans "wandering in fear".[85] Each year, in June, the English Committee held a public meeting in London, which was addressed in encouraging terms by missionaries on leave and men from public life. "I have been all my life, or for the greater part of it, interested in the Melanesian Mission," declaimed Archbishop Davidson in 1921. "Bishop Selwyn, his work and enterprise, were the inspiration of my own school days, and the murder of Bishop Patteson in the year when I took my degree at Oxford gave a new start to missionary thought and enterprise ..."[86] Popular reports in the church press were less restrained:

> They will be glad in Melanesia when they hear of what happened at the Church House in London on June 11 [1926] ... The bishops will tell the priests, and the priests will tell the natives; those shining, dark faces will glisten when they hear of the three great speeches that their friends made in the great capital of the little island in the North ...[87]

But what the English supporters lacked in knowledge of Melanesia, they made up in enthusiasm. Hundreds joined the Associates of Melanesia for a small annual subscription, or paid £10 each year towards the support of individual scholars, teachers and clergy, or joined sewing groups to make clothes for school pupils and cassocks and surplices for island churches. A Miss Emery of Leamington Spa composed a "Melanesian March" for organ or piano, royalties from which earned £151 for the general fund. The English edition of the *Southern Cross Log* carried private advertisements offering used postage stamps, weather cards, "Melanesian Mission Lotto" (a game for four to eight players), Persian kittens, home-made sweets and fresh-picked snowdrops in February: all proceeds to the Mission.

Goodwill and the proceeds of bazaars were insufficient to save the Melanesian Mission from financial confusion. In 1922, Steward took ill during a visit to England, underwent a series of operations for cancer and was absent from the diocese for more than two years. Expenditure consistently exceeded income, resulting in a running annual deficit of £6000. Accounting was inefficient. No one knew exactly how much was owing, and when an ill-paid clerk in the London office retired, it was found that he had embezzled £900 of mission funds in his last three years alone. There was no yearly budget and no limitation on orders for stores and equipment sent in by island missionaries, many of whom, it was complained, had "no idea of business whatever".[88] Steward himself was in the habit of "lending" large sums (a total of £2370) from his private income to pay outstanding bills or for extra projects dear to his heart.

New Zealand churchmen were estranged by rumours of Melanesian maladministration and extravagance.[89] In high places, the loss of confidence was so serious that in 1924, the primate, Archbishop Julius, took the unprecedented step of asking Steward to resign. Meanwhile, an inquiry commissioned by General Synod into the chaotic business operations of the Mission recommended the establishment of a Finance Board based in Auckland, with power to control its financial administration, though not its internal management. This was constituted in 1925, with high hopes that the crisis was at last solved.[90] By 1928, however, the debt was up to £7000 and Steward was complaining bitterly of the high-handed attitude of New Zealand church authorities towards the affairs of an independent diocese. Between bishop and Finance Board, there was a state of war.

When Steward resigned in August 1928, oppressed by administrative worries and in bad health, he was remembered with affection in Melanesia, but not in New Zealand. His successor, appointed by the New Zealand bishops after nomination by the Melanesian synod, was Frederick Merivale Molyneux, who had come from England in 1925 to be Assistant Bishop, with responsibility for the New Hebrides.

It was increasingly obvious that a principal reason for the Mission's notorious failure to live within its income was the huge expense of running a twenty-year-old steamship. For four months each year, the *Southern Cross* lay idle at Auckland. The two annual voyages, each of 14,000 kilometres were planned casually, following no natural geographical lines, according to the conflicting demands of school headmasters who wanted their boarding pupils returned and collected from widely scattered places. In the six years from 1918 to 1923, the ship cost £50,000 in wages, coal and maintenance, out of a total mission income of £112,000. "It cannot be too strongly stressed", reported the Finance Board in 1928, "that no marked economies of working the Mission are possible, other than in connection with the Mission steamer ..."[91]

Once again, the white staff divided, traditionalists versus

250   *God's Gentlemen*

Fredrick Merivale Molyneux (From the Melanesian Mission English Committee *Annual Report*, 1924)

modernizers. The steamship, which to the latter was an unjustifiable extravagance, was to Steward and a few others a loveable physical embodiment of the Mission's hallowed traditions and *lingai*. Since 1903, *Southern Cross V* had been known throughout the diocese as *akanina* ("our ship"), and as such it was a source of pride. Realism eventually triumphed over romance. In 1931, a staff conference decided in favour of two much smaller ships, one operating in the New Hebrides, the other (to keep the name *Southern Cross*) for the Solomons, with use of Burns, Philp & Co. steamers for connection between the two and for transport of stores from Sydney.

In the meantime had come the Depression. New Zealand subscriptions fell away markedly.[92] Debt, which had only just been extinguished by a special appeal, soared again, so that by 1931, the long-suffering Auckland merchants who supplied the Mission were again owed thousands of pounds in overdue accounts. In the islands, copra prices collapsed and revenue from school plantations and church collections shrank to nothing. Molyneux, shielded from poverty by his own comfortable background, proved to be a spendthrift, incapable of making economies. In mid-1931, following the example of governments and other missionary societies, the Finance Board demanded drastic retrenchments: reduction of missionary stipends and teachers' pay by 10 per cent, closure of the Pamua school and reduction of numbers at other central schools by one-third, cutting of orders and supplies, and no replacements for staff who resigned. In November 1931, Molyneux himself resigned. "Financial strain, owing to the diminished income, is doubtless the cause," announced a puzzled New Zealand missionary paper, with more kindness than truth, for the accusations of homosexuality, which were the real reason for the bishop's dramatic departure in a state of breakdown, were not widely known.[93] It was not an auspicious time to seek out a successor. If the Mission were not to be destroyed by maladministration, it was clear to all that no bishop should in future be appointed without an eye to his financial and organizing ability—practical qualities that had never before been considered as relevant. The days of gentleman adventurers and romantic visionaries were over.

NOTES AND REFERENCES

1. *M.M.R.*, 1919, pp. 9–11.
2. J.M. Steward, *John Steward's Memories*, ed. M.R. Newbolt, pp. 10, 79–110. For Cecil Wilson's comments, see Wilson, Diary, 8 October 1903, 16 October 1907, in possession of Mrs Qona Clifton. See also Charles E. Fox's vivid sketch, *Lord of the Southern Isles*, pp. 64–65; and Bishop G. Sharp to H. Newton, 18 May 1922, Anglican Archives, University

of Papua New Guinea Library, Port Moresby. The author owes this reference to Dr David Wetherell.
3. *S.C.L.E.*, July 1921, p. 90.
4. *S.C.L.*, March 1916, pp. 664-66; December 1919, p. 3; *A.B.M. Review* 10 (1919): 124-25.
5. *M.M.R.*, 1919, pp. 15-17; Melanesian Mission English Committee Minutes, 2 December 1919; *S.C.L.E.*, August 1922, p. 89. For Anglican and Protestant thinking on the relationship between "younger" and "older" churches, see *Report of the Jerusalem Meeting of the International Missionary Council, March 24th-April 8th, 1928* (London: Oxford University Press, 1928), vol. 3.
6. J.M. Steward, *The Primary Charge of the Right Reverend John M. Steward, Bishop of Melanesia*, pp. 3-4. Melanesian priests were then paid £10 annually; Europeans received between £100 and £120.
7. Alexander Don, comp., *Light in Dark Isles: A Jubilee Record and Study of the New Hebrides Mission of the Presbyterian Church of New Zealand* (Dunedin: Foreign Missions Committee, 1918), pp. 140-41.
8. D.L. Hilliard, "Protestant Missions in the Solomon Islands, 1849-1942" (Ph.D. thesis), pp. 338-40, 458-60; Hugh M. Laracy, *Marists and Melanesians*, pp. 89-91, 147, 159.
9. R.E. Tempest, "Melanesia, 1877-1919", p. 11, Melanesian Mission English Committee Office.
10. T.C. Cullwick in *S.C.L.*, January 1917, pp. 6-8.
11. J.M. Steward, *Hints on District Work*, p. 14.
12. R.E. Tempest, "Memories" p. 14, Melanesian Mission English Committee Office.
13. *S.C.L.E.*, August 1925, p. 123. See also his obituary in *S.C.L.*, July 1931, pp. 6-7; and Fox, *Lord of the Southern Isles*, p. 201. Personal communication, Geoffrey White, University of California, San Diego, 29 August, 1975.
14. Steward, *Hints*, p. 15; *S.C.L.E.*, January 1920, p. 15. Interview with Rev. D. Lloyd Francis, Hove, Sussex, September 1970.
15. *S.C.L.E.*, January, 1921, front cover; August 1922, p. 94.
16. David M. Paton, ed., *Reform of the Ministry: A Study in the Work of Roland Allen* (London: Lutterworth Press, 1968), pp. 89-90.
17. W.C. Groves, "Report on a Survey of Education in the British Solomon Islands Protectorate", sect. 1, p. 1; sect. 6, p. 7, Barr Smith Library. See also H.K. Colebatch, "Educational Policy and Political Development in Australian New Guinea", in *Melbourne Studies in Education, 1967*, ed. R.J.W. Selleck (Carlton: Melbourne University Press, 1968), pp. 103-16; D.J. Dickson, "Murray and Education: Policy in Papua, 1906-1941", *New Guinea* 4, no. 4 (December 1969-January 1970), pp. 15-40. On racial attitudes, see Amirah Inglis, *"Not a White Woman Safe": Sexual Anxiety and Politics in Port Moresby, 1920-1934* (Canberra: A.N.U. Press, 1974), ch. 1. There are, as yet, no comparable studies of the British Solomon Islands.
18. C. Wilson to H.H. Montgomery, 16 January 1895, Wilson-Montgomery Correspondence, U.S.P.G. Archives; William Sinker, "In the Islands of

Melanesia: A Sailor's Testimony", *The East and the West* 12 (1914): 188-89; R.P. Wilson in *S.C.L.E.*, August 1918, pp. 93-95.
19. Florence Coombe, *School-days in Norfolk Island*, p. 37; Durrad in *S.C.L.*, April 1916, p. 21; Drummond in *S.C.L.*, March 1909, p. 149.
20. R. Godfrey to G.A. Joy, 23 January 1930, W.P.A., file no. N.H. 85/1930.
21. *S.C.L.*, July 1936, p. 40.
22. A.I. Hopkins, Autobiography, p. 203, Church of Melanesia Archives.
23. D.C. Horton, *The Happy Isles: A Diary of the Solomons* (London: Heinemann, 1965), p. 28.
24. Charles E. Fox, *Kakamora*, p. 45, and generally ch. 4. For an educationalist's assessment, see W.C. Groves, Report on All Hallow's Training College, Pawa, enclosure in Groves to Acting Resident Commissioner, 6 November 1939, W.P.A., file no. W.P.H.C. 2736/1939.
25. Eugene Stock, "Thirty Years' Work in the Non-Christian World ... 1872 to 1902', *The East and the West* 1 (1903): 455; W.N. Gunson, "Victorian Christianity in the South Seas: A Survey", *Journal of Religious History* 8 (1974-75): 193-94. See also World Missionary Conference, 1910, *Report of Commission III*, ch. 8.
26. The differing attitudes of missionaries in Papua towards industrial training are discussed by D.F. Wetherell, "Christian Missions in Eastern New Guinea: A Study of European, South Sea Island and Papuan Influences, 1877-1942" (Ph.D. thesis), ch. 9.
27. Welchman's views on industrial training are expounded in *S.C.L.*, March 1906, pp. 9-12; April 1906, pp. 11-12; May 1906, pp. 11-12; June 1906, pp. 4-7; August 1906, p. 35; September 1906, pp. 47-48.
28. *S.C.L.E.*, May 1925, p. 69.
29. Edward Jacomb, *The Future of the Kanaka*, pp. 143, 148-50.
30. A.I. Hopkins, ed., *Melanesia To-day*, pp. 96-107; Clifford W. Collinson, *Life and Laughter 'midst the Cannibals* (London: Hurst & Blackett, 1926), ch. 7; *S.C.L.*, October 1927, p. 27; Woodford Papers, bundle 18, 2/50, Department of Pacific and Southeast Asian History, A.N.U.
31. *S.C.L.*, June 1946, pp. 22-23.
32. For contemporary accounts, see Margaret Lycett, *Brothers*; J.M. Steward, *"The Brothers", Melanesian Mission*; and *John Steward's Memories*, ed. Newbolt, pp. 111-22.
33. Lycett, *Brothers*, p. 24.
34. *S.C.L.*, January 1936, p. 15.
35. See Fox's accounts: *S.C.L.*, June 1946, pp. 21-24; *Kakamora*, ch. 8; "Companions and Brothers", *Melanesian Messenger*, January 1964, pp. 27-29; and *The Melanesian Brotherhood*.
36. Raymond Firth, *Rank and Religion in Tikopia*, p. 342; Ben Bani, "Early Days with the Heathen on Raga", *Melanesian Messenger*, Easter 1965, pp. 18-20.
37. Henry Welchman, Diary, 11 August 1905, Melanesian Mission English Committee Office.
38. *M.M.R.*, 1907, p. 11.
39. Kenneth Gregory, *Stretching Out Continually: A History of the New*

Zealand Church Missionary Society, 1892–1972 (Christchurch: N.Z.C.M.S., 1972), pp. 21–22.
40. See, generally: E.R. Morgan, ed., *Essays Catholic and Missionary* (London: S.P.C.K., 1928); Stacy Waddy, "The Oxford Movement in the Empire and in the Mission Field", in *Northern Catholicism: Centenary Studies in the Oxford and Parallel Movements*, eds. N.P. Williams and Charles Harris (London: S.P.C.K., 1933), pp. 117–29.
41. *S.C.L.*, May 1912, p. 343, For an account of the Anglo-Catholic revival of ritual in English churches, see Owen Chadwick, *The Victorian Church*, pt. 2, pp. 308–25, 347–58.
42. *S.C.L.*, April 1917, p. 19. The worship at Maravovo is described by Fox, *Lord of the Southern Isles*, pp. 234–35.
43. Melanesian Mission, *The Faith of the Church*, p. 17.
44. J.M. Steward, *A Melanesian Use, together with Notes on Ceremonial*; *S.C.L.*, October 1926, pp. 23–24. For example, the English Committee did not think it "advisable" to associate itself publicly with the 1926 Anglo-Catholic Congress, though invited to do so.
45. On the Sisters of the Cross, see Melanesian Mission, *The Community of the Cross*; Sister Margaret of the Cross, Autobiography, 1887–1966, microfilm, Pacific Manscripts Bureau, A.N.U.; Sister M. Gwen [Shaw], *God, Truth and Thirteen (A Conversion Story)*, (Melbourne: Australian Catholic Truth Society, 1956); Laracy, *Marists*, pp. 162–63. Their educational work at Bungana received praise from W.C. Groves in his 1939 survey of Solomons education, "Report on a Survey of Education in the British Solomon Islands Protectorate", sect. 3, p. 5; sect. 5, p. 3. For an Anglican reaction to their secession, see Fox to Durrad, 14 and 28 August 1950, in Introduction to C.E. Fox, "A Missionary in Melanesia", Durrad Papers, Alexander Turnbull Library.
46. *S.C.L.E.*, January 1908, p. 187.
47. *S.C.L.*, April 1917, p. 15.
48. Melanesian Mission, *Report of the Fourth Conference of the Melanesian Mission and of the First Synod of the Missionary Diocese of Melanesia*, pp. 21–25. This system of public penance was heavily revised in the 1960s, and the terms "putting out of church" and "lesser excommunication" were explicitly forbidden.
49. *S.C.L.E.*, November 1921, p. 5; Melanesian Mission, *A Handbook of the Melanesian Mission* (1926), p. 5.
50. J.M. Steward to Acting Resident Commissioner, 18 February 1921, W.P.A., file no. W.P.H.C. 2049/1921.
51. *A.B.M. Review* 15 (1923): 9, 82; Melanesian Mission English Committee Minutes, 20 June 1923, 15 November 1923; W.P.A., file nos. W.P.H.C. 2929A/1920, 1448/1922, 190/1923.
52. S.G.C. Knibbs, *The Savage Solomons as they were & are* (London: Seeley, Service, 1929), p. 19; Report of Sir Hunter Rodwell on his visit to the Solomons and New Hebrides, W.P.A., file no. W.P.H.C. 2787/1920.
53. Charles E. Fox, "The Church of Melanesia", *East and West Review* 28 (1962): 39.

54. Melanesian Mission English Committee Minutes, 25 October 1927, 24 January 1928; A.E. Corner to Major H.S.N. Robinson, 1 November 1927, A.E. Corner to R.E. Tempest, 15 February 1928, New Zealand Office Letterbooks, Church of Melanesia Archives. On the Bell murder, see Report of Lieut.-Colonel Sir H.C. Moorhouse, in Great Britain, *Parliamentary Papers*, vol. 5, 1928-29, [C.3248], and the forthcoming study by Professor Roger Keesing of the A.N.U. and Dr Peter Corris.
55. D.E. Graves to J.B. Steel, League against Imperialism, 17 September 1931, W.P.A., file no. W.P.H.C. 1701/1932.
56. Steward, *Hints*, p. 12.
57. J.C. Barley, Memorandum on mission influence in the Solomons, 24 November 1933, W.P.A., file no. W.P.H.C. 3808/1933; W.H. Baddeley to F.N. Ashley, 4 November 1933, W.P.H.C. 1876/1933.
58. *S.C.L.E.*, June 1908, p. 267; December 1908, p. 370; *S.C.L.*, January 1912, p. 271. For the political background, see Edward Jacomb, *France and England in the New Hebrides: The Anglo-French Condominium* (Melbourne: George Robertson, 1914); Linden A. Mander, "The New Hebrides Condominium: 1906 to the Present", *Pacific Historical Review* 13 (1944): 151-67; Deryck Scarr, *Fragments of Empire*, ch. 8.
59. *M.M.R.*, 1911, p. 50.
60. For accounts of the missions' campaign against the Condominium, see Charles W. Forman, "Missionaries and Colonialism: The Case of the New Hebrides in the Twentieth Century", *Journal of Church and State* 14 (1972): 81-88; G.S. Parsonson, "La Mission Presbytérienne des Nouvelles-Hébrides: Son Histoire et son Role Politique et Social", *Journal de la Société des Océanistes* 12 (1956): 133-36; Roger C. Thompson, "Australian Imperialism and the New Hebrides, 1862-1922" (Ph.D. thesis), pp. 546-632. For expressions of Anglican opinion, see, e.g., *Sydney Morning Herald*, 27 July 1911; *A.B.M. Review* 4 (1913): 152, 202-3; Melanesian Mission English Committee Minutes, 28 November 1911, 23 January 1912, 21 January 1914.
61. William Gunn, *The Gospel in Futuna: With Chapters on the Islands of the New Hebrides, the People, their Customs, Religious Beliefs, etc.* (London: Hodder & Stoughton, 1914), pp. 299-308.
62. Secretary of Anti-Slavery Society to Edward Jacomb, 8 January 1921, British and Foreign Anti-Slavery and Aborigines Protection Society Papers, G.397, Rhodes House Library.
63. Great Britain, *Parliamentary Debates* (Commons), 5th series, vol. 136 (1920): 80-81, 1787-88.
64. E.g., Report of delegation to Colonial Office, 5 December 1922, W.P.A., file no. W.P.H.C. 305/1923 Confidential; *A.B.M. Review* 15 (1924): 166; Melanesian Mission English Committee Minutes, 9 May 1928.
65. A.I. Hopkins, "The Call from the South Seas", *The East and the West* 24 (1926): 217.
66. R.E. Tempest to Duke of Devonshire, 10 February 1923, W.P.A., file no. W.P.H.C. 2028/1923 Confidential.
67. E.g., Bishop Molyneux in *S.C.L.*, July 1927, p. 21; R.E. Tempest, Paper on the New Hebrides Condominium, W.P.A., file no. W.P.H.C.

1362/1925; R. de Voil, "Slavery in the New Hebrides", W.P.H.C. 2604/1931.
68. Minute by H. Vaskess, 19 September 1925, on Tempest's paper, ibid.
69. See the cases in W.P.A., file nos. N.H. 27/1924, 95/1924, 155/1924, 289/1927, 361/1930, 439/1930, 196/1934, 234/1934, 129/1936, 228/1938, W.P.H.C. 3731/1930.
70. Joy to Molyneux, 26 October 1927, W.P.A., file no. N.H. 289/1927.
71. W.P.A., file no. W.P.H.C. 3686/1928.
72. W.G. Ivens in *S.C.L.* August 1906, p. 34.
73. *S.C.L.*, December 1919, pp. 3-4; July 1921, pp. 3-4; *M.M.R.*, 1919, pp. 11-12; *John Steward's Memories*, ed. Newbolt, pp. 19-21; [L.B. Radford], Bishop of Goulburn, *Missionary Problems of the Western Pacific*. As a half-way measure, however, the New Zealand General Synod in 1922 empowered the bishops of its associated missionary dioceses to appoint one or more assistant bishops.
74. Melanesian Mission English Committee Minutes, 8 January 1919; Melanesian Mission English Committee, *Memorandum on the Future of the Melanesian Mission*.
75. *S.C.L.*, February 1920, p. 4.
76. *M.M.R. & I.V.*, 1892, p. 20.
77. *A.B.M. Review* 15 (1928): 4.
78. *S.C.L.E.*, September 1920, pp. 119-20. For other resolutions, see *A.B.M. Review* 10 (1919): 60; Melanesian Mission English Committee Minutes, 8 January 1919, 2 December 1919, 27 January 1920; *S.C.L.E.*, November 1922, pp. 126-29; December 1922, pp. 137-38.
79. A.B.M. Minutes, 14-15 June 1922, 19-20 August 1925, A.B.M. Archives; Melanesian Mission English Committee, *Annual Report*, 1925, pp. 8-9.
80. *A.B.M. Review* 15 (1929): 228.
81. *A.B.M. Review* 16 (1929): 93. Interview with H.W. Bullen, Auckland, January 1969.
82. W.H. Baddeley to Chairman, A.B.M., 27 August 1934, Mandated Territory Papers, Church of Melanesia Archives.
83. *Church Gazette* 63, no. 1 (January 1933): 8. The precise nature of the relationship of the missionary dioceses of Melanesia and Polynesia with the New Zealand General Synod, and the matters on which their voices should be heard, was the subject of legal debate and special inquiry during these years; see Church of the Province of New Zealand, *Proceedings of General Synod*, 1922, pp. 94-97; 1928, pp. 4-10; 1931, pp. 162-69; 1934, pp. 252-53.
84. In 1924, the president of the English Committee was the Archbishop of Canterbury. Vice-presidents included the Archbishop of York and five other bishops, the headmaster of Eton, C.M. Woodford and Sir Bickham Sweet-Escott. The seventeen-man executive committee, chaired by Bishop Harmer of Rochester, included two other diocesan bishops and Admiral Sir Wilmot Fawkes.
85. The opening verse ran:
    Isles of sunshine! Isles of darkness!
    Far away they lie,

       Scattered o'er the Southern Ocean,
       'Neath the tropic sky;
       There God's Melanesian children
       Live, and grow, and die.
    S.C.L., January 1928, pp. 20-21.
86. *S.C.L.E.*, July 1921, p. 81. Woodford addressed the English Committee's London meeting in 1916; his successor as Resident Commissioner of the British Solomon Islands, Charles Workman, spoke in 1921. The Eton Association's time-honoured St. Barnabas' Day meeting at Eton College was suspended during the First World War, as the "old supply of visitors was dying out". The last Melanesian Mission meeting at Eton was held in June 1920.
87. Undated newspaper report [London, 1926], newspaper cuttings book, in possession of Rev. D. Lloyd Francis.
88. Melanesian Mission English Committee Minutes, 27 February 1923, 15 January 1929; Corner to Robinson, 11 September 1929, New Zealand Office Letterbooks.
89. See correspondence between Steward and Archbishop Averill, Selwyn Papers, folder 6, Auckland Institute and Museum Library; undated note, Bishop's Correspondence, New Zealand Office Letterbooks.
90. Church of the Province of New Zealand, *Proceedings of General Synod,* 1925, pp. 3-4, 47-53. The Finance Board was dissolved by General Synod in 1934.
91. "Melanesian Mission: Report of Commission appointed by Standing Committee of General Synod ... 1923", Church of the Province of New Zealand Records, 7/4, National Archives of New Zealand; Report of Melanesian Mission Finance Board, in Church of the Province of New Zealand, *Proceedings of General Synod,* 1928, pp. 221-35.
92. Income from New Zealand parishes, channelled through the Anglican Board of Missions, was £8500 in the financial year 1928-29, £7000 in 1931-32, £6000 in 1932-33.
93. *Reaper* 9, no. 11 (December 1931): 5; Major H.S.N. Robinson to D.E. Graves, 27 November 1931, Assistant Bishop J.H. Dickinson to Robinson, 3 December 1931, New Zealand Office Letterbooks. Interview with Rev. W.F. Browning, Greatworth, Oxfordshire, November 1970.

9
"The Redemption of the Whole Man"

In the 1930s, the prevailing mood of English-speaking Protestant missions was less dogmatic, more earth-centred than it had been in 1900. In the major churches of Great Britain and the United States, it was the late summer of pre-Barthian liberal theology, whose followers rejected exclusive claims to final truth as spiritual arrogance and who sought to apply a "social gospel" to build a kingdom of God on earth. True Christianity did not belong to the church sanctuary, they said; it was a world-bettering programme of action that should embrace the whole of life. In relation to the great non-Christian religions, there was new talk of the possibility of co-operation in a common search for complete truth and to combat materialistic secularism.[1] At the same time, among ordinary church-goers, there was widespread though seldom explicit support for the proposition that "all religions are just as good", with the corollary that conventional missions to the heathen were unnecessary, "one of the frills of the Church".[2] To refute such objections, and reflecting the theological preoccupations of the day, many missionary apologists stressed the social utility of Christian expansion into non-Western societies. Christianity, they claimed, was the only basis for a moral and social transformation, which alone could prevent demoralizing disintegration under the impact of materialistic Western civilization.

In the South Seas, one of the earliest exponents of the "modern missionary outlook" was John Wear Burton. When he joined the Methodist Indian mission in Fiji in 1902, he was impelled not by a desire to save the heathen from eternal damnation, but by the "unhappy condition of people who, ignorant of the good news, were living without the joy and happiness that Christ alone could give"—a view for which he was publicly castigated by the veteran Presbyterian missionary John G. Paton, for presuming to preach a "lukewarm Gospel". Thirty years later, however, when Burton had become general secretary of the Australian Methodist missionary organization, Paton's stark vision of eternity had "dropped right out of missionary thinking and expression" in all but the most conservative Evangelical circles.[3]

A semi-official expression of the missionary mind of the Church of England was the *World Call* series of study books, the final volume of which, in 1928, included a restatement of the missionary task in which social reform was placed equal in importance to the salvation of souls:

> ... the Christianizing of the world involves the creation of sanitary conditions, of an educational system, of social, economic, and political welfare, in which life and life abounding may come to its full personal and corporate development; that salvation involves not the saving of men's souls alone, but the bringing of the whole human race in every aspect of its existence into conformity with the will of God; that nothing less than full physical, artistic, intellectual, moral, and spiritual "godliness" is necessary if we are all to attain to the measure of the stature of the fullness of Christ.[4]

As already demonstrated in the abortive plans for industrial work earlier in the 'twenties, a missionary strategy that exalted social, economic and political change was not one that assimilated easily with the entrenched ethos of the Melanesian Mission. No Anglican station in the Solomons, for example, rivalled the Methodist headquarters at Roviana or the Seventh-day Adventist at Batuna as show-places of mission-inspired progress. The goal of the Mission was a spiritual one, affirmed Hopkins in 1927: "the salvation of Melanesia from within, a long, slow, patient task, by means of a native Christianity". "No great material future can be predicted," he added; though it was possible to hope for the evolution of a village-centred "native civilization" suited to the Melanesian climate and social environment.[5]

The official outlook of the Mission did not change until the end of 1932, when Walter Baddeley arrived at Siota as seventh bishop. As before, it had not been easy to find an episcopal candidate for Melanesia. Under a new system of appointment, imposed by the New Zealand General Synod in 1922, the wishes of the Mission's clergy were represented by a delegation that conferred with the New Zealand bishops, whose direct say in

Walter Hubert Baddeley
(Permission New Zealand Anglican Board of Missions)

the appointment was increased. In May 1932, the Archdeacon of Colombo, N.C. Christopherson, who was known to some of the English missionaries, had been nominated in Melanesia, only to be vetoed in New Zealand. At a meeting in Wellington with the two delegates from Melanesia, the bishops offered the see to Fox, who declined, then by cable to Baddeley, the successful vicar of a large artisan parish in industrial Yorkshire, who accepted.[6]

In personality, Baddeley shared many traits with George Augustus Selwyn. He was autocratic, brisk, self-assured, "the very picture of health", with an unsentimental, hearty manner, which impressed men of affairs. "He is full of 'go' and keeps all who come in contact with him, cheerful and care-free," commented an Australian missionary after their first meeting.[7] Like his immediate predecessors in Melanesia, Baddeley was a moderate Anglo-Catholic, but the Christian supernaturalism, which had been central to Steward, was overshadowed by his belief in "redemption of the whole man". "For my part," he said, "I don't think the Christian Gospel is primarily concerned with the life hereafter. I think the Christian Gospel is profoundly concerned with men's lives here and now."[8] His aggressive approach to missionary work is well illustrated by the sermons he delivered while on a visitation of school villages in Guadalcanal in 1935, during which he advised his hearers to remember that they were called to be workers for God in His church; that churches, villages and persons must be kept "clean and neat"; that "they must stand up for their Catholic Heritage, and resist to the utmost unwanted sects who try to intrude in our villages".[9]

Baddeley placed a high premium on publicity at home, and in special articles, sermons, platform addresses and radio broadcasts he spelt out a "here-and-now" justification for the Mission's existence.[10] Its goal was a regenerated Melanesia of "strong peoples", "better Melanesians", resistant to alien diseases, social decay and Western secularism. To churchmen who thirsted for news of social progress amongst savages, or who followed Bishop de Witt Batty of Newcastle in seeing vigorous Christian churches in New Guinea and the Pacific Islands as a "rampart for Christ" blocking the future southward advance of atheistic Bolshevism, Baddeley's forward-looking propaganda was satisfying and reassuring.[11] Anglican schools in Melanesia, he declared, were proudly producing an English-speaking élite for training in Fiji or New Guinea in agriculture, wireless and village medicine, to "serve their own people". A few might go further afield for higher education, one day to take a share in the government of their own islands ("Why should they not?"): "Maybe the time will come when, in my little Sussex vicarage ... I shall be able to put up, during his vacs. from Oxford, one of our Maravovo–Pawa lads. That's not impossible."[12] For the largest mission in the region, however, the actual numbers involved were small enough. By 1941, about a dozen former pupils of Pawa school had been sent beyond the Solomons by the protectorate government for specialized training, most of them to Suva to qualify as Native Medical Practitioners.

The "whole of life" to be ensouled included political life. This was one non-religious area in which the Melanesian Mission was no stranger, with the difference that whereas Steward had talked of mediation, it was characteristic that Baddeley should stress the need for partnership and co-operation between government and mission. During his episcopate, English church and British administration in the Solomons were linked more closely than ever before. He was a high-ranking Freemason, active in the Tulagi lodge, possessed a distinguished war record (as a combatant officer, decorated D.S.O., M.C. and Bar) and enjoyed the company of planters and officials. At the biennial sessions of the Advisory Council, his contributions to discussion and voting were rarely distinguishable from his non-official colleagues, and by 1940, when he became the recognized spokesman for the non-officials, his acceptability to all parties was assured. In public, the alliance was secure. In "no part of Melanesia", said Baddeley in 1936, "is there justification for an opinion often popularly held that missions and governments are hostile one to the other".[13]

Working relations between Anglican mission and protectorate government during the 1930s were never ruptured, though sometimes strained. Common to each episode of conflict was the resistance of missionaries to any externally imposed regulation that threatened their influence over their Melanesian adherents, against attempts by government officials to demonstrate the supremacy of secular authority. In 1933, for example, there was a noisy clash when the Acting Resident Commissioner, by means of a clumsy Native Passes Regulation, sought to prevent all missionary access to the unevangelized Polynesian outliers of Rennell and Bellona. The stated intentions of the administration were humanitarian—to protect the hitherto isolated islanders from the likelihood of devastating infectious diseases. In the eyes of Baddeley, however, the move was a bureaucratic, rationalist-inspired attempt to curtail the propagation of Christian truth, and he led a successful protest to the High Commissioner with a much-quoted telegram grandly signed "Melanesia": "Sorry to conflict but Christ's Kingdom recognizes no boundaries. Moreover Letters Patent included Rennell in Melanesia's Mandate."[14]

Likewise, in the cause of mission independence, Baddeley resisted plans for a government-supervised education scheme for the Solomons. In 1931, the Resident Commissioner, F.N. Ashley, had put forward a proposal that mission schools under a trained European teacher should be eligible for small grants-in-aid, together with remission of senior pupils' poll taxes, provided that they followed a prescribed academic curriculum, were open to official inspection and complied with other specified conditions. For the next seven years, while the scheme was under discussion, the Anglicans remained strongly opposed—as did the Marists and the S.S.E.M. (The small Seventh-day Adventist mission was alone in favour; the Methodist response was ambiguous.) The government grants would be on too small a scale, Baddeley told Ashley, "to make it worth while surrendering our present freedom".[15] Moreover, among missionaries who had long been accustomed to being the sole controllers of education in their own districts, government regulations or government schools were to be feared as vehicles for anti-Christian secularism. For whereas religious teaching was central to mission schooling at every level, to the government secular subjects were paramount.

> To neglect the primacy of the spiritual side of human nature and to concentrate on man's intellectual and social elements is to tend to the creation of a race of "clever devils" to whom God is fiction or at best unnecessary.[16]

They were theocratic assumptions, which in the post-war years produced strong Anglican opposition to successive efforts by the administration to introduce a unified education scheme for the whole protectorate.

There were differences of principle, too, in the area of marriage. Whereas the Church of England taught that Christian marriage was indissoluble, the Solomons government sanctioned civil divorce (a legal provision that both Wood and Steward had objected to, as a source of "confusion" to simple people[17]), and for years it refused to recognize the legal validity of marriages performed by indigenous clergy or teachers. Legally, Melanesians could be married only by "native custom", by a registered European minister or by a civil celebrant. In most Anglican villages, where a service of blessing by a local teacher or clergyman followed the customary presentation of bride price ("native custom"), the government's marriage regulations posed no difficulty. On Santa Isabel, however, there was a unique problem. This was because the giving of bride price had ceased in Welchman's time, to be replaced solely by a blessing of the marriage in church. Virtually every marriage therefore fell into no permissible category, and despite the fact that the Santa Isabel people considered themselves validly married, their unions were in fact extra-legal, unrecognized by the administration or its courts for sanctioning divorce or punishing adultery. It was a Gilbertian situation, much relished by visitors to the protectorate, in which an entire island of church-going Anglicans was in the eyes of the law "living in sin". One solution, first put forward by Steward, was to include within the definition of native custom that form of marriage that had been conducted on Santa Isabel for the previous thirty years by native clergymen; however, this was rejected by High Commission lawyers as contrary to their own definition of custom as "a thing of slow growth" and indigenous origin. The sole feasible alternative was the registration of Santa Isabel priests as marriage officers. Officials initially rejected the proposal as "novel and undesirable", but as a last resort it was reluctantly agreed to in 1938.[18]

Meanwhile, there were signs of a warmer attitude towards the white population of the Solomons. Personal relations between Anglican missionaries and individual settlers had usually been cordial, especially in isolated places, always assuming the English clerical preference for employees of the big firms, who were thought to be "fair to the natives" and "not hostile" to the Mission, over the majority of small independent traders and planters.[19] But there had been little instinctive sympathy between the assumptions and objectives of secular business and the village-oriented vision of the churchmen. Plantation life "does the native no good", was Hopkins' hostile verdict.

> He earns money that he does not need, to buy goods that he is better without, and does not learn to like work, though he likes, of course, getting and spending money. He would be much better learning to do more work in his own village under his village chief.[20]

Others deplored the racist ethos of island commerce:

> A trader does not look at the native as does the Missionary. To the former they are "hands" rather than a collection of individual personalities. They are "niggers" who are useful for work and nothing else. He looks on them with almost a feeling of contempt; much as he may try to disguise it.[21]

It was also objected that plantations were effectively closed to religious influence, for a Christian teacher was not wanted unless he was also a recruited labourer, taking services and school in the evenings.

The two worlds thus rarely overlapped. Anglican missionaries as a group showed little apparent interest in those issues that aroused the passions of the white commercial community of the Solomons during the 'twenties and 'thirties—the charges of government extravagance and unfair competition from Chinese traders, the demands for imported labour and for elective representation on a new Legislative Council, resentment against "Tulagi-ism" (as the symbol of bureaucratic centralism) and the condescending behaviour of English officials towards Australian-born settlers.[22]

For their part, most planters and traders had been openly sceptical about the practical value of missionary work. That the missions were "spoiling the natives" was a perennial allegation: "It is often the small amount of real knowledge half-gained at some Mission School, which induces these natives to swelled heads."[23] Missionaries of the Melanesian Mission in particular —men of liberal education, who should know better—were thought to be wasting their time among "those utterly hopeless Melanesians". Few settlers or officials were willing church-goers, and whenever English services were held at Tulagi, recalled an officiant, "if you had a dozen you were doing well".[24] A plan to appoint a permanent chaplain for the five hundred European residents came to nothing. The "primary duty" of the Mission was to the Melanesians, reported Steward when tackled by the S.P.G. on the subject of "Our Own People Overseas", and in any case, the whites had "never shewn any startling desire to be ministered to".[25]

Baddeley, by contrast, actively cultivated good relations with the traders and planters. In his first annual report, he paid tribute to the Resident Commissioner, the managers of Levers, and Burns, Philp & Co., and the white population in general, regretting that the Melanesian Mission had hitherto failed to realize its "responsibilities" towards them. He collected money for a handsome church at Tulagi—as "the shopwindow of the Solomons"—and when in the neighbourhood, he conducted English services there himself.[26]

The public identification of the Melanesian Mission with the British political and commercial presence in the Solomon Islands reached its peak during the Pacific war. In December 1941, the Japanese armed forces bombed Pearl Harbour and commenced their rapid advance into South-east Asia. At the end of January 1942, they had captured Rabaul and were preparing to seize the British Solomons, as a further step towards the invasion of Australia and New Zealand. At Tulagi, a Japanese bombing attack was rumoured to be imminent. Everywhere in the protectorate, there was confusion as the European community made a hasty evacuation in overcrowded boats. Planters abandoned their plantations, the S.S.E.M., Methodist and Adventist missions withdrew most of their staff, while the Solomon Islanders who witnessed the white man's panic were officially reported to be "rather nervous".[27] "Unless the Govt. do something to show that they still function there will be trouble all along the coast," Fox noted in his diary. "The people think there is now no Govt."[28] It was at this point of crisis, relates a popular war history published by the British government, that the Resident Commissioner, W. S. Marchant, visited the new Anglican headquarters station at Taroaniara, Nggela, "to see his friend the Bishop of Melanesia. He needed advice."[29] As the Solomons Islands were almost totally undefended against invasion, resistance was useless: was the protectorate government therefore to retreat altogether before the Japanese army? Baddeley, the former colonel, was adamant that the administration should not withdraw: "My own mind is made up. I am staying in the Solomons." Marchant was thus fortified in his decision to remain; and he moved his headquarters to Malaita when the Japanese bombed, and in May occupied, Tulagi. But after the American victories of 1943, it was Baddeley who was to receive the principal credit for having "inspired" the tattered government not to abdicate its imperial responsibilities: "I think if our Bishop had not taken a stand and refused to go, everyone would have gone ... We were very thankful, because it did lend stability and kept the British flag flying."[30] Both church and state had "every reason to feel proud" of the Bishop of Melanesia, announced the *Southern Cross Log* in 1947, when Baddeley resigned and returned to England to become Suffragan Bishop of Whitby.[31]

A general concern for the temporal interests of the Melanesians seemed naturally to imply a commitment to their physical health. Medical missions as such had first become part of Protestant missionary strategy in the 1840s, much of the initial impetus having come from Scottish Presbyterians associated with the Edinburgh Medical Missionary Society. By the early 1900s, when there were some five hundred mission hospitals and a thousand dispensaries, the combination of preaching with medicine was widely hailed as an "integral and essential" part of Christian missionary enterprise, a demonstration of the "gospel in action" and—because cures often led to conversions—a proven agency of evangelism.[32]

In the Melanesian Mission, little was done during the nineteenth century. It throws light on the tradition of amateur doctoring favoured by the Anglicans to read John Selwyn's advice to a Cambridge lecture audience in 1896. Although it was a counsel of perfection that every mission should have its own trained medical man, he said, for uncivilized peoples who knew no better there was no need for professional treatment.

> There is great virtue in Epsom Salts administered with no niggard hand; Castor Oil, poured out of the bottle into the mouth, can hurt no one; Cockle's Pills, Painkiller, are potent remedies. And, above all, nursing and hot water are unknown quantities in most wild lands.[33]

Medical missions as such had "no place" in Melanesia, insisted Ivens in his *Hints to Missionaries* (1907), despite the example of the Presbyterians, who by this time ran three hospitals in the New Hebrides.[34] At length, in 1913, a small hospital in memory of Welchman was opened on mission-owned land at Maravovo. As it was the first permanent hospital in the Solomons, the range of cases it treated was wide: gunshot wounds, crocodile bites, leprosy, malaria, measles, dysentery, elephantiasis and eye diseases. The choice of site, however, was an unsuitable one, isolated from the largest concentrations of population and without an all-weather anchorage. In 1916, when the two nurses married and the doctor recruited for war service, the hospital was closed. For the next ten years, there was talk of reopening it elsewhere as the Mission's "first duty", but without adequate funds or trained medical staff nothing could be done.[35]

Meanwhile, sensitive men were perturbed by evidence that suggested that population decline, though not confined to Christian islands, could in some places be correlated with the advance of Christianity. In three districts of north Malaita, for example, where population changes were watched carefully over two years (1920-22), the Christian communities had an excess of thirty-one deaths over births, whereas in neighbouring pagan villages there were ten more births than deaths.[36] Although the total reason was unclear, the fact that school villages of every mission were generally larger than pagan settlements, often built on low-lying and therefore less healthy sites near the shore, was almost certainly a contributary cause. It was also true that those who came down from the interior bush to join Christian villages included a high proportion of the old and infirm, who were attracted by the prospect of a less strenuous life on the coast. "Every ship seemed to bring some germ or other," observed Ellen Wilson, the sister of R.P. Wilson. *Southern Cross V* in particular was notorious for spreading influenza.[37] Anthropologists and medical experts blamed the adoption of unsuitable and unhygienic European dress by Christian converts as a common cause of disease, for it was not until the 1920s that elaborate clothing was universally condemned by missionaries as an "evil custom".

It was obvious that little was to be expected of the inferior (two-doctor) medical department of the Solomon Islands administration. A growing number of missionaries of all denominations were therefore attracted by the idea that the Church itself had a "duty" to play a "fundamental" part in the battle against Melanesian depopulation.[38] The first mission hospital of this period was opened by the Methodists at Roviana in 1927. A Seventh-day Adventist hospital was established in 1938, also in the western Solomons. Plans for a new Anglican hospital took shape in 1928, following the arrival of a young Cambridge medical graduate, L.M. Maybury, who had volunteered for work in Melanesia. The protectorate government promised an annual subsidy of £200, together with a free supply of certain drugs, on condition that patients of all religious beliefs received equal treatment.[39] Building commenced at a new site, in north Malaita, at Fauambu. But there was more than a touch of incompetence about the hospital project, first demonstrated by the spending of £2000 given by an English lady benefactor for foundation expenses on elaborate houses for the doctor and nurses, whereas the actual hospital wards were found to be of "unsubstantial and insanitary" native construction. The imbalance was corrected by an embarrassed Finance Board only after the angry donor threatened press publicity and legal action for misapplication of funds.[40]

Baddeley's approach to medical work was more positive, more aggressive, than that of any previous bishop. It was an "absolute necessity", more effective than any pulpit: "How are we to preach the Love of God to folk whose bodies are covered with yaws, or have limbs partially eaten away with horrible sores, or whose desire to live has been sapped by fever, leprosy or tuberculosis?"[41] Medical facilities were diversified. To combat the high (one in four) infantile death-rate, he encouraged a "mothercraft school", begun in 1938 at Siota, where a dozen or more girls were instructed in Western techniques of nursing and mothercraft, in order to teach others in their home villages.[42] A few nurses went on village rounds from temporary medical-aid posts. Hospital services were extended under European nursing sisters to Omba (at Lolowai), Uki and New Britain.

To supply money and buildings was not enough. Everything at Fauambu depended on the calibre of a single doctor, and with three changes of direction within the first seven years, there was no continuity of policy. A leprosarium begun by Maybury was found to be beyond the Mission's inadequate resources and was closed in 1933, to be reopened on a smaller scale in 1938. For some years, moreover, the hospital made small impact on the surrounding area. Nurses (mainly New Zealand-trained) were energetic and resourceful, but some were prone to scold village people within reach for being utterly callous to their children, lazy and dirty—"but we do our best to train them".[43] The inhabitants of the surrounding Kwara'ae district, attached to their own well-tested remedies, were reluctant to entrust themselves to in-patient treatment and feared the violation of customary taboos. When a woman first gave birth at the hospital, instead of withdrawing from the community into seclusion, there was an uproar among pagans employed there, and because of the strong opposition of the local people, it was not possible to begin the training of young women as nurses until 1941. Nor did the medical staff always receive the gratitude that they were inclined to think was their due. When a hospital superintendent exhorted a Malaitan Christian to help his own people because the Mission had helped him, the reply was unexpectedly blunt:

> We did not ask you to come. You came because you wanted to, and not because we wanted you to come. As for you, you come here to give us medicine. You get paid for doing it. It is just your job.[44]

The protectorate government also had misgivings. When the medical programmes of the Seventh-day Adventist, Methodist and Anglican missions visibly outpaced their own lack-lustre efforts, officials were quick to spot opportunism or threats to government prestige in any request for financial aid. A contribution of any kind to Christian medical work, commented the senior medical officer, "allows of their diverting more of their own resources to the narrower field of evangelism". Ashley regretted that the practice of subsidizing mission hospitals had ever begun. Under such a scheme, he complained, the administration was looked upon as a mere chemist's shop, and he was opposed to "any recognition that the Mission Societies are undertaking work which places us under an obligation to assist them".[45]

Nevertheless, by 1940, largely as a result of the various mission-sponsored medical services, the people of the New Hebrides and Solomons had access to Western medicine to a greater degree than ever before. In places within reach of a hospital or a dispensary, there had been a slow but perceptible rise in the general level of health. In the northern New Hebrides, for example, it was said to be rare to see children covered with sores, which had been a commonplace sight twenty years earlier.[46] Yaws were fast disappearing as the result of regular mass injections inaugurated in the late 'twenties by teams from the Rockefeller Assisted Yaws Campaign and carried on by government and mission agents. There was no more talk of inevitable population decline. Yet many problems remained unsolved. The gulf between institutionalized Western medicine and village life was unbridged. Preventive measures were hardly thought of; maternal and infant mortality remained high; and in Anglican Santa Isabel, there was no regular medical work at all.

During the 1930s, the ethos of the Melanesian Mission under-

Melanesian Mission Headquarters station at Siota, Nggela, c. 1935
(Permission: New Zealand Anglican Board of Missions)

went an observable change. There was a new social consciousness, but at the same time there were fewer opportunities than before for close relations between Europeans and Melanesians. This was partly a consequence of a staff conference decision in 1931 to resolve the long-standing language debate, by replacing Mota with English as the language of instruction in the Solomon Islands central schools. In addition, as more Melanesian clergy were ordained for village pastoral work, white missionaries came to be employed almost exclusively at central schools and colleges. New recruits found themselves appointed to English-speaking institutions, where they were permanently engaged in teaching, medical and administrative duties and seldom travelled far afield. With no incentive to master even one Melanesian language, a growing number of missionaries thus lost the possibility of intimate contact with indigenous teachers and clergy who themselves spoke Mota, but knew little or no English. Reflecting this decline in missionary knowledge of local languages, vernacular translations printed by the mission press at Maravovo during the 'thirties declined in both scope and quality.

In the early 1900s, the Melanesian Mission had an exaggerated reputation among traders for being "very wrong-headed, insisting on the horrible doctrine of equality of races and putting their doctrine into practice".[47] It was not an accusation that would have come easily thirty years later. Anglican stations were better equipped than before, but more separated from the village society around them. Married couples were replacing the itinerating bachelor missionaries of the previous generation. The typical missionary residence of the 'thirties was a self-conscious European outpost, with house-girls, schoolboy servants and a closely observed routine for work and leisure, to which Melanesians were rarely admitted as equals. One Australian headmaster corresponded regularly with 108 different people at home, his wife with 67. Anglo-Saxon exclusiveness, as experienced at Siota by one Melanesian clergyman, was not confined to the episcopal headquarters.

> When an English priest goes to see the Bishop he finds him perhaps standing at the top of the stairs of his verandah, and as soon as the Bishop sees him he says, "Come in, old chap, and have a cup of tea." But if I, or another Melanesian priest, goes to see him he stands at the top of the stairs and says, "Well, what have you come here for?"[48]

The racial division was accentuated on *Southern Cross VII*, which arrived, with a new captain, in 1933 (*Southern Cross VI* having been wrecked in the New Hebrides on its maiden voyage in October 1932).[49] On this vessel, the time-honoured custom of European and Melanesian clergy eating meals together in brotherly unity was discontinued, allegedly because the growing number of Melanesians eligible made it too expensive. To dine with the bishop on board was a special privilege, no longer to be taken for granted. Voyages were more hurried than previously, so that the ship rarely stayed more than a few hours, or overnight at most, in any one place. On an episcopal visit to Mota in 1936, for example, five new churches were dedicated at different places within forty-eight hours.

The new spirit was partly a reflection of Baddeley himself. He was broad in his sympathies, efficient in business (financial chaos was a thing of the past), but without first-hand experience of Melanesian village life.[50] His grasp of the old *lingua franca* was very limited. "I talk to him in English which he does not understand," commented an elderly Nggela priest, "and he to me in Mota which I don't understand."[51] A five-day episcopal tour to bush villages in New Britain in 1938 had an entourage of twenty porters to carry beds, food and utensils, and when it came to the hourly rest, "woe betide the boy who was not at hand with a deckchair when the Bishop wanted to sit down".[52]

The same contradiction was evident in his readiness to ordain large numbers of Melanesian clergy as the basis for a "native church" (there were 28 indigenous priests and deacons in 1932, 49 in 1936, 81 in 1947), while at the same time refusing to delegate power.[53] He called no synods or diocesan conferences. Melanesians thus lost their sole opportunity of formally participating in the government of their own church, while Europeans chafed under the reversion to episcopal autocracy and looked back to Steward's golden days, when their voice had been listened to. Encounters between itinerating bishop and resentful subordinates became notorious as occasions for rancorous disputes. "I thanked God to see the last of him & the ship," R.P. Fallowes confided to his diary after one such exchange. "What a Bishop! What a Ship! What a diocese!"[54]

Guardians of the Mission's traditional ethos disappeared from the scene. It was no secret that Baddeley wanted a new European staff around him. Veteran missionaries—"Old Melanesians" they called themselves—who were venerated for length of service and their affection for the old ways, were encouraged to resign, to make way for more pliable men. Graves went in 1933, after 19 years; Godfrey and Tempest in 1935 (17 and 18 years respectively); Warren in 1938 (25 years) and Mason in 1941 (27 years). Of the seventy missionaries who arrived in Melanesia in the 1930s, the proportion of women—most of them trained nurses—increased, while the number of university graduates declined. Apart from the bishops, only four clergymen with university degrees joined the mission staff betwen 1929 and 1942. Almost half of the new recruits were New Zealanders. Their social background was more homogeneous than their English-born predecessors and their missionary assumptions were generally less idealistic, less tradition-conscious.[55] Fox, himself a New Zealander and the last of those on the old staff who had taught at Norfolk Island, privately voiced his regret at the changed face of the Mission:

> In Melanesia I am rather the ghost of a past generation; noone of our time is left; ... the old traditions are largely unknown to the present white staff. There was a great break—a new Bishop, a new ship, a new Captain all at once. And Norfolk Island gone, and then Mota gone from the schools. Only the Melanesians are the same.

Charles Elliot Fox, c. 1950 (Permission: Provincial Secretary, Church of Melanesia)

> Still, that is something after all. It is the "Inina" ["we" inclusive] feeling that is lacking.[56]

A comparison of Anglican statistics for 1934 with those for 1918 (for none are available for the intervening years) shows that the largest numerical gains had been recorded in Pentecost, Santa Cruz, the Reef Islands, Tikopia, Santa Isabel and north Malaita. The rate of growth increased. There were 14,000 baptized

Anglican Melanesians in 1918, 29,000 in 1934 and an estimated 35,000 in 1942. Within the borders of the British Solomon Islands Protectorate (1931 population: 93,415) the Melanesian Mission was still the largest mission, claiming some 22,000 baptized members in 1942, compared with 15,000 adherents of the S.S.E.M., 14,000 baptized Roman Catholics, 9000 Methodists and 4300 Seventh-day Adventists.[57]

Church growth was aided by four factors that had not been present a generation earlier. Since the mid-1920s, *Pax Britannica* had been established over the whole of the Solomons, which meant an end to pagan persecution of Christian minorities. There were more senior mission schools to supply teachers, a new supply of indigenous evangelists in the Brothers and a slight overall increase in population numbers.

By the 1930s, missionaries were confident that the Melanesian islands would soon be totally Christianized, the question being not so much "When?" as "By whose agency?" Evangelists of four denominations had their eyes on Malaita, where there was a pagan population estimated at 30 000. "Christianity is like an epidemic; there is no escape from it," a bush chief told a group of Brothers; "We are like fish in a net," lamented another.[58] Pagan attitudes were in fact more varied. H.I. Hogbin, who was doing anthropological research at Malu'u in 1934, believed that Christianity no longer had the prestige that it had enjoyed thirty years before as the religion of the conquering European: "But now the natives know us better this is not so, and I had the impression that some of the younger men have a feeling of revulsion from it and are building up a more tenacious loyalty to their old faith."[59]

On the other hand, under colonial rule there was a new incentive for pagans to accept Christianity as the bearer of Western education. Although older men, as evangelists discovered, usually wished to continue with the religion of their ancestors, a growing number were prepared to allow their own children to attend a mission school, knowing that they would eventually succumb to Christianity in the process. The reasons were invariably practical. Only at a school could children learn the ways of the white men, in order to be able to meet them on a more equal footing. There was a specific desire to learn English, for to be able to read and write it made one eligible for higher wages as a trader's clerk or storeman, instead of working as an unskilled plantation labourer. Literacy was also seen in religious terms as a key to the mystery of unlimited European wealth. "You white men are like us," Hogbin was told by a young Guadalcanal pagan.

> ... How are you different? Because you can read books. That is why you can buy axes, knives, clothing, ships and motor-cars ... You do not have to work hard; you pay us a little money and we work for you, carrying heavy boxes on our backs ... If we could read your books we would have money and possessions.[60]

As there were no government schools in either the Solomons or the New Hebrides, mission schools were the only places where young Melanesians could acquire even the most rudimentary education. "The native is desperately keen on learning to read and write," reported the Guadalcanal District Officer in 1934, "but some resent being forced to join a mission body in order to attain their object."[61]

As paganism became a minority religion, converts were increasingly drawn to Christianity through their daily contacts with an expanding Christian community that loudly proclaimed its moral and religious superiority. This may be illustrated from the experience of the Polynesian society of Tikopia, where the advance of Anglican Christianity and the decline of the pagan religious system has been studied over a generation with magisterial scholarship by Raymond Firth.[62] There was no other mission on the isolated island, south-east of Santa Cruz.

At the time of Firth's first visit to Tikopia in 1929, half the population—643 out of 1300—was either baptized or attended church, mainly as a consequence of the conversion five years earlier of a chief, the Ariki Tafua, who had been followed by the people of his district. In 1939, the number of Christians had grown to 911; in 1952, there were 1540 Christians and 210 pagans, and four years later, the traditional religion was abandoned altogether. Conversions, as observed by Firth, were undertaken for a variety of reasons. These included the expectation of economic benefit, the anticipation by some ambitious men of superior status in the Christian congregation, intellectual persuasion, the pressure from mission teachers who were outsiders and from within by social superiors. During the transition period, many converts, facing a radical change in religious allegiance, reported disturbing dreams in which they were confronted by traditional gods or symbolic figures of the new religion. Young people in particular were attracted by the corporate activities of the Church: daily religious services, singing, festival celebrations and "a general sense of 'belonging' to a wide organization reaching out beyond Tikopia and the Solomons to the lands of the Europeans".[63] The Mission also provided the sole pathway by which selected boys could proceed to English schooling at Pawa. The bishop, with his air of authority and elaborate robes for confirmations and other services, was held in great respect as an *ariki* (chief) of the highest rank.

Buoyed up by the assurance of external support, the Christians —led by a Mota Lava-born priest, Ellison Tergatok—were aggressive. The pagans, by contrast, were on the defensive, compelled to rely on their own resources. Despite a fair degree of mutual accommodation in everyday relations, there was a constant pressure on the diminishing band of pagans to conform to the majority religion of the island. Christians launched drives to bring in those outside the fold and badgered their pagan relatives to be baptized. In both communities, the view was expressed that religious division was socially harmful, a possible reason for natural disasters. It was to this persistent external pressure that Tikopia paganism finally succumbed.

The ill-conceived Mandated Territory mission seemed to defy all attempts at revival. When Baddeley arrived in Melanesia, the stations on New Britain were virtually moribund, and despairing missionaries in the Solomons had urged total withdrawal. Baddeley refused to accept the advice. There was a need, he maintained, to continue ministrations to the white people of Rabaul (a geographical parish misleadingly described by its clergyman as "the biggest in the world"), while the pagan south coast of New Britain would provide a future outlet for the missionary zeal of "old Melanesia".[64] The spectacular discovery of "new tribes" in the New Guinea Highlands in 1933 was further hailed as a "challenge" to the Melanesian Mission to take its due share in their evangelization as an imperial responsibility. Both aims were frustrated in 1936, when the Mandated Territory administration applied an existing immigration regulation, insisting on the withdrawal of all "foreign" teachers hitherto brought in from the British Solomon Islands.[65] In a vigorous round of episcopal protest to Rabaul and Canberra, Baddeley claimed that the regulation was "contrary to British justice", for no such restrictions were placed upon the entry of European "foreign" missionaries from France and Germany. He received only the minor concession that a few "local natives" could be removed to the Solomons for training. Unlike the established Methodist and Roman Catholic missions on New Britain, therefore, the Anglicans had no convenient source of evangelists and were compelled to rely on hastily trained first-generation converts. Teachers and schools had initially been promised to all coastal villages within reach, but without external reinforcements none could be provided. "Now—having got so far—we cannot very well withdraw," it was lamented, "but we are handicapped for want of teachers to put down in villages which we visit."[66] The Melanesian Mission lost what prestige it had, and the gaps were filled by a newly arrived and better-equipped mission of the Sacred Heart Fathers.

Reports from New Britain nevertheless told of "splendid" progress and forward movements. Baddeley strengthened the European organization by placing the region under the charge of an archdeacon with extensive powers, and new recruits from England and Australia were sent to staff six small stations scattered along the Arawe coast between Gasmata and Sag Sag. The first few converts were baptized in 1933. In Rabaul, however, where services were strictly segregated and thinly attended, the church atmosphere was described as wholly "depressing".

> I blush with shame at the blank contradiction of all our teaching, and for my boys to see but three whites, and but four natives, conscious of their C. of E. & Catholic privileges, or even duties. I *hope* Rabaul goes a long, long way away, with its Godlessness & vice; frivolity and snobbery ...[67]

Geographical isolation produced further difficulties. Communications between Rabaul and the south-coast stations were irregular and expensive, and each annual visit of the *Southern Cross* from the Solomons cost an extra £750. An admission by Baddeley in 1938 that the Anglican work in New Britain would henceforth be intensive rather than extensive, contained a tacit confession of failure: "The more I see of the Mandated Territory the more sad I am that it was not possible for the church in Australia to go in in reasonable strength in the early days of the Mandate."[68] In 1940, when three stations were vacant, therefore not functioning as teaching centres, reports were circulating in Australian church circles of the "practical abandonment" by the Melanesian Mission of its work in the northern archdeaconry. During the Japanese occupation from 1942 to 1944, one of the two remaining missionaries, John Barge, was captured and beheaded by Japanese soldiers, and the other, Bernard Moore, died of privation. After the war, what was left of the Mandated Territory mission was handed over without regret to the Australian missionary diocese of New Guinea.[69]

In the decade before the Pacific war, it became a commonplace observation that the Solomon Islands were undergoing rapid social changes. As early as 1927, Fox wrote of a "New Solomons" coming to birth in the wake of government control and the suppression of fighting: "The murder of Bell marks the end of the old and the beginning of the new era."[70] "It is not generally recognised with what speed the native is 'growing up'," reported a District Officer from Guadalcanal in 1934, without enthusiasm, "but I can observe great changes in the short space of six years since I first came to this district. The native is thinking for himself and is critical alike of government and mission."[71]

In the New Georgia group, there was a striking demand for Sydney mail-order catalogues, New South Wales lottery tickets, clothing and bicycles. Among the people of Nggela, a District Officer recognized a deep-rooted "retaliatory" feeling of "Melanesia for the Melanesians".[72]

It was one thing to detect new attitudes and aspirations, quite another to know how best to meet them. For the Melanesian Mission, this was nowhere more apparent than on Santa Isabel, which was lauded by publicists as an Anglican Zion, peopled by descendants of converted head-hunters: a model Christian island of clean villages, finely decorated churches, with inlaid pearl-shell furniture and ornaments, and an esteemed native clergy who carried on Welchman's methods of strict discipline and constant visitation. Beneath the placid surface, however, there was growing a current of frustration and disenchantment. The Anglican mission had introduced a new religious faith, a new social order based upon the ideology of peace, new occasions for festivities on holy days and a new leadership of priests and deacons. On the other hand, it had done little to introduce the Santa Isabel people to secular knowledge that would be useful outside the mission context or that would assist their material prosperity. By the 1930s, the level of teaching in village schools was admitted to be much lower than in the days of Welchman. The first generation of teachers, who had received systematic instruction in Scripture at Norfolk Island or from "the Doctor" at Mara na Tambu, were dying out, and many of their successors had received no special training for teaching. The school classes they held for an hour or two each day struggled on without a formal syllabus, without supervision and without incentives to improve. Attendance was irregular. Teaching materials had been the same for forty years, confined to alphabet charts, slates, translations of the New Testament and the Book of Common Prayer, and a few other printed religious works in the Mota and Bugotu languages. The establishment of a few district boarding-schools in the late 1930s to prepare older boys for Maravovo and Pawa suffered equally from a lack of external co-ordination and encouragement. The schools and teachers of Santa Isabel were "negligible as educational influences outside the religious field", reported W.C. Groves in 1939, during an official investigation of education in the protectorate.

> They are mostly inadequately trained for the conduct of even the very elementary teaching required of them; and they do not, in fact, carry out even this rudimentary school work conscientiously or on any regular plan. The schooling situation in the villages is one of stalemate if not of retrogression.[73]

The situation was not unique to Santa Isabel, but it was in sharp contrast with the eagerness of its people to achieve the benefits of a Western-style standard of living. The rich natural resources of the island in coconuts and trochus-shell (purchased by Chinese trading vessels) had for fifty years made it possible for coastal-dwellers to become keen traders. Accordingly, there was little inducement for young men to take employment as plantation labourers, either in Queensland or within the

Solomons. In 1908, Welchman had regretted that the inhabitants of one off-shore island were "too busy making copra or searching for bêche-de-mer for sale, to take the trouble to build canoes".[74] By the 1930s, Western goods were no longer luxuries but necessities; metal kitchen utensils had virtually replaced native manufactures, small launches were supplanting canoes and there was a rising demand for tinned food. By 1937, there were fifty-two native-owned trading stores on the island. Church collections were invariably the highest in the diocese—£471 in 1926, when copra prices were high.

Open dissatisfaction with the existing order surfaced in 1931, when the touring High Commissioner, Sir Murchison Fletcher, was petitioned by the headmen of Bugotu—men of "intelligent appearance and shrewd observations"—to establish a government school (under European supervision), which would teach English, carpentry, elementary marine engineering and other modernizing skills.[75] This appeal to the government was especially significant, for Santa Isabel had been the scene of tension between the representatives of religious and secular authority ever since the establishment of a government station on the island in 1918. Successive District Officers had resented the influence in day-to-day affairs exerted by Hugo Hembala and other native clergy, who in turn had scorned the government's headmen as usurpers of power—"mission outcasts, people of evil reputation or white man's pimps".[76] Wilfred Fowler, appointed District Officer in 1930, had sought to restore the balance: to have the government recognized by the Santa Isabel people as the "fount of progress" and its supremacy asserted over every aspect of native life.[77] He encouraged the petition for a government school and convened several meetings to discuss the question, but nothing was done.

Fowler's missionary contemporary was Richard Fallowes, a young Englishman, Cambridge-educated, who had come to the Solomons in 1929 from a curacy in South London. He was inexperienced, paternalistic—"a white chief" with his "flock of brown children"—and fired with a grand vision of an Anglo-Catholic Melanesian society.[78] As a means of strengthening the discipline of the Santa Isabel church, he instituted in 1931 the office of "church chief" (or churchwarden) in each village. These

Richard Prince Fallowes, c. 1929 (Permission the Reverend R.P. Fallowes)

vunagi kiloau were elected by the people, then commissioned by the local priest to report cases of "immorality" and to superintend the material affairs of the church. A Melanesian constable complained to Fowler that in some villages the new division of authority had produced confusion: "Some say mission headman is number one in the place and some say Government headman is number one ... People are asking who is boss—King George or Archbishop?"[79] It is significant that cricket matches were held at the government headquarters between church and police elevens.

Fallowes left the Mission in 1935, after a severe mental breakdown. In 1938, he returned to Santa Isabel independently (unlicensed by the bishop), where he encouraged the island's leading men to hold a mass meeting or "parliament" to discuss common needs and grievances, which could then be submitted to the Resident Commissioner. His motivation was religious.

Convinced that the protectorate government was unjustly neglecting the welfare of its Melanesian subjects in favour of the white commercial community, he maintained that it was his duty as a priest to engage in political activities in the cause of a just society, the Kingdom of God on earth.[80]

The first such "parliament" was held on Santa Isabel at the beginning of 1939, and others followed on Savo in April and on Nggela in June. Anglican teachers, "church chiefs" and clergy —led by Ben Hageria and Stephen Talu on Santa Isabel and by George Gilandi on San Cristobal (himself an important village leader from Bugotu)—took a prominent part in the proceedings. Numbers and enthusiasm grew rapidly, for there had been nothing like it since the last great assemblies of the Nggela *vaukolu* thirty years earlier. At Fallowes' suggestion, parliamentary procedure was adopted to regulate debate, with an elected "speaker" and an elaborately carved wooden chair. The latter was given "an almost superstitious reverence", so catching the imagination of supporters that the movement came to be known as "Chair and Rule".

The discussions at these meetings gathered up the discontents and frustrated aspirations of the people of the central Solomons: their lack of economic and educational opportunities and the failure of both British government and Church of England mission, despite taxes and church collections over many years, to give them the means of achieving that economic, political and social equality with Europeans that, they believed, had been the intention of "the leading people in England".

> In the year 1702 [sic] Queen Anne began two societies in England (1) S.P.C.K. (2) S.P.G. to carry out the commands of Jesus ...
>
> In the year 1820 [sic] Bishop Selwyn commenced the commandments of Jesus and the law Queen Anne had laid down in England and taught and instructed the heathen of New Zealand called Maoris. After 50 years they were allowed equality with white men in regards to wages and prices ...
>
> In the year 1801 [sic] Bishop Selwyn and Bishop Patteson promised to minister like that among the heathen of Melanesia following the words of Jesus; and the law of Queen Anne which she had laid down to the people of England, to teach them the Way of Jesus, and to instruct them about work and wages, and after 50 years to give them equality with whites in the matter of wages and prices ...

We have only been taught the Gospel, but nothing yet about trade
and commerce. We have been Christianised for 78 years now. The
Church people are anxious for collections, and the [Government]
for taxes, but where is the money? Here in the Islands wages and
prices are very small, not enough for taxes and church collections.[81]

The islanders' demands therefore included a general increase in plantation wage rates (from 5d. a working day, or £6.10.4d. a year, to 9/2½d. a working day and £155 a year), an increase in the price paid for village-produced copra and shell, the establishment of a government technical school, dispensaries staffed by native medical practitioners throughout the islands and the redress of specific administrative grievances.

As the news of Fallowes and his "parliament" spread further afield, as far as San Cristobal, with inevitable exaggeration, the heads of both church and state united in opposition. Government officers ridiculed the islanders' demands as absurd and impracticable—"a distorted Utopia"—and attacked the movement as subversive to established government and good order.[82] Among the white staff of the Melanesian Mission, Steward's vision of the missionary as mediator was almost forgotten. With the exception of Fox, none of Fallowes' former European colleagues sympathized with his aim of creating a permanent assembly to represent indigenous viewpoints. Only a few months previously, Baddeley had stated in a Sydney radio broadcast that he was looking "forward to the day when Melanesians will be able to take their part in the government of the islands".[83] Back in the Solomons, however, he was embarrassed by the presence of a clerical activist outside his jurisdiction and accepted without hesitation the government's negative verdict on the movement. To Fallowes' supporters he became the symbol of white hostility:

Clergy and teachers, chiefs and people belonging to the Solomon
Islands have said together, "we follow Fallowes. Whoever is foolish
shall follow the Bishop and Hipkin [H.S. Hipkin, a missionary]
who desire to blind our eyes and shut our ears, and want us different
from the people of England ..."[84]

At this point, Sir Harry Luke, the High Commissioner, arrived in the Solomons on his first official visit. A few days after the Nggela assembly, Fallowes was summoned to his presence at Tulagi, lectured like an errant schoolboy for his "dangerous and irresponsible" meddling in politics and deported from the protectorate by the next steamer. Among his former supporters, however, Fallowes was still held in honour. For many months afterwards, stories were in circulation that the King was about to send him back to the Solomons by special aeroplane to raise the price of copra. In the post-war years, when the powerful proto-nationalist movement, Marching Rule, spread from Malaita to Nggela and Santa Isabel, his name and teachings were popularly associated with it.[85]

C.S. Belshaw, a District Officer who later turned anthropologist, described the Fallowes movement as a "primitive, abortive manifestation, constituting no danger to the government, not warranting repressive measures, and even capable of beneficial results had it been handled by enlightened administrators".[86] He could also have included Baddeley and other missionaries in his indictment, for their uncomprehending opposition.

That the Fallowes movement passed without mention in any mission publication was due partly to embarrassment, partly to a belief among Europeans that the whole affair was analogous to an adolescent rebellion and as such best forgotten. The same incomprehension and secrecy surrounded the "Danielites"—a prophetic movement that flourished on Pentecost during the same period.[87]

North Pentecost (Raga), like Santa Isabel, had a reputation as one of the strongest districts in the Mission, more like an established parish than a missionary district. The last pagans were baptized in the 1920s. By 1930, there were 45 school villages, 80 teachers and 4 native-born clergy, led by Matthias Tarileo. The only resident Anglican missionaries were women, based at the Lamalanga station, where they held regular classes for women and girls of the district.

The Danielites took their name from a village teacher named Daniel Tambe—"the Prophet"—who at Easter 1931, after Lenten prayer, announced that he had heard a voice from heaven: "The island of Raga [is] still with its custom." There were two groups of people on the island, he proclaimed: "the one group belongs to Jesus and the other group belongs to Satan". To him had come God's personal call to purify the church. Justified by divine direction and by his own study of the Bible, he proceeded to launch an attack on the continued practice of Kava-drinking, night dancing and *sukwe* rites, which were carried on in Anglican villages despite years of missionary-imposed prohibitions. He denounced bride price ("Marriage is free according to what Adam and Eve had shown us in the beginning. We must obey this."), infant baptism ("He must know the meaning of what we call 'born again'.") and the eating of pigs ("the Holy Spirit ... told him that the evil spirit has given power to the pigs"). Christians should study the Bible, attend school and plant coconuts.

Daniel's prophecies were an important ingredient in his success. He predicted that in the future there would be a war and that Simeon Langlangmele, a Pentecost priest, would go away from his home village for many years, before returning there to die—both predictions eventually being fulfilled. There was a guarantee of Anglican paramountcy: the Roman Catholics and every other church would one day be absorbed into the Anglican Church, and the Brothers would preach the gospel throughout the world, "right to the beginning where Jesus was born". Another of his prophecies, reportedly revealed in a dramatic dream, is evidence of a deep-rooted but frustrated desire for Melanesian autonomy:

> "I saw the heavens opened, and there were two letters H and P." He said that this is the token that the Melanesians will rule themselves in the future and the Europeans will be under them. He said also about the islands of Raga [Pentecost] that the Church on Raga will disappear, there will be no Church left, then after that the Church on Raga will grow up better than this time, and will finish the island of Raga. He said all islands will have their own kings and Bishops, and they will rule themselves until the end of the world, or last day.[88]

Daniel died in 1934, having trained some of his followers, led by his widow, to carry on his teachings. During the years following, the movement gained two or three hundred followers in north and central Pentecost. The Danielites held their own services in village churches separately from those conducted by mission-appointed teachers They rejected remonstrations from the Pentecost priests and deacons, refusing to listen to "a mere man", for they followed "the voice of a spirit". By 1940, when

Simeon Langlangmele declared himself on the side of the Danielites, the Pentecost church was in a state of confusion "because so many Christians ... began to fall away from the Faith".[89] A.E. Teall, the senior missionary in the New Hebrides, resident at Lolowai, dismissed what little of "Silon Daniel" that came to his ears as "absolutely ridiculous". They were "rebels against authority", he told the British District Agent, who were foolishly convinced that their "puritan ideas" were the only right ones, and they acted as they did merely out of a desire to be "different" from established methods.[90] Meanwhile, Christians who stayed with the Mission complained of harrassment. Tension finally erupted in 1942, in a week of open fighting in north Pentecost, in which the Christian party, led jointly by a chief Alfred Hukwe, and a priest, Henry Tavoa, drove out the Danielites from the district where they were living. The latter then settled in another village, but after Langlangmele's death in 1947, the movement gradually dwindled under pressure from energetic village priests and through reabsortion of younger members into the Anglican fold by marriage. Twenty years later, there was a Danielite remnant living in four villages, and by 1975, there were only two small groups left.

The Danielites were only incidentally heterodox. The prophetic movement had begun in the Christian revival tradition, in a campaign for religious purity. Daniel's command to plant coconuts and attend school seemingly points to a desire for Western-style economic progress. There was a vision of an earthly millennium, ushering in an age in which Melanesians would rule themselves and the island of Pentecost would achieve a pre-eminence. As with the Fallowes movement in the Solomons, the Danielites had embodied indigenous goals that Baddeley's mission was ill-equipped to understand.

During the 1930s, many Anglican churchmen saw the creation of a Christianized social order as an essential part of missionary strategy. In this, they sought to counterbalance what they took to be the "other-worldly" pietism implicit in much previous missionary practice. In the Melanesian Mission, social Christianity powerfully motivated the extension of medical services. If the war had not intervened, it is likely that the same activist spirit would have broadened and improved the Mission's educational system. The weakness of the doctrine of the "redemption of the whole man" in the Melanesian context was that the "whole man" was a European construction. It failed to advance racial equality within the church organization, nor did it produce a greater understanding by European missionaries of Melanesian aspirations for political and economic betterment.

NOTES AND REFERENCES

1. Gerald H. Anderson, ed., *The Theology of the Christian Mission* (New York: McGraw-Hill, 1961), pp. 3-16; Stephen Neill, *A History of Christian Missions*, pp. 454-56.
2. See, e.g., *S.C.L.*, January 1932, pp. 8-10; October 1932, p. 8.
3. John Wear Burton, *Modern Missions in the South Pacific* (London: Livingstone Press, 1949), p. 12.
4. Church of England, Missionary Council of the Church Assembly, *The Call to West and East: The Sixth and Final Report of the World Call Series*, p. 166.
5. A.I. Hopkins, ed., *Melanesia To-day*, p. 114.
6. A.E. Teall, Diary, 11 May 1932, 6 July 1932, Melanesian Mission English Committee Office; C.E. Fox to W.J. Durrad, 1 September 1953, Durrad Papers, Alexander Turnbull Library.
7. E.A. Codd to his family, 3 July 1934, Codd Letters, in possession of Rev. E.A. Codd. See also *Church Standard*, (Sydney), 22 March 1935, p. 21; Charles E. Fox, *Lord of the Southern Isles*, pp. 85-87. Interviews with Archdeacon E.A. Codd, Adelaide, December 1969; Rev. D. Lloyd Francis, Hove, East Sussex, September 1970; Miss N. Stead, Sydney, March 1965.
8. *S.C.L.*, January 1944, p. 35.
9. ibid., April 1935, p. 10.
10. See, e.g., W.H. Baddeley, *Melanesia, by the Bishop of Melanesia; S.C.L.*, October 1938, pp. 8-12; January 1944, pp. 31-38; June 1947, pp. 7-9; Church of the Province of New Zealand, *Proceedings of General Synod, 1943*, pp. 12-19.
11. *A.B.M. Review* 18 (1931): 106-7.
12. ibid., 26 (1939): 186.
13. W.H. Baddeley, "Melanesia", *East and West Review* 2 (1936): 326.
14. Telegram, Bishop of Melanesia to High Commissioner, 17 November 1933, W.P.A., file no. W.P.H.C. 2866/1933. For a detailed account, see David Hilliard, "The Battle for Rennell Island: A Study in Missionary Politics", in *W.P. Morrell: A Tribute*, eds. G.A. Wood and P.S. O'Connor, pp. 105-24. See also S.M. Lambert, *A Doctor in Paradise* (London and Melbourne: Dent, 1942), pp. 303-78.
15. W.H. Baddeley to F.N. Ashley, 27 August 1936, W.P.A., file no. W.P.H.C. 951/1934. On Ashley's education policy, see W.P.A., file nos, W.P.H.C. 1410/1930, 2594/1931, 951/1934, 3052/1937, 1195/1939.
16. *S.C.L.*, April 1951, p. 8. On post-war educational developments in the British Solomon Islands, see Hugh M. Laracy, *Marists and Melanesians*, ch. 8.

17. E.g., C.J. Wood to Resident Commissioner, 4 July 1918, W.P.A., file no. W.P.H.C. 229/1919.
18. See W.P.A., file nos. W.P.H.C. 536/1916, 229/1919, 1804/1925, 27/1928, F49/11; H. Ian Hogbin, *Experiments in Civilization*, p. 213.
19. R.E. Tempest to A.E. Corner, 31 December 1927, New Zealand Office Letterbooks, Church of Melanesia Archives.
20. A.I. Hopkins, *In the Isles of King Solomon*, p. 224; and id., "Native Life in the South-west Pacific: From Two Points of View", *International Review of Missions* 17 (1928): 547-48.
21. W.J. Durrad in *S.C.L.E.*, May 1920, p. 63.
22. For expressions of discontent, see, e.g., "The Humble Petition of the Settlers of the Solomon Islands", W.P.A., file no. W.P.H.C. 1976/1923; *Pacific Islands Monthly* 17, no. 2 (September 1946): 10, 14.
23. *S.C.L.*, June 1914, p. 355; Joseph H.C. Dickinson, *A Trader in the Savage Solomons: A Record of Romance and Adventure* (London: H.F. & G. Witherby, 1927), p. 103.
24. E.g., *S.C.L.E.*, January 1922, p. 9; Roy Struben, *Coral and Colour of Gold* (London: Faber & Faber, 1961), p. 125. Interview with Bishop S.G. Caulton, London, January 1971.
25. J.M. Steward to Stacy Waddy, 28 June 1927, S.P.G. Letters Received, U.S.P.G. Archives.
26. *S.C.L.*, July 1934, pp. 17-18. Interview with H.W. Bullen, Auckland, January 1969. For missionary tributes to traders, see *Pacific Islands Monthly* 4, no. 5 (December 1933): 40; and 6, no. 6 (January 1936): 42.
27. W.S. Marchant to Sir Harry Luke, 27 April 1942, Marchant Papers, Rhodes House Library. For accounts of the European evacuation, see D.C. Horton, *Fire over the Islands: The Coast Watchers of the Solomons* (Sydney and Wellington: A.H. & A.W. Reed, 1970), pp. 13-18; and K. Dalrymple-Hay in *Pacific Islands Monthly* 42., no. 7 (July 1971): 53-55.
28. C.E. Fox, Diary, 20 February 1942, Bishop Patteson Theological Centre Library. Fox was then living in north Malaita.
29. [Harold Cooper], *Among those Present: The Official Story of the Pacific Islands at War* (London: H.M.S.O., 1946; repr. Honiara, [1973]), pp. 7-11. For Baddeley's account, see *S.C.L.*, April 1943, pp. 5-15; July 1945, pp. 32-33.
30. E. Field to M. Rice, 28 October 1945, "Letters to Miss Rice", Melanesian Mission English Committee Office.
31. *S.C.L.*, March 1947, p. 3. See also *Pacific Islands Monthly* 17, no. 9 (April 1947): 28; and Baddeley's obituary in *The Times*, 12 February 1960.
32. C.F. Harford, "Fifty Years of Medical Missions", *The East and the West* 13 (1915): 325-31; R. Fletcher Moorshead, *The Appeal of Medical Missions* (Edinburgh: Oliphant, Anderson & Ferrier, 1913), pp. 18-20, 45-46; World Missionary Conference 1910, *The History and Records of the Conference*, vol. 9 of the collected *Reports of Commissions*, pp. 113-20.
33. J.R. Selwyn, *Pastoral Work in the Colonies and the Mission Field*, p. 130.
34. W.G. Ivens, *Hints to Missionaries to Melanesia*, p. 31. The first

Presbyterian hospital was opened at Ambrym in 1897.
35. The Anglican medical work is described more fully by Fox, *Lord of the Southern Isles*, ch. 18; and D.L. Hilliard, "Protestant Missions in the Solomon Islands, 1849-1942" (Ph.D. thesis), pp. 200-203, 206-8.
36. W.P.A., file no. W.P.H.C. 2703/1922; *S.C.L.E.*, December 1922, pp. 141-42.
37. Stuart W. Artless, ed., *The Church in Melanesia*, p. 71.
38. *Reaper* 1, no. 5 (June 1923): 4; A.I. Hopkins, "The Call from the South Seas", *The East and the West* 24 (1926): 215.
39. W.P.A., file no. W.P.H.C. F70/92/1.
40. Melanesian Mission English Committee Minutes, 11 December 1930, 28 April 1931.
41. Melanesian Mission, *In the Solomons and other Islands of Melanesia*, p. 7.
42. See infant mortality statistics in W.P.A., file no. W.P.H.C. 1050/1936.
43. *New Zealand Woman's Weekly*, 1 March 1934, in D.L. Francis, newspaper cuttings book, in possession of Rev. D. Lloyd Francis.
44. *Reaper* 16, no. 8 (September 1938): 4.
45. Comment on W.H. Baddeley to Senior Medical Officer, 18 November 1936, W.P.A., file no. W.P.H.C. 1050/1936; Minute by F.N. Ashley, 22 May 1937, W.P.A., file no. B.S.I.P. F46/36.
46. *Reaper* 16, no. 2 (March 1938): 2-3.
47. Bohun Lynch, ed., *Iles of Illusion: Letters from the South Seas* (London: Constable, 1923), p. 51; also Edward Jacomb, *The Future of the Kanaka*, pp. 150-52.
48. Charles E. Fox, *Kakamora*, p. 134.
49. Charles E. Fox, "A Missionary in Melanesia", pp. 106-7, Durrad Papers.
50. Annual income rose from £26, 000 in 1936 to £33, 000 in 1940. Much of the increase was due to the subdivision and sale of land owned by the Melanesian Mission Trust Board in the new eastern suburbs of Auckland. In 1934, the business office of the Mission was moved from Auckland to Sydney, which was the headquarters of Burns, Philp & Co's interisland shipping line, the Finance Board was dissolved, and all Mission property was transferred to the Bishop of Melanesia as a corporation sole. There was no further problem of divided control of funds.
51. Fox, *Lord of the Southern Isles*, p. 85.
52. Fox, *Kakamora*, p. 100.
53. Baddeley's views on the "native ministry" are expounded in *S.C.L.*, July 1933, p. 6; *M.M.R.* 1938, pp. 8-10.
54. R.P. Fallowes, Diary, 18 March 1934, N.L.A.
55. There were 8 New Zealanders on the European staff (out of 46) in 1929; 15 in 1933; 23 in 1940, in a total of 54.
56. Fox to Durrad, 17 August 1938, in Introduction to Fox, "A Missionary in Melanesia", Durrad Papers.
57. *S.C.L.*, May 1919, p. 18; *M.M.R.*, 1934, pp. 6, 8, 16. For additional statistics, and comparison with other missions, see Hilliard, "Protestant Missions ...", pp. 232, 344-45, 407-9, 465-66; Laracy, *Marists*, pp. 65-66. For population statistics, see British Solomon Islands Protectorate,

Report on the Census of the Population, 1970 (Honiara, n.d.), ch. 1.
58. *S.C.L.*, April 1934, pp. 6-7.
59. Hogbin, *Experiments in Civilization*, p. 183.
60. ibid., pp. 180-81.
61. Guadalcanal District Report, 1934, W.P.A., file no. W.P.H.C. 1589/1935.
62. Raymond Firth, *We, the Tikopia*, ch. 2; id., *Social Change in Tikopia*, chs. 1, 9; id., *Rank and Religion in Tikopia*, chs. 11-15.
63. Firth, *Rank and Religion*, p. 324.
64. *S.C.L.*, July 1934, pp. 26-27; *A.B.M. Review* 18 (1932): 201.
65. A.B.M. Minutes, 4-5 November 1936, 14-15 April 1937, A.B.M. Archives; Telegram, Brigadier-General W. McNicoll to Prime Minister, 3 February 1936; W.H. Baddeley to Senator G.P. Pearce, undated [April 1936] and 3 September 1936, Australian Archives, Canberra, A1 822/1. The author owes this reference to Dr Hugh Laracy.
66. Notes on Gasmata district, Mandated Territory Papers, Church of Melanesia Archives.
67. C.V. Longden to E.A. Codd, 23 March 1938, Codd Letters; *A.B.M. Review* 25 (1938): 147.
68 *S.C.L.*, July 1938, p. 15; Melanesian Mission English Committee, *Annual Report*, 1938, p. 20.
69. *S.C.L.*, April 1941, pp. 29-30. On the wartime "martyrs", see Dorothea Tomkins and Brian Hughes, *The Road from Gona* (Sydney: Angus & Robertson, 1969), pp. 64-67. The mainland portion of the Mandated Territory, which included a chaplaincy at the Wau goldfield, was incorporated into an enlarged diocese of New Guinea in 1939. New Britain and the other New Guinea islands were transferred from Melanesia in 1949.
70. Fox to Durrad, 17 December 1927, in Introduction to Fox, "A Missionary in Melanesia", Durrad Papers.
71. Guadalcanal District Report, 1934, W.P.A., file no. W.P.H.C. 1589/1935.
72. Gizo District Report, 1932, W.P.A., file no. W.P.H.C. 1522/1933; D.G. Kennedy, "Marching Rule in the British Solomon Islands Protectorate ...", Rhodes House Library.
73. W.C. Groves to Acting Resident Commissioner, 28 July 1939, W.P.A., file no. W.P.H.C. 2736/1939.
74. *S.C.L.E.*, January 1909, p. 387.
75. Report of Sir Murchison Fletcher on tour, W.P.A., file no. W.P.H.C. 3058/1931; Notes of discussion at Tunabuli, Ysabel, 18 July 1931, W.P.H.C. 2588/1931; J.C. Barley to High Commissioner, 9 December 1932, W.P.H.C. 2594/1931.
76. Wilfred Fowler, *This Island's Mine* (London: Constable, 1959), p. 41. For examples of conflict, see *S.C.L.*, May 1919, p. 17; R.B. Hill to High Commissioner, 22 February 1924, W.P.A., file no. W.P.H.C. 849/1924.
77. Ysabel District Report, 1930, W.P.A., file no. W.P.H.C. 1103/1931.
78. See R.P. Fallowes, Letters, 1929-34, and Diary, 1931-34, N.L.A.
79. Fowler, *This Island's Mine*, p. 40. In this work, the names of all Europeans

have been changed. There is an unsympathetic portrait of Fallowes as the missionary "Woodley".
80. This account of the Fallowes movement is based principally upon: W.P.A., file nos. B.S.I.P. F43/14/1 Confidential (originally W.P.H.C. 2811/1939); Ysabel, Guadalcanal and Eastern Solomons District Reports, 1939, W.P.H.C. 2195/1940; Sir Harry Luke to C.O., 27 November 1939, W.P.H.C. 3307/1938; R.P. Fallowes, personal communications, 25 January 1966, 20 November 1970, 8 January 1971, 23 June and 28 July 1975.
81. Statement of John Palmer Pidoke, "Chief of Gela", June 1939, enclosure in R.P. Fallowes to High Commissioner, 15 June 1939, W.P.A., file no. B.S.I.P. F43/14/1.
82. Eastern Solomons District, Report for quarter ended 30 June 1939, W.P.A.
83. *S.C.L.*, October 1938, p. 11.
84. Statement of John Palmer Pidoke, loc.cit.
85. C.H. Allan, "The Marching Rule Movement in the British Solomon Islands Protectorate" (Dip. Anthrop. thesis, Cambridge University, 1950), pp. 27-29, 60, 77; Hugh M. Laracy, "Marching Rule and the Missions", *Journal of Pacific History* 6 (1971): 96-114.
86. Cyril S. Belshaw, "Native Politics in the Solomon Islands", *Pacific Affairs* 20 (1947): 189-90.
87. The following account of the Danielites is based upon Oscar Arthur Toa, "Strange Religion on Raga", *Melanesian Messenger*, August 1965, pp. 23-26; Michael Henry Tavoa, "Church on Raga and Short Account of Selwyn and Patteson and their Melanesian Mission" (Dip. Theol. essay).
88. Toa, "Strange Religion on Raga", p. 25.
89. Tavoa, "Church on Raga ...".
90. A.E. Teall to Adam, 10 January and 11 February 1941, New Hebrides British Service, Central District No. 2, General Correspondence 1933-50, 32/4, W.P.A.

Epilogue

At the dedication in London in July 1932 of the sixth *Southern Cross*, Archbishop Lang of Canterbury described the Melanesian Mission as "the most romantic" of missions of the Church of England.[1] It was an extravagant tribute, which its missionaries, and their metropolitan supporters, were accustomed to hear and to applaud. For throughout its first ninety years, the Melanesian Mission had no doubt of its high quality and unique character among the Christian missions of modern times. In the South Pacific, it was not just one mission among many, but in a class of its own: "God's instrument" for the evangelization of northern Melanesia.[2] This tradition of religious primacy went back to G.A. Selwyn's grandiose scheme for a mission to embrace every island from New Caledonia to New Guinea. It derived also from the "halo of glory ... cast over the work" by the martyrdom of Patteson,[3] from the statistics of numerical dominance over other denominations in the British Solomon Islands and from the assured world-view of clergymen of a privileged national church.

The Melanesian Mission at the outbreak of the Pacific war embodied the results of an Anglican missionary presence in the south-west Pacific, which in many island communities already extended back beyond a single lifetime. Since the 1850s, some seventy thousand islanders had received Anglican baptism. At every stage, and in every place, its history had been shaped by the interaction between an inherent desire to expand throughout northern Melanesia on the one hand, and the constrictions imposed by the Melanesian physical and social environment, inflexible organization and inadequate supplies of finance and personnel on the other.

Beneath the fluctuations of local success and failure, however, the ultimate goal of the Mission did not change. The Anglicans saw their task as the creation of a self-governing church—"a native one and not a mere exotic"[4]—that would conserve and not destroy the indigenous social and cultural order. To this end, a remarkable succession of missionary clergymen studied Melanesian society with sensitivity and depth, and looked for points of contact between Western Christianity and Melanesian religious beliefs. Yet the practical steps that the Anglicans took to achieve their avowed objectives were hesitant and often inconsistent. An enlightened attempt by missionaries of the first generation to replace mid-nineteenth-century doctrines of Anglo-Saxon superiority by a commitment to social equality and Melanesian leadership was largely swept away in a resurgence of European paternalism at the close of the nineteenth century. "What little we did was I think on the right lines, but it has gone a very little way," was Codrington's regretful verdict, fifty years after Patteson's death.[5] Likewise, the goal of an indigenous Christianity was obscured by the almost universal missionary expectation that the Church on the mission field should be a purer version of the parent church in England. The future "native church" was to be Anglican first and Melanesian second.

Despite the legal connection between the diocese of Melanesia and the Anglican Church in New Zealand, the distinctive ethos and attitudes of the Melanesian Mission were, until the 1930s, moulded by churchmen who shared the values of the English upper-middle-class. Traces of this ethos survive in the self-governing Church of Melanesia, which in 1975 became headed by its first Melanesian-born archbishop. As a body, the Melanesian Mission preferred decent reticence and self-restraint to colourful stories of spiritual progress and displays of religious emotion. Its worship was ordered and liturgical. It was enthusiastic about its links with the public schools, the ancient universities, the Royal Navy and the rulers of the British Empire, while at the same time, it stood aloof from the everyday world of commerce and economic development. Its interventions in secular politics combined a judiciously balanced defence of Melanesian interests with a deference to established authorities. It cherished the memory of great events and great men in its own past. The Anglican missionaries respected the traditions of Melanesian villagers because they revered their own.

NOTES AND REFERENCES

1. *The Times*, 27 July 1932.
2. Melanesian Mission, *Hand-Book of the Melanesian Mission* (1907), p. 22. Cf. Austin Coates, *Western Pacific Islands*, p. 220.
3. Alfred Barry, *The Ecclesiastical Expansion of England in the Growth of the Anglican Communion* (London, 1895), p. 204.
4. [Ellen Wilson], *The Isles that Wait*, p. v.
5. R.H. Codrington to C.H. Brooke, 4 November 1921, Codrington Papers, Rhodes House Library.

Biographical Notes

Between 1849 and 1942, more than three hundred ordained and lay missionaries worked in the Melanesian Mission. To supplement biographical information contained in the text, the careers of a selection of these men and women are outlined below:

Abbreviations
- *A* Parochial or other appointments
- *B* Place of birth
- *E* Place of higher education and/or theological training
- *M* Marriage
- *O* Place and dates of ordination as deacon and priest
- *P* Profession
- *S* Period of missionary service, with principal places of work
- *W* War service

Baddeley, Walter Hubert (1894-1960)
- *B* Portslade, Sussex, England
- *E* Keble College, Oxford: B.A., 1920; Cuddesdon Theological College; Hon. Doctor of Sacred Theology, Columbia University, New York, 1944; D.D., Lambeth, 1955
- *W* 1914-19: M.C., 1917 (Bar, 1918); D.S.O., 1918. Hon. Chaplain, Fiji Military Forces, 1943-45; U.S. Medal of Freedom, 1945
- *O* Ripon, 1921
- *A* Dioceses of Ripon and York, 1921-32
- *S* Bishop of Melanesia, 1932-47
- *M* Mary Katherine Thomas, 1935
- *A* Bishop of Whitby, 1946-54; Bishop of Blackburn, 1954-60

Bice, Charles (1844-1922)
- *B* St Enoder, Cornwall, England
- *E* St Augustine's College, Canterbury
- *O* Melanesia, 1868, 1870
- *S* 1867-91: Norfolk Island; Omba-Maewo, 1871-90

- M Susannah Eliza Maunsell, 1871
- A Organizing Secretary for Melanesian Mission in Australia, 1891-94; Organizing Secretary, A.B.M., 1894-97; Diocese of Newcastle, N.S.W., 1897-1911

Codrington, Robert Henry (1830-1922)
- B Wroughton, Wiltshire, England
- E Wadham College, Oxford: B.A., 1852; Hon. D.D., 1885; Fellow of Wadham College, 1855-87; Hon. Fellow, 1901-22
- O Oxford, 1855, 1857
- A Diocese of Nelson, New Zealand, 1860-64
- S 1867-87, 1892-93: Headmaster, Norfolk Island; Acting-Head of Melanesian Mission, 1871-77
- A Diocese of Chichester, 1887-1922

Comins, Richard Blundell (1848-1919)
- B Tweston, Devonshire, England
- E Bishop Hatfield's Hall, Durham: L.Th.; Hon. D.D., Durham University, 1902
- O Lincoln, 1873, 1874
- S 1877-1912: Eṁae, 1877-80; San Cristobal, 1880-94; Siota, 1895-1902; Chaplain to Norfolk Islanders, 1903-12; Archdeacon of Northern Melanesia, 1900-10
- M Alice Forrest, 1882

Coombe, Florence Edith (1870-1953)
- B England
- S 1905-19: Norfolk Island, 1905-11, 1915-19; Mota, 1911-15
- A Travelling Secretary for Melanesian Mission, England, 1920-25

Cullwick, Thomas Cartwright (1862-1948)
- B Hadley, Shropshire, England
- O Melanesia, 1886, 1889
- S 1886-1913: Banks Islands, 1887-1902; Headmaster, Norfolk Island, 1903-13; Archdeacon of Southern Melanesia, 1902-10
- M Bessie Palmer, 1896
- A Diocese of Waiapu, New Zealand, 1914-37

Drummond, Henry Nelson (1880-1941)
- B Rockhampton, Queensland, Australia
- E St Barnabas' Theological College, Adelaide, 1913-14: Th.L., 1914
- O Melanesia, 1904, 1907
- P Mining engineer, Wallaroo Mines, South Australia
- S 1903-12, 1914-20: Reef Islands, 1903-5; Pentecost, 1905-11; Santa Cruz, 1910; Headmaster, Norfolk Island, 1914-19

A Dioceses of Auckland and Adelaide, 1921-41

Durrad, Walter John (1878-1954)
B Highgate, Middlesex, England
E Jesus College, Cambridge: B.A., 1900
O Chichester, 1901, 1902
S 1905-19: Torres Islands, 1905-10; Tikopia, 1910; Vureas school, 1911-18
M Margaret Bridges, 1911
A Organizing Secretary, New Zealand Anglican Board of Missions, 1919-25; Diocese of Wellington, 1925-46

Fallowes, Richard Prince (1901-   )
B Worthing, Sussex, England
E Pembroke College, Cambridge: B.A., 1923; Dorchester Missionary College
O Southwark, 1924, 1925
S 1929-35: Santa Isabel
A Dioceses of York, Southwell, Zululand, 1939-68

Fox, Charles Elliot (1878-1977)
B Stalbridge, Dorset, England
E University of New Zealand: M.A., 1901; Litt.D., 1922; St John's College, Auckland: L.Th., 1902
O Melanesia, 1903; Auckland, 1906
S 1902-5, 1907-73: Norfolk Island, 1903-5, 1907-11; Pamua school, 1911-14; San Cristobal, 1915-24; Pawa school, 1924-32; Melanesian Brotherhood, 1932-43, 1975-77; Siota, 1943-49; Fiu, 1949-52; Tambalia, 1952-54, Taroaniara, 1954-73; Canon of Melanesia, 1956; M.B.E., 1952; C.B.E., 1974

Hopkins, Arthur Innes (1869-1943)
B Cheltenham, Gloucestershire, England
E St Catharine's College, Cambridge: B.A., 1891
O York, 1892, 1893
S 1900-25: Norfolk Island, 1900-2, 1915-19; North Malaita, 1902-14; Maravovo, 1919-21; Siota Theological College, 1921-25
A Secretary for Melanesian Mission, London, 1926-29

Ivens, Walter George (1871-1939)
B Waikuku, Canterbury, New Zealand
E University of New Zealand: M.A., 1894; Litt.D., 1919; Litt.D., University of Melbourne, 1923; Fellow of the Royal Anthropological Institute, 1931
O Christchurch, 1894; Melanesia, 1896

- S   1895–1909: Ulawa and south Malaita
- M   Eleanore Barrett, 1899
- A   Organizing Secretary for Melanesian Mission in New Zealand, 1909–10; Superintendent, Yarrabah Aboriginal Mission, North Queensland, 1910–12; Diocese of Melbourne, 1912–24; Research Fellow, University of Melbourne, 1924–28; Travelling Secretary for Melanesian Mission, England, 1928–35; Diocese of Canterbury, 1935–39

Molyneux, Frederick Merivale (1885–1948)
- B   Christchurch, Hampshire, England
- E   Keble College, Oxford: B.A., 1908; Cuddesdon Theological College
- O   Ripon, 1909, 1911
- A   Diocese of Leeds, 1909–13; Diocese of Oxford, 1913–25
- W   Army Chaplain, 1916–19; M.B.E., 1917
- S   1925–32: Assistant Bishop, 1925–28; Bishop of Melanesia, 1928–31

Palmer, John (1837–1902)
- B   Oxfordshire, England
- E   St John's College, Auckland; B.D., Lambeth, 1893
- O   Melanesia, 1863, 1867
- S   1863–1902: Banks Islands, 1863–91; Norfolk Island, 1867–1902 (Headmaster, 1887–1902); Acting-Head of Melanesian Mission, 1892–94; Archdeacon of Southern Melanesia, 1894–1902
- M   (1) Sarah Ashwell, 1868; died 1874
      (2) Mary Ashwell, 1877; died 1892

Patteson, John Coleridge (1827–71)
- B   London
- E   Balliol College, Oxford: B.A., 1849; D.D., 1861; Fellow of Merton College, 1852–71
- O   Exeter, 1853, 1854
- S   1855–71: Bishop of Melanesia, 1861–71

Penny, Alfred (1845–1935)
- B   Bubbenhall, Warwickshire, England
- E   Trinity Hall, Cambridge: B.A., 1868
- O   Rochester, 1868, 1869
- A   Dioceses of Rochester and Lichfield, 1868–74
- S   1875–86: Nggela and Santa Isabel
- A   Diocese of Lichfield, 1888–1935

Pritt, Lonsdale (1822–85)
- B   Lancashire, England

E	Trinity College, Cambridge: B.A., 1844
O	1845
A	Diocese of Nelson, New Zealand, 1858–61
S	1861–67: Kohimarama, Auckland
M	Mary Otterson, 1863
A	Diocese of Auckland, 1867–85

Selwyn, George Augustus (1809–78)

B	Hampstead, Middlesex, England
E	St John's College, Cambridge: B.A., 1831; D.D., 1841; Fellow of St John's College, 1833–39; Hon. D.D., Oxford, 1841
O	London, 1833, 1834
M	Sarah Richardson, 1839
A	Bishop of New Zealand, 1841–69; Bishop of Lichfield, 1868–78

Selwyn, John Richardson (1844–98)

B	Waimate North, New Zealand
E	Trinity College, Cambridge: B.A., 1866; D.D., 1885
O	Lichfield, 1869, 1870
S	1873–91: Bishop of Melanesia, 1877–91
M	(1) Clara Innes, 1872; died 1877
	(2) Annie Mort, 1885; died 1930
A	Master of Selwyn College, Cambridge, 1893–98

Steward, John Manwaring (1874–1937)

B	Southampton, Hampshire, England
E	Magdalen College, Oxford: B.A., 1896; Ely Theological College
O	St Albans, 1900, 1901
S	1902–28: Guadalcanal, 1903–6; Nggela, 1906–11; Maravovo and Theological College, 1911–19; Bishop of Melanesia, 1919–28

Tempest, Roger Ernest (1891–1966)

B	Ipswich, Suffolk, England
E	Selwyn College, Cambridge: B.A., 1912; Leeds Clergy School
O	St Edmundsbury, 1914, 1915
S	1917–35: Banks Islands, 1918–24; Siota Theological College, 1925–35
A	Diocese of St Edmundsbury and Ipswich, 1936–66

Warren, George Thomas (1887–1954)

B	Ryde, Isle of Wight, England
A	Church Army, 1908–13
O	Melanesia, 1921, 1924
S	1913–16, 1920–38: Pamua school, 1913–15; Maravovo school, 1920–38
M	1920 Hilda Hulke, 1918

A   Dioceses of Oxford and Birmingham, 1941–45; General Secretary of Melanesian Mission English Committee, 1945–54

Welchman, Henry Palmer (1850–1908)
B   Lichfield, Staffordshire, England
E   Queen's College, Birmingham; M.R.C.S. (England), 1876
P   General practitioner, Lichfield
O   Auckland, 1892, 1893
S   1888–1908: Santa Isabel, 1890–1908; Siota, 1896–1900
M   Helen Rossiter, 1896; died 1897

Wilson, Cecil (1860–1941)
B   London
E   Jesus College, Cambridge: B.A., 1883; Hon. D.D., 1908
O   Winchester, 1886, 1887
A   Diocese of Winchester, 1886–94
S   1894–1911: Bishop of Melanesia
M   Alice Julius, 1899
A   Archdeacon and Assistant Bishop of Adelaide, 1911–17; Bishop of Bunbury, Western Australia, 1917–37

Wilson, Ellen (1861–1954)
B   Staffordshire, England; sister of Robert Paley Wilson
S   1904–27: Norfolk Island, 1904–7; Pentecost, 1907–9; Bungana school, 1910–19; Siota, 1922–26

Wilson, Robert Paley (1855–1947)
B   Staffordshire, England
P   Solicitor
E   Emmanuel College, Cambridge: B.A., 1892
O   Lichfield, 1892, 1893
S   1895–1927: San Cristobal, 1896–1906; Bungana school, 1909–18; Administrator of diocese, 1918–19; Siota, 1922–26

Wood, Cecil John (1874–1957)
B   London
E   Peterhouse, Cambridge: B.A., 1896; Hon. D.D., 1912
O   Canterbury, 1897, 1898
A   Dioceses of Canterbury, London, Southwark, 1897–1912
S   1912–18: Bishop of Melanesia
M   Marjorie Bell, 1919
A   Dioceses of St Edmundsbury, Newcastle and Chichester, 1924–46

Full details of the ecclesiastical careers of all Anglican clergymen will be found in *Crockford's Clerical Directory*.

Bibliography

Entries are arranged under the following headings:

MANUSCRIPT SOURCES

1. Official Manuscripts
2. Collected Private Papers and Unpublished Works
3. Papers in Private Possession
4. Unpublished Theses

PRINTED SOURCES

1. Official Publications
2. Annual Reports
3. Newspapers and Periodicals
4. Books, Pamphlets and Articles by Missionaries and other Participants
5. Other Published Works

INTERVIEWS

MANUSCRIPT SOURCES

Official Manuscripts

Barr Smith Library, University of Adelaide
Groves, W.C., "Report on a Survey of Education in the British Solomon Islands Protectorate", mimeographed (Tulagi, 1940).

Public Record Office, London
Colonial and Foreign Office Correspondence
  C.O. 225. Original Correspondence, Western Pacific, 1877–1913.
  (Microfilm, N.L.A.)
  F.O. 58/147. Consular and Associated Correspondence, Pacific Islands, 1875. (Microfilm, N.L.A.)

Western Pacific Archives, Suva, Fiji
British Solomon Islands Protectorate
  District Office, Eastern; Annual Reports, Quarterly Reports, 1919–42.
  District Office, Malaita; Correspondence, 1909–45.
  District Office, Santa Cruz; Annual Reports, Quarterly Reports, 1928–42.
  Office of the Resident Commissioner; General Correspondence, 1935–52.
New Hebrides British Service
  British District Agency, Central District No. 2; General Correspondence, 1933–50.
  British District Agency, Northern District; General Correspondence, 1936–48.
  Office of the Resident Commissioner; General Correspondence, 1907–42.
Western Pacific High Commission
  Inward Correspondence, General, 1875–1941.
  General Correspondence, F. series, 1942–54.

Collected Private Papers and Unpublished Works

Collections marked thus * are described fully in Phyllis Mander-Jones, ed., *Manuscripts in the British Isles relating to Australia, New Zealand and the Pacific* (Honolulu: University Press of Hawaii, 1972).

Alexander Turnbull Library, Wellington
Colenso, Elizabeth, Diaries, letterbooks and notebooks, 1862–95.
Durrad, Walter John, Papers and letters relating to C.E. Fox, 1920–55. (Collection includes an unpublished typescript by Fox entitled "A Missionary in Melanesia", with introduction and notes by Durrad.)
Melanesian Mission Correspondence (seven letters), 1849–1918. (Microfilm)
Selwyn, George Augustus, Letters to W.E. Gladstone, 1828–60. (Microfilm of correspondence in the Gladstone Papers)

Auckland Institute and Museum Library
Atkin, Mary, "Miss Atkin's Notes on the Early History of Mission Bay". (Typescript)
Jackson, Robert Simeon, Letters to the Rev. R.S. Jackson, mainly from members of the Melanesian Mission, 1863-79. (Manuscript and typescript copies)
Patteson, J.C., Letter to F. Max Müller, 8 June 1866. (Photocopy).
Selwyn Papers. For a description of this collection, see Enid Evans, "The Selwyn Papers", *Journal of Pacific History* 5 (1970): 153-57.
The collection comprises two series: (i) "Letters from the Bishop of New Zealand and Others, 1842-1867" (Typescript copies); (ii) Papers by or concerned with Bishop G.A. Selwyn.
Southern Cross (vessel), Logbooks, 1870-71, 1910-32.
Vigors, Philip D., "Private Journal of a Four Months Cruise through some of the South Sea Islands and New Zealand in H.M.S. 'Havannah' ", 1850. (Typescript)

Auckland Public Library
Nihill, William, "Journal of a Voyage to the New Hebrides, New Caledonia and the Loyalty Islands in the Bishop of New Zealand's Schooner 'Undine' ", 1850. (Manuscript and typescript copies)
——, "Journal of a Voyage from Auckland, N.Z. to the New Hebrides and Loyalty Islands", 1851. (Manuscript and typescript copies)

Australian Board of Missions, Stanmore, New South Wales
A.B.M. Archives. These include:

A.B.M. Executive Council Minutes, 1886-1917.
A.B.M. Minutes, 1921-41.
Melanesian Mission Sub-committee Minutes, 1915-26.
Papers relating to Melanesia and South Pacific Province, 1918-45.

Australian National University, Canberra. Department of Pacific and Southeast Asian History
Woodford Papers.

Australian National University, Canberra, Pacific Manuscripts Bureau
Microfilm copies of the following are available in member libraries of the Pacific Manuscripts Bureau:
Margaret of the Cross, Sister, Autobiography, 1887-1966 (PMB 145).
New Hebrides Presbyterian Mission, Synod Minutes, 1857-1938 (PMB 31).
Records of the Melanesian Mission at Lolowai, Aoba, New Hebrides (PMB 43).
Wilson, Cecil, Diary, 1894-1911 (PMB 530).

Bishop Patteson Theological Centre Library, Kohimarama, Solomon Islands
Fox, Charles Elliot, Diary, 1942-63.
——, History of the Melanesian Mission. (Typescript)
Ruddock, David, Diary, 1880-84.

*Bodleian Library, Oxford
Samuel Wilberforce Papers.

*British Museum Library
Gladstone Papers.

*Church Missionary Society, London
C.M.S. Archives. These include:

Home Committee Minutes, vol. 28, 1850-52.
Home Letterbooks, Outward, 1852.
Norfolk Island Papers.
Outward Letterbooks: New Zealand, 1845-62.
Papers of missionaries: G.A. Kissling.

Church of Melanesia Provincial Office, Honiara, Solomon Islands
Church of Melanesia Archives. These include:

Comins, Alice, and Comins, R.B. Letters to Charles Palmer, 1895-1910.
Hopkins, Arthur Innes, Autobiography. (Typescript; on microfilm, Department of Pacific and Southeast Asian History, A.N.U.)
Mandated Territory Papers.
Melanesian Mission, Medical Officer's Reports, 1930-33. (Mimeographed)
Melanesian Mission, Sydney Advisory Committee, Minutes, 1940-46.
New Zealand Mission Office Letterbooks:
 English Committee, 1921-31.
 Bishops, 1924-32.
 D.E. Graves, 1931-33.
Palmer, John, Journals of mission voyages, 1863, 1866.
Patteson, J.C., Miscellaneous letters, 1868-1871.
Swabey, Frances Edith, "Elizabeth Colenso: Her Work for the Melanesian Mission". (Typescript)

Hocken Library, Dunedin
Dudley, Benjamin Thornton, "Journal of a winter spent on Amota, Banks [Islands] ... ", 1860.
——, "Journal of my 4th Melanesian voyage in the 'Southern Cross'

with the Bishop of N.Z.—commenced Sept. 17th 1858".
Nihill, William, Letters to his family, 1841-54.

Lambeth Palace Library, London
Benson Papers.
Davidson Papers.
Tait Papers.
Frederick Temple Papers.

Melanesian Mission English Committee Office, Watford, Hertfordshire
Most of the English Committee collection has been microfilmed by the Australian Joint Copying Project, N.L.A.: AJCP M802-5.

English Committee Minutes, 1872-1934.
Hobhouse, Edmund, Letters to Bishop Patteson, 1868-70. (Manuscript and typescript copies)
Miscellaneous letters, 1871-74, mainly relating to the death of Bishop Patteson.
Rice, M., Letters to Miss Rice and others, mainly from women missionaries, 1941-52. (Typescript copies)
Teall, Alfred Ernest, Diary, 1923-37, 1952-64.
Tempest, Roger Ernest,"Melanesia, 1877-1919". (Typescript)
——, "Memories". (Typescript)
Welchman, Henry, Diary, 1889-1892, 1896-1908.
——, Letters to his mother, 1887-88.

Mitchell Library, Sydney
Denison, Sir William Thomas, Correspondence and related papers, 1856-57. (Microfilm, AJCP M671)
Godden, Charles Christopher, Papers, 1832-1965.
Nobbs, George Hunn, Papers, 1824-85.
Patteson Memorial Endowment Fund of the Melanesian Mission, Papers, 1871-1906.
Penny, Alfred, Diary, 1876-86.
Sharp, L.M., "See of Islands: The Story of John Coleridge Patteson and the Melanesian Mission from 1854 to 1871". (Typescript)
Stephen Family Correspondence, 1812-1961.

National Library of Australia, Canberra
Fallowes, Richard Prince, Account of voyage, 1929.
——, Diary, 1931-34.
——, Letters to his sister, 1929-34. (Typescript copies)
Thurston Papers.

National Archives of New Zealand, Wellington
Church of the Province of New Zealand Records:
  Series 7 — Papers relating to Melanesia.

Presbyterian Church of New Zealand, Wellington
Committee of Mission Overseas Archives:
  New Hebrides Condominium correspondence, 1909-29.

*Rhodes House Library, Oxford
Ashley, F.N., Papers, 1931-38.
British and Foreign Anti-Slavery and Aborigines Protection Society Papers:
  New Hebrides correspondence, 1909-33.
Clemens, W.F.M., Diary, 1942.
Codrington, Robert Henry, Diaries, letters, lectures, 1867-1922.
Kennedy, D.G., "Marching Rule in the British Solomon Islands Protectorate: A Memorandum on the Origin of the Term".
Marchant, William Sydney, Papers, 1942-43.

St Augustine's College, Canterbury
Personal files of students.

St John's College Library, Auckland
Patteson, J.C., Letters to G.A. Selwyn, 1858-59.

*Selwyn College Library, Cambridge
Patteson, J.C., Diary, 1866, 1870.
Selwyn, G.A., Papers. (Microfilm, Australian Joint Copying Project, N.L.A.: AJCP M590)

*Society for Promoting Christian Knowledge, London
Foreign Translation Committee Minutes, 1902-17.
Standing Committee Minutes, 1861-1929.

*United Society for the Propagation of the Gospel, London
U.S.P.G. Archives. These include:

Letters Received, 1859-1933.
Patteson Papers. Letters from John Coleridge Patteson to his father and sisters, 1855-71. (Microfilm, Department of Pacific and Southeast Asian History, A.N.U.)
Reports from Missionaries, 1858-84.
Standing Committee Minutes, 1852-84.
Wilson, Cecil, Letters to Bishop H.H. Montgomery, 1894-1906.

University of Auckland Library
Fox, C.E., Letters to Sir Douglas Robb, 1968-69.
Patteson, J.C., Letters to Dr Goldsboro', 1867-70.

*University of London, School of Oriental and African Studies
Archives of the Council for World Mission (incorporating the London Missionary Society):
   L.M.S. South Seas, Incoming Letters, 1848-59. (Microfilm, M.L.)

Papers in Private Possession

Blencowe, John Walcot, Papers, mainly 1908-11.
Bury, Guy F., "Home Letters".
In the possession of Mrs M. Blencowe, Uckfield, East Sussex. (Microfilm, Australian Joint Copying Project, N.L.A.: AJCP M824)

Codd, Ernest Appleby, Diary, 1933-35.
——, Letters from E.A. and N. Codd, 1933-38.
——, Letters to E.A. Codd, 1938.
In the possession of the Reverend E.A. Codd, Prospect, South Australia.

Edgell, William Henry, Diary, 1897-1901.
In the possession of Mrs R. Rowland, Turnditch, Derby. (Microfilm: Australian Joint Copying Project, N.L.A.: AJCP M721)

Farr, Julia, Diary, 1894.
In the possession of Mrs Mary Clift, Walkerville, South Australia.

Francis, David Lloyd, Letters, 1941-44.
Newspaper cuttings relating to the Melanesian Mission, 1925-49.
In the possession of the Reverend D. Lloyd Francis, Hove, East Sussex.

Pinson, Wilfred John, "A Check List of Books printed 1855-1975 by the Anglican Church in Melanesia, on the Mission Press". (Typescript)
In the possession of the Reverend W.J. Pinson, Warrnambool, Victoria.

*Selwyn Family Papers. Papers and letters relating to George Augustus Selwyn, his wife Sarah Harriet, and his son John Richardson Selwyn.
In the possession of the Reverend H. Selwyn Fry, Sherston, Wiltshire.

Welchman, Henry, Diary, 1892-95.
In the possession of the Reverend W.F. Browning, Greatworth, Oxfordshire. (Microfilm, Australian Joint Copying Project, N.L.A.: AJCP M728)

Wilson, Cecil, Diary, 1894-1914.

In the possession of Mrs Qona Clifton, Arthur River, Western Australia. (Microfilm, Pacific Manuscripts Bureau, A.N.U.: PMB 530)

Wilson, Cecil, Extracts from letters to his wife, 1900, 1903, 1904, 1909. (Typescript copies)
In the possession of the Reverend Canon J.C.J. Wilson, Otane, New Zealand.

Unpublished Theses

Clark, Wendy Patricia, " 'A Truly Christian Spirit?': Christchurch and the Melanesian Mission, 1868-1875" (M.A. long essay, University of Otago, 1966).

Gunson, W.N., "Evangelical Missionaries in the South Seas, 1797-1860" (Ph.D. thesis, A.N.U., 1959).

Hagesi, Robert, "Towards Localization of Anglican Worship in the Solomon Islands" (B.D. thesis, Pacific Theological College, Suva, 1972).

Hilliard, D.L., "Protestant Missions in the Solomon Islands, 1849-1942" (Ph.D. thesis, A.N.U., 1966).

Howe, K.R., "Culture Contacts on the Loyalty Islands, 1841-1895" (Ph.D. thesis, A.N.U., 1973).

Jackson, K.B., "Head-hunting and Santa Ysabel, Solomon Islands, 1568-1901" (B.A. Hons thesis, A.N.U., 1972).

Parsonson, G.S., "Early Protestant Missions in the New Hebrides, 1839-1861" (M.A. thesis, University of New Zealand, 1949).

Pinson, Wilfred John, "Diocese of Polynesia, 1868-1910" (B.D. thesis, Pacific Theological College, Suva, 1970).

Prebble, A.E., "George Augustus Selwyn, the Apostle of Melanesia" (M.A. thesis, University of New Zealand, 1931).

Sayes, Shelley, "The Ethnohistory of Arosi, San Cristobal" (M.A. thesis, University of Auckland, 1976).

Tavoa, Michael Henry, "Church on Raga and Short Account of Selwyn and Patteson and their Melanesian Mission" (Diploma of Theology essay, Bishop Patteson Theological Centre, 1973).

Thompson, Roger C., "Australian Imperialism and the New Hebrides, 1862-1922" (Ph.D. thesis, A.N.U., 1970).

Wetherell. D.F., "Christian Missions in Eastern New Guinea: A Study of European, South Sea Island and Papuan Influences, 1877-1942" (Ph.D. thesis, A.N.U., 1974).

——, "A History of the Anglican Mission in Papua, 1891-1941" (M.A. thesis, A.N.U., 1970).

Bibliography 311

PRINTED SOURCES

Official Publications

British Solomon Islands Protectorate
 Annual Reports, London, 1912–42.
 Handbook of the British Solomon Islands Protectorate (Suva, 2nd edn, 1923).

Great Britain
Hansard's *Parliamentary Debates*, 3rd series, vols. 209–11 (Commons) 1872; 5th series, vol. 136, 1920.
Parliamentary Papers:
 Vol. 39, 1872 [C.542]: Report of the proceedings of H.M. ship "Rosario", during her cruise among the South Sea Islands, between 1st November 1871 and 12th February 1872.
 Vol. 43, 1872 [C.496]: Further correspondence respecting the deportation of South Sea Islanders.
 Vol. 50, 1873 (244): Communications respecting outrages committed upon natives of the South Sea Islands.
 Vol. 56, 1892 [C.6686]: Correspondence relating to Polynesian labour in the Colony of Queensland.
 Vol. 70, 1895 [C.7912]: Further correspondence relating to Polynesian labour in the Colony of Queensland.
 Vol. 5, 1928–29 [C.3248]: British Solomon Islands Protectorate. Report of Commissioner appointed by the Secretary of State for the Colonies to inquire into the circumstances in which murderous attacks took place in 1927 on government officials on Guadalcanal and Malaita.

Annual Reports

Church of England, Central Board of Missions, *Annual Reviews*, 1908–21.
Church of England, Missionary Council of the Church Assembly, *Annual Reports*, 1923–40.
Church of the Province of New Zealand, *Proceedings of General Synod*, 1859–1949.
Diocese of Auckland, *Year Books*, 1919–47.
Eton Association of the Melanesian Mission, *Annual Reports*, 1872–1912.
Melanesian Mission, *Annual Reports*, Auckland or Sydney, 1852–1942 (from 1897, sometimes published in the *Southern Cross Log*).
——, *The Island Voyage*, Ludlow, 1874–90.

Melanesian Mission English Committee, *Annual Reports*, London, 1899-1939.
Society for the Propagation of the Gospel, *Annual Reports*, 1849-1881.

Newspapers and Periodicals

A.B.M. Review (Sydney), 1910-42.
Australasian Missionary News (Sydney), 1888-90.
Church Gazette for the Dioceses of Auckland and Melanesia (Auckland), 1872-91; cited as *Church Gazette*.
Colonial Church Chronicle (London), 1847-74.
Gospel Missionary (London), 1851-1902.
Guardian (London), 1871-72, 1908.
Melanesian Mission, *Occasional Paper* (Ludlow), 1892-97.
Mission Field (London), 1856-1941.
Mission Life (London), 1866-90.
Missionary Notes of the Australian Board of Missions (Sydney), 1895-1909.
Net Cast in Many Waters (London), 1866-96; cited as *The Net*.
Pacific Islands Monthly (Sydney), 1930-47.
Reaper (Wellington), 1923-47.
St Augustine's College, Canterbury, *Occasional Papers*, 1867-1935.
Southern Cross Log (Australia and New Zealand edn, Auckland), 1895-1904, 1913-34, 1947-72; (Sydney), 1904-13, 1934-47.
Southern Cross Log (English edn, London), 1900-47.

Books, Pamphlets and Articles by Missionaries and Other Participants

Aborigines Protection Society, *The Polynesian Labour Traffic, and the Murder of Bishop Patteson: The Proceedings of a Public Meeting held in London on the 13th of December, 1871, with the Private Diary of Mr Consul March, of Fiji, and an Introduction* (London, 1872).
Artless, Stuart, W., ed., *The Church in Melanesia* (London: Melanesian Mission, 1936).
Ashwell, B.Y., *Journal of a Visit to the Loyalty, New Hebrides, and Banks' Islands, in the Melanesian Mission Schooner the "Southern Cross", with an Account of the Wreck of that Vessel* (Auckland, 1860).
Baddeley, W.H., *Melanesia by the Bishop of Melanesia*, The Bishops' Books no. 1 (London: Church Literature Association, 1936).
——, "Melanesia", *East and West Review* 2 (1936): 325-32.
——, "Melanesia", *East and West Review* 14 (1948): 105-9.

Bani, Ben, "Early Days with the Heathen on Raga", *Melanesian Messenger* (Taroaniara), Easter 1965 pp. 18-20.
Bice, C., "The Church's Duty to the Heathen—(1) In Australasia—(2) In Other Lands", in *The Official Report of the Church Congress held at Hobart on January 23rd, 24th, 25th, and 26th, 1894* (Hobart, 1894), pp. 272-77.
Bice, C., and Brittain, A., *Journal of Residence in the New Hebrides, S.W. Pacific Ocean: Written during the Year 1886* (Truro, 1887).
Bishop, F.R., *Work in the Mandated Area, Territory of New Guinea* (Westminster, 1928).
[Brooke, C.H.], *Percy Pomo: or, the Autobiography of a South Sea Islander* (London, [1881]).
Brown, Charles Hunter, *The Melanesian Mission: A Letter to the Editors of the Australian Churchman* (Nelson, N.Z., 1869).
Browning, C.W., "Amongst the Savages of the Solomon Islands", *Evangelist Monthly*, no. 111 (1901), pp. 66-70; no. 112, pp. 92-95; no. 113, pp. 105-7; no. 114, pp. 140-43; no. 115, pp. 153-55.
——, "More about the Solomon Islands", *Evangelist Monthly*, no. 118 (1901), pp. 223-25; no. 119, pp. 249-51.
Church of England in Australia, *Minutes of Proceedings at a Meeting of the Metropolitan and Suffragan Bishops of the Province of Australasia, held at Sydney, from October 1st to November 1st, A.D. 1850* (Sydney, [1850]).
Codrington, R.H., *Lecture delivered at Nelson, N.Z., September 25, 1863*; published with address by J.C. Patteson (Torquay, n.d.).
——, *The Melanesian Languages* (Oxford, 1885).
——, *The Melanesians: Studies in their Anthropology and Folk-lore* (Oxford, 1891).
——, "Religious Beliefs and Practices in Melanesia", *Journal of the Anthropological Institute* 10 (1880-81): 261-316.
——, "Various Forms of Paganism", in *The Official Report of the Missionary Conference of the Anglican Communion ... 1894*, ed. George A. Spottiswoode (London, 1894), pp. 112-16.
Coombe, Florence, *Islands of Enchantment: Many-sided Melanesia* (London: Macmillan, 1911).
——, *School-days in Norfolk Island* (London: S.P.C.K., 1909).
Coote, Walter, *The Western Pacific: Being a Description of the Groups of Islands to the North and East of the Australian Continent* (London, 1883).
Cosh, James, *The Martyrs of Melanesia: A Sermon preached in St Andrew's Presbyterian Church, Auckland ... on the Occasion of the Death of Bishop Patteson, the Rev. Joseph Atkin, and a Teacher named Stephen—who were Killed by the Natives of Nukapu, 20th September, 1871* (Auckland, [1871]).

Cowie, W.G., *Notes of a Visit to Norfolk Island, the Headquarters of the Melanesian Mission, in November, 1872: From the Journal of the Bishop of Auckland* (Auckland, 1872); for private circulation.

Drummond, H.N., *John Coleridge Patteson: An Account of his Death at Nukapu, and Description of S. Barnabas Chapel, Norfolk Island, Dedicated to his Memory* (Parkstone [Dorset]: Ralph & Brown, 1930).

Dudley, B.T., "The Church's Duty to the Heathen—(1) In Australasia—(2) In Other Lands", in *The Official Report of the Church Congress held at Hobart on January 23rd, 24th, 25th, and 26th, 1894* (Hobart, 1894), pp. 277-82.

——, *Love in Self Sacrifice: A Sermon preached at Christ Church, Nelson, N.Z., on the First Sunday in Lent, 1877, being the Occasion of the Consecration of the Right Rev. John Richardson Selwyn, M.A., Missionary Bishop of Melanesia* (Christchurch, 1877).

——, *The Martyrs of Santa Cruz: A Sermon preached in Auckland, 5th November, 1871, 22nd Sunday after Trinity, with Appendix* (Auckland, 1871).

——, *"Who is Sufficient for these Things?": A Sermon preached in S. Paul's Cathedral Church, Auckland, N.Z., on S. Barnabas' Day, June 11, 1873, on the Occasion of the Ordination of George Sarawia, the First Native Clergyman of Melanesia, to the Priesthood ...* (Auckland, 1873).

Durrad, W.J., *The Attitude of the Church to the Suqe*, Melanesian Mission Occasional Papers no. 1 (Norfolk Island, 1920).

——, "Notes on the Torres Islands", *Oceania* 10 (1939-40): 389-403; 11 (1940-41): 75-109, 186-201.

Edgell, W.H., *Diocese of Melanesia: New Hebrides Islands District. Diary of Island Voyage in the South Pacific Ocean* [1898] (Kingston-on-Thames, 1899); for private circulation.

Fox, Charles E., "The Church of Melanesia", *East and West Review* 28 (1962): 35-47.

——, "Companions and Brothers", *Melanesian Messenger* (Taroaniara), January 1964, pp. 27-29.

——, *Introduction to the Study of the Oceanic Languages* (Norfolk Island: Melanesian Mission Press, 1910).

——, *Kakamora* (London: Hodder & Stoughton, 1962).

——, *Lord of the Southern Isles: Being the Story of the Anglican Mission in Melanesia, 1849-1949* (London: A.R. Mowbray, 1958).

——, *The Melanesian Brotherhood*, rev. Brian Macdonald-Milne (London: Melanesian Mission, 2nd edn, [1972]).

——, *The Story of the Solomons* (Taroaniara: D.O.M. Publications, 1967).

———, *The Threshold of the Pacific: An Account of the Social Organization, Magic and Religion of the People of San Cristoval in the Solomon Islands* (London: Kegan Paul, Trench, Trubner, 1924).

Freeth, Robert E., "Christian Influences on a Dying Race", *The East and the West* 14 (1916): 382-94.

[Harvey, B.W.], *A Sermon preached in St Paul's Church, Wellington, on Sunday, 5th November, 1871 on the Death of Bishop Patteson* (Wellington, 1871).

Hogg, Lewis M., *A Letter to His Grace the Duke of Newcastle, Secretary of State for the Colonies ... on behalf of the Melanesian Mission of the Bishop of New Zealand, and also on behalf of Missions to the Aborigines of Australia* (London, 1853).

Hopkins, A.I., "The Call from the South Seas", *The East and the West* 24 (1926): 215-22.

———, *From Heathen Boy to Christian Priest* (London: S.P.C.K., 1930).

———, *In the Isles of King Solomon: An Account of Twenty-five Years spent amongst the Primitive Solomon Islanders* (London: Seeley, Service, 1928).

———, ed., *Melanesia To-day: A Study Circle Book* (London: S.P.C.K., 1927).

———, (with Johann Flierl), "Native Life in the South-west Pacific: From Two Points of View", *International Review of Missions* 17 (1928): 543-49.

Howard, Cecil W., "The Church's Mission in Melanesia", in Church of England, *Pan-Anglican Papers: Being Problems for Consideration at the Pan-Anglican Congress, 1908* (London, 1908), 2, sect. S.E., 4 (f), pp. 1-7.

———, "The Islands of Melanesia", *The East and the West* 6 (1908): 283-91.

Ivens, W.G., *Darkness and Dawn: A Missionary Play in Three Acts, descriptive of the Work of the Melanesian Mission* (Sydney: Australian Board of Missions, 1914).

———, *Dictionary and Grammar of the Language of Sa'a and Ulawa, Solomon Islands*, Carnegie Institute of Washington, Publication no. 253 (Washington, 1918).

———, "The Diversity of Culture in Melanesia", *Journal of the Royal Anthropological Institute* 64 (1934): 45-56.

———, *Hints to Missionaries to Melanesia* (London: Melanesian Mission, 1907).

———, *The Island Builders of the Pacific: How & Why the People of Mala construct their Artificial Islands, the Antiquity & Doubtful Origin of the Practice, with a Description of the Social Organization, Magic & Religion of their Inhabitants* (London: Seeley, Service, 1930).

——, *Melanesians of the South-east Solomon Islands* (London: Kegan Paul, Trench, Trubner, 1927).
Marau, Clement, *Story of a Melanesian Deacon: Clement Marau, written by Himself*, trans. R.H. Codrington (London, 1894).
Martin, Lady [Mary], *Our Maoris* (London, 1884).
Mason, Etta, *On Our Island* (London: S.P.C.K., 1925).
Melanesian Mission, *About Melanesia: A Brief Survey of the Present Situation in the Mission Field* [1930], (Auckland, 1930).
——, *About Melanesia, no. 2: Life in a Mission Native School* (Auckland, n.d.).
——, *About Melanesia, no. 3: The Daily Task of a Missionary in Melanesia* (n.p., n.d.).
——, *About Melanesia, no. 4: Medical Work in Melanesia* (n.p., n.d.).
——, *About Melanesia, no. 6: "Lady Missionaries and One of the Empire's Best"*, being an Extract from *"A Trader in the Savage Solomons"* (n.p., n.d.).
——, *About Melanesia, no. 7: Native Women of the Solomons, "Mothers' Union Work"* (Sydney, n.d.).
——, *About Melanesia, no. 8: Training Young Melanesians*, being an Address to the Annual Meeting of the English Committee, Church House, Westminster, London, May 29th, 1935, by the Reverend Geo. Warren, Melanesian Mission (Sydney, n.d.).
——, *About Melanesia, no. 9: A Brief Survey of the Present Situation in the Mission Field, 1937* (Sydney, 1937).
——, *About Melanesia, no. 10: Melanesia, by the Bishop of Melanesia* (Sydney, 1937).
——, *The Canons of Discipline of the Diocese of Melanesia, as Revised at the Synod of 1962* (Taroaniara, [1963]).
——, *A Catechism: With Prayers to be used by those preparing for Holy Baptism and Confirmation, and for Catechumen's Class* (Maravovo, 1935).
——, *The Community of the Cross* (London, [1946]).
——, *Consecration of Memorial Chapel: A Week at St. Barnabas', Norfolk Island* (Sydney, [1881]).
——, *The Constitutions, Canons and Regulations of the Missionary Diocese of Melanesia together with such Canons and other Proceedings of the General Synod of the Church of New Zealand as affect the Missionary Diocese of Melanesia* (Auckland, [1924]).
——, *A Course of Six Lessons on the Work of the Church in Melanesia for Children under 10*, comp. Marjorie B. Wright (Westminster, [1925]).
——, *District Clergy in Melanesia*, Southern Cross Booklet no. 3 (London, n.d.).

——, *Education in Melanesia*, Southern Cross Booklet no. 4 (London, n.d.).
——, *The Faith of the Church: Lessons in the Faith for Junior Schools in the Diocese of Melanesia* (Summer Hill, N.S.W., [1949]).
——, *Form for the Consecration of the Church of St Barnabas, Norfolk Island, built in Memory of John Coleridge Patteson D.D., First Bishop in Melanesia, St Andrew's Day 1880* (Norfolk Island, 1880).
——, *Hand-Book of the Melanesian Mission* (Westminster, 1907; 2nd edn, 1923).
——, *A Handbook of the Melanesian Mission* (Auckland, [1926]).
——, *In the Solomons and other Islands of Melanesia* (Sydney, 1943).
——, *Isles of the Pacific: Account of the Melanesian Mission and of the Wreck of the Mission Vessel. Also the Bishop of New Zealand's Sermon on the Consecration of the Rev. J.C. Patteson, M.A., in St Pauls Church, Auckland, N.Z., with a Letter from the Missionary Bishop* (Melbourne, 1861).
——, *Journal of the Mission Voyage to the Melanesian Islands of the Schooner "Southern Cross": Made in May–October, 1866* (Auckland, 1866).
——, *Leprosy in Melanesia*, Southern Cross Booklet no. 6 (London, n.d.).
——, *Medical Work in Melanesia*, Southern Cross Booklet no. 7 (London, n.d.).
——, *Melanesia: Historical and Geographical*, Southern Cross Booklet no. 1 (London, n.d.).
——, *The Melanesian Mission: Some Testimony to the Efficacy of its Work in Humanizing, Civilizing, and Christianizing the Natives of the Islands of the S.W. Pacific Ocean* (London, [1899]).
——, *The Melanesian Mission, 1849 to 1939* (Auckland, 1939).
——, *Mothercraft in Melanesia*, Southern Cross Booklet no. 8 (London, n.d.).
——, *Pacific Progress, 1849–1949: Being the Illustrated Centenary Book of the Diocese of Melanesia* (Chatham: Parrett & Neves, 1949).
——, *The Printed Word*, Southern Cross Booklet no. 4a (London, n.d.).
——, *Records and Documents relating to the Consecration of a Missionary Bishop for the Western Islands of the South Pacific Ocean* (Auckland, 1861).
——, *Religion and Customs in Melanesia*, Southern Cross Booklet no. 2 (London, n.d.).
——, *Report of the Fourth Conference of the Melanesian Mission and of the First Synod of the Missionary Diocese of Melanesia held at Siota, Oct. 24th until Nov. 8th, 1921* (n.p., n.d.).
——, *St Andrew's College, Mission Bay, Kohimarama, Auckland, N.Z.* (Auckland, 1929).

——, *The Story of the Melanesian Mission* (Auckland, [1926]).

——, *Suggestions for the Revision of the Prayer Book and for Additional Forms of Service ... submitted for Consideration preparatory to the Discussion of the Subject at the 1921 Conference* (Maravovo, 1920).

——, *Syllabus for Study Circle* (Westminster, [1914]).

——, *"Ta'ina", or Some Lines on a New Movement in Melanesia* (Sydney, 1935).

Melanesian Mission English Committee, *Memorandum on the Future of the Melanesian Mission* (London, 1919); for private circulation.

Montgomery, H.H., "The Anglican Church in the South Pacific", *The East and the West* 1 (1903): 402–12.

——, *The Light of Melanesia: A Record of Thirty-five Years' Mission Work in the South Seas, written after a Personal Visitation made by Request of the Right Rev. John Selwyn, D.D., late Bishop of Melanesia* (London, 1896).

The New Zealand Church Almanac for the Year of Our Lord 1852 (Auckland, 1852).

The New Zealand Church Almanac for the Year of Our Lord 1853 (Auckland, 1853).

Norfolk Island: Correspondence between His Excellency Sir W. Denison, K.C.B., Governor General of Australia, and the Bishop of New Zealand; with other Documents relating to Norfolk Island, and its Present Inhabitants (Auckland, 1857); for private circulation.

O'Ferrall, W.C., *Santa Cruz and the Reef Islands* (Westminster: Melanesian Mission, [1908]).

Oldham, L.L., "San Cristoval (Solomon Islands)", *Walkabout* 2, no. 3 (January 1936): 29–31.

Patteson, J.C., *The Abiding Comforter: A Sermon preached in St. Mary's Church, Auckland, on the Evening of Sunday, 3rd March, 1861 (being the day of his Consecration), by the late Right Reverend John Coleridge Patteson, D.D., Missionary Bishop of Melanesia* (1861; repr. Auckland, 1871).

——, "'Christian Principles': A Sermon preached by Bishop Patteson of Melanesia at Christ Church, Sydney, on the 15th of October, 1865. Taken from his own notes", *Australasian Church Quarterly Review* 1 (1910–11): 223–33.

——, *A Letter from the Right Reverend John Coleridge Patteson, D.D. to **** [11 Nov. 1862] (Auckland, n.d.).

——, *A Letter from the Rt Rev. John Coleridge Patteson, D.D.* ([Auckland], n.d.)

——, *Letters with Extracts from the Bishop of Lichfield's Sermon* (Eton, [1872]).

——, *The Melanesian Mission* (address delivered at St Mary's

Schoolroom, Balmain, Sydney, 2 April 1864; published with lecture by R.H. Codrington), (Torquay, n.d.).

———, *A Sermon preached at Saint Paul's Church, Auckland, on Whitsunday, 1862, by the Rt Rev. John Coleridge Patteson D.D., Fellow of Merton College, Oxford: Missionary Bishop of the Melanesian Islands* (n.p., n.d.).

Peacocke, Ponsonby, "A Cruise in the 'Southern Cross' ", *New Zealand Illustrated Magazine* 6 (1902): 274–84.

Penny, Alfred, *The Headhunters of Christabel: A Tale of Adventure in the South Seas* (London, [1903]).

———, *Ten Years in Melanesia* (London, 1887).

[Radford, L.B.], *Missionary Problems of the Western Pacific: Memorandum by the Bishop of Goulburn* (n.p., [1920]); for private circulation.

Rivers, W.H.R., ed., *Essays on the Depopulation of Melanesia* (Cambridge: Cambridge University Press, 1922).

Robin, L.P., "Something about the Melanesian Mission", *Evangelist Monthly*, no. 97 (1900), pp. 11–15; no. 98, pp. 36–41; no. 99, pp. 58–62; no. 101, pp. 107–10; no.102, pp. 139–42.

Sarawia, George, *They Came to My Island: The Beginnings of the Mission in the Banks Islands*, trans. from Mota by D.A. Rawcliffe (Siota: Diocese of Melanesia Press, 1968).

Selwyn, G.A., *A Charge delivered to the Clergy of the Diocese of New Zealand, at the Diocesan Synod, in the Chapel of St John's College, on Thursday, September 23, 1847* (London, 2nd edn, 1849).

———, *Letter from Bishop Selwyn* [St Barnabas' Day, 1853], ([Eton], 1853); for private circulation.

———, *Letters on the Melanesian Mission in 1853* (London, 1855).

———, *Sermon preached at the Consecration of the Rev. John Coleridge Patteson, M.A., Fellow of Merton College, to act as Missionary Bishop among the Western Islands of the South Pacific, on the Festival of St Matthias, Feb. 24, 1861, by George Augustus, Bishop of New Zealand and Metropolitan* (Auckland, 1861).

———, *Two Letters from Bishop Selwyn* (Eton, 1850).

———, *The Work of Christ in the World: Four Sermons preached before the University of Cambridge ... 1854* (Cambridge, 1855).

Selwyn, G.A., et al, *Extracts from New Zealand Letters during the Years 1851–2* (Eton, 1853).

Selwyn, J.R., "Australasian and South Sea Problems", in *The Official Report of the Missionary Conference of the Anglican Communion ... 1894*, ed. George A. Spottiswoode (London, 1894), pp. 257–61.

———, *Bishop Patteson*, repr. from the Selwyn College Calendar (Cambridge, 1895; for private circulation.)

—, "The Islands of the Western Pacific", *Journal of the Royal Colonial Institute* 25 (1894): 587–607.

—, *The Lessons of the Holy Sepulchre: A Sermon preached in the Church of the Holy Sepulchre, Auckland, on the Eighth Anniversary of its Dedication, Wednesday, August 27, 1873* (Auckland, 1873).

—, "Letters from the Right Reverend the Lord Bishop of Melanesia", *Australasian Month* 1 (1884): 343–52.

—, *Melanesian Mission: Its Mode of Work and Present Position* ([Sydney], n.d.).

—, *Pastoral Work in the Colonies and the Mission Field* (London, 1897).

—, *Personal Recollections of Bishop George Augustus Selwyn*, repr. from the Selwyn College Calendar (Cambridge, 1894; for private circulation.)

[Shaw], Sister Gwen, "The Girls' School in the Solomon Islands", *Overseas Education* 22, no. 1 (October 1950): 2–8.

Sinker, William, *By Reef and Shoal: Being an Account of a Voyage amongst the Islands in the South-western Pacific* (London: S.P.C.K., 1904).

—, "In the Islands of Melanesia: A Sailor's Testimony", *The East and the West* 12 (1914): 184–92.

Steward, John Manwaring, "The Anglican Communion: New Zealand", in *Episcopacy, Ancient and Modern*, ed. Claude Jenkins and K.D. Mackenzie (London: S.P.C.K., 1930), pp. 262–67.

—, *"The Brothers", Melanesian Mission* (Auckland, 1928).

—, *Hints on District Work*, Melanesian Mission Occasional Papers no. 4 (Maravovo, 1926).

—, *John Steward's Memories: Papers written by the Late Bishop Steward of Melanesia*, ed. M.R. Newbolt (Chester: Phillipson & Golder, 1939).

—, "Melanesia", in *The Anglican Communion throughout the World: A Series of Missionary Papers from the Field*, repr. from *The Living Church*, ed. Clifford P. Morehouse (Milwaukee and London: Morehouse, 1927), pp. 201–9.

—, *Melanesia in Pictures* (Leeds: Hunters Armley, 1931).

—, *A Melanesian Use, together with Notes on Ceremonial, etc.*, Melanesian Mission Occasional Papers no. 3 (Maravovo, 1926.

—, *The Primary Charge of the Right Reverend John M. Steward, Bishop of Melanesia* (Norfolk Island, 1919).

Toa, Oscar Arthur, "Strange Religion on Raga", *Melanesian Messenger* (Taroaniara), August 1965 pp. 23–26.

Uthwatt, [W.A.], Archdeacon, *Life in Melanesia: Education of People steeped in Heathenism and Witchcraft, Cannibals and Child Murderers* (n.p., [1913]).

Uthwatt, W.A., "The Melanesian Mission in the Solomons", *Australasian Church Quarterly Review* 1 (1910-11): 234-43.
Veronica of the Cross, Sister [Wilson, Beatrice], *The School Island* (London: S.P.C.K., 1949).
Waddy, P. Stacy, *A Visit to Norfolk Island* (Westminster: Melanesian Mission, [1906]).
Webb, A.S., "The People of Aoba, New Hebrides", *Mankind* 2 (1937): 73-80.
Welchman, H., "The Dancers", *Evangelist Monthly*, no. 136 (1903): 78-79.
———, "Soga's Canoe House", *Evangelist Monthly*, no. 157 (1905): 10-12.
Wench, Ida, *Mission to Melanesia* (London: Elek Books, 1961).
Wilson, Cecil, "Cricket in the Solomon Islands", in *Imperial Cricket*, ed. Pelham F. Warner (London: London & Counties Press Association, 1912), pp. 419-27.
———, "Missions to the Heathen in and near Australia", in *The Official Report of the Proceedings of the Adelaide Church Congress held from September 29 to October 3, 1902* (Adelaide, 1903), pp. 192-96.
———, *My Last Voyage* (London: Melanesian Mission, [1912]).
———, *The Wake of the Southern Cross: Work and Adventures in the South Seas* (London: John Murray, 1932).
———, *Women of Melanesia* (Sydney, n.d.).
Wilson, Ellen, *Dr Welchman of Bugotu* (London: S.P.C.K., 1935).
[———], *The Isles that Wait, by a Lady Member of the Melanesian Mission* (London: S.P.C.K., 1912).
———, *Sketches from Life in Melanesia* (London: S.P.C.K., [1927])
[Wood, Cecil J.], *A Form of Spiritual Communion compiled by the Bishop of Melanesia* (Auckland, 1916).

Other Published Works

Allen, M.R., "The Establishment of Christianity and Cash-Cropping in a New Hebridean Community", *Journal of Pacific History* 3 (1968): 25-46.
Allen, W.O.B., and McLure, Edmund, *Two Hundred Years: The History of the Society for Promoting Christian Knowledge, 1698-1898* (London, 1898).
Armstrong, E.S., *The History of the Melanesian Mission* (London: Isbister & Co., 1900).
Artless, Stuart W., *The Story of the Melanesian Mission* (London: Melanesian Mission, 3rd edn, 1948).
Awdry, Frances, *In the Isles of the Sea: The Story of Fifty Years in Melanesia* (London: Bemrose & Sons, 3rd edn, 1911)

——, *The Story of a Fellow Soldier: Being a Life of Bishop Patteson narrated for the Young* (London, 1874).
Australian Board of Missions, *The Jubilee Festival of the Australian Board of Missions, 1850-1900: The Commemoration in Sydney. Illustrated Handbook and Programme of Services and Meetings, August 19th to August 26th inclusive* (Sydney, 1900).
Belshaw, Cyril S., "Changes in Heirloom Jewellery in the Central Solomons", *Oceania* 20 (1949-50): 169-84.
——, *Changing Melanesia: Social Economics of Culture Contact* (Melbourne: Oxford University Press, 1954).
——, "Native Politics in the Solomon Islands", *Pacific Affairs* 20 (1947): 187-93.
Black, Robert H., "Christianity as a Cross-Cultural Bond in the British Solomon Islands Protectorate as seen in the Russell Islands", *Oceania* 33 (1962-63): 171-81.
Bogesi, George, "Santa Isabel, Solomon Islands", *Oceania* 18 (1947-48): 208-32, 327-57.
Boodle, R.G., *The Life and Labours of the Right Rev. William Tyrrell, D.D.: First Bishop of Newcastle, New South Wales* (London, 1881).
Boreham, F.W., *George Augustus Selwyn, D.D.: Pioneer Bishop of New Zealand* (London: S.W. Partridge, [1911]).
Burton, John Wear, *Missionary Survey of the Pacific Islands* (London: World Dominion Press, 1930).
Chadwick, Owen, *The Victorian Church*, in 2 parts (London: Adam & Charles Black, 1966-70).
Charles [Elizabeth] Rundle, *John Coleridge Patteson* (London: S.P.C.K., 1927).
Church of England, *Authorised Report of the Second Missionary Conference held at Oxford, May 2nd and 3rd, 1877* (London, [1877]).
Church of England, Missionary Council of the Church Assembly, *The World Call to the Church*, 6 vols. (Westminster: Church Assembly, 1926-28).
Church of England, United Boards of Missions, *The Official Report of the Missionary Conference of the Anglican Communion: on May 28, 29, 30, 31 and June 1, 1894*, ed. George A. Spottiswoode (London, 1894).
——, *Reports of the Boards of Missions of the Provinces of Canterbury and York on the Mission Field* (London, 1894).
——, *A Study of Some Missionary Problems: Being a Report issued by the United Boards of Missions of the Provinces of Canterbury and York* (London, 1903).
Clarke, H. Lowther, *Constitutional Church Government in the Domin-*

ions beyond the Seas and in other Parts of the Anglican Communion (London: S.P.C.K., 1924).

Coates, Austin, *Western Pacific Islands* (London: H.M.S.O., 1970).

Corris, Peter, "Kwaisulia of Ada Gege: A Strongman in the Solomon Islands", in *Pacific Islands Portraits*, ed. J.W. Davidson and Deryck Scarr (Canberra: A.N.U. Press, 1970), pp. 253-65.

———, *Passage, Port and Plantation: A History of Solomon Islands Labour Migration, 1870-1914* (Carlton: Melbourne University Press, 1973).

Curteis, G.H., *Bishop Selwyn of New Zealand, and of Lichfield: A Sketch of his Life and Work with some further Gleanings from his Letters, Sermons, and Speeches* (London, 1889).

Davenport, William, "Notes on Santa Cruz Voyaging", *Journal of the Polynesian Society* 73 (1964): 134-42.

———, "Two Social Movements in the British Solomons that Failed and their Political Consequences", in Fourth Waigani Seminar, *The Politics of Melanesia*, ed. Marion W. Ward, (Port Moresby and Canberra: University of Papua New Guinea and Research School of Pacific Studies, A.N.U., 1970), pp. 162-72.

Davidson, N.J., *Patteson of the South Sea Islands: The Story of the First Bishop of Melanesia ...* (London: Seeley, Service, 1931).

Davis, John King, *History of St. John's College, Tamaki, Auckland, New Zealand* (Auckland: Abel Dykes, 1911).

———, *The Melanesian Mission*, Jubilee Leaflets no. 7 (Christchurch, 1907).

Debenham, Mary H., *Patteson of the Isles* (London: Oxford University Press, 1921).

Evans, John H., *Churchman Militant: George Augustus Selwyn, Bishop of New Zealand and Lichfield* (London: George Allen & Unwin, 1964).

Finney, R.C., *I'll Have a Hurricane: John Coleridge Patteson*, Eagle Books no. 70 (London: Edinburgh House Press, 1955).

Firth, Raymond, *Rank and Religion in Tikopia: A Study in Polynesian Paganism and Conversion to Christianity* (London: George Allen & Unwin, 1970).

———, *Social Change in Tikopia: Re-study of a Polynesian Community after a Generation* (London: George Allen & Unwin, 1959).

———, *We, the Tikopia: A Sociological Study of Kinship in Primitive Polynesia* (London: George Allen & Unwin, 1936).

Forman, Charles W., "Missionaries and Colonialism: The Case of the New Hebrides in the Twentieth Century", *Journal of Church and State* 14 (1972): 75-92.

Gladstone, W.E., "Bishop Patteson", in *Gleanings of Past Years* (London, 1879), vol. 2, pp. 213-63.

Godden, Ruth, *Lolowai: The Story of Charles Godden and the Western Pacific* (Sydney: Wentworth Press, 1967).
Grierson, E.W., *Bishop Patteson of the Cannibal Islands* ... (London: Seeley, Service, 1927).
Gunson, W.N., "A Missionary Comity Agreement of 1880", *Journal of Pacific History* 8 (1973): 191-95.
——, "Missionary Interest in British Expansion in the South Pacific in the Nineteenth Century", *Journal of Religious History* 3 (1964-65): 296-313.
——, "The Theology of Imperialism and the Missionary History of the Pacific", *Journal of Religious History* 5 (1968-69): 255-65.
——, "Victorian Christianity in the South Seas: A Survey", *Journal of Religious History* 8 (1974-75): 183-97.
Guppy, H.B., *The Solomon Islands and their Natives* (London, 1887).
Gutch, John, *Martyr of the Islands: The Life and Death of John Coleridge Patteson* (London: Hodder & Stoughton, 1971).
Harris, S.F., "The Martyred Bishop of Melanesia", in his *A Century of Missionary Martyrs: Being an Account of Some who have suffered Martyrdom for the Truth during this Century of Missionary Work* (London, 1897), pp. 53-68.
Hilliard, David, "The Battle for Rennell Island: A Study in Missionary Politics", in *W.P. Morrell: A Tribute. Essays in Modern and Early Modern History presented to William Parker Morrell, Professor Emeritus, University of Otago*, eds. G.A. Wood and P.S. O'Connor, (Dunedin: University of Otago Press, 1973), pp. 105-24.
——, "Bishop G.A. Selwyn and the Melanesian Mission", *New Zealand Journal of History* 4 (1970): 120-37.
——, "Colonialism and Christianity: The Melanesian Mission in the Solomon Islands", *Journal of Pacific History* 9 (1974): 93-116.
——, "John Coleridge Patteson: Missionary Bishop of Melanesia", in *Pacific Islands Portraits*, ed. J.W. Davidson and Deryck Scarr (Canberra: A.N.U. Press, 1970), pp. 177-200.
——, "The South Sea Evangelical Mission in the Solomon Islands: The Foundation Years", *Journal of Pacific History* 4 (1969): 41-64.
Hogbin, H. Ian, *Experiments in Civilization: The Effects of European Culture on a Native Community of the Solomon Islands* (1939; repr. London: Routledge & Kegan Paul, 1969).
——, *A Guadalcanal Society: The Koaka Speakers* (New York: Holt, Rinehart & Winston, 1964).
——, *Social Change* (London: Watts, 1958).
How, F.D., *Bishop John Selwyn: A Memoir* (London, 1899).
The Island Mission: Being a History of the Melanesian Mission from its Commencement, repr. from *Mission Life* (London, 1869).

Jackson, K.B., "Head-hunting in the Christianization of Bugotu, 1861-1900", *Journal of Pacific History* 10 (1975): 65-78.
Jacobs, Henry, *Colonial Church Histories: New Zealand. Containing the Dioceses of Auckland, Christchurch, Dunedin, Nelson, Waiapu, Wellington, and Melanesia* (London, [1889]).
Jacomb, Edward, *The Future of the Kanaka* (Westminster: P.S. King, 1919).
Japp, Alexander Hay, "John Coleridge Patteson and the South Pacific", in his *Master Missionaries: Chapters in Pioneer Effort throughout the World* (London, [1880]), pp. 294-362.
Jones, Muriel, *Married to Melanesia* (London: George Allen & Unwin, 1974).
Kent, Graham, *Company of Heaven: Early Missionaries in the South Seas* (Wellington: A.H. & A.W. Reed, 1972).
Laracy, Hugh M., "The First Mission to Tikopia", *Journal of Pacific History* 4 (1969): 105-9.
———, "Marching Rule and the Missions", *Journal of Pacific History*, 6 (1971): 96-114.
———, *Marists and Melanesians: A History of Catholic Missions in the Solomon Islands* (Canberra: A.N.U. Press, 1976).
———, "Roman Catholic 'Martyrs' in the South Pacific, 1841-55", *Journal of Religious History* 9 (1976-77): 189-202.
———, Xavier Montrouzier: A Missionary in Melanesia", in *Pacific Islands Portraits*, ed. J.W. Davidson and Deryck Scarr (Canberra: A.N.U. Press, 1970), pp. 127-45.
Lycett, Margaret, *Brothers: The Story of the Native Brotherhood of Melanesia* (London: S.P.C.K., 1935).
McLean, Archibald, "John Coleridge Patteson", in his *Epoch Makers of Modern Missions* (St Louis: United Christian Missionary Society, 1912), pp. 133-56.
Miller, R.S., *Misi Gete: John Geddie, Pioneer Missionary to the New Hebrides* (Launceston: Presbyterian Church of Tasmania, 1975).
Morrell, W.P., *Britain in the Pacific Islands* (Oxford, Clarendon Press, 1960).
———, *The Anglican Church in New Zealand: A History* (Dunedin: Anglican Church of the Province of New Zealand, 1973).
Neill, Stephen, *Colonialism and Christian Missions* (London: Lutterworth Press, 1966).
———, *A History of Christian Missions* (Harmondsworth: Penguin, 1964).
Page, Jesse, *Bishop Patteson, the Martyr of Melanesia* (London, [1891]).
Paget, Elma K., *The Story of Bishop Patteson*, Children's Heroes Series (London and New York: T.C. & E.C. Jack, 1920).

Palmer [Edwin], *Bishop Patteson: Missionary Bishop and Martyr* (London, [1872]).
Parnaby, O.W., *Britain and the Labor Trade in the Southwest Pacific* (Durham, N.C.: Duke University Press, 1964).
Parsonson, G.S., "La Mission Presbytérienne des Nouvelles-Hébrides: Son Histoire et son Role Politique et Social", *Journal de la Société des Océanistes* 12 (1956): 107-37.
Pascoe, C.F., *Two Hundred Years of the S.P.G.: An Historical Account of the Society for the Propagation of the Gospel in Foreign Parts, 1701-1900*, 2 vols. (London: S.P.G., 1901).
Paton, Frank H.L., *Patteson of Melanesia: A Brief Life of John Coleridge Patteson, Missionary Bishop* (London: S.P.C.K., [1930]).
Peterson, Nicholas, "The Church Council of South Mala: A Legitimized Form of Masinga Rule", *Oceania* 36 (1965-66): 214-30.
Prebble, A.E., *About Melanesia: The Ships of the Mission, 1849-1932* (Auckland: Melanesian Mission, [1933]).
Purchas, H.T. *A History of the English Church in New Zealand* (Christchurch: Simpson & Williams, 1914).
Rayner, K., "The Home Base of the Missions of the Church of England, 1830-50", *Journal of Religious History* 2 (1962-63): 29-48.
Rivers, W.H.R., *The History of Melanesian Society*, 2 vols. (Cambridge: Cambridge University Press, 1914).
Ross, Angus, *New Zealand Aspirations in the Pacific in the Nineteenth Century* (Oxford: Clarendon Press, 1964).
Scarr, Deryck, *Fragments of Empire: A History of the Western Pacific High Commission, 1877-1914* (Canberra: A.N.U. Press, 1967).
———, "Recruits and Recruiters: A Portrait of the Labour Trade", in *Pacific Islands Portraits*, ed. J.W. Davidson and Deryck Scarr (Canberra: A.N.U. Press, 1970), pp. 225-51.
Shineberg, Dorothy, *They Came for Sandalwood: A Study of the Sandalwood Trade in the South-west Pacific, 1830-1865* (Carlton: Melbourne University Press, 1967).
Society for Promoting Christian Knowledge, *Bishop Patteson: Missionary Bishop and Martyr*, Little Books on Religion no. 26 (London, 1925).
———, *Bishop Selwyn*, Mission Heroes Series (London, n.d.).
———, *Bishop Selwyn*, Little Books on Religion no. 59 (London, 1928).
———, *Life of Bishop Patteson* (London, n.d.).
———, *Sketches of the Life of Bishop Patteson of Melanesia: A Revised Edition of "The Life of Bishop Patteson"* (London, 1873).
Society for the Propagation of the Gospel, *Diocese of Melanesia*, Historical Sketches, New Series (Westminster, 1917).

——, *Melanesia*, Historical Sketches, Missionary Series, no. 5 (Westminster, 2nd edn, 1889).
——, *The Story of a Martyr*, Missionary Stories no. 1 (London, [1921]).
Srawley, J.H. *Some Memorials of Bishop G.A. Selwyn and Bishop Patteson*, repr. from the Selwyn College Calendar, 1908-9 (Cambridge, [1909]).
Steel, Robert, *The New Hebrides and Christian Missions: With a Sketch of the Labour Traffic and Notes of a Cruise through the Group in the Mission Vessel* (London, 1880).
Stewart, P.J. "New Zealand and the Pacific Labour Traffic, 1870-1874", *Pacific Historical Review* 30 (1961): 47-59.
Stock, Eugene, "Thirty Years' Work in the Non-Christian World: A Brief Survey of Protestant Missions, 1872 to 1902", *The East and the West* 1 (1903): 438-62.
Thompson, H.P., *Into All Lands: The History of the Society for the Propagation of the Gospel in Foreign Parts, 1701-1950* (London: S.P.C.K., 1951).
Tippett, A.R., *Solomon Islands Christianity: A Study in Growth and Obstruction* (London: Lutterworth Press, 1967).
Tucker, H.W., *Memoir of the Life and Episcopate of George Augustus Selwyn, D.D.: Bishop of New Zealand, 1841-1869, Bishop of Lichfield, 1867-1878*, 2 vols. (London, 1879).
Twitchell, Joseph Hopkins, *Coleridge Patteson of Melanesia: A Modern Knight* (New Haven: Yale Foreign Missionary Society, 1906).
Warren, Max, *Social History and Christian Mission* (London: S.C.M. Press, 1967).
Wetherell, David, *Reluctant Mission: The Anglican Church in Papua New Guinea, 1891-1942* (St Lucia: University of Queensland Press, 1977).
Whonsbon-Aston, C.W., *Pacific Irishman: William Floyd Inaugural Memorial Lecture given in Holy Trinity Anglican Cathedral, Suva, Fiji, on August 28, 1970* (Stanmore: Australian Board of Missions, [1971]).
Williams, C.P.S., *From Eton to the South Seas* (London, n.d.).
Woodford, Charles Morris, *A Naturalist among the Head-Hunters: Being an Account of Three Visits to the Solomon Islands in the Years 1886, 1887, and 1888* (London, 1890).
World Missionary Conference, 1910, *Reports of Commissions*, 9 vols. (Edinburgh and London: Oliphant, Anderson & Ferrier, 1910).
Yonge, Charlotte Mary, *Life of John Coleridge Patteson: Missionary Bishop of the Melanesian Islands*, 2 vols. (London, 1874).

Yonge, Charlotte F., "The Melanesian Brotherhood", *East and West Review* 1 (1935): 344–51.

Young, Florence S.H., *Pearls from the Pacific* (London and Edinburgh: Marshall Brothers, [1925]).

INTERVIEWS

Bishop Leonard Alufurai, Auki, Solomon Islands; April 1965.
Rev. W.F. Browning, Greatworth, Oxfordshire; November 1970.
Mr H.W. Bullen, Auckland; December 1964, January 1969.
Bishop S.G. Caulton, London; January 1971.
Archdeacon E.A. Codd, Adelaide; December 1969.
Mr N.C. Deck (S.S.E.M.) Sydney; July 1963, March 1965.
Sister Mary Dismas (formerly Sister Veronica of the Sisters of the Cross); Suva, February 1970.
Rev. Dr C.E. Fox, Taroaniara, Solomon Islands; April 1965.
Rev. D. Lloyd Francis, Hove, East Sussex; September 1970, January 1971.
Rev. Robert Hagesi, Kohimarama, Solomon Islands; January 1974
Bishop A.T. Hill, Honiara, Solomon Islands; April 1965.
Bishop D.A. Rawcliffe, Lolowai, New Hebrides; January 1974.
Archdeacon H.V.C. Reynolds, Honiara, Solomon Islands; April 1965.
Archdeacon R.C. Rudgard, Basingstoke, Hampshire; January 1971.
Miss N. Stead, Sydney; March 1965.
Mrs H.O. Warren, London; October 1970, February 1971.

Index

Abel, Charles, 225
Adams, Hedley Vicars, 200–201
Adelaide, 45, 112
Admiralty, First Lord of (fifth Earl Spencer), 109
Admiralty Islands, 4
Ako, Arthur, 181
Alamemea, 183
All Hallows School, Pawa. *See* Pawa school
Alite Island, 85–86
Allen, Roland, 221
Alufurai, Leonard, 221
Ambrym, 68, 98-99, 290n
Ambuofa, Peter, 178
Andrews, George Henry, 161n
Aneityum, 5–7, 47, 99
Anglican Church in New Zealand, 1, 3, 23–25
  General Synod of, 25, 44, 54, 79, 127–29, 210, 247, 249, 256–56n, 259. *See also* New Zealand
Anglican missionaries in Melanesia, 297–302
  attitudes to British annexation, 6, 107–8, 110–11, 133
  attitudes to economic development, 57–59, 101, 174, 224–27, 259, 280, 283, 294
  attitudes to labour recruiting, 63–65, 68, 103–7, 130, 178, 240, 242, 264–65
  attitudes to Melanesian religion and customs, 37, 50, 54–58, 96, 112, 164–65, 182, 190–203, 286, 294
  churchmanship, 2–4, 14, 30, 46, 57, 75, 127, 140, 181, 183, 208, 232–35, 260–61, 281
  life in islands, 11, 47–51, 81–82, 116n, 145–49, 271–72
  numbers, 10, 31, 115, 125, 127, 129, 144, 153, 163, 208, 217, 273
  plans for indigenous church, 8, 10, 61–62, 153–57, 194, 215–23, 273, 293–94
  racial attitudes, 10, 41–43, 153–55, 190, 222–23, 231, 271–74, 288, 294
  salaries, 146, 252n
  secular European views of, 113–14, 176, 264–65, 271
  social backgrounds, 31–33, 36, 38, 102, 124–27, 136, 144–45, 151, 208, 221, 226, 273, 290n, 293–94
  women missionaries, 34, 112, 123, 149–53, 234–35, 267–69, 273, 285. *See also* British Solomon Islands Protectorate government; Eton College; New Hebrides Condominium; Melanesian Mission; Melanesians in Anglican ministry; Royal Navy; names of individual missionaries; traders; trading vessels
Anglican missions
  adaptation to non-Western cultures, 56–57, 122, 194–95
  appointment of missionary bishops, 23–26, 126, 245
  indigenous leadership, 61, 123, 126, 155–56, 217, 221
  Day of Intercession for missions, 73, 121
  home organization, 121–24, 156
  missionary recruitment and training, 124–26
  missionary theology, 2–3, 121, 123, 194–95, 258–59, 287
Anglo-Catholicism, in Melanesia,

181, 208, 232–35, 254n, 260–61, 281. *See also* Oxford Movement; Tractarianism
Anthropology, contribution of Anglican missionaries to, 37, 190–96. *See also* Codrington, R.H.; Fox, C.E.; Ivens, W.G.
Anti-Slavery Society, 240–41
Aola, Guadalcanal, 230
Archibald, Isaac, 4
Armstrong, E.S., 138
Arosi district, San Cristobal, 82, 196
Ashley, Francis Noel, 262–63, 270
Associates of Melanesia, 248
Ata'a Cove, Malaita, 177
Atkin, Joseph, 38, 48, 65–67, 79 82, 85
Auckland, 25, 40, 62–63, 71, 101, 127, 249, 251
  Bishop of (M.R. Neligan), 124
  headquarters of Melanesian Mission at, 9–11, 14–15, 17, 20–21, 30–36, 45, 47, 49
  support for Melanesian Mission from, 12–13, 45, 129, 247, 290n
Auki, Malaita, 181
Australia, support for Melanesian Mission from 13–14, 43–45, 53n, 111–12, 127–29, 183, 244–47, 279
Australian (Australasian) Board of Missions, 13–14, 46, 112, 244–47

Baddeley, Bishop Walter Hubert, 260, 266, 269, 272–73, 277–79, 282, 284–85, 287
  appointed Bishop of Melanesia, 259–60
  biographical notes, 297
  personality and religious views, 260–61, 269, 272
  relations with B.S.I.P. government and traders, 261–66
Banks Islands, 17, 37
  Christian population of, 96, 115, 156
  labour recruiting from, 63–64, 104–7, 164, 179
  Melanesian Mission in, 11, 17, 47–51, 58–62, 96–98, 144, 164, 233, 235–36
  mission scholars and teachers from, 18, 34, 38, 41, 51, 58–62, 96–97, 104–5, 185
  missionary opposition to *sukwe*, 198–202. *See also* Kwasvarong, W.; Marau, C.; Pantutun, R,; Sarawia, G.; Tagalad, H.; Wogale, E.; names of individual islands
Barge, John Frederick, 279
Barker, Bishop Frederic, 44
Batty, Bishop F. De Witt, 261
Bell, W.R., 238, 279
Bellona Island, 15, 262
Belshaw, Cyril, S., 198, 285
Benson, Archbishop E.W., 126
Bera, 87–89
Bice, Charles, 38, 39, 40–41, 45, 81, 88, 99–100, 104, 137, 150, 182
  biographical notes, 297–98
Bishops, appointment of, 1, 23–26, 79, 126–27, 206–8, 213n, 214, 246, 249, 256n, 259–60
Bismarck Archipelago, 243, 246. *See also* New Britian
Bitama, Malaita, 197
Blencowe, John Walcot, 147, 163, 187, 205
Bollen, Frank, 161n, 191–92
Border Maid, 11
Borneo Mission, 7, 24, 115
Bougainville, 101, 137. *See also* German Solomon Islands
Bowen, Sir George, 45
Bower, Lieutenant, 91
Brisbane, bishops of, 105, 131
British New Guinea, 134
British Solomon Islands Protectorate, 110–11, 132, 186, 266, 275, 293
British Solomon Islands Protectorate government
  Advisory Council, 237, 262
  and Christianity, 132–35, 166–70, 181, 275
  and Fallowes movement, 282–85
  education, 222, 261–63, 276, 281
  legislation, 237–38, 262–64
  medical work, 237, 268, 270
  relations with Melanesian Mission, 132–36, 159n, 237–39, 261–64, 266, 268, 270, 281–85
Brittain, Arthur H., 81, 129–30, 161n
Brook, Charles Hyde, 38, 48, 65–66, 89–90, 150, 165, 210
Brothers, Brotherhood. *See* Melanesian Brotherhood
Brown, George, 137–38, 193, 211n
Browne, C.G.D., 161n

Browning, Charles William, 110, 132, 144
Bugotu district, Santa Isabel. *See* Santa Isabel
Bula, 19
Bundaberg, 106, 130–31
Bungana, Nggela
  conference (1911), 202–3, 205
  school, 144, 205, 235, 254n
Burns, Philp & Co. Ltd., 179, 251, 265, 290n
Burton, John Wear, 258–59
Bury, Guy Francis, 144–45, 161n, 187
Bwarat(Bwaxat), 46
Bwatvenua, Pentecost, 100

Cakobau (chief of Bau, Fiji), 88
Canterbury, archbishops of, 24, 73, 126. *See also* Benson, E.W.; Davidson, R.T.; Howley, W.; Lang, C.G.
Central Schools. *See* Norfolk Island; St. Andrew's College, Kohimarama St. John's College, Auckland
Child, Gwendolen, 153
Cho, John, 19
Choiseul, 101, 110, 138
Christianity, conversion to
  and British power, 51, 91, 108–11, 133–35, 166–70, 275
  and disease, 60, 101, 156, 169, 186, 268
  and peace, 51, 88, 93, 98, 169–70, 181, 280
  and social change, 51, 57–61, 93–95, 97–98, 101–2, 174, 194–95, 198, 224–27, 258–59, 261, 280, 283–84
  and trade goods, 21–22, 49–50, 82, 89, 165–66
  and Western education, 275–77
Christopherson, Noel Charles, 260
Church Congresses
  Adelaide (1902), 112
  Hobart (1894), 137
Church discipline, 147, 154, 174, 182, 203, 235–36, 254n
Church Missionary Associations, 112, 140, 232. *See also* Church Missionary Society
Church Missionary Society, 7, 44, 112, 115, 123–24, 126, 151, 155–56, 161n, 221
  New Zealand Mission, 1, 13, 31, 33, 41, 57, 144, 149

  relations with G.A. Selwyn, 3, 9, 13–14, 18
Church of England missions. *See* Anglican missions
Church of the Province of New Zealand. *See* Anglican Church in New Zealand
Church services, 33, 38–40, 59, 94–97, 179, 196–97, 203, 208, 232–34
Churches, in Melanesian villages, 97, 172–73, 182, 196, 197
Churches of Christ mission, New Hebrides, 141, 184, 225, 240
Clayton, J.E., 130
Clothing, adoption of by Melanesian Christians, 19, 35, 58, 94, 97, 101–2, 114, 131, 151, 194, 268
Codrington, Robert Henry, 15, 36, 79, 294
  attitude to Melanesian religion and customs, 37, 95, 165, 191, 199
  biographical notes, 298
  headmaster at Norfolk Island, 36–38, 40–41, 111, 222
  in England, 126, 147, 161n, 210
  translations, 146, 171, 223
  views on labour recruiting, 64, 68, 103–5
  visits to islands, 51, 60, 89, 93, 97
Colenso, Elizabeth, 149–50
Coleridge, Sir John Duke, 72
Colonial Bishoprics Council, Colonial Bishoprics Fund, 1, 23
Colonial Office, 2, 5, 24, 65, 103, 105, 134, 238, 240
Colonies, Secretaries of State for, 72, 242
Comins, Richard Blundell, 82–83, 86, 104, 110–11, 131, 165, 206, 207
  biographical notes, 298
Coombe, Florence Edith, 222
  biographical notes, 298
Cordelia, H.M.S., 48
Cormorant, H.M.S., 91
Corner, Arthur Edward, 238, 247
Creagh, Stephen Mark, 11, 46
Crowther, Bishop Samuel, 155–56
Cullwick, Thomas Cartwright, 199, 206
  biographical notes, 298
Curacoa, H.M.S., 111
Curtis Island, 35
Cust, Dr. Robert Needham, 126

332 God's Gentlemen

Daisy Chain, The 30, 44
"Danielites", 285−87
Dausuke, James, 177
Davidson, Archbishop Randall T., 112, 207−8, 247−48, 256n
Denison, Sir William Thomas, 24
Devonshire, ninth Duke of, 242
Dictionary of the Language of Mota, 37, 146
Didimang, William Nihill, 10−11, 20−21, 36
Dido, H.M.S., 3−4
Diseases, 6, 8, 50, 60, 82, 101, 131, 143, 145, 149, 156, 169, 185−86, 262, 267−70
Dixon, Norman, 161n
Doane, Bishop G.W., 23
Doraadi, Andrew, 85
Dorawewe, 85
Drew, Frederick Henry, 144, 161n
Drummond, Henry Nelson, 145, 153, 182, 196, 222
  biographical notes, 298−99
Dudley, Benjamin Thornton, 31, 33, 49−50, 109
Durrad, Walter John, 148, 156, 167, 180, 198, 202, 206, 222, 226, 233,
  biographical notes, 299

East and the West, The, 123
Edgell, William Henry, 133, 145
  missionary on Pentecost, 110, 139, 141, 153, 181−83, 236,
Edinburgh Missionary Conference (1910), 191, 217
Education,
  B.S.I.P. government policy, 222, 262−63
  in village schools, 51, 59−60, 83, 93, 100, 165−66, 203, 280
  objectives of Melanesian Mission, 30−31, 38−40, 222−23, 261, 263
  Solomon Islanders' demand for (1930s), 275−77, 281, 283−84.
  See also Mota language
Efate, 47, 68, 242
Elliot Smith, Professor Grafton, 192
Emae, 18, 19, 98−99
Emerald, H.M.S., 91
Emma Bell, 66, 68
England
  support for Melanesian Mission
    from, 44, 53n, 127, 129, 247−48. *See also* Melanesian MIssion English Committee
English language, teaching of, 9−10, 19, 34, 131, 203−5, 208, 261, 271, 276−77, 281
Epalle, Bishop Jean-Baptiste, 6
Epi, 99
Erromango, 4, 19, 47, 108
Erskine, Captain John Elphinstone, 10
Espiritu Santo, 98−99
Essays on the Depopulation of Melanesia, 226
Eton College
  Anglican missionaries educated at, 1, 15, 16, 25, 31, 72, 104, 144
  connections with Melanesian Mission, 44, 127, 158n, 256−57n
Evangelicals, 3, 7, 14, 23, 44, 57, 78n, 112, 121, 140, 183, 190, 196, 232, 259
Excommunication. *See* Church discipline

Fagani, San Cristobal, 85, 107, 168, 198
Fallowes, Richard Prince, 273, 281−85, 282, 292n
  biographical notes, 299
"Fallowes movement", 282−85
Fauambu hospital, 268−70
Fawkes, Admiral Sir Wilmot H., 256n
Fenualoa, Reef Islands, 170
Ferguson, Captain Alexander, 101−2
Fiji, 6, 88, 156, 183, 243, 261
  High Commissioner for the Western Pacific based at, 107, 238
  labour recruiting for, 63−66, 68−69, 86, 103−6
  mission work on plantations, 105−6, 112, 131, 137, 177, 230
Finance
  mission income, 13, 44−45, 53n, 111−12, 126, 129, 246−49, 251, 257n, 290n
  salaries and wages, 62, 146−47, 155, 180, 252n
  self-support in Melanesian church, 97, 203, 219, 226, 251, 281, 284
Finance Board, *See* Melanesian Mission Finance Board
Firth, Raymond, 194, 276
Fison, Lorimer, 68

Fiu, Malaita, 177, 179, 181, 239
Fletcher, Sir Murchison, 262, 281
Floyd, William, 106
Fly, H.M.S., 10
Forrest, Actaeon E.C., 69, 71, 161n, 185–86, 189n
Foui'a, Malaita, 180
Fowler, Wilfred, 281–82
Fox, Charles Elliot, 144, 224, 260, 266, 273–74, 279, 284
  as anthropologist and linguist, 146, 192–93
  biographical notes, 299
  and Melanesian Brotherhood, 227, 231
  missionary on San Cristobal, 85, 149, 170, 195–96, 198, 227, 238
Frodsham, Bishop G.H., 178
Futuna, 6

Gaeta district, Nggela, 90–93
Gariri, Benjamin, 20, 36
Gasmata district, New Britian, 246, 278
Gavutu, Nggela, 132, 167
Geddie, John, 4
General Synod. *See* Anglican Church in New Zealand
German New Guinea, 110, 134, 243–45. *See also* New Britain; New Guinea
German Solomon Islands, 110, 141, 243–44. *See also* Bougainville
Gilandi, George, 283
Gito, Ellison, 176
Gladstone, William Ewart, 7, 72
Godden, Charles, 145, 182–84
Godfrey, Richard, 273
Goldie, John Francis, 194, 238–39
Goodenough, Commodore J.G., 60, 184
Gordon, Sir Arthur Hamilton (first Baron Stanmore), 161n
Gororagwia, 96
Gorovaka, Hugo, 88, 135
Graciosa Bay, Santa Cruz, 63, 184
Graves, Douglas Eccleston, 145, 273
Gray, Bishop Robert, 24
Grey, Sir George, 5–6, 13, 14
Groves, W.C. 254n, 280
Grunling, Charles, 240
Guadalcanal, 86, 111, 115, 137–38, 164, 187, 276, 279
  and Melanesian Brotherhood, 227, 229–30, 232
  labour recruiting from, 103, 137, 177
  Melanesian Mission on, 15, 18, 88, 135, 139, 149, 177, 192, 261
  rivalry with Roman Catholics on, 139–42
  traders and planters on, 101–2, 167. *See also* Maravovo
Guppy, H.B. 113

Hageria, Benjamin, 218, 283
Halavo, Nggela, 93–94
Hale, Bishop Mathew, 105
Hannington, Bishop James, 78n
Harmer, Bishop J.R., 256n
Hart, Harold Langley, 233
Havannah, H.M.S., 10, 20
Head-hunting raids, 87-89, 138, 167, 173
Hembala, Hugo, 176, 218–19, 220, 281
Heuru, San Cristobal, 85, 197
Hints to Missionaries to Melanesia, 145, 267
Hipkin, Howard Stockdale, 284
History of the Melanesian Mission, The, 138
History of Melanesian Society, The, 192
Hiu, Torres Islands, 180
Hobart, 71, 137
Hodgson, Reginald, 145, 238
Hogbin, H. Ian, 275–76
Holmes, J.H., 193, 211n
Homosexuality, 90, 155, 185–86, 251
Honggo, Nggela, 89, 95
Honolulu, bishops of, 26, 137
Hopkins, Arthur Innes, 195, 223, 227, 241, 259, 264
  and labour trade, 177–79
  biographical notes, 299
  missionary in north Malaita, 135, 141, 147, 166–67, 178, 181
Hospitals
  Fauambu, 268–70
  Welchman Memorial, 176, 267
Howard, Fred, 109
Howley, Archbishop William, 1, 7
Hukwe, Alfred, 287

im Thurn, Sir Everard, 189n

In the Isles of King Solomon, 195
Industrial missions, 122–23, 174, 224–27, 259. *See also* Anglican missionaries in Melanesia; traders, trading vessels
Inglis, John, 18, 64
Island Builders of the Pacific, The 193
Isle of Pines, 4–8
Ivens, Walter George, 82, 145–46, 154, 166, 185, 204, 267
  as anthropologist and linguist, 22, 146, 193
  biographical notes, 299–300
  missionary in south Malaita, 147 49, 197
Ivo, James 181

Jackson, Robert Simeon, 82–83
Jacob, Bishop Edgar, 126, 213n
Jacomb, Edward, 194, 205, 226
Japanese invasion, 266, 279
Jeffrey, Sarah, 161n
Jones, John, 11
Joy, G.A., 242
Julius, Archbishop J.C., 249

Kalekona, 90–92
Kaye, Alan Lister, 69
Keble, John, 30, 44, 73
Kerr, Thomas 33
Kia, Santa Isabel, 169
Kimberley, (first Earl of), 72
Kissling, G.A., 14
Knowles, Lees, M.P., 111
Kohimarama, Auckland. *See* St. Andrew's College
Kohimarama, Mota. *See* Mota Christian village
Kopuria, Ini, 227–32, 228
Kwaisulia, 180
Kwalges, Simon, 199
Kwaratu, Edmund, 96
Kwasvarong, William, 59, 97, 235–36

Labour recruiting, colonial, 62–66, 85–87, 95, 100–101, 103, 106, 177, 184–85, 280–81
  and death of Patteson, 65–72
  attitudes of Anglican missionaries to, 63–65, 68, 103–7, 130, 178
  British regulation of, 65, 71–72.
  See also Returned labourers

Labour recruiting, inter-island, 167, 230, 280-81, 284
  attitudes of Anglican missionaries to, 240, 242, 264–65. *See also* Planters
Lamalanga, Pentecost, 151, 182, 242, 285
Lambeth Conferences
  (1897), 56–57, 122
  (1908), 122
  (1920), 245
Lang, Archbishop C.G., 293
Langalanga Lagoon, Malaita, 85, 177
Langgo, Nggela, 90–91
Langlangmele, Simeon, 286–87
Lau Lagoon, Malaita, 177, 180, 193
Levers Pacific Plantations Ltd., 265. *See also* Planters
Levuka, Fiji, 106, 131
Lifu, 7, 46–47, 61
  mission scholars from 10–11, 18–19, 49
Light of Melanesia, The, 112
Light-Hearts, Guild of, 247, 256–57n
Limai, George, 177
Livingstone, David, 57, 121
Loh, Torres Islands, 96, 148
Lolowai, Omba, 183, 217, 223, 269, 287
Lombu, Alfred, 93–94,
London
  English Committee annual meetings at, 149, 192, 247–48, 257n
  Melanesian Mission office at, 127, 247–48
London Missionary Society, 1–2, 4, 6–7, 22, 41, 46–47, 95, 136, 146, 193, 225
  and G.A. Selwyn, 4, 7, 11, 46
  Patteson's views on, 30–31, 41, 46–47
  Polynesian teachers of, 4, 6–8, 11, 19, 30, 46
Long, William Fortescue, 145, 161n
Loyalty Islands, 4, 6–7, 10, 18, 22, 30, 46–48, 58. *See also* Lifu; Mare
Luke, Sir Harry, 284
Lush, Vicesimus, 13

MacGregor, Sir William, 134, 137
Mackay, Queensland, 129, 131, 178
Mackenzie, Bishop Charles F., 26, 45, 57, 245

Maewo, 81, 96, 98–101, 115, 141, 150, 156
Makira Bay, San Cristobal, 6, 83
Malaita, 101, 115, 139, 156, 184, 187, 238–39, 266, 268, 275, 285
  labour recruiting from, 103–4, 177–81
  Melanesian Mission on, 48, 85–86, 109, 132, 135, 138, 147, 164, 166–67, 173, 177–81, 193, 197, 227, 230–31, 239, 268–70, 274–75
  S.S.E.M. on, 135, 141, 178
Malakula, 11–12, 63, 99
Malayta Company, 225
Malu'u, Malaita, 178, 275
Mandated Territory of New Guinea, Melanesian Mission in, 243–46, 277–79, 291n
Maoris in Melanesian Mission, 4, 11, 129
Maramasike Passage, Malaita, 109
Mara na Tambu, Santa Isabel, 175, 176, 280
Marau, Clement, 41, 86, 154, 171–73, 172, 219
Marau, Martin, 173, 218
Marau Sound, Guadalcanal, 15, 230
Maravovo, Guadalcanal, 135, 139, 151, 214, 227, 271
  conferences, 205, 209–10
  hospital (Welchman Memorial), 176, 267
  school, 224, 226–27, 233, 261, 280
Marchant, William Sydney, 266
Marching Rule, 285
Mare, 7, 10–11, 18, 46. *See also* Wadrokal, M.
Margaret of the Cross, Mother (Margaret Wilson), 235
Markham, Lieutenant Albert Hastings, 73–75
Marists. *See* Roman Catholic missions
Maros, 96, 98, 154–55
Marriage
  B.S.I.P. legislation on, 263–64
  bride price, 196, 263, 286
Marsden, Samuel, 57
Martin, Lady Mary, 12 13, 19, 33
Martin, Sir William, 13, 45
Mason, Albert, 145, 239, 273
Matema, Reef Island, 186

Max Müller, Friedrich, 54–55
Maybury, Lawrence Montague, 268–69
Mboli (Boli), Nggela, 89–90, 131, 165
Medical work, 81, 122–23, 151, 169, 174–76, 231, 261, 267–70, 284
Melanesia, bishops of. *See* Baddeley, W.H.; Molyneux, F.M.; Patteson, J.C.; Selwyn, J.R.; Steward, J.M.; Wilson, C.; Wood, C.
Melanesia,, foundation of, diocese of, 23-26. *See also* Anglican Church in New Zealand
Melanesian Brotherhood, 227–32, 228, 229, 275, 286
Melanesian Languages, The, 37
Melanesian Mission
  comparisons with other missions, 8, 18, 98, 115–16, 125, 136–37, 146–47, 155–56, 164, 190, 193–95, 206, 208, 215–18, 275, 293
  mission statistics of, 115, 156, 163–64, 273–75. *See also* Church Missionary Society; London Missionary Society; Methodist missions: Presbyterian mission; Roman Catholic missions; Seventh-day Adventist mission; South Sea Evangelical Mission; Universities' Mission to Central Africa
Melanesian Mission English Committee, 44, 119n, 127, 145, 210, 213n, 226, 238, 241, 244–45, 247–48, 254n, 256n, 257n
Melanesian Mission Finance Board, 249, 251, 257n, 269, 290n
Melanesian Mission Trust (board), 44, 53n, 54, 146, 247, 290n
Melanesians, The, 37
Melanesians, in Anglican ministry, 10, 61–62, 92–94, 99, 153–57, 171–73, 172, 200, 215–24, 234, 271–73, 279, 281, 283, 285–87
  numbers, 115, 154, 209, 217, 273
  wages, 62, 155, 180, 252n
  See also names of individual Melanesians
Melanesians, first contacts with Melanesian Mission, 5, 11–12, 15–22, 48–51. *See also* Christianity, conversion to

Melanesians of the South-east Solomon Islands, 193
Melbourne, 44, 71
Mendaña, Alvaro de, 184
Mere Lava, 41, 86, 96, 98, 173, 218–19
Methodist missions, 1, 4, 22, 31, 95, 136, 259
  Fiji, 106, 137, 258
  New Britain, 137, 151, 193, 246, 278
  Papua, 137, 151
  Solomon Islands, 134–35, 137–38, 164, 194, 218, 225, 238–39, 259, 263, 266, 268, 270, 275
  and Melanesian Mission, 135, 137–38
Milne, Peter, 141
Minipa, James, 66–67
Mission ships. *See Border Maid; Ruth; Southern Cross; Undine*
Moltata, Peter, 181
Molyneux, Bishop Frederick Merivale, 242, 249–51, 250
  biographical notes, 300
Montgomery, Bishop Henry Hutchinson, 112, 123
  and Cecil Wilson, 130, 138, 206
  views on Melanesian Mission, 85, 112, 136, 143, 186, 244
Moore, Bernard William Farren, 279
Mota, 18, 47, 96, 107, 109, 131, 151, 154, 272
  Christian village (Kohimarama), 58–61, 61–62, 82, 96
  Patteson at, 49–51, 58–61, 65, 67
  population of, 49, 50, 60, 96, 115, 156
  sukwe, 49, 50, 96, 198–202
  teachers from, 96, 100, 106
Mota language
  as teaching language of Melanesian Mission, 34, 36, 98, 112, 131, 151, 182, 185, 199, 203–5, 208, 221–23, 234, 271–72
  translations, 40, 140, 146, 219, 223, 280
Mota Lava, 59, 96, 115, 200
  teachers from 97, 99, 277
Moto, 66–67
Murray, Sir Hubert (J.H.P.), 134
Murua (Woodlark Island), 6
Mwadjo'a, Ulawa, 171–73
Mwata, San Cristobal, 11, 20–21, 102

Natei, 184
Navkoe, Mota, 96
Nduindui, Omba, 141
Nelua, Santa Cruz, 184, 186
Nevill, Bishop S.T. 210
New Britain, 7, 47, 230, 243–46, 269, 272, 277–79, 291n,
  Methodist mission on, 137, 151, 193, 246, 278
New Caledonia, 4, 6–7, 10, 46, 53n, 106
New Georgia, 48, 87, 115, 138, 173, 279. *See also* Roviana
New Guinea, 7, 47, 110, 134, 166, 244, 261, 277. *See also* German New Guinea; Mandated Territory of New Guinea; Papua
New Guinea Mission, 112, 151, 179, 194, 244–45, 279, 291n
New Hanover, 7
New Hebrides, 4–8, 22, 58, 143, 187, 190, 193, 198, 267, 270, 272, 276
  French annexation of, 107–8, 241
  labour recruiting from 63–64, 100-101, 103, 106, 129, 181–83,
  Melanesian Mission in, 47, 98–101, 107, 141, 144, 181–84, 215, 217, 223, 239–42, 249, 251
  mission scholars from, 10, 18–20, 38, 39, 98
  Selwyn's voyages to, 4–5, 10–12. *See also* Banks Islands Presbyterian mission; names of individual islands; Torres Islands; traders
New Hebrides Condominium, attitudes of Anglican missionaries to, 239–42
New Ireland, 4, 7
New Zealand
  support for Melanesian Mission from, 12–14, 43–45, 53n, 111–12, 127–29, 158n, 210, 234, 247, 249, 251, 257n, 273, 290n. *See also* Anglican Church in New Zealand
New Zealand Anglican Board of Missions, 247, 257n
Nggela (Florida), 150, 156, 279, 283–85
  and British protectorate, 110–11, 132–33

labour recruiting from, 66, 89, 95, 105
Melanesian Mission on, 48, 65, 89–95, 101, 114–15, 131–33, 164–65, 169, 177, 196, 266
reputation of Christians of, 114–15, 132, 137
teachers and clegy from, 92–94, 114, 132–33, 135, 140, 180–81, 231, 272
vaukolu ("parliament"), 95, 133, 283
women's mission station on, 151, 152, 153. *See also* Bungana; Siota; Tulagi
Ngongono, John, 66, 96
Ngorefou, Malaita, 166, 181
Nguna, 141
Nifiloli, Reef Islands, 68, 184
Nihill, William, 11, 46
Nobbs, Edwin, 63
Norfolk Island
Melanesian mission headquarters at, 24, 35–36, 43, 54, 58, 65, 68, 79, 81, 90, 92, 94, 100, 106, 114–15, 130, 145–46, 200, 202–3, 205–7, 214, 232–33, 244; headquarters transferred from, 206, 208, 215
St. Barnabas' Chapel at, 73, 74, 75, 97, 173, 205–6, 208, 215
St. Barnabas' College at, 35–43, 39, 42, 45, 54, 59, 63, 81, 83, 86, 89, 98, 111–12, 127, 130–31, 142–44, 155, 165, 171, 177, 184–85, 187, 205, 215, 222, 224, 227, 273, 280; former scholars of, 58, 60, 81, 83–87, 89–90, 96–97, 150, 163–64, 182, 210; training of girls at, 149–50, 152, 207
Notere, Eric, 173–74
Nukapu, Reef Islands, 66–71, 73–75, 108, 186
Nupani, Reef Islands, 68, 184

O Sala Ususur, 204
Omba, 102, 109, 202
Melanesian Mission on, 47, 98–100, 141, 182–84, 230, 240
other missions on, 141, 184, 225. *See also* Lolowai
Ontong Java, 230

Oxford Movement, 2, 72, 232. *See also* Anglo-Catholicism; Tractarianism

Paddon, James, 5
Palmer, John, 33, 38, 104, 111, 113
at Mota, 50–51, 59–61, 96, 98, 199
biographical notes, 300
Pamua, San Cristobal
conference (1911), 202–3
school, 144, 227, 251
Pantutun, Robert, 49, 62, 96, 107, 200, 201
Papua, 134, 137, 151, 193, 225. *See also* New Guinea
Patteson, Bishop John Coleridge, 15, 16, 18, 21, 25, 36, 41, 44–45, 55, 61–63, 79, 89, 232
and G.A. Selwyn, 15, 35, 63, 73
and L.M.S., 30–31, 41, 46–47
and labour trade, 63 65, 105
and Melanesian languages, 15, 31, 34, 41, 49, 55, 204, 234
appointed Bishop of Melanesia, 23–26, 126
as teacher, 19–20, 30–33, 39–40, 80, 171, 222
at Mota, 49–51, 58–61, 65, 67
attitude to Melanesian religion and customs, 50, 54–59, 109–91, 98, 199, 225
biographical notes, 300
his death and its consequences, 62–63, 65–75, 79, 112, 115–16, 121, 183–84, 205–6, 248, 293
memorials, 70, 71, 73, 74, 75, 244
modifies Selwyn's mission plan, 33–35, 47–48
views on British power, 107–9
voyages to Melanesia, 15–17, 48, 82, 98, 230
Paton, John G., 64, 259
Pawa school, Uki, 224, 227, 238, 261, 277, 280
Pek, Vanua Lava, 59, 97
Penny, Alfred, 87–88, 90, 92, 101–2, 104
biographical notes, 300
Pentecost, 109–10, 156, 202, 242
indigenous clergy of, 218, 236, 285–87
Melanesian Mission on, 81, 96, 98–100, 141, 151, 153, 164,

167, 181–82, 230–31, 274, 285–87
  other missions on, 139, 141–43
Perry, Bishop Charles, 44
Pidgin English, 104–5, 129, 140, 178–79, 182, 203–4
Pileni, Reef Islands, 68
Pirihandi, Santa Isabel, 87, 175
Pitcairners (Norfolk Island), 24, 35, 40, 63
Plant, John Holford, 92, 95, 109–10
Planters, 134, 142, 166–67, 176, 223, 238, 240, 242, 246, 264–66. *See also* Labour recruiting, inter-island
Population, decline of, 82, 101, 156–57, 164, 225–26, 268. *See also* Mota
Polynesia, diocese of, 243, 256n
Port Adam, Malaita, 184, 197
Port Patteson, Vanua Lava, 17, 48
Presbyterian mission, New Herbrides, 4, 7, 47, 58, 64, 98, 103, 107–8, 115, 136, 146, 194, 218, 259 267, 289–90n
  and Melanesian Mission, 18, 47, 99, 141
  opposition to Condominium, 239-41
Pritt, Francis Dinkall, 130
Pritt, Lonsdale, 33–34, 36–37
  biographical notes, 300–301

Queensland
  Curtis Island school, 35
  labour recruiting for, 63–65, 86, 103–7
  mission work on plantations, 105–6, 112, 129–31, 178–80
  repatriation of Pacific Islanders from, 177–83
Queensland Kanaka Mission, 106, 131, 134, 140, 178–79. *See also* South Sea Evangelical Mission

Ra, Mota Lava, 59, 96
Rabaul, New Britain, 245–46, 266, 277–78
Raga district, Pentecost. *See* Pentecost
Reef Islands, 66, 68, 170, 184–86, 274. *See also* Nukapu
Rennell Island, 15, 262
Returned labourers, 97, 194
  Christian influence of, 106–7, 130, 141, 164, 177–83

Ridding, Bishop George, 155
Ritual, introduction of, 232–34. *See also*. Anglo-Catholicism; Oxford Movement; Tractarianism
Rivers, W.H.R., 192, 226
Robinson, Mary Goodwin, 129, 131, 178, 180
Rodwell, Sir C. Hunter, 238
Roman Catholic Church, 72, 190, 218, 235
Roman Catholic missions, 1, 6, 46, 151
  and Melanesian Mission, 7, 12, 139–41, 195
  in New Britain, 246, 278
  in New Hebrides, 139, 141–43, 184, 286
  in Solomon Islands, 6–7, 83, 134–36, 138–39, 142–43, 164, 193–94, 218, 231, 263, 275
Rosario, H.M.S., 73–75, 108
Roviana, New Georgia, 138, 259, 268
Rowa, 59, 97, 235–36
Royal Navy, association with Melanesian Mission, 10, 20, 48, 51, 73–75, 83, 91, 107–11, 113, 167, 247, 294
Rua Sura, Guadalcanal, 139
Ruddock, David, 82, 116
Russell Islands, 229
Ruth, 176

Sa'a Malaita, 48, 85–86, 109, 193
Sage, Charles, 161n, 178
Sag Sag, New Britain, 278
St. Andrew's College, Kohimarama, Auckland, 30–35,
St. Augustine's College, Canterbury, 38, 125, 145
St. Barnabas' Association, 129
St. Barnabas' Chapel, Norfolk Island, 73, 74, 75, 97, 173, 205–6, 215
St. Barnabas' College, Norfolk Island, 35–43 *See also* Norfolk Island
St. Boniface College, Warminster, 145
St. John's College, Auckland, 9, 12–13, 19, 30, 33
Sakelrau, Edwin, 59
Samoa, 4, 106
San Cristobal, 109, 139, 156, 238, 283–84
  Melanesian Mission on, 11, 48, 65, 82–85, 107, 149, 164, 166,

169–70, 177, 195–96, 198, 227
mission scholars from, 10–11
15, 18–21, 36, 48, 82–83
traders at, 82, 101–2, 109. *See also*
C.E. Fox; Pamua
Sandalwood traders, 4–5, 10, 48
Sandfly, murders (Nggela), 90–91
Santa Catalina, San Cristobal, 166
Santa Cruz, 11, 47, 63, 106, 110
and death of Patteson, 66–71
Melanesian Mission on, 66, 145, 147, 184–87, 230, 274
Santa Isabel, 110, 134, 270
Melanesian Mission on, 48, 87–89, 101–2, 115, 137–38, 142, 164, 173–76, 182, 196, 219, 274, 279–85
mission-government relations on, 263–64, 282–85
reasons for conversion on, 88–89, 169, 170, 177, 283–84
teachers and clergy from, 138, 174–76, 218–19, 229, 231–32, 263–64, 279, 281, 283
Santa Maria, 96, 98, 115, 154–55
Sapimbuana, Charles, 90, 92–93
Sarawia, George, 17, 21, 51, 58–62, 96, 115, 127, 201
Sarawia, Sarah, 58, 60, 150
Savo, 48, 86–88, 102, 283
Selwyn, Bishop George Augustus, ii, 1, 25, 44, 63, 73, 79, 158n, 232, 248, 260
and J.C. Patteson, 15, 35, 63, 73
and L.M.S., 4, 7, 11, 46
appointed Bishop of New Zealand, 1–2
biographical notes, 301
foundation of diocese of Melanesia, 23–26
missionary strategy, 2–4, 6–14, 18, 22–23, 34, 43, 57, 61, 153, 190, 244, 293; its weaknesses, 17–22, 43–44
religious views, 2–4, 13–14, 46
views on British power, 5–6, 108
voyages to Melanesia, 3–5, 10–12, 15–17, 46, 48, 66, 98–99
Selwyn, Bishop John Richardson, 69, 71, 80, 83, 88–89, 99, 111, 126, 137, 154, 190, 267
appointed Bishop of Melanesia, 79, 126
attitude to trade and labour recruiting, 101–4, 106

biographical notes, 301
personality and religious views, 79–81
views on British power, 91, 108–9, 114, 123
Selwyn Mission, Mackay, 129–31, 178–79
Sepi, Santa Isabel, 88
Seventh-day Adventist mission, Solomon Islands, 134, 194, 218, 259, 263, 266, 268, 270, 275
Shaw, Gwen (Sister Gwen), 235
Shortland Islands, 135
Sikaiana, 230
Sili, James, 181
Simmons, Robert John Andrew, 145
Sinker, Captain William, 148
Siota, Nggela, 215, 217, 234, 246, 259, 269, 271, 272
St. Luke's School, 131–32, 144, 205
training college, 217, 223
Sisters of the Cross, 234–35
Society for Promoting Christian Knowledge, 146
Society for the Propagation of the Gospel, 44, 73, 112, 123–25, 143, 265
Society of Mary (Marists). *See* Roman Catholic missions
Soga, 88–89, 173–74, 219
Solomon Islands, 4, 22, 35, 142–43, 166–67, 218, 275, 279
anthropological study in, 190–96
British protectorate of, 110–11, 132–36, 166–70, 181, 186, 222, 237–39, 261–66, 268, 270, 275–76, 281–85
European settlement in, 86, 101–3, 142, 166–67, 181, 206, 264–65
expansion of Christianity in, 163–64, 166–70, 187, 275–76
first mission scholars from, 10–11, 15, 18–21, 35–36, 38, 41, 48–49,
labour recruiting from, 65–66 85, 103–6, 177
medical work in, 176, 267–70
Melanesian Mission in, 47–48, 82–95, 113–15, 129, 131–44, 147, 163–64, 171–81, 202–3, 214–15, 217, 224, 233–35, 251, 259, 275–77, 279–85, 293. *See also* British Solomon Islands Protectorate government;

340 God's Gentlemen

Labour recruiting; Methodist missions; Planters; Roman Catholic missions; Seventh-day Adventist mission; South Sea Evangelical Mission; names of individual islands, traders, trading vessels
South Sea Evangelical Mission, 134–36, 178, 194, 225, 231, 263, 266, 275
and Melanesian Mission, 140–41, 194–95. *See also* Queensland Kanaka Mission
Southern Cross, 21, 34, 40, 73, 79, 140, 148, 206, 250–51, 293
as carrier of disease, 156, 268
costs of, 111, 113, 144, 146, 206, 249–50, 278
life on board, 81–82, 114, 174, 272
voyages of, 15, 17, 22, 36, 37, 47–48, 62–63, 65–68, 81, 85, 89, 91, 98, 100, 106, 112, 118n, 127, 135, 138, 142, 177, 192, 200, 272
Southern Cross Log, 129, 248
Sprott, Rudolph, G.M., 145, 170
Staley, Bishop Thomas Nettleship, 26
Stanley, Dean A.P., 121
Steward, Bishop John Manwaring, 141, 195, 215, 216, 226, 232, 243–50, 265, 273
and indigenous ministry, 217–21
and Melanesian Brotherhood, 227–30, 229
appointed Bishop of Melanesia, 214 15
biographical notes, 301
personality and religious views, 215, 234, 260–61
political interventions, 237–39, 241, 262–64, 284
Still, John, 68, 79, 82, 85, 213n
Stock, Eugene, 161n
Story of a Melanesian Deacon, 171
Sulufou, Malaita, 180
Sulukavo, 135
sukwe (graded society), 49–50, 96, 198–202, 286
Suva, 131, 177, 261
Svensen, Captain Oscar, 102
Sweet-Escott, Sir E. Bickham, 238, 256n

Sydney, 13–14, 20–21, 40, 83, 101, 137–38, 143, 186
and Melanesian Mission, 13–14, 44, 71, 145, 182, 251, 290n

Tafua, Ariki, 276
Tagalad, Henry, 59, 62, 96–97, 115, 127, 154
Tahiti, 2, 22, 46, 95
Tait, (Arch)bishop Archibald Campbell, 56, 73
Taki, 83–85, 84
Takibaina, Martin, 195–96
Takua, 89–90, 117n
Talofuila, Jack, 180
Talu, Stephen, 283
tamate (secret society), 96, 198–99
Tambalia, Guadalcanal, 230
Tambe, Daniel, 285–86
Tambukoro, David, 95
Tanna, 47, 63, 68, 108
Tanoriki (Tanrig), Maewo, 100–101
Taratoa, Henry, 11
Taribwatu, Charles, 100
Tarileo, Matthias, 218, 236, 285
Tariliu, Louis, 100, 181
Taroaniara, Nggela, 266
Taroaniara, Stephen, 48, 66–67, 82
Tavoa, Henry, 287
Tawatana, San Cristobal, 48
Te Motu, Santa Cruz, 184
Teall, Alfred Ernest, 287
Teandule, 67
Tega, Santa Isabel, 87
Tegua, Torres Islands, 186
Teilo, Benjamin, 186
Tempest, Roger Ernest, 187, 218–19, 241–42, 273
biographical notes, 301
Tergatok, Ellison, 277
Thol, John, 10–11
Threshold of the Pacific, The, 192
Thurston, Sir John Bates, 69–71, 109, 114–15, 131–32
Tikopia, 17, 69, 156, 231, 274, 276–77
Tonbridge Association, 127, 136
Tonbridge School, 127, 136
Tonga, 4, 6, 22, 137
Torres Islands, 47, 96, 164, 180, 186
Tractarians, Tractarianism, 2, 9, 14, 96

23, 44, 232. *See also* Anglo-Catholicism; Oxford Movement
Traders, trading vessels, 4–5, 10, 21–22, 48, 83, 86–87, 89, 97, 100–103, 109, 113, 132, 142, 166–67, 176, 185, 195–96, 225, 230, 271, 280
  attitudes of Anglican missionaries to, 5, 10, 12, 17, 48, 101–2, 238, 264–65. *See also* Industrial missions; Planters
Translations, 11, 31, 34, 40, 93, 140, 146, 171, 182, 185, 196, 219, 223, 271, 280
Tuffnell, Bishop Edward, 105
Tulagi, Nggela, 132–33, 135, 167, 176, 215, 230, 262, 265–66, 284
Turnbull, Robert Monilaws, 88
Tuti, Dudley, 221
Tyrrell, Bishop William, 11, 13

Uki, 102, 109, 269. *See also* Pawa school
Ulawa, 17, 65–66, 68, 71, 86, 164, 171–73, 193, 218
Ulgau, Thomas, 96, 100, 181
Undine, 10
Universities' Mission to Central Africa, 24, 26, 45, 57, 115, 125, 194, 221, 233
Ureparapara, 199
Uthwatt, Archdeacon William Andrews, 153, 163
Utupua, 186

Vaget, William, 218
Vanikolo, 186
Vanua Lava, 17, 21, 48, 59, 61, 97, 179. *See also* Sarawia, G.; Vureas school
Vaturanga, Guadalcanal, 88
Vella Lavella, 138, 148
Venn, Henry, 18, 155
Vila, Efate, 242
Visale, Guadalcanal, 139, 141
Vureas school, Vanua Lava, 144, 233

Waaro, Walter, 86
Wadrokal, Mano, 49–50, 87, 184
Walurighi, Omba, 99
Wango, San Cristobal, 48, 66, 82–85, 196
Warren, George Thomas, 233, 273

  biographical notes, 301–2
Wate, Joseph, 85, 109
Wawn, William T. 107
Welchman, Henry Palmer, 110, 131, 133, 138, 140–41, 151, 161n, 232, 267
  biographical notes, 302
  misssionary on Santa Isabel, 89, 142, 146, 173–76, 175, 182, 219, 235, 279–81
  views on industrial missions, 174, 225–26
Wench, Ida, 153
Wesleyan missions. *See* Methodist missions
Western Pacific High Commission, 107, 114, 157, 238, 242, 264. *See also* Gordon, A.H.; Fletcher, M.; im Thurn, E.; Luke, H.; Rodwell, C.H.; Sweet-Escott, E.B.; Thurston, J.B.
Whalers, 4, 17, 48, 83, 102
Wilberforce, Bishop Samuel, 24, 25
Williams, Archdeacon Samuel, 111
Williams, Henry, 144
Williams, John, 2, 4, 6, 57
Williams, Percy Temple, 130, 135, 144
Willis, Bishop Alfred, 137
Wilson, Bishop Cecil, 112, 128, 131–36, 138, 141, 146, 148, 175, 183, 191–92, 196, 206, 232, 236, 239
  and indigenous church, 153–54, 157, 222
  and labour trade, 129–31, 179
  appeals for missionaries, 124–25, 127, 144–45, 163
  appointed Bishop of Melanesia, 126–27
  biographical notes, 302
  missionary policies, 127–29, 143, 149–51, 201, 206, 226, 232
  views on individual missionaries, 174, 185, 214–15
Wilson, Ellen, 268
  biographical notes, 302
Wilson, J.M., 235
Wilson, Margaret (Mother Margaret of the Cross), 235
Wilson, Robert Paley, 144, 204–5, 268
  biographical notes, 302
Wilton, Bishop Edward Nowill, 246

Winnington-Ingram, Bishop A.F., 125
Wogale, Edward, 62, 96, 106
Wood, Bishop Cecil, 153, 205, 208–10, 226, 233, 263
  appointed Bishop of Melanesia, 206–8
  biographical notes, 302
  resignation, 209–10, 214
Woodford, Charles Morris
  and Melanesian Mission, 94–95, 113–14, 120n, 132–36, 143, 149, 163, 206, 256n, 257n
  as Resident Commissioner, 132–35, 156–57, 166–67, 173, 186
Workman, Charles, 257n
Woser, Walter, 99

Yengen, New Caledonia, 10, 46
Yiewene Kicini Bula, 11
Yonge, Charlotte Mary, 30, 44, 73, 75, 112
Young, Fisher, 63
Young, Florence S.H., 106, 178
Young, Sir John, 35

www.ingramcontent.com/pod-product-compliance
Lightning Source LLC
Chambersburg PA
CBHW051524020426
42333CB00016B/1776